HEROES IN HOOPS

QPR
Who's Who
1899 ~ 2003

By John Marks

Published by:
Yore Publications
12 The Furrows, Harefield,
Middx. UB9 6AT.

British Library Cataloguing-in-Publication Data.
A catalogue record for this book
is available from the British Library.

ISBN 1 874427 844

The Cromwell Press
Trowbridge, Wiltshire

Front cover:

Players, clockwise from top...
Alfred Hitch, George Goddard, Alec Stock, Peter Angell, Rodney Marsh, Stan Bowles, Clive Allen, Les Ferdinand, Ian Holloway and Kevin Gallen.

Rear cover

Players from bottom left to top left...
Tony Hazell, Phil Parkes, Gary Waddock, Paul Parker, Alan McDonald, Andy Sinton, Ray Wilkins, Chris Plummer and Clarke Carlisle

And....

The players with 'special attributes':
Peter Molloy (Fairground boxer),
Gordon Reed (Dance band leader)
John Hartburn (Three minute hat-trick)
Mike Pinner (52 Amateur caps)
Fred Pentland (Son of the Lord Mayor)
Andrew Wilson (Capped from hospital)
Allan Glover (30 second loan)
Clarke Carlisle (Brainiest footballer)
Percy Varco (Cornish town Mayor)
Ivor Powell (Subbed by an Englishman)
George Seeley (Entered a lion's cage)

I dedicate this work to my wife Ann without whose patience and understanding I could never have completed it.
JOHN C. G. MARKS
August 2003

John Marks

John has been a lifelong follower of Q.P.R.; not surprising they were the team he chose as a boy since he lived in Macfarlane Road, Shepherds Bush (just a few hundred yards from Loftus Road), from where, *"You could hear when a home goal was scored."* He first watched the team as a schoolboy during the Second World War, *"When I used to bunk in for the last part of the game for free"* (the gates having to be left open in case of air-raids). For three seasons, from 1946/47, he saw every home game and many local away matches, but then, due to shift working, this attendance record was broken. John continued to live in London after marrying, until the 1970's when his work, as a Power Station Engineer took him North to Burnley. Since then his supporting has been from afar. He retired in 1992, when he moved with his wife to Spalding in Lincolnshire, where he still lives. John's passion for statistics, with particular reference to players, has led to this book which has taken in total around 15 years in its preparation.

KEY

The following facts and details relating to a player are given where known:

Player's full name (popular abbreviated or nicknames are referred to where relevant).

Playing positions recorded relate to the terminology of that era, ie: a midfield player of today would be a wing half, or an inside forward of the fifties. Modern terminology has been shown under the players name, whilst the earlier equivalent is in brackets. Height and Weight (in feet and inches, and stones [one stone = 14 pounds = c.6.4 kilos.] and pounds) follow.

Date and place of birth are included, likewise that of the player's death.

The clubs for which each player has played for are listed in date order and type of move and details, i.e. trials, loans, transfer fees, etc. have been included, followed by the joining date. Note: accurate transfer fees are often not known and/or conflicting figures are often quoted from different source references. Where a year only is given for a joining date, this is most likely during the close season, and hence could be June, July or August.

Q.P.R. appearances for all matches (as detailed below) are included, and split as shown. These include substitutions, which have been considered a full appearance and added to the total. Under 'Other' these consist other first team cup competitions plus Charity matches and acknowledged first team Friendly games.

SURNAME Christian names

(Old) & New positions. height & weight
b.= born, place & date. d = death, place & date

Club played for type of transfer and fee Joining date

Q.P.R. details type of transfer and fee Joining date
(Appearances - Goals) League F.A.Cup Football League Cup Other Totals

Honours:

(Short biography relating to the player)

Debut: (For Q.P.R.) Date... opponants.....result.... competition/division

General Notes:

Normally, June2003 has been taken as a 'cut-off' point for statistical and other details. However, where a player's move is known to have been made later during the Summer of 2003, this information is briefly appended, within brackets, at the end of the player's biography.

Transfer fees and dates: Accurate fees are not always made available, and are estimated (normally by the press). Inevitably, different sources will vary and therefore the figures given should often be assumed to be approximate. Where a transfer month is known this information is given, however, different sources again may quote different months, or is often during the close season, therefore some dates may be only approximate.

Acknowledgements

The author and publisher would like to thank, in particular:

Gordon Macey for his help and assistance in finalising the book, and for providing many of the photographs.

Mike Pink and Phil Harris at the Club for their help and co-operation.

Photographs: Many thanks to Gerard Farrell for his permission to use a number of the photographs. It is often difficult to trace the source of photographs, therefore apologies are offered should copyright have been inadvertently infringed. Notification to the Publisher will ensure that this error is remedied in the event of a reprint/revised edition.

Contents

Football League Players A-Z

ABBOTT Harry

(I.L) Mid 5' 9" 11st 4lbs
b. Blackburn, Lancashire in 1883
Padiham
Blackburn Rovers
Q.P.R. 1904
Southern League: 27-4. FAC: 1-0. FLC: 0-0. Others: 0-0.
Total: 28-4.
Burnley
Bolton Wanderers 1905
Swindon Town 1907

Harry came to the notice of Blackburn Rovers after some sterling performances for Padiham in the Lancashire Combination League. However he never turned out for the first eleven and drifted south to Q.P.R. He was somewhat impressive as a play-maker, until the arrival of Milward in the side when he was relegated to the reserves. According to the 1905 edition of the *" Men Famous in Football"* he drifted back north again and was taken on the books of Burnley. However he never turned out for them but he did play for Bolton Wanderers in their promotion campaign of 1905. In 1906 he returned to the Southern League to play for Swindon Town.
Debut: 3. 9.1902 v. Wellingborough (H) 2-0 SL Div. 1.

ABBOTT Ronald W.

Mid
b. Lambeth, London 2. 8.1953.
Q.P.R. 1971
Football League: 46-4. FAC: 5-0. FLC: 3-0. Others: 0-0.
Total: 54-4.
Drogheda 1979

Ron made a dream start to his career at the club by scoring the winning goal on his first team debut. West Ham United were beaten in exciting fashion on their own ground by three goals to two in a First Division clash in September 1973. Used as a substitute for most of his time at the club, he proved to be a good stand-in. The arrival of Steve Burtenshaw as manager in 1978 saw the end of his time at Q.P.R. and he left for Drogheda.
Debut: 10.9.1973. v. West Ham United (A) 3-2. Div.1

ABBOTT Shirley Wray

(L.B.) Def. 5' 9" 12st 7lbs.
b. Alfreton, Derbyshire 10. 2.1880. d. 26. 8.1947
Alfreton Town Sep 1906
Sheffield Wednesday (Trial) 1910
Derby County 1911
Portsmouth Aug 1920
Q.P.R. May 1923
Football League: 12-0. FAC: 0-0. FLC: 0-0. Others: 0-0.
Total: 12-0.
Chesterfield Sep 1924

It seemed that the capture of the Portsmouth captain in 1923 was a shrewd move by the then manager of Q.P.R , Ned Liddell. He thought that Abbott would be a calming influence in the Rangers defence, having been the captain of the south coast team when they won the Southern League title in 1920. Now at the age of 33 he had the experience of playing in every defensive position including goalkeeper. Alas of the 12 matches that he was involved in not one was won and indeed 30 goals were conceded in the process. At the start of the following season he joined Chesterfield and became captain of the side until 1927, becoming trainer in 1928. Whilst trainer, promotion was gained twice, in 1931 and again in 1936. Abbott held the job until May 1939 when he was sacked by the new manager Norman Bullock. Moving back south to Portsmouth he took a job in the dockyard and worked there throughout the 2nd World War. He died at the early age of 58.
Debut: 6.10.1923 v. Swansea Town (A). 0-2. Div. 3 (S)

ABEL Samuel Charles

(C.F./R.B.) Striker/Def. 5' 11" 12st 0lbs.
b. Neston, Cheshire. 30.12.1908. d. London. 26. 9.1959
Neston Brickworks
Bury Oct 1929
Accrington Stanley Jul 1930
Chesterfield (£100) Feb 1931
Fulham (£500) May 1933
Q.P.R. (£400) May 1934
Football League: 36-6. FAC: 1-0. FLC: 0-0. Others: 5-0.
Total: 42-6.

Honours: Metropolitan Police v. Royal Navy 20. 5.1942.

On joining the Loftus Road club, Sam suffered a most horrendous injury in a League match, which kept him out of the game for eighteen months. When he fully was recovered he returned to the side as a right back and found that he dominated in that position, until the end of World War Two.

Sam appeared in over 170 matches during the conflict appearing for Brighton & Hove Albion, Chelsea, Crystal Palace and Fulham. In between matches he played golf and during the summer cricket. During the war, his days were spent as a Special Constable, for the Harlesden district of west London.
Debut: 15. 9.1934 v. Brighton & H.A. (H). 2-1. Div.3(S)

ADAMS Ernest W.

(O.R.) Wing
b. Willesden 3. 4.1922
P.N.E.

Fulham	Mar 1947
Q.P.R.	Sep 1947

Football League: 5-0. FAC: 0-0. FLC: 0-0. Others: 0-0.
Total: 5-0.

A diminutive winger who played for the senior squad on two occasions during the latter part of the championship season of 1948. He appeared in the 2nd Division three times the following season but nothing was heard of him after 1950.
Debut: 24.4.1948 v.Newport County (H).1-0.Div. 3 (S)

ADDINALL Albert William

(C.F.) Striker 5' 11" 12st 1lb
b. Marylebone, London 30. 1.1921.
British Oxygen Company

Q.P.R.	1943

Football League: 150-59. FAC: 6-2. FLC: 0-0. Others: 0-0.
Total: 156-61.

Brighton & Hove Albion	Jan 1953
Crystal Palace	Jul 1954
Snowdon Colliery	Jan 1955

Bert was known as a rugged and fearless player, who was full of running and a firm favourite of the crowd. Representing Middlesex & London at school he was quickly snapped-up by the club. Addinall made his debut for Q.P.R. in the latter stages of the 2nd World War, in which he served as a P.T. instructor. Bert was soon representing the Army, playing against the Belgium Army in 1946. Perhaps his most memorable match for the club was their first home match in the 2nd Division after promotion. Leicester City were visiting Loftus Road when the Rangers played havoc with their defence, and during the first 45 minutes of the match Bert scored a hat-trick; Rangers won the match 4-1. In 1953 he was transferred, along with Harry Gilberg, to Brighton in exchange for centre forward Ron Higgins and a four figure sum. In retirement he became a taxi driver in London and for a time was the landlord of the Ferry Inn in Shoreham, before returning once again to his cab.
Debut: 25. 9.1946 v. Bournemouth & B. 3-0. Div. 3 (S)

ADLAM Leslie William

(L.H.) Mid. 5' 10" 12st 7lbs.
b. Guildford, Surrey 24. 6.1897
Farnham Breweries

Guildford United	1920
Oldham Athletic	Mar 1923
Q.P.R.	Nov 1931

Football League: 56-0. FAC: 8-0. FLC: 0-0. Others: 0-0.
Total: 64-0.

Cardiff City	Dec 1933

The manager of the club at the time, Archie Mitchell, negotiated the transfer of the season when he secured the two half backs from Oldham Athletic for £1,500 for the pair. One, Adlam, was a wholehearted player who had cost the Lancashire club the sum of £300 in 1923. Now at the age of 34 he was still worth his weight in gold for his experience alone. With these two players in the side, Adlam and Goodier, the team rose from bottom of the table in January to thirteenth place by the end of the season. Having done his job, Adlam was sold to Cardiff City for £100 in 1933. A year later he was coaching in France.
Debut: 14.11.1931 v. Cardiff City (A). 4-0. Div. 3 (S).

AGOGO Manuel (Junior)

Mid. 5' 11" 11st 9lbs.
b. Accra, Ghana 1. 8.1979
Willesden Constantine

Sheffield Wednesday	1996
Oldham Athletic (Loan)	1999
Chester City (Loan)	1999
Chesterfield (Loan)	1999
Lincoln City (Loan)	1999
Colarado Rapids, USA	2000
San Jose Earthquakes, USA	
Q.P.R.	Mar 2002

Football League: 2-0. FAC: 0-0. FLC: 0-0. Others: 0-0.
Total: 2-0.

Barnet	Jul 2002

After spending two years in the U.S.A. Manuel joined the club on a non-contract basis, where his time was spent mostly on the substitutes bench. After his move to Barnet, he became one of the top Conference goalscorers in the 2002/03 season. (Moved to Bristol Rovers Summer 2003)
Debut: 6. 4.2002 v. Swindon Town (A). 1-0. Div. 2.

AINSWORTH Charles

(O.L.) Wing
b. Ashbourne, Derbyshire in 1885. d. in 1955
Junior Football

Q.P.R.	1908

Southern League: 2-2. FAC: 0-0. FLC: 0-0. Others: 0-0.
Total: 2-2.

Derby County	1909
Grimsby Town	1910

Charlie was tall and well built for one who played on the wing, however he earned glowing praise in the papers of his day. Ainsworth was a first-class player who had a rare turn of speed, scoring in both of the matches that he played in.
Debut: 25. 1.1908 v. Crystal Palace (H). 1-2. SLDiv. 1.

ALLEN Bradley James

Striker 5' 8" 11st 0lbs.
b. Harold Wood, Essex 13. 9.1971.

Q.P.R.	Sep 1988

Football/Premier League: 81-27. FAC: 5-0. FLC: 7-5.
Others: 0-0. Total: 93-32.

Charlton Athletic	(£400,000)	Mar 1996
Colchester United	(Loan)	Feb 1999
Grimsby Town		Jul 1999
Peterborough United		
Bristol Rovers		Nov 2002

Honours: England schoolboy, Youth and U21 caps.

Bradley forced his way into the Q.P.R. side at 20 years of age. He was a hard worker and was comfortable on the ball, showing good awareness in the opponents penalty area. Perhaps his best period with the Rangers was in October 1993 when he scored 7 goals in 6 matches. In 1996 he was transferred to Charlton where he sustained many injuries, which kept him out of the senior squad. Later, further moves took him to four clubs in the lower divisions.
Debut: 14. 1.1989 v. Wimbledon (A). 0-1. Div. 1.

ALLEN Clive Darren

Striker 5' 10" 12st 3lbs.
b. Stepney, London 20. 5.1961

Q.P.R.	Sep 1978

Football League: 49-32. FAC: 1-0. FLC: 5-2. Others: 0-0.
Total: 55-34.

Arsenal	(£1,250,000)	Jun 1980
Crystal Palace	(£1,250,000)	Aug 1980
Q.P.R.	(£700,000)	Jun 1981

Football League: 87-40. FAC: 8-7. FLC: 7-2. Others: 0-0.
Total: 102-49.

Tottenham Hotspur	(£700,000)	Aug 1984
Bordeax, France	(£1,000,000)	Mar 1988
Manchester City	(£1,000,000)	Jul 1989
Chelsea	(£250,000)	Dec 1991
West Ham United	(£275,000)	Mar 1992
Millwall	(£75,000)	1994
Carlisle United	1995	

Honours: England school caps. 15 Youth caps. 3 U21 caps. 5 full caps. Football League cap. 2 FAC runners-up medals. 2nd Div. championship medal. FLC runners-up medal. Footballer of the year for 1987. Football Writers Association Footballer of the year 1987.

The son of the ex-Q.P.R. player manager Les., Clive played for Havering, Essex and London schools before making his debut for Rangers. His prowess as a goalscorer was evident from an early age and all the major clubs were eager to sign him. Arsenal bought and sold him for over £1,000,000 in 1980 (at 19, he was the youngest six figure valued player) without his playing a match, within a 65 day period. Clive packed such a tremendous shot in either foot he broke Jimmy Greaves' scoring record at Spurs with 49 goals in the 1986/87 season. Clive's father Les played for Spurs and Q.P.R., his uncle Dennis played for Reading, his cousin Martin for Q.P.R. and West Ham, his younger brother Bradley for Q.P.R., and his cousin Paul for West Ham, Spurs and Southampton.
Debut: 4.11.1978 v. Chelsea (H). 0-0. Div. 1.

ALLEN James

(R.H.) Def. 5' 10"
b. Amble, Northumberland 18. 8.1913 d. London 1979
Stakeford Albion
Huddersfield Town Mar 1934
Q.P.R. Apl 1935
Football League: 44-1. FAC: 1-0. FLC: 0-0. Others: 1-0. Total: 46-1.
Clapton Orient May 1937

Jimmy Allen was a member of a very good team put together by manager Billy Birrell in 1935. They challenged for the 3rd Division (South) title a year later, but in the event Q.P.R. finished the season in 4th position and Allen moved across London in 1937.
Debut: 14. 9.1935 v. Aldershot 5-0. Div. 3 (S).

ALLEN Joseph

(I.R.) Mid. 5' 9" 11st 4lbs.
b. Bilsthorpe, Notts. 30.12.1909.d.29.11.1978
Bilsthorpe Colliery
Mansfield Town Aug 1929
Bilsthorpe Colliery 1930
Tottenham Hotspur Aug 1932
Northfleet (Loan)
Q.P.R. Apl 1933
Football League: 51-6. FAC: 3-1. FLC: 0-0. Others: 4-0. Total: 58-7.
Mansfield Town Aug 1935
Racing club de Roubaix, FranceNov 1935
Clapton Orient 1937

Joe played for Mansfield Town before they entered the League and went on to Spurs, scoring a goal in his only first team appearance. After a loan period at Northfleet, Mick O'Brien, the manager of Q.P.R. at the time, brought him to Loftus Road. He became part of a very good side side that finished the season 4th in the League in the early 1930s. Joe played cricket during the summer for Bilsthorpe and continued playing football for Mansfield Town during the 2nd World War.
Debut: 30. 9.1933 v. Exeter City (A). 1-1. Div. 3. (S).

ALLEN John C. (Ian)

(O.R.) Wing
Elderslie, Scotland 27. 1.1932
Beith Juniors 1951
Q.P.R. 1952
Football League: 1-1. FAC: 0-0. FLC: 0-0: Others: 0-0. Total: 1-1.
Bournemouth & Boscombe Ath. Jul 1954

His only match for Q.P.R. was at Bournemouth in a 3rd Division (South) League match and the home team liked what they saw. John, or Ian as he was also known, had just finished his National Service and took to the sea air, scoring the only goal in a 1-0 victory for the Rangers. He was to enjoy a happy sojourn at the seaside town until he was sacked by the new manager in May 1956.
Debut: 7. 4.1954 v. Bournemouth & B. A. 1-0. Div.3 (S).

ALLEN Leslie

(I.F.) Mid/Striker 5' 10" 11st 5lb.
b. Dagenham, Essex 4. 9.1937
Briggs Sports
Chelsea Sep 1954
Tottenham Hotspur (£20,000) Dec 1959
Q.P.R. (£21,000) Jul 1965
Football League: 128-55. FAC: 8-3. FLC: 15-4. Others: 0-0. Total: 151-62.
Woodford Town 1971

Honours1 England U23 cap. 1 Football League cap. 1st Div. championship medal. 1 F.A.Cup winners medal. 1 Football League Cup medal. 1 3rd Div. Championship medal.

Les was a neat ball playing inside forward with a quiet temperament. As a sixteen year-old he was a member of the Briggs Sports team that reached the semi-final stages of the FA Amateur Cup in 1954. He joined Chelsea the following season but was never part of the set-up there. However, along came Bill Nicholson the manager of Spurs, exchanged him for English International Johnny Brooks, and so the "Double" team of 1961 was formed. In the summer of 1965 he joined Q.P.R. where his experience was invaluable in bringing on a young side that rose to the 1st Division from the 3rd in successive seasons, including the winning of the League Cup.

After the brief and stormy appointment of Tommy Docherty as manager, for just 28 days, Les was to become the third manager within a month which lasted until 1971, when he resigned to become player/manager of Woodford Town. The managership of Swindon Town followed before he took a similar job in Greece for a time. In later life he worked as a model maker in the car industry.
Debut: 21. 8.1965 v. Brentford (A). 1-6. Div. 3.

ALLEN Martin James

Mid. 5' 10" 11st 0lbs.
b. Reading, Bucks. 4. 8.1965

Q.P.R.	May 1983	
Football League: 136-16. FAC: 10-1. FLC: 18-0. Others: 3-1. Total: 167-18.		
West Ham United	(£675,000)	Aug 1989
Portsmouth	(Loan)	1995
Portsmouth	(£500,000)	Feb 1996
Southend United	(Loan)	1997

Honours: 3 England youth caps. 2 U21 caps.

Martin came from a long line of footballers related to the Allen family. His father Denis played for Charlton Athletic, Reading and Bournemouth and his uncle Les and cousins Bradley and Clive have already been included. He was a vigorous, hard shooting, midfield player who loved to be involved in the match. Unfortunately Martin never saw eye to eye with the manager at the time, Trevor Francis, who quickly had him transferred. In 1999 an appeal to the League for unfair dismissal was granted to him, winning him the sum of £200,000 from Portsmouth. When his playing career finished he joined the coaching staff at Reading before becoming the Barnet manager.
Debut: 23. 3.1985 v. Luton Town (A). 0-2. Div. 1.

ALLEN Reginald Arthur

(Goal) 6' 0" 12st 12lbs.
b. Marylebone, London 3. 5.1919
Corona F.C.

Bromley		1937
Q.P.R.		May 1938
Football League: 183-0. FAC: 18-0. FLC: 0-0. Others: 2-0. Total: 203-0.		
Manchester United	(£11,000)	Jun 1950
Altrincham		Jun 1953

Honours: 1 Football League cap. 1st Div. Championship medal. 3rd Div.(South) Championship medal.

From the beginning it was obvious that Reg was to become a first-class goalkeeper, but the boy himself, modest to a fault, was lacking in confidence. Feeling that he let the side down in his first game for the club as an amateur at Clapton, he slipped off and made his own way to London instead of joining the arranged get-together after the match. However, the club invited him back to join the players in training. He was then asked to appear in the annual Brentford Hospital Cup match and played such a great game, that the scouts of other clubs were soon buzzing around. The club decided to sign him - behind closed doors - the same evening. A few weeks later Reg made his debut as a professional in the reserve side at West Ham and their centre forward scored six goals! West Ham won the game 7-1. What a sad debut for the young Allen but his worth was apparent to anyone in the game and he was soon to take over from Mason as the first team goalkeeper. Undoubtably the best uncapped goalkeeper in the land during the post-war era. Matt Busby was relentlessly chasing him until the club gave way to their offer (the highest fee ever to be paid for a goalkeeper up until that time). Reg was cool under pressure and dealt with the most difficult crosses with ease. He played for the British Army twice during the war while serving as a commando. Allen was taken prisoner during a raid on the North African coast and spent three years in a P.O.W. camp.
Debut: 3.12.1938 v. Newport County (A). 0-2. Div.3(S)

ALLUM Albert
(O.R.) Wing
b. Notting Hill, London 15.10.1930

Brentford	Oct 1952
Dover	
Q.P.R.	Jun 1957

Football League: 1-0. FAC: 0-0. FLC: 0-0. Others: 0-0.
Total: 1-0.

Dover	1958

Allum deputised for Longbottom who in turn took the injured Bobby Cameron's place in midfield. Albert's one match for Rangers, was played before floodlights were made compulsory and the score at Layor Road, Colchester was 1-1 with just a minute to go. The afternoon was so gloomy that Springett in the Rangers goal claimed it was so dark that he never saw the match winner.
Debut: 2. 9.1957 v. Colchester United (A). 1-2. Div.3 (S)

ANDERDSON Edward T.
(I.F.) Mid.
b. Scotland in late 1881

St. Mirren	
Woolwich Arsenal	Nov 1903
Fulham	1904
Willington	
Sheffield United	1905
Q.P.R.	1906

Southern League: 19-3. FAC: 0-0. FLC: 0-0. Others: 0-0.
Total: 19-3.

Although Eddie stayed at Arsenal for just six weeks or so, he seemed to be a fast and skilful player. At Fulham he found himself included in the general clearout of players by the new manager. Whilst at Q.P.R. he played in all three inside forward positions, scoring on his debut.
Debut: 1.9.1906 v. Luton Town (A) (1-1). SLDiv.1.

ANDERSON George Edward
(O.L.) Wing 5' 8" 11st 4lbs
b. Sunderland in 1881

Sunderland schools		
Sunderland Albion	(Trial)	
Sunderland Royal Rovers		
Birmingham		1905
Brentford		Aug 1909
Q.P.R.		May 1912

Southern League: 3-1. FAC: 0-0. FLC: 0-0. Others: 0-0.
Total: 3-1.

Aberdeen	1913

A very skilful player who supported his home town club Sunderland but they never signed him. He usually played on his best form when he was pitted against them. His wife suffered from a long term illness and while he was reluctant to leave her at home in Sunderland (players rarely lived near their clubs) permission was granted to let Anderson visit his wife as often as he liked and to permit compassionate leave if her condition was to become much worse at anytime during the season. In fact he was forced to take some leave to visit his ailing wife. He then had his absence extended, by what was his own illness, followed by a leg injury. By this time he was just a shadow of himself and he was allowed to travel back to Scotland.
Debut: 7. 9.1912 v. Norwich City (H). 1-0. SLDiv. 1.

ANDERSON Thomas Cowan
(O.R.) Wing 5' 9" 11st 7lbs
b. Haddington, Scotland 24. 9.1934

Heart of Midlothian	
Queen of the South	Sep 1955
Watford	Dec 1956
Bournemouth & Boscombe Athletic	Jun 1958
Q.P.R.	Nov 1958

Football League: 10-3. FAC: 0-0. FLC: 0-0. Others: 0-0.
Total: 10-3.

Torquay United	Jul 1959
Stockport County	Jun 1960
Doncaster Rovers	Nov 1961
Wrexham	Mar 1962
Hellos, Australia	Feb 1963
Barrow	Dec 1963
Hellos, Australia	Feb 1964
Watford	Dec 1964
St. Mirren	Oct 1965
Melbourne George Cross, Australia	Dec 1965
Leyton Orient	Jul 1967
Limerick	Jan 1968

Honours: 1 Scottish schoolboy cap.

After finishing his National Service he was quickly snapped-up by Watford. He was described as a very fast winger with blistering pace and nimble footwork an attribute which brought him second place in the 1957 Powderhall Sprint race. Gradually, Tommy became known as "Soccer's Happy Wanderer". Eventually he is believed to have gone to South Africa, before finally settling down in Australia, becoming a Sydney soccer reporter and later hosted his own radio programme.
Debut: 29.11.1958 v. Hull City (A). 0-1. Div. 3.

ANDERTON Sylvan James

(H.B.) Mid. 5' 9" 12st 0lbs
b. Reading, Bucks 23.11.1934
Battle Athletic

Reading		Jun 1951
Chelsea	(£15,000)	Mar 1959
Q.P.R.	(£5,000)	Jun 1962

Football League: 4-0. FAC: 0-0. FLC: 0-0. Others: 0-0.
Total: 4-0.
Dover 1963

A product of Ted Drake's youth policy at Reading, it was the same man that captured him for Chelsea in 1959, when he was manager there. Anderton was a strongly built, hard tackling half back. At Q.P.R. he deputised for Angell when he was out of the squad and stayed until the end of the season. He currently lives in Bideford, Devon, where he writes poetry and also scouts for Reading.
Debut: 20. 1.1962 v. Crystal Palace (H). 1-0. Div.3.

ANDREWS Cecil J.

(L.H.) Def. 5' 11" 13st 3lbs
b. Alton, Hampshire 1.11.1930

Portsmouth	Jan 1949
Crystal Palace	Jun 1952
Q.P.R.	Jun 1956

Football League: 58-1. FAC: 4-0. FLC: 0-0. Others: 3-0.
Total: 65-1.
Sittingbourne 1959

Signed by the manager, Jack Taylor, he was a big, hefty old-fashioned defender, who gave no quarter nor did he ask for any. Alec Stock's arrival at Loftus Road, heralded his departure. Nicknamed ' Archie' , after the popular radio ventriloquist at the time.
Debut: 18. 8.1956 v. Reading (A). 0-1. Div. 3. (S).

ANDREWS James Patrick

(O.L.) 5' 5" 10st 10lbs.
b. Invergordon, Scotland 1. 2.1927
Dundee

West Ham United	(£4,750)	Nov 1951
Clapton Orient		Jun 1956
Q.P.R.		Jun 1959

Football League: 82-16. FAC: 4-1. FLC: 1-0. Others: 1-0.
Total: 88-17.

Honours: Hertfordshire X1 v. F.A.X1. 22. 5.1940

Jimmy joined Alec Stock at Q.P.R. in 1959. At 32 years of age he was a fast and nimble winger, who was given the job of chief coach to the reserve team. It was to make a tremendous impact on the future of the club. Eventually Andrews became the team manager while Stock became the General Manager. The set-up lasted just 77 days before Jimmy quit the job in 1965 to become a coach at Chelsea, then Luton Town in 1967, followed by Spurs five years later. Finally he took the job of coach at Cardiff City in 1973. Within four months he became the manager and stayed as such until he was sacked in November 1978. Since then Andrews has remained in Wales as chief scout to Southampton.
Debut: 22. 8.1959 v. Swindon Town (H). 2-0. Div. 3.

ANGELL Brett

(F) Striker 6' 2" 13st. 11lbs
b. Marlborough, Wiltshire 20. 8.1968
Portsmouth
Cheltenham Town

Derby County	(£40,000)	1987
Stockport County	(£33,000)	1988
Southend United	(£100,000)	1990
Everton	(loan)	1993
Southend United		1993
Everton	(£500,000)	1993
Sunderland	(£600,000)	1994
Sheffield United	(loan)	1995
W.B.A.	(loan)	1995
Sunderland		1996
Stockport County	(£120,000)	1996
Notts County	(loan)	1999
P.N.E.	(loan)	1999
Walsall		2000
Rushden & Diamonds		2002
Port Vale		2002
Q.P.R.		2002

Football League: 13-0: FAC: 0-0. FLC: 0-0. Others: 0-0.
Total: 13-0.
Linfield 2003

Angell appeared an awkward looking player in possession of the ball, nevertheless he has the ability to be in the right place at the right time. Despite scoring over 160 goals in a long career he failed to notch one at Loftus Road.
Debut: 23.11.2002 v. Luton Town (A). 0-0. Div. 2.

ANGELL Peter F.

(L.H.). Def. 5' 10" 11st 2lbs
b. Chalvey, Buckinghamshire 11. 1.1932 d. 1979
Slough Town
Q.P.R. Jul 1953
Football League: 417-37. FAC: 27-1. FLC: 6-2. Others: 7-0.
Total: 457-40

Peter was originally a left winger at Slough Town when Charlton Athletic took an interest in him. But after a few games at the Valley in the London Mid-Week League he was allowed to join Q.P.R., where he signed professional forms in 1953. He was one of the most reliable players the club was to have in their post-war history. Noted as the best defender in the lower divisions during the fifties and sixties, he could in fact play in any position he was asked to and for several years was the club captain. Angell was also an expert penalty taker and seldom missed. He played week after week with almost boring consistency, and eventually totalled over 460 matches during his 12 year period at Q.P.R. When his playing days were over he went to Charlton Athletic as a coach.
Debut: 12. 9.1953 v. Walsall (H). 2-0. Div. 3. (S).

ARCHER Arthur

(R.B.) Def. 5' 9" 12st 7lbs
b. Ashby-de-la-Zouch, Derbyshired. 1940

Burton St. Edmonds		1892
Tutbury Hampton		1894
Swadlincote Town		
Burton Wanderers		1895
Small Heath	(£50)	Aug 1897
New Brompton	(£40)	Mar 1902
Wingfield House		
Q.P.R.	Aug 1903	

Southern League: 52-0. FAC: 1-0. FLC: 0-0. Others: 0-0. Total: 53-0.

Tottenham Hotspur	(Loan)	Aug 1903
Norwich City		Aug 1905
Brighton & Hove Albion		Aug 1907
Millwall		Aug 1908

Honours: Staffordshire Cup winners medal. Kettering & Bass Cup winners medal.

One of the most colourful characters to come out of this period of football. A tough, uncompromising player with a huge kick and a fearless tackle. A big man in stature and in heart, who was extremely popular wherever he went. He signed for Q.P.R. and Spurs simultaneously playing mid-week for the latter in the London League and for Rangers, in the Southern League. Arthur retired in 1909 to coach in Germany and Belgium before the 1st World War and in Italy after it, finally becoming the Watford trainer in 1924.
Debut: 5. 9.1903 v. Brentford (H). 1-0. SLDiv. 1.

ARDILES Osvaldo Cesar

Mid. 5' 6" 9st. 10lbs.
b. Cordoba, Argentina 3. 8.1952

Red Star, Cordoba		
Institute de Cordoba		
Huracan, Argentina		1975
Tottenham Hotspur	(£325,000)	Jul 1978
Paris St. Germain	(Loan)	1982
Blackburn Rovers	(Loan)	1988
Q.P.R.		Aug 1988

Football League: 8-0. FAC: 1-0. FLC: 1-0. Others: 0-0. Total: 10-0.

Fort Lauderdale, U.S.A.		Jun 1989
Swindon Town		Jul 1989

Honours: Argentian International and member of the World Cup squad in 1978 and 1982. UEFA Cup winners medal. F.A. Cup winners medal. F.A.Cup runners-up medal.

A World Cup International who graced the game with his unique style of play, and his ability to ride tackles while he was running with the ball, he reached Q.P.R. at the age of 36 years on a free transfer. Ossie had moved to Spurs ten years earlier along with Ricardo Villa, a centre forward, the pair causing quite a sensation. After only a few matches for Q.P.R. Ossie suffered a broken leg. Swindon Town then offered him the manager's chair, which he took and he soon guided them to promotion. In March 1991 he took over at Newcastle United but he was given the sack 12 months later, the same fate awaited him at W.B.A. in 1992 and at Spurs in 1993. Ossie was last heard of as being the manager of Guadalajara, Mexico, in 1995.
Debut: 27. 8.1988 v. Manchester United (A). 0-0. Div. 1.

ARMITAGE Stanley

(I.L.) Mid.
b. Woolwich, London 5. 6.1919

Charlton Athletic	1939
Q.P.R.	1946

Football League: 2-0. FAC: 0-0. FLC: 0-0. Others: 0-0. Total: 2-0.

Gravesend & Northfleet	1948

As happened with many young players in 1939, Stan was called to arms, losing the best part of his career during the conflict. He eventually played in non-League football but retired shortly afterwards.
Debut: 14. 9.1946 v. Reading (H). 2-0. Div. 3. (S).

ARMSTRONG James Harris

(C.H.) Def. 6' 0" 12st 2lbs
b. Lemington, Nr. Newcastle 8. 3.1904
d.Watford 13. 4.1971

Easington Colliery	1925
Clapton Orient	Nov 1926
Q.P.R.	May 1928

Football League: 122-5. FAC: 11-0. FLC: 0-0. Others: 0-0. Total: 133-5.

Watford	May 1933

Honours: Hertfordshire F.A. X1 v. F.A.X1 22. 5.1940

Jimmy was ideally built for the role of centre half and was a stalwart in the middle of the defence in the early thirties. He became a casualty, when the new manager, Mick O'Brien, cleared out a lot of players when he arrived at the club. Watford immediately signed Jimmy and the club never regretted it, for he was on their books until 1941. When his career at Watford ended he took a job at Universal Asbestos and they employed him for the rest of his life.
Debut: 10.11.1928 v. Exeter City (A). 1-1. Div.3 (S).

ASHFORD Herbert E.

(L.H.) Mid
b. Southall, Middlesex

Brentford	1919
Q.P.R.	1920

Football League: 10-0. FAC: 0-0. FLC: 0-0. Others: 0-0. Total: 10-0.

Not much is known about this player, Bert was a reserve at Brentford and at Q.P.R., standing in for either Mitchell or O'Brien when one or other of them was out of the team.
Debut: 12. 2.1921 v. Plymouth Argyle (A). 0-1. Div.3(S)

ASHMAN Donald

(L.B.) Def. 5' 10" 11st 12lbs
b. Staindrop, Durham 9.10.1902d. 1984

Cockfield Athletic		
Middlesbrough	(£10)	May 1924
Q.P.R.	(£500)	May 1932

Football League: 75-0. FAC: 5-0. FLC: 0-0. Others: 4-0. Total: 84-0.

Darlington	May 1935

Honours: 2 2nd Div. Championship medals.

Cool, unruffled and undoubtably the best full back playing in the division at the time. When signed by Middlesbrough, Don was known as an inside forward but turned out to be an excellent full back and became an established part of their promotion winning side in 1927 and 1929 seasons. He finally ended his playing career appearing for Darlington in the middle thirties.
Debut: 27. 8.1932 v. Brentford (H). 2-3. Div. 3. (S).

ASTON Charles Lane

(R.B.) Def.
b. Bilston, Staffordshire in July 1875
d. Leytonstone 9. 1.1931

Bilstoe United	
Walsall	Dec 1895
Aston Villa	Apl 1898
Q.P.R.	Jun 1901

Southern League: 25-1. FAC: 3-0. FLC: 0-0. Others: 0-0. Total: 28-1.

Burton United	Aug 1902
Gresley Rovers	1903
Burton United	Jun 1904
Watford	May 1905
Leyton	Jun 1908

Honours: 1st Div. Championship medal

A very efficient player who was an expert at floating the ball down the line or across the pitch rather than giving it a hefty punt up-field. Charlie enjoyed going forward with the attack and seemed to have plenty of stamina to do so. At Aston Villa he was the reserve to the great Howard Spencer and deputised for him on 14 occasions when they won the championship in 1899.
Debut: 7. 9.1901 v Watford (H). 0-1. SLDiv. 1.

BAILEY Dennis L.

(C.F.) Striker 5' 10" 11st 6lbs
b. Lambeth, London 13.11.1965
Tulse Hill Comprehensive
Watford
Barking

Fulham		Nov 1986
Farnborough Town		
Crystal Palace	(£10,000)	Dec 1987
Bristol Rovers	(Loan)	Feb 1989
Birmingham City	(£80,000)	Aug 1989
Bristol Rovers	(Loan)	Mar 1991
Q.P.R.	(£150,000)	Jul 1991

Football / Premier League: 39-10. FAC: 5-3. FLC: 2-1. Others: 2-0. Total: 48-14.

Charlton Athletic	(Loan)	Oct 1993
Watford	(Loan)	Mar 1994
Brentford	(Loan)	Jan 1995
Gillingham	(£25,000)	Aug 1995
Lincoln City		Mar 1998
Cambridge City		
Forest Green		

Honours: Leyland Daf Cup winners medal

His close ball control and ability to take on defenders in tight situations were decidedly the main factors for Q.P.R. buying him. Dennis proved the point when he scored the equaliser at Highbury on the opening day of the 1991/92 season. Scoring a hat-trick against Manchester United at Old Trafford on New Year's Day 1992, was the highlight of his career at the club, and the whole match was televised across the land. Yet after various loan periods he was finally transferred to Gillingham.
Debut: 17. 8.1991 v. Arsenal (A). 1-1. Div. 1.

BAILEY Sidney

(L.B.) Def. 5' 9" 11st 8lbs
b. London
Q.P.R. 1921
Football League: 1-0. FAC: 0-0. FLC: 0-0. Others: 0-0. Total: 1-0.

The only fact known about this player was that he was an amateur. Sid's sole outing in the senior squad was late in the season.
Debut: 22. 4.1922 v. Merthyr Town (H). 0-0. Div.3 (S).

BAIN Kenneth

(L.B.) Def. 5' 8" 11st 8lbs
b. Scotland
Mid Rhondda
Q.P.R. 1921
Football League: 91-0. FAC: 7-0. FLC: 0-0. Others: 0-0. Total: 98-0.

Ken was the regular left back in the early 1920s when the club ended the season bottom of Division 3. (South) in 1924, and he was included in the general clear-out of players by manager Ned Liddell.
Debut: 12.11.1921 v. Aberdare Athletic (H).1-0. Div.3 (S)

BAKER Peter R.

(R.B.) Def
b. Walthamstow, London 24. 8.1934
Tottenham Hotspur

Sheffield Wednesday	Nov 1954
Q.P.R.	Mar 1961

Football League: 27-0. FAC: 0-0. FLC: 1-0. Others: 0-0. Total: 28-0.
Romford 1963

Peter was the cousin of Peter Russell Baker, (hence both men shared the same initials), only Peter Russell played for the famous Spurs double team in the early sixties. The two of them both turned out for Spurs reserves in the 1950s as amateurs. However , unlike his famous cousin, the Q.P.R. Baker achieved few first team games wherever he played.
Debut: 4. 3.1961 v. Port Vale (H). 1-0. Div. 3.

BAKHOLT Kurt

Mid
b. Odense, Denmark 12. 8.1963
Vegle, Denmark

Aston Villa	1985
Q.P.R.	1986

Football League: 1-0. FAC: 0-0. FLC: 0-0. Others: 0-0. Total: 1-0.
Bronby, Denmark 1987

Honours: Danish U21 International

Kurt did not play a match for Aston Villa, instead he was given a contract at Q.P.R. Coming on as a substitute at Main Road in February 1986, replacing Robbie James in the second half. His contract was not renewed at the end of the season.
Debut: 8. 2.1986 v. Manchester City (A). 0-2. Div. 1.

BALDOCK John William N.

(L.H.) Mid
b. Shadwell, London in 1893
Q.P.R. 1913
Southern/Football League: 57-8. FAC: 0-0. FLC: 0-0. Others: 0-0. Total: 57-8.

John was a somewhat clever player and made no fewer than 150 appearances for the club during the 1st World War. Drafted directly into the senior squad from the juniors, he caused a sensation by scoring on his debut. His early days were spent in the forward line but he settled down into a solid midfield player.
Debut: 6.12.1913 v. Coventry City (H). 3-0. SLDiv. 1.

BALLANTYNE John

(I.F.) Mid 5' 8" 11st 0lbs
b. Glasgow, Scotland 27.10.1899
Glasgow Ashfield
Partick Thistle
Boston Wonder Workers
Partick Thistle 1929
Falkirk
Q.P.R. 1935
Football League: 25-3. FAC: 1-0. FLC: 0-0. Others: 0-0.
Total: 26-3.

Honours: Scottish League v. Irish League. Scottish Cup runners- up medal.

An experienced inside left who had played some of his soccer in the U.S.A. in the 1920s while he was working there as an engineer. John rejoined Partick Thistle when he returned and played in the 1930 Scottish Cup Final. At Q.P.R. he was at the heart of a very good team that ended the season in fourth place in the title race.
Debut: 16.11.1935 v. Northampton T. (A).4-1.Div. 3(S)

BALOGUN Jesilimi

(C.F.) Striker
b. Nigeria, Africa 27. 3.1931
Skegness Town 1954
Peterborough United 1955
Q.P.R. 1956
Football League: 13-3. FAC: 2-2. FLC: 0-0. Others: 1-2.
Total: 16-7.
Holbeach United 1957

The competition for the place of centre forward at the club was intense at this period in time. Tesi lasted the season, after scoring on his debut. His early career was marked by his refusal to wear anything on his feet during a match. On another occasion, while he was appearing in a reserve match, it snowed and not having encountered the stuff before, Balogun ran off the pitch refusing to go back until he was convinced that the cold powder was harmless!
Debut: 13.10.1956 v. Watford (H). 3-1. Div. 3. (S).

BANKOLE Ademola

(G.) 6' 3" 12st 10lbs
b. Abeokuta, Nigeria 9. 9.1969
Shooting Stars, Ibadan, Nigeria
Doncaster Rovers Nov 1995
Leyton Orient Dec 1995
Crewe Alexandria Sep 1996
Q.P.R. (£50,000) Jul 1998
Football League: 1-0. FAC: 0-0. FLC: 0-0. Others: 0-0.
Total: 1-0.
Bradford City (Loan) Mar 2000
Crewe Alexandria Aug 2000

A very unorthodox but agile goalkeeper who was released back to his former club in August 2000, where he became first choice.
Debut: 9.10.1999 v. Tranmere Rovers (H). 2-1. Div. 1.

BANKS Reginald

(O.L.)
b.
W.B.A. 1934
Q.P.R. 1935
Football League: 12-3. FAC: 0-0. FLC: 0-0. Others: 0-0.
Total: 12-3.
Tunbridge Wells Rangers 1937

Honours: 1 England Amateur cap v. Wales.

Reg remained an amateur during the days he was with W.B.A., however, he never did appear in the senior squad for them. When he signed for Q.P.R. he became a professional.
Debut: 31. 8.1935 v. Millwall (H). 2-3. Div. 3. (S).

BANNER William Henry

(C.H.) Def
b. Barnsley, Yorks. in 1878 d. Holmewood 28. 6.1936
Poolsbrook United
Dronfield Town Aug 1898
New Wittingham Exchange Apl 1900
Chesterfield Town Aug 1901
Q.P.R. 1903
Southern League: 4-0. FAC: 0-0. FLC: 0-0. Others: 0-0.
Total: 4-0.
Chesterfield Town Jul 1904
Hardwick Colliery Sep 1908
Denby United Sep 1908
Hardwick Colliery

A powerful, elegant and versatile player who was able to play anywhere in defence. However, he was only called upon to play in four matches, so after one season he returned to Saltergate. Retiring at the age of 30 he continued to play for Hardwick Colliery until the start of the 1st World War.

Bill was quiet an introspective man who won many friends in the Holmeswood community for his services to local sport as a football and cricket coach.
Debut: 28.12.1903 v. Northampton T. (A). 1-2. SLDiv.1

BANNISTER Gary

Striker 5' 8" 11st 10lbs
b. Warrington , Cheshire 22. 7.1960

Coventry City		May 1978
Detroit Express	(Loan)	Apl 1980
Sheffield Wednesday	(£100,000)	Aug 1981
Q.P.R.	(£200,000)	Aug 1984

Football League: 136-56. FAC: 9-1. FLC: 23-9. Others: 4-6.
Total: 172-72.

Coventry City	(£300,000)	Mar 1988
W.B.A.	(£250,000)	Mar 1990
Oxford United	(Loan)	Mar 1992
Nottingham Forest		Aug 1992
Stoke City		May 1993
Hong Kong		1994
Lincoln City		1994
Darlington		1995

Honours: 1 cap at U21 level. 2nd Div. runners-up medal. League Cup runners-up medal.

A product of Hollins Green, near Warrington, he made only 22 appearances for Coventry City prior to his £100,000 transfer to Sheffield Wednesday in 1981. However, Gary made an immediate impact by scoring 22 goals in his first season and 66 goals in all. Q.P.R. paid £200,000 for him in 1984 and he settled well at Loftus Road, scoring 72 goals before he returned to Coventry in 1988 for a substantial fee. He was arguably the best signing made by Alan Mullery during his reign as manager at Loftus Road. Gary was rather short for a striker, nevertheless, he made up for this with his quick, intelligent play. Bannister was always on the look-out for mistakes made by opposing defenders and would punish them with his quick reflexes.
Debut: 25. 8.1984 v. W.B.A. (H). 3-1. Div. 1.

BARACLOUGH Ian R.

(W.B.) 6' 1" 12st 2lbs
b. Leicester 4.12.1970

Leicester City		Dec 1988
Wigan Athletic	(Loan)	Mar 1990
Grimsby Town	(Loan)	Dec 1990
Grimsby Town		Aug 1991
Lincoln City		Aug 1992
Mansfield Town		Jun 1994
Notts County		Oct 1995
Q.P.R.	(£50,000)	Mar 1998

Football League: 125-1. FAC: 7-0. FLC: 7-0. Others: 0-0.
Total: 139-1.

Notts County	Aug 2001

Honours: England Youth caps. 3rd Div. Championship medal.

A striker who was turned into an attacking full back at Mansfield Town. He opened his scoring account with one of the most remarkable goals ever witnessed at Field Mill - a free kick from fully 50 yards. A tall defender who liked to get forward as often as possible. Ian became a dead-ball specialist and was a favourite of the spectators during his three years at Loftus Road, where he operated on the left hand side of the pitch. He moved to Notts County for the 2001/02 season and immediately established himself as a first team player.
Debut: 21. 3.1998 v. Stoke City (A). 1-2. Div. 1.

BARBER Michael J.

(O.L.) Wing
b. Kensington, London 15. 8.1941

Arsenal	
Q.P.R.	Dec 1959

Football League: 63-11. FAC: 2-2. FLC: 4-0. Others: 0-0.
Total: 69-13.

Notts County	Jul 1963

A fast two-footed winger who indeed could play on both sides of the park. Mike would interchange with the opposite winger on several occasions during the course of a match.
Debut: 5. 9.1960 v. Coventry City (A). 4-4. Div. 3.

BARDSLEY David John

(W.B.) 5' 10" 10st 0lbs
b. Manchester 11. 9.1964

Blackpool	Nov 1982	
Watford	(£150,000)	Nov 1983
Oxford United	(£265,000)	Sep 1987
Q.P.R.	(£500,000)	Sep 1989

Football League: 253 -4. FAC: 19-0. FLC: 20-1. Others: 3-1.
Total: 295-6.

Blackpool	Jul 1998

Honours: 2 England Youth caps. 2 England International caps. F.A.Cup runners-up medal.

Dave was ever-present in the F.A.Cup run of Watford, which took them to Wembley. He scored the first two League goals of his career in his 100th appearance for the Vicarage Road club, as a substitute in a 5-1 victory at Chelsea. The England Youth manager Graham Taylor signed him for Watford, and nine years later capped him at senior level. After nearly four years in Hertfordshire, he moved on to Oxford United where he stayed for two seasons, before becoming a big signing at Loftus Road. An excellent full back with a vast amount of pace and good attacking flair, who had the ability to cross the ball on the run. Dave was also very steady in his defensive role and although some of his tackling was somewhat crude at times, he was a huge asset to the team and gave very many fine performances. After nine years and nearly 300 appearances, Dave moved back to his first League club Blackpool, after an absence of 15 years.
Debut: 16. 9.1989 v. Derby County (H). 0-1. Div. 1.

BARKER Simon

(Mid) 5' 9" 11st 0lbs
b. Farnworth, Lancashire 4.11.1964

Blackburn Rovers		Nov 1982
Q.P.R.	(£400,000)	Jul 1988

Football League: 315-33. FAC: 23-3. FLC: 31-5. Others: 7-0.
Total: 376-41.

Port Vale	Sep 1998

Honours: 4 England U21 caps. Football Milk Cup final medal.

In July 1988 QPR broke Blackburn Rovers transfer record when they paid £400,000 for the midfielder. However, he initially found it difficult to break into the first team at Loftus Road, but once he had settled down, Simon developed a formidable partnership with Ray Wilkins. An attacking player who passed the ball intelligently and was capable of opening the tightest of defences. Simon was a good skilful player on his day and had an astute football brain. His stay at Loftus Road lasted ten years, during which time he made close to 400 appearances (at a very high average of 38 per season in all first team matches), the most during the 1994/95 season. He enjoyed a benefit match v. Jamaica in 1998, which produced record receipts for a Q.P.R. player, and later that year moved on to the Potteries, and Port Vale.
Debut: 27. 9.1998 v. Manchester United (A). 0-0. Div. 1.

BARLEY Derek Charles

(C.F.) Striker
b. Highbury, London 20. 3.1932
Maidenhead United

Arsenal	Dec 1951
Q.P.R.	May 1953

Football League: 4-0. FAC: 0-0. FLC: 0-0. Others: 0-0.
Total: 4-0.

Aldershot	Jul 1954
Headington United	1955

Honours: 2 England Youth caps.

The son of a pre-war Arsenal player who seemed to be a very bright prospect indeed, reaching the East Anglian Cup final in 1952 and helping Arsenal win the London Midweek League in the following year. However, that was Derek's sole achievement in football, and he failed to make the grade at a high level.
Debut: 29. 8.1953 v. Aldershot (H). 0-2. Div. 3. (S).

BARNES William Edwin

(O.L.) Wing 5' 9" 10st 4lbs
b. West Ham 20. 5.1879

Leyton	1899
Thames Ironworks	1900
Sheffield United	1901
West Ham United	1902
Luton Town	1904
Q.P.R.	1907

Southern League: 261-26. FAC: 15-1. FLC: 0-0. Others: 3-0.
Total: 234-27.

Southend United	1913

Honours: F.A. Cup winners medal. 2 Southern League championship medals. Represented the Southern League v. the Scottish League.

A very tricky and experienced winger who was made captain as soon as he arrived at the club, and gave good service for six years. Retiring from playing in 1915, William had to wait until after the hostilities of the 1st World War before he could take-up a coaching appointment in Spain with Bilbao.
Debut: 2. 9.1907 v. Tottenham Hots. (H).3-3. SLDiv. 1.

BARR Hamid

(Mid)
b. London 1980
Fisher Athletic

Q.P.R.	Oct 2001

Football League: 0(1) FAC: 0-0. FLC: 0-0. Others: 0-0.
Total: 1-0

Gravesend & Northfleet	Oct 2002
Tonbridge	

Made one solitary substitute appearance, in the Associate Members Cup before moving back into non-League football.
Debut: 16. 10. 2001 v. Yeovil Town (A).0-3. LDV Trophy

BARR John M.

(C.H.) CD 6' 0" 12st 7lbs
b. Glasgow, Scotland
Third Lanark

Q.P.R.	1939

Football League: 4-0. FAC: 0-0. FLC: 0-0. Others: 0-0.
Total: 4-0.

Dundee United	Nov 1947

John was unfortunate, for the 2nd World War interrupted his career at Q.P.R. as soon as he joined the club. He was called up to join the army and was taken prisoner by the Germans in the Western desert. John was forced to work in a concrete factory and had little chance of playing football. After arriving back in Britain at the end of the war, his transfer back to his native Scotland was his main concern.
Debut: 2.11.1946 v. Notts County (A). 2-1. Div. 3. (S).

BARR William

(C.H.) CD
b.
London Caledonians

Q.P.R.	1925

Football League: 2-0. FAC: 0-0. FLC: 0-0. Others: 0-0.
Total: 2-0.

Honours: Amateur Cup winners medal.

Billy Barr was the centre half who turned out for the London Caledonians when they lifted the F.A. Amateur Cup by beating Evesham Town 2-1 in extra time in 1923. At Q.P.R. he was released after the team finished last in the table with 21 points.
Debut: 5. 9.1925 v. Merthyr Town (H). 1-1. Div.3 (S).

BARRIE Walter B.

(R.B.) Def. 5' 10" 11st 8lbs
b. Kirkcakly, Scotland 9. 8.1909

Hibernian	
Arthurlie	
U.S.A. soccer	
West Ham United	1931
Q.P.R.	1932

Football League: 157-1. FAC: 12-0. FLC: 0-0. Others: 3-0.
Total: 172-1.

Carlisle United	Mar. 1938

Honours: London Challenge Cup winners medal.

Walter was a part-time pro with Hibs and he was one of the many Scotsmen to sample soccer in the U.S.A. in the 1920s. At West Ham he remained a reserve for his two year period there, but at Q.P.R. he was regarded as a first rate defender who became part of a very good squad that challenged for promotion just before the 2nd World War. After six years and 157 League appearances, he moved to the north-west and joined Third Division (North) Carlisle United in 1938. When not playing football he enjoyed a round of golf and sketching was another of his hobbies.
Debut: 24. 2.1932 v. Watford (H). 2-1. Div. 3. (S).

BARRON Paul George

Goal 6' 2" 13st 5lbs
b. Woolwich, London 16. 9.1953

Erith Grammar school		
Borough Road College		
Wycombe Wanderers		1973
Slough Town		1975
Welling United		
Plymouth Argyle		Jul 1976
Arsenal	(£40,000)	Jul 1978
Crystal Palace	(£200,000)	Aug 1980
W.B.A.	(£60,000)	Dec 1982
Stoke City	(Loan)	Jan 1985
Q.P.R.	(£35,000)	Mar 1985

Football League: 32-0. FAC: 1-0. FLC: 0-0. Others: 0-0.
Total: 33-0.

Reading	(Loan)	Dec 1986
Welling United		1988
Cheltenham Town		1989
Welling United		1990

Honours: Charity Shield runners-up medal. League Cup runners-up medal.

A big, strong and very experienced goalkeeper who took over the No. 1 spot during Jim Smith's reign at the club. With the transfer of David Seaman as the first choice goalkeeper in 1986, Paul was made redundant and drifted into non-League football.
Debut: 28. 9.1985 v. Birmingham City (H). 3-1. Div. 1.

BARTLETT Frederick Leslie

(C.H.) CD. 6' 0" 12st 0lbs
b. Reading, Buckinghamshire 5. 3.1913 d.1968

Q.P.R.	1933

Football League: 48-0. FAC: 2-0. FLC: 0-0. Others: 1-0.
Total: 51-0.

Clapton Orient	1937
Gloucester City	1948

Fred was earmarked in the late 1930s as the best young player in the country. Tall and elegant he dominated the centre of the pitch. Over 200 wartime appearances were notched-up by him for the Orient club.
Debut: 3.11.1934 v. Millwall (A). 0-2. Div. 3. (S).

BEAN Marcus.

Mid. 5' 11" 11st. 6lbs
b. Hammersmith, London 2.11.1984
Q.P.R. Schoolboy signing
Football League: 7-0. FAC: 0-0. FLC: 0-0. Others: 1-0.

Marcus joined the club at a professional level at the start of the 2002/03 season, and had the indignity of being sent-off in his debut match!
Debut: 26. 8.2002 v. Wycombe Wand's (A).1-4. Div.2.

BEATS Edwin

(C.F.) Striker
b.

Aston Villa	1925
Q.P.R.	1927

Football League: 1-1. FAC: 0-0. FLC: 0-0. Others: 0-0.
Total: 1-1.

Honours: 2 England Schoolboy International caps.

An English Schoolboy International who played against Scotland and Wales in the 1920s. His only match for Q.P.R. was the 6-1 defeat at Millwall. Eddie scored the only goal for Rangers, the match report revealing: *"That a rasping shot from the visitor's centre forward was deflected off Len Graham, the Millwall left half and beat the goalkeeper for the Q.P.R. goal."*
Debut: 10. 3.1928 v. Millwall (A). 1-6. Div. 3. (S).

BECK John Alexander

Mid. 5' 10" 11st 9lbs
b. Edmonton, London 25. 5.1954

Q.P.R.		May 1972

Football League: 40-1. FAC: 5-0. FLC: 2-0. Others: 0-0. Total: 47-1.

Coventry City	(£40,000)	Jun 1976
Fulham	(£80,000)	Oct 1978
AFC Bournemouth		Sep 1982
Cambridge United		Jul 1986

John was a dangerous midfield schemer who was an expert at dead ball situations and a specialist at crossing the ball. John Beck is well known as a manager for taking his club, Cambridge United, to the quarter finals of the F.A.Cup in 1990 and to the brink of the Premiership in 1992. His impact as a manager can only be described as sensational, but his long ball style of play was not liked by the purists. Other manager postions included those at Preston North End in 1992, Lincoln City in 1995 and Barrow in 1998.
Debut: 26.12.1972 v. Leyton Orient (H). 3-1. Div. 2.

BECK Mikkel Venge

Striker 6' 2" 12st 9lbs
b. Arhus, Denmark 12. 5.1973

B1909, Denmark		1992
Fortuna Koln, Germany	(£25,000)	1993
Middlesbrough		Sep 1996
Derby County	(£500,000)	Mar 1999
Nottingham Forest	(Loan)	Nov 1999
Q.P.R.	(Loan)	Feb 2000

Football League: 11-4. FAC: 0-0. FLC: 0-0. Others: 0-0. Total: 11-4.

Aalborg	(Loan)	Apl 2000
Lille, France		May 2000

Honours: 19 Danish International caps. 2nd Div. Championship medal.

A striker who is willing, hard working and promising but never quite delivers the real thing. Helped B1909 to win promotion to the Danish 1st Division but was sold to solve a cashflow problem. Mikkel was transferred to Middlesbrough under the free 'Bosman' ruling. After two loan periods, including that at Q.P.R., he settled in French football with Lille. His father Carl played for the Danish side AGF.
Debut: 12. 2.2000 v. Stockport County (H). 1-1. Div. 1.

BEDFORD Noel Brian

(C.F.) Striker 5' 11" 11st 8lbs
b. Ferndale, Wales 24.12.1933
Beddau Youth club, South Wales

Reading	Apl 1954
Southampton	Jul 1955
Bournemouth & Boscombe Ath.	Aug 1956
Q.P.R.	Jul 1959

Football League: 258-161. FAC: 16-13. FLC: 8-6. Others: 1-0. Total: 283-180.

Scunthorpe United	Sep 1965
Brentford	Sep 1966
Atlanta Chiefs, U.S.A.	Apl 1967
Bexley United	Nov 1968

Alec Stock paid £750 to acquire his services from Bournemouth after he had scored 32 goals in 75 League games. At Q.P.R. he scored 180 goals in 294 matches, which repaid his fee many times over. A busy, bustling player, who was a handful for any opposing defender. Brian had a fierce shot and scored approximately 25 goals a season throughout his time at the 'Bush'. After short periods at Scunthorpe and Brentford, he moved across the Atlantic and joined Atlanta Chiefs. But on his return from the U.S.A., in 1967, Brian found himself banned from playing by the F.A. due to the fact that the American Football Association was then not affiliated. It took a year for him to successfully appeal against the ban, however, in 1968 he was forced to retire owing to a severe knee injury. After his retirement from football he became a professional tennis coach. Bedford became the stadium manager at Loftus Road until 1992 when he was made redundant.
Debut: 22. 8.1959 v. Swindon Town (H). 2-0. Div. 3.

BEDINGFIELD Frank

(C.F.) Striker 5' 8" 12st 7lbs
b. Sunderland in 1877 d. Nov 1904
South Shields schools
Yarmouth
Kirkley
Rushden
Aston Villa 1898
Q.P.R. 1899
Southern League: 24-17. FAC: 8-4. FLC: 0-0. Others: 0-0.
Total: 32-21.
Portsmouth 1900

Honours: County cap.

Short and stocky for a centre forward, Frank was very fast off the mark and had a wholehearted attitude towards the game. At Q.P.R. he became the top goalscorer for the club in their first season in the Southern League. During the following season he played for Portsmouth and in 1901he was tragically struck down with consumption. Cash was raised to send him to South Africa to recuperate in the sun but it was too late to avert his premature death.
Debut: 9.9.1899 v. Tottenham Hotspur (A). 0-1. SLDiv.1

BEECHAM Ernest Cromwell

Goal 5' 9" 11st 7lbs
b. Hertford 24. 8.1896 d. Hertford Aug 1985
Hertford Town 1918
Fulham Oct 1923
Q.P.R. May 1932
Football League: 86-0. FAC: 9-0. FLC: 0-0. Others: 0-0.
Total: 95-0.
Brighton & Hove Albion Sep 1935
Swindon Town Nov 1935

Honours: Represented an English X1 in Holland. Played for the Professionals v. the Amateurs. London Combination winners medal.

A fearless goalkeeper, short in stature but big in heart, who possessed a massive pair of hands and a huge kick. Ernest's career was renewed at Q.P.R. after he had suffered a particularly nasty spinal injury with his previous club. Then in 1934 he broke his arm and decided to retire, however, he was signed by Brighton & Hove Albion in 1935 but never played for them. He did turn out for Swindon Town, when their goalkeeper was injured. Ernest died in the same house as he was born in.
Debut: 27. 8.1932 v. Brentford (H). 2-3. Div. 3. (S).

BELLINGHAM James

(R.B.) Def 6' 0" 13st 7lbs
b. Falkirk, Scotland in 1878
Falkirk Excelsior 1899
Falkirk Hawthorn 1899
Woodlane Rovers 1900
Falkirk 1900
Q.P.R. 1900
Southern League: 15-0. FAC: 2-0. FLC: 0-0. Others: 0-0.
Total: 17-0.
Grimsby Town May 1901
Brentford 1903
Willesden Town 1905

Honours: Scottish inter-County player. Scottish Junior International trialist.

Bellingham had a fine knowledge of the game and was able to play anywhere in the defence. Although he was tall and heavy, he was very quick on his feet for a big man. James was a blacksmith by trade.
Debut: 8. 9.1900 v. Swindon Town (H). 7-1. SLDiv. 1.

BEN ASKER Aziz

CD 6' 2" 13st 5lbs
b. Chateau Gontier, France 30. 3.1976
Stade Lavallois, France
QP.R. (Loan) Aug 2001
Football League: 18-0. FAC: 0-0. FLC: 1-0. Others: 1-0.
Total: 20-0.
Srade Lavallois, France May 2002

Ben Asker came on a one year loan from France and was subsequently dropped from the squad after he received an injury, whereupon he returned to his club.
Debut: 11. 8.2001 v. Stoke City (H). 1-0. Div. 2.

BENNETT Edward Ernest

Goal 5' 10" 10st 13lbs
b. Kilburn, London 22. 8.1925

Southall	
Q.P.R.	Feb 1949

Football League: 2-0. FAC: 0-0. FLC: 0-0. Others: 0-0. Total: 2-0.

Southall	
Watford	Dec 1953
Gravend & Northfleet	1956

Honours: 11 England Amateur caps. Olympic winners medal in 1952. F.A. tour of the West Indies.

The club were very lucky to have this man on their books when the regular goalkeeper, Reg Allen, was out of the squad, injured. Later Ted turned professional when he signed for Watford.
Debut: 19. 3.1949 v. West Ham United (A). 0-2. Div. 2.

BENSTEAD Graham Mark

(Goal) 6' 1" 13st 7lbs
b. Aldershot, Hants. 20. 8.1963

Mayford Athletic		
Tudor Rovers		
Wimbledon		
Q.P.R.		Jul 1981

Football League: 0-0. FAC: 1-0. FLC: 0-0. Others: 0-0. Total: 1-0.

Norwich City		Mar 1985
Colchester United	(Loan)	Aug 1987
Sheffield United		Mar 1988
Brentford		Jul 1990
Kettering Town		
Rushden & Diamonds		
Kingstonians		

Honours: 1 England youth cap. 3 semi-pro caps.

A bricklayer by trade, Graham was a personable and bubbly character. Tommy Docherty first noticed the goalkeeper when Q.P.R. were playing a friendly against Southern League opponents Wimbledon in a floodlight match. Later he signed professional forms with Terry Venables.
Debut: 8. 1.1983 v. W.B.A. (A). 2-3. FAC. 3rd Rnd.

BENSON George Herdman

(O.L.) Wing 5' 8" 10st 9lbs
b. Garstang, Lancashire 26. 5.1893
d. Lancashire 19.12.1974

Accrington Stanley	
Blackburn Rovers	1920
Stalybridge Celtic	1921
Q.P.R.	1923

Football League: 17-0. FAC: 0-0. FLC: 0-0. Others: 0-0. Total: 17-0.

Port Vale	Feb 1924
Chorley	

George was just one of six players to be tried on the left wing during this re-election season. He was released halfway into the season and was given a one month trial at Port Vale but failed to impress and moved into the Lancashire League.
Debut: 25. 8.1923 v. Brentford (H). 1-0. Div. 3 (S).

BENTLEY Roy Frank Thomas

(R.B.) Def 5' 10" 12st 0lbs
b. Bristol 17. 5.1924

Portway		
Bristol Rovers		1937
Bristol City		Aug 1938
Newcastle United	(£8,500)	Jun 1946
Chelsea	(£12,500)	Jan 1948
Fulham		Sep 1956
Q.P.R.		Jun 1961

Football League: 45-0. FAC: 6-0. FLC: 1-0. Others: 0-0. Total: 52-0.

Honours: 12 English International caps. 2 B caps. 3 Football League caps. Great Britain v. The Rest of Europe. Football League Championship medal. 2 2nd Div. Promotion medals.

Roy was the son of a noted rugby player, who became one of the hottest properties of the post-war era. He started out as an inside forward and became one of the first 'roaming centre forwards', of the '50s. A fine header of the ball with a potent right-foot shot he became the most expensive signing to come out of the lower Divisions. Eighteen months after Newcastle had signed him, Chelsea offered, what was then a staggering fee, for Bentley. He became their leading goalscorer for the next eight seasons, and was the club captain when they won the League championship.

At Fulham he resorted to centre half for the next five years and covered that position with some success. At the age of 33, Bentley was persuaded by manager Alec Stock to continue his career and fill in at right back and help to bring along the youngsters that Q.P.R. had at the time. Bentley later became the Reading manager, until 1969, and in 1970 he took Swansea Town to promotion as their manager, where he stayed until 1972. Roy then took over the reins at Thatcham Town before becoming the secretary of Reading in 1977. His last job before he retired, was that of secretary of Aldershot in 1985.
Debut: 19. 8.1961 v. Brentford (H). 3-0. Div. 3.

BERRY P.

Goal
b.
Q.P.R. 1919
Southern League: 4-0. FAC: 0-0. FLC: 0-0. Others: 0-0. Total: 4-0.

Berry played throughout the month of February 1920 during the club's last Southern League season, replacing the injured Merrick. Berry was never once on the winning side.
Debut: 14. 2.1920 v. Swansea Town (A). 1-3. SLDiv. 1.

BEST Thomas H.

(C.F.) Striker
b. Milford Haven 23.12.1920
Milford Haven United
Chester City Jul 1947
Cardiff City Oct 1948
Q.P.R. Dec 1949
Football League: 13-3. FAC: 1-0. FLC: 0-0. Others: 0-0. Total: 14-0.
Hereford United 1950

Tommy was built small and compact, like a pocket battleship, and he was never really in the running for a place in the senior side. He left at the end of the 1949/50 season moving into the non-League scene.
Debut: 10.12.1949 v. Blackburn Rovers (A). 0-0. Div. 2.

BEVAN Frederick Edward T. Walter

(C.F.) Striker 5' 8" 12st 0lbs
b. Hackney, London 27. 2.1879 d. Hackney 10.12.1935
Millwall St. Johns
Millwall Athletic May 1899
Manchester City Apl 1900
Reading May 1903
Q.P.R. May 1904
Southern League: 58-30. FAC: 1-0. FLC: 0-0. Others: 0-0. Total: 59-30.
Bury (£340) May 1904
Fulham Aug 1907
Derby County Nov 1907
Clapton Orient May 1909
Chatham 1914

Honours: Lancashire Combination winners medal. Western League Championship medal.

Fred was a strong, burly player who was very bold and had a devastating shot in either foot. The 1905 edition of "*Men Famous in Football*", noted him as a '*clever dribbler*'. At Clapton Orient he was made captain as soon as he arrived there and was chosen as a reserve for the Football League v. the Southern League in 1910. He retired during the Great War to become the coach at Clapton Orient where he stayed until 1923.
Debut: 3. 9.1904 v. Plymouth Argyle (H).2-1. SLDiv.1.

BIGNOT Marcus

C.D. 5' 10" 11st 2lbs
b. Birmingham 22. 8.1974
Kidderminster Harriers
Crewe Alexandria (£150,000) Sep 1997
Bristol Rovers Aug 2000
Q.P.R. Mar 2001
Football League: 54-1. FAC: 1-0. FLC: 1-0. Others: 1-0. Total: 57-1.
Rushden & Diamonds Nov 2002

Bignot followed his manager to the club from Bristol Rovers and played at the heart of the Rangers defence where his ball winning talents were much in evidence. Despite making over 50 appearances for the Rangers, Marcus became part of the general clearout at the club at the end of the 2001/02 season. After a one month loan at Rushden & Diamonds, in August 2001, he subsequently signed a long term contract with the Northants. Club.
Debut: 17. 3.2001 v. Grimsby Town (H). 0-1. Div. 1.

BIRCH James

(I.R.) Striker 5' 7" 11st 2lbs
b. Blackwell, Derbyshire in 1888 d. in 1940
Stourbridge
Aston Villa 1912
Q.P.R. 1912
Southern/Football League: 328-123. FAC: 29-19. FLC: 0-0. Others: 0-0. Total: 357-142.
Brentford 1926

Jimmy was a somewhat compact player who was very stocky and was a natural successor to the captaincy after Archie Mitchell. Manager James Cowan signed the striker after he had scored 40 goals for Aston Villa reserves in 1912. and had also notched two goals in his first team debut standing in for Harry Hampton, the Villa regular centre forward. He proved to be one of the finest servants the club ever had. Jimmy possessed a deceptive body swerve and could beat opponent after opponent without deviating from a straight line. For many years his deadly shooting made him the club's leading goalscorer from the inside right position.
Debut: 5. 9.1912 v Plymouth Argyle (H). 2-1. SLDiv. 1.

BIRCHAM Marc Stephen John.

Mid. 5' 10" 12st 4lbs
b. Wembley, Mddx. 11. 5.1978.

Millwall	1996
Q.P.R.	2002

Football League: 39 - 2. FLC: 0-0. FAC: 2-0. Others: 0-0.

Honours: 13 Canada (full) caps & 1 U23 cap.

Marc supported the Rangers as a youngster, and became the first member of the 'Q.P.R. Loyal Supporters Association' to play for the club. However, he in fact joined the club from Millwall. The only two goals he scored in the 2002/03 season were both against Brentford. He is a hard working, strong running midfielder who always gives 100% in a match, which goes down well with the Q.P.R. fans. At one time he dyed his hair blue, white and black!
Debut: 10. 8.2002 v.Chesterfield (H). W. 3-1. Div. 2.

BLACK Samuel

(O.L.) Striker 5' 6" 11st 0lbs
b. Motherwell, Scotland 18.11.1905 d.1977

Kirkintillock Rob Roy	
Plymouth Argyle	1924
Q.P.R.	1938

Football League: 5-0. FAC: 0-0. FLC: 0-0. Others: 0-0. Total: 5-0.

A famous name in the history of Plymouth Argyle, so much so that he became something of a legend. His control was so good and Sammy was such a beautiful striker of the ball with either foot that he could find the back of the net from any angle which other players would consider impossible. During his Argyle career he scored 185 goals in 491 matches. At the age of 34, Black arrived at Loftus Road but he was all burnt out. He soon retired from the game, and went back to Plymouth where he found employment in the docks as a storekeeper and stayed there until after the 2nd World War.
Debut: 31.12.1938 v. Bristol Rovers (A). 0-0. Div.3 (S).

BLACKMAN Frederick Ernest

(R.B.) Def 5' 10" 12st 7lbs
b. Brixton, London 8. 2.1884

Woolwich Arsenal		
Hastings & St. Leonards		1907
Brighton & Hove Albion		May 1909
Huddersfield Town		May 1911
Leeds City	(£1,000)	Feb 1914
Q.P.R.		1919

Southern/Football League: 60-0. FAC: 2-0. FLC: 0-0. Others: 0-0. Total: 62-0.

Honours: Southern League Championship winners medal. 2 caps for the Southern League v. Football League. Played in an England trial match.

Fred was described in the, "Athletic News", as quick on his feet, with a sound kick and a fearless tackle. During the 1st World War he played over 100 matches for Fulham, and played in the last London Victory Cup Final of 1919. Fred retired in 1922 to pursue his trade as a carpenter and cabinet maker.
Debut: 30. 8.1919 v. Bristol Rovers (A). 2-0. SLDiv. 1.

BLACKMAN John James

(C.F.) Striker 5' 9" 12st 4lbs
b. Bermondsey, London in January 1911

Weston United	
Q.P.R.	1932

Football League: 108-62. FAC: 8-7. FLC: 0-0. Others: 4-2.
Total: 120-71.

Crystal Palace	1936
Guildford City	

Blackman was snapped up by Q.P.R. after having won cup and league medals in the Brixton Sunday League. He was a keen, bustling forward with a sizzling shot whose scoring rate was approximately one in every other match. Jack, as he was known, was also noted as a good all round athlete who had also won medals and trophies for boxing, running and jumping. He scored twice on his debut for the club and then five in the next six matches.
Debut: 13. 1.1932 v. Reading (A). 2-3. Div. 3. (S).

BLACKWOOD John

(C.F.) Striker 5' 9" 12st 0lbs
b. Maine, U.S.A. in 1875

Perterhill		
Celtic		Sep 1899
Partick Thisle	(Loan)	Oct 1899
Celtic		May 1900
Woolwich Arsenal		May 1900
Reading		May 1901
Q.P.R.		1902

Southern League: 46-33. FAC: 0-0. FLC: 0-0. Others: 0-0.
Total: 46-33

West Ham United	1904
Royal Albert	Sep 1905

John's parents happened to be living in the U.S.A. at the time of his birth, however, he came home in time to be educated in Scotland and joined Petershill F.C. at the age of 20. A keen, bustling player who had a hard shot and a nose for scoring. John was a real favourite of the spectators at Park Royal.
Debut: 29.11.1902 v. Northampton T. (H). 0-0. SLDiv.1.

BLAKE Albert George

(L.H.) Mid 5' 8" 11st 0lbs
b. Fulham, London in 1900

Fulham	May 1928
Watford	Jul 1929
Q.P.R.	Aug 1933

Football League: 81-9. FAC: 5-0. FLC: 0-0. Others: 3-1.
Total: 89-10.

Tunbridge Wells	Aug 1936

The latter part of Albert's career at Watford followed a strange pattern. He was re-engaged for the 1932/33 season after being given a free transfer, but not recalled until the final game of that season after two years out of the first team. He was then released again immediately afterwards, whereupon he signed for Q.P.R. Albert was the product of the London amateur game, and looked very classy going forward. At defending however, it was another story. After four years service at Loftus Road, when William Birrell took over, Blake was one of those whose contract was ended.
Debut: 26. 8.1933 v. Brighton & H. A.(H).2-0. Div.3 (S).

BLAKE F. J. C.

(C.F.) Striker
b.

Ilford	
Q.P.R.	1913

Southern League: 2-0. FAC: 0-0. FLC: 0-0. Others: 0-0.
Total: 2-0.

Ilford	
Walthamstow Grange	1923
Clapton	1924

Honours: Represented London League v. London Combination 2 Amateur Cup Final winners medals.

Blake remained an amateur throughout his career. He joined the army at the outbreak of war and rose to the rank of captain and fought on the Western Front. On his return to civilian life he rejoined Ilford.
Debut: 26. 3.1914 v. Portsmouth (H). 1-0. SLDiv. 1.

BLAKE Sidney

(O.L.) Mid
b. Whitley Bay, near Newcastle

Willington Athletic		
Whitley Athletic		Oct 1904
Newcastle United		Jan 1905
Q.P.R.		1906

Southern League: 14-0. FAC: 0-0. FLC: 0-0. Others: 0-0.
Total: 14-0.

Whitley Athletic		1907
North Shields Athletic		1908
Newcastle United	(£30)	May 1909
Coventry City		May 1914

This man was an outside left when he appeared for Q.P.R. in 1906, but four years later after joining Newcastle United from South Shields, for the sum of £30, he had become a goalkeeper. Sid moved to Coventry in 1914 as a player but retired to become their trainer in 1918.
Debut: 1. 9.1906 v. Luton Town (A). 1-1. SLDiv. 1.

BLIZZARD Leslie William B.

(R.H.) Def 6' 0" 12st 2lbs
b. Acton, Mddx. 13. 3.1923 d. Northampton 1996
Q.P.R. 1944
Football League: 5-0. FAC: 0-0. FLC: 0-0. Others: 0-0.
Total: 5-0.
Bournemouth & Boscombe Athletic 1947
Yeovil Town 1948
Leyton Orient 1950
Headington United 1956

Honours: 3rd Divi. Championship medal

Les was with Q.P.R. during the war years and played alongside Alec Stock. Later when Stock became manager of Yeovil Town in 1948, Blizzard became part of the team, following him to Clapton Orient in 1950. Making a name for himself under the manager, Stock later spoke highly of the player, saying that Orient's promotion would not have been possible without Les's great efforts. Les was known as being a highly committed player.
Debut: 1. 3.1947 v. Norwich City (A). 1-0. Div. 3. (S).

BOLAM Robert C.

(O.R.) Mid 5' 8" 11st 7lbs
b. Birtley, County Durham in 1896 d. in 1964
Birtly 1919
Sheffield United 1919
Darlington 1922
Q.P.R. 1924
Football League: 2-0. FAC: 0-0. FLC: 0-0. Others: 0-0.
Total: 2-0.

Ned Liddell's reign as manager of Q.P.R. ended in 1925 and Bob Hewison became the new boss. A general clear out of players was the order of the day. Bolam was one among many others to get his marching orders. It is believed that he immediately drifted out of the professional game.
Debut: 6.12.1924 v. Bristol City (H). 3-0. Div. 3. (S).

BONASS Albert Edward

(O.L) Wing 5' 8" 10st 7lbs
b. York 1911 d. 8.10.1945 Tockwith, Yorkshire
Dringhouses FC. York
York Wednesday
Darlington Jan 1933
York City May 1933
Hartlepool United Aug 1934
Chesterfield Apl 1936
Q.P.R. Jun 1939
Football League: 0-0. FAC: 0-0. FLC: 0-0. Others: 59-7.
Total: 59-7.

Albert, like a lot of his team mates, became a war reserve policeman shortly after war broke out. In 1943 he joined the RAF and served in Wellington bombers as a wireless operator, and he was forced to bale out of his aircraft over Manchester. He lost his life on active service, when the Stirling bomber in which he was a crew member crashed on a training flight. The trio of Football League matches that he was involved in were not recognised by the F.A., the 1939/40 season being abandoned after three games, and therefore he had no Football League debut for the club, but he still merits inclusion for his 59 Q.P.R. matches that were all made during wartime.

BONNOT Alexandre

C.D. 5' 8" 11st 6lbs
b. Poissy, France 31. 7.1973
SCO Angers, France
Watford 1998
Q.P.R. Aug 2001
Football League: 22-1. FAC: 1-0. FLC: 1-0. Others: 1-0.
Total: 25-1.
France Feb 2002

Alex arrived on a three month contract in the summer of 2001. His contract was extended on a month by month basis until financial considerations led to him being released at the end of February 2002.
Debut: 11. 8.2001 v. Stoke City (H). 1-0. Div. 2.

BOTT Wilfred E.

(O.L.) Striker 5' 7" 11st 2lbs
b. Edlington, Yorkshire 25. 4.1907
Edlington Colliery Welfare
Doncaster Rovers Mar 1927
Huddersfield Town (£1,000) Mar 1931
Newcastle United (£1,500) Dec 1934
Q.P.R. (£750) May 1936
Football League: 75-34. FAC: 9-1. FLC: 0-0. Others: 4-1.
Total: 88-35.
Lancaster Town 1939
Colchester United 1945

Wilf was considered to be the fastest footballer in the country during the early thirties. He was always among the top scorers at the end of each season and indeed headed the scoring list for Q.P.R. during the 1937/38 season. Wilf played in over 100 matches during the 2nd World War.
Debut: 29. 8.1936 v. Bristol City (A). 2-3. Div. 3. (S).

BOTTOMS Michael C.

(I.L.) Mid
b. Harrow, Mddx. 11. 1.1939.

Harrow Town	1959
Q.P.R.	1960

Football League: 2-0. FAC: 0-0. FLC: 1-0. Others: 0-0. Total: 3-0.

Oxford United	1961

Given a trial in the senior squad by manager Alec Stock. Mike never seemed to gell with the team, so he drifted out of the Football League scene.
Debut: 5. 9.1960 v. Coventry City (A). 4-4. Div. 3.

BOWERS Alfred George W.

(L.H.) Def 6' 1" 12st 6lbs
b. Canning Town, London in May 1895

Hoffmans Athletic	
Chelmsford	
Mile End Albion	
Bromley Celtic	
Charlton Athletic	May 1919
Bristol Rovers	May 1925
Q.P.R.	May 1926

Football League: 1-0. FAC: 0-0. FLC: 0-0. Others: 0-0. Total: 1-0.

Alf was an amateur until he signed for Charlton Athletic. He made just nine appearances in his entire career as a professional.
Debut: 2.10.1926 v. Bournemouth(A). 2-6. Div. 3. (S)

BOWLES Stanley

(I.L.) Mid 5' 10" 11st 4lbs
b. Mosten, Manchester 24.12.1948

Manchester City		Jan 1967
Bury	(Loan)	Jul 1970
Crewe Alexandria		Sep 1970
Carlisle United		Oct 1971
Q.P.R.	(£110,000)	Sep 1972

Football League: 255-71. FAC: 25-8. FLC: 27-7. Others: 8-11. Total: 315-97.

Nottingham Forest	(£250,000)	Dec 1979
Leyton Orient	(£90,000)	Jul 1980
Brentford	(£25,000)	Oct 1981

Honours: 5 England International caps. 2nd Div. Runners-up medals. 1st Div. Runners-up medal.

Prior to his move to Loftus Road in September 1972, Stan played for Carlisle, where, despite only 11 months and 36 appearances at Brunton Park, he is still one of their best remembered players. At Q.P.R., Stan was probably the brightest among a team of stars. With his magical feet and tremendous vision he was really a genius on the field of play; a class above the average player. However, off the pitch he was something of a wayward character with a weakness for gambling. He was always the most charismatic of players at all his clubs. Although there was always doubt about his temperment, Stan was indeed a wonderful player and left many magical moments for all supporters to savour over the years. At his last club, Brentford, he was a given a benefit match (the Bees v. Rangers) in May 1987, and it is a mark of the respect that supporters had for 'Mr.Entertainment', that the attendance of 7,049 was the second highest at Griffin Park that season. In total Stan made a total of 507 career League appearances, netting 127 goals. Presently he acts as ' mine host ' on matchdays in Q.P.R.'s hospitality suites and he is as popular as ever at the club.
Debut: 16. 9.1972 v. Notts Forest (H). 3-0. Div.2.

BOWMAN John William

(R.H) Mid 5' 8" 12st 0lbs
b. Middlesbrough 23. 4.1879 d. Sudbury 26. 1.1943

Sheldon Juniors
Hanley St. Judes
Burslam Park
Burslam Port Vale Feb 1899
Stoke City Aug 1899
Q.P.R. Jun 1901
Southern League: 103-2. FAC: 7-0. FLC: 0-0. Others: 0-0.
Total: 110-2.
Norwich City Apl 1905

A good athlete and a strong swimmer. According to the Bells magazine (the sporting paper of the day), they wrote that he was '*a brainy and intelligent player, who only makes for the good of the game*'. John became the club secretary in 1903, but in 1905 he took the job of manager of Norwich City. Bowman later became the Croydon Common manager until the start of the 1st World War, when the club had to close. After the war he owned a sports outfitters shop in the City of London as well as becoming a Q.P.R. director. Despite his ill-health, John took over as manager of the club for a short spell in 1931.
Debut: 7. 9.1901 v. Watford (H). 0-1. SLDiv. 1.

BOXSHALL Daniel

(O.R.) Striker
b. Bradford, Yorkshire 2. 4.1920
Q.P.R. Jan 1944
Football League: 29-14. FAC: 8-3. FLC: 0-0. Others: 0-0.
Total: 37-17.
Bristol City (£2,575) May 1948
Bournemouth & Boscombe Athletic Jul 1950
Rochdale Jul 1952
Chelmsford 1953

Honours 3rd Div. (South) Championship medal.

Danny was a New Years Day signing in 1944 and within three months he was in France winning the Military Medal. Boxshall was a very fast winger with a deadly shot whose favourite position was centre forward. His tally of eleven goals in the championship side of 1948 was precious.
Debut: 26.12.1946 v. Watford (A). 2-0. Div. 3. (S).

BRADSHAW James

(I.R.) Striker 5' 7" 10st 7lbs
b. Burnley, Lancashire in 1880
Woolwich polytechnic
Woolwich Arsenal
West Norwood
Southampton
Fulham Mar 1904
Chelsea May 1909
Q.P.R. 1910
Southern League: 2-2. FAC: 0-0. FLC: 0-0. Others: 0-0.
Total: 2-2.
Southend United 1911

Jimmy burst onto the scene at Q.P.R. by scoring two goals in his debut match, but almost immediately he was on his way to Southend United to become manager of the club. After military service in the Great War he became manager of Swansea Town in 1919 guiding them to promotion in 1925. Fulham in 1926 was his next club, followed by Bristol City in 1929. In 1932 he left the football scene to take up work in the insurance business.
Debut: 3. 9.1910 v. Coventry City (H). 5-0. SLDiv. 1.

BRADSHAW John Henry

(O.R.) Mid
b. Burnley, Lancashire 28. 6.1892
Burnley
Southend United May 1913
Watford Oct 1919
Luton Town Feb 1920
Aberdare Athletic 1920
Q.P.R. Aug 1921
Football League: 5-0. FAC: 0-0. FLC: 0-0. Others: 0-0.
Total: 5-0.
Burnley
Southend United 1922
Swansea Town 1923

Small with red hair, Jack as he was known was just one member of a prominent footballing family. His manager at Southend United was his brother John and when Jack played for Watford, his father was manager there. His father also managed Woolwich Arsenal and Fulham, and was also secretary of the Southern League. At Southend, Jack took the job of trainer, nevertheless there was still one appearance left for him in 1923, on the wing.
Debut: 24. 9.1921 v. Reading (A). 1-0. Div. 3. (S).

BRADY Patrick J.

(R.B.) Def 5' 7" 10st 6lbs
b. Dublin, Eire 11. 3.1936
Home Farm F.C. Eire
Millwall 1959
Q.P.R. 1963
Football League: 62-0. FAC: 5-0. FLC. 3-0. Others: 0-0.
Total: 70-0.
Gravesend & Northfleet 1965
Honours: 4th Div. Championship medal.

Pat had a very cultured left foot and indeed was the brainy one of the two brothers, having studied at Dublin University for a B.A. in Science. He was a schoolboy international and it was something of a coup when Alec Stock captured the brothers in 1963.
Debut: 30.10.1963 v. Hull City (A). 0-3. Div. 3.

BRADY T. Raymond

(C.D.) 6' 0" 12st 2lbs
b. Dublin, Eire 3. 6.1937
Transport F.C., Eire

Millwall	Jul 1957
Q.P.R.	Jul 1963

Football League: 88-0. FAC: 6-1. FLC: 3-0. Others: 0-0. Total: 97-1.
Hastings United

Honours: 6 caps for Eire. 4th Div. Championship medal.

Ray's rugged, uncompromising defending and fearless tackling proved an inspiration at Loftus Road. Brady tackled furiously, using his height splendidly and he was to show real constructive skill as he moved up field to supply a stream of smooth passes. One of the seven sons of a Dublin docker who produced three footballers, the third being Liam of Arsenal and Juventus. After his retirement from football Ray went on to run a public house in Kent.
Debut: 24. 8.1963 v. Oldham Athletic (A). 1-2. Div. 3.

BRAZIER Matthew Ronald

(Mid) 5' 8" 10st 7lbs
b. Whipps Cross, London 2. 7.1976

Q.P.R.		Jul 1994

Football League: 49-2. FAC: 3-0: FLC: 5-1. Others: 0-0. Total: 57-3.

Fulham	(£65,000)	Mar 1998
Cardiff City	(Loan)	Aug 1998
Cardiff City	(£100,000)	Jul 1999
Leyton Orient	(£100,000)	Jan 2002

A midfield player come defender who is at his best going forward. His battling qualities soon enabled him to establish himself. Unfortunately, Matt found it difficult to live up to inflated expectations and at times he has looked somewhat lightweight at his other clubs.
Debut: 28.10.1995 v. Notts. For. (H). 1-1. Prem. Lge.

BRAZIL Alan Bernard

(For.) 5' 11" 13st 1lb
b. Glasgow, Scotland 15. 6.1959
Celtic boys youth club, Glasgow

Ipswich Town	Aug 1975
Detroit Express, U. S.A.	May 1978
Tottenham Hotspur	Jan 1986
Q.P.R.	Jun 1986

Football League: 4-0. FAC: 0-0. FLC: 2-1. Others: 0-0. Total: 6-1.

Witham Town	1988
Woolongong City, Australia	
Chelmsford City	1988
F.C. Baden, Switzerland	1988
Southend Manor	1989
Bury Town	1989
Stambridge	1990
Chelmsford City	1991
Saffron Waldon	1991
Wivenhoe Town	1991

Honours: Scottish Youth & U21 International caps. 13 Scottish International caps. 2 1st Div.runners-up medals. UEFA Cup winners medal.

A powerfully built player with a rugged determined nature. However, Alan didn't quite seem able to capture the form at Q.P.R. that he had shown at his other League clubs. He suffered an unfortunate back injury in January 1987 while he was at the club and this forced his retirement from the fully professional game. He eventually became the proprietor of the Black Adder Inn, in Ipswich.
Debut: 23. 8.1986 v. Southampton (A). 1-5. Div. 1.

BREACKER Timothy Sean

(R.B.) Def 6' 0" 13st 0lbs
b. Bicester, Oxfordshire 2. 7.1965

Luton Town		May 1983
West Ham United		Oct 1990
Q.P.R.	(Loan)	Oct 1998

Football League: 2-0. FAC: 0-0. FLC: 0-0. Others: 0-0. Total: 2-0.

Q.P.R.	Feb 1999

Football League: 32-2. FAC: 2-0. FLC: 2-0. Others: 0-0. Total: 36-2.

Honours: 2 England U21 caps. League Cup winners medal.

A placid and unassuming man who was nevertheless a strong muscular player. Tim had a powerful attacking and adventurous nature and a liking to overlap. A leg injury, which he suffered in the middle of the 1999/2000 season unfortunately kept him out for the rest of the campaign, and led to his retirement from playing, whereupon he became the Q.P.R. reserve team coach.
Debut: 3.10.1998 v. Grimsby Town (H). 1-2. Div. 1.

BREVETT Rufus Emanuel

Def 5' 8" 11st 0lbs
b. Derby, Derbyshire 24. 9.1969

Doncaster Rovers		Jul 1988
Q.P.R.	(£250,000)	Feb 1991

Premier/Football League: 152-1. FAC: 8-0. FLC: 10-0. Others: 0-0. Total: 170-1.

Fulham	(£375,000)	Jan 1998
West Ham United		Feb 2003

Rufus is a stocky marauding left-sided wing back, who is strongly committed and enjoys all he contributes to the game including taking the ball to the opposition when the opportunity occurs. He is a no nonsense defender who likes to go in where it hurts and although he may have lacked finesse or great passing ability, he was one of the best defenders at the club. However, at Fulham , in the flat back-four system, Rufus was less likely to cross the halfway line, especially in tight situations. A big money buy from Doncaster Rovers in 1991, Rufus enjoyed nearly eight years at Loftus Road, where he appeared in 170 first team matches, before a short journey took him to Fulham, and five years later to West Ham.
Debut: 23. 3.1991 v. Tottenham H. (A). 0-0. Div. 1.

BREWIS Robert

C.F. Striker
b. circa 1885

Q.P.R.	1905

Southern League: 7-2. FAC: 0-0. FLC: 0-0. Others: 0-0. Total: 7-2.

Lincoln City	1907
Burnley	1908
Merthyr Tydfil	1909
Hartlepool United	1912
Luton Town	1913

Not a lot is known about Brewis. However, his most successful period was at Lincoln City, where he notched 11 goals in 22 matches.
Debut: 7.10.1905 v. Tottenham H. (A). 1-2. SLDiv. 1.

BRIDGES Barry John

Striker 5' 9" 11st 3lbs
b. Horsford, Norfolk 29. 4.1941
Norfolk boys

Chelsea		May 1958
Birmingham City	(£55,000)	May 1966
Q.P.R.	(£50,000)	Aug 1968

Football League: 72-31. FAC: 4-1. FLC: 6-3. Others: 0-0. Total: 82-35.

Millwall	(£40,000)	Sep 1970
Brighton & Hove Albion	(£29,000)	Aug 1971
Highlands Park, South Africa 1974		
Bexhill Town		Jan 1976

Honours: 7 Schoolboy caps. 14 youth caps. 4 England caps. Football League cap. League cup winners medal.

Barry was the sprint champion at school, so one can imagine the pace of the player during a match. It was the most striking thing about him, whether he was in a good position or not when he received the ball. His prodigious turn of speed was quite phenomenal and he had good ball control and was a dangerous shot to boot. Bridges would drift from wing to wing during the course of a match and leave his marker completely bewildered. His ceaseless intelligent wandering to create space for others always gave the attack elbow room. At the end of his career he took the job of player/manager at St. Patrick's Athletic in 1976, then Sligo Rovers manager in 1978. The manager's job at Dearham Town followed, then Kings Lynn and finally Horsford. He was last heard of running a hotel in Eastbourne.
Debut: 24. 8.1968 v. Manchester City (H). 1-1. Div. 1.

BRINDLEY Horace

(O.L.) Mid 5' 9" 11st 9lbs
b. Knutton, Staffordshire 1. 1.1885 d. Stoke, Staffs 1971
Knutton Villa

Stoke	Nov 1904
Crewe Alexandria	1905
Norwich City	Jan 1906
Blackpool	Jun 1907
Q.P.R.	Aug 1910

Southern League: 17-0. FAC: 1-0. FLC: 0-0. Others: 0-0. Total: 18-0.

Sutton Town	
Lincoln City	May 1911
Chester	1914

Honours: Central League championship winners medal.

The East Anglian Football Gazette wrote of Horace that he was a hard running, speedy winger, who packed a fierce shot.
Debut: 3. 9.1910 v. Coventry City (H). 5-0. SLDiv. 1.

BROCK Kevin Stanley

Mid 5' 9" 10st 2lbs
b. Bicester, Oxfordshire 9. 9.1962

Oxford United		May 1979
Q.P.R.		Aug 1987

Football League: 40-2. FAC: 4-1. FLC: 6-0. Others: 2-0.
Total: 52-3.

Newcastle United		Dec 1988
Cardiff City	(Loan)	Feb 1994
Stockport County	(Loan)	Sep 1994
Stevenage Borough		Nov 1994
Marlow	(Loan)	1994
Yeovil Town		Feb 1995
Rushden & Diamonds		1995
Banbury United		1999

Honours: 8 England youth caps. 4 U21 caps. 1 B cap. 3rd Div. championship medal. 2nd Div. championship medal. League Cup winners medal.

Kevin followed manager Jim Smith on his journey from Oxford to Q.P.R. and on to Newcastle. Brock was a good solid all round performer who scored on his debut for the club. He was last heard of as being the manager of Banbury United in 1999.
Debut: 15. 8.1987 v. West Ham United (A).3-0. Div. 1.

BROOMES Marlon Charles

Def 6' 0" 12st 12lbs
b. Birmingham 28.11.1977

Blackburn Rovers		Nov 1994
Swindon Town	(Loan)	Jan 1997
Q.P.R.	(Loan)	Oct 2000

Football League: 5-0. FAC: 0-0. FLC: 0-0. Others: 0-0.
Total: 5-0.

Grimsby Town	(Loan)	Sep 2001
Sheffield Wednesday		Dec 2001
Preston North End		Aug 2002

Honours: England school & youth caps. 2 U21 caps.

Marlon quickly became popular with the Loftus Road faithful in his short stay with the club. He put in some fine performances and a deal was underway but a transfer fee couldn't be agreed.
Debut: 25.10.2000 v. Sheffield Wed. (H) 1-2. Div. 1.

BROSTER John

Def 5' 8" 11st 2lbs
b. Earlstone, Lancashire

Chorley	
Q.P.R.	1913

Southern League: 68-3. FAC: 4-0. FLC: 0-0. Others: 0-0.
Total: 72-3.

Rochdale	1920
Wigan Borough	
Rochdale	1922
Earlstone L.M.S.	

John came to the fore during the war and plied his sevices throughout the 1914 to 1918 conflict. Described as a serviceable intervener by a local paper he consequently served clubs in the north until he retired from the game.
Debut: 12. 3.1914 v. Swindon Town (H). 4-2. SLDiv. 1.

BROWN Albert Richard

(O.L.) Striker 5' 5" 10st 0lbs
b. Pegswood, Northumberland 14. 2.1911

Alnwick United	1928
Rochdale	1929
Sheffield Wednesday	1930
Blyth Spartans	1931
Q.P.R.	1932

Football League: 60-20. FAC: 9-1. FLC: 0-0. Others: 1-2.
Total: 70-23.

Northampton Town	1934
Nottingham Forest	1936

Honours: Northumberland County schoolboy cap.

Bert was plucked out of the mines to become a pro. for Rochdale in 1929. He became a very fast winger who had won prizes as a sprinter.
Debut: 27. 8.1932 v. Brentford (H). 2-3. Div. 3. (S).

BROWN Arthur F.

(C.F.) Striker 5' 11" 12st 10lbs
b. Tamworth, Warwickshire in 1879

Atherton Star	
Tamworth Swifts	
Brownhill Albion	
W.B.A.	
Aston Villa	1898
Southampton	May 1901
Q.P.R.	Oct 1902

Southern League: 30-11. FAC: 1-1. FLC: 0-0. Others: 0-0.
Total: 31-12.

P.N.E.	May 1904
Blackpool	Mar 1906

Honours: F.A.Cup runners-up medal.

Known as the Tamworth Flyer, Arthur was a popular member of the team among the spectators in the early days of the club. At Southampton his scoring rate was phenomenal, netting 29 goals in 34 matches. However, he sustained an injury and during the summer of 1902 he was quickly transferred to Q.P.R. Although Arthur's scoring rate was not as good as at Southampton, he nevertheless brought together what had been a very disorganised side, and introduced method into it. Plagued by injuries Brown became disenchanted with the club and the club with him, and he moved on in 1904.
Debut: 25.10.1902 v. Reading (H). 1-3. SLDiv.. 1.

BROWN Charles

(O.R.) Mid 5' 8" 10st 0lbs
b. Stakeford, North'land 14.1.1898
d. Southampton 2. 1.1979

Stakeford United	
Southampton	Mar 1920
Q.P.R.	Aug 1924

Football League: 67-3. FAC: 6-0. FLC: 0-0. Others: 0-0. Total: 73-3.

Poole F.C.	Aug 1926
Supermarine Sports	1927

Honours: 3rd Div. South Championship medal.

Described as quick and crafty with subtle ball control, he had a way of unsettling his marker. Unfortunately, Charlie was a member of the team during that period in the history of the club when they were at their lowest. After retirement in 1936 he was employed by Vosper Thornycroft until 1967.
Debut: 30.8.1924 v. Newport County (A). 0-0. Div. 3 (S)

BROWN Harold Archer

(C.F.) Striker
b. Shildon, County Durham in 1897

Shildon	1922
Sunderland	1922
Leadgate Park	
Shildon Colliery	1923
Q.P.R.	1924

Football League: 13-3. FAC: 0-0. FLC: 0-0. Others: 0-0. Total: 13-3.

Nothing at all is known about this player, except that he was only on the winning side twice. It is not known where he went to after he left Q.P.R.
Debut: 30. 8.1924 v. Newport County (A). 0-0. Div.3. (S).

BROWN Harold Thomas

Goal 6' 1" 12st 4lbs
b. Kingsbury, London 9. 4.1924d. Abingdon in June 1982

Q.P.R.	1942
Notts County	1946
Derby County	Oct 1949
Q.P.R.	Aug 1951

Football League: 189-0. FAC: 11-0. FLC: 0-0. Others: 0-0. Total: 200-0.

Plymouth Argyle	Aug 1956
Exeter City	Sep 1958

Honours: Played for an F.A.X1 in 1943 & 1944.

A wartime signing who made approximately eighty appearances for Q.P.R. during the hostilities of the 1939/45 war. Harry was a very alert and agile goalkeeper with a daring disposition. As a 17 year old, Brown was introduced to first team football on the 15th November 1941 v. Millwall in a wartime London League match at Loftus Road in which Q.P.R. won 4-1. With Reg Allen in the army he became the No.1 for Q.P.R. He was the man that mysteriously filled-in for Arsenal's Griffiths in the second half of the Moscow Dynamo match at foggy White Hart Lane in which Arsenal lost 4-3.
Debut: 18. 8.1951 v. West Ham Utd. (H). 2-0. Div. 2.

BROWN Wayne Lawrence

CD 6' 0" 12st 6lbs
b. Barking, Essex 20. 8.1977

Ipswich Town		May 1996
Colchester United	(Loan)	Oct 1997
Q.P.R.	(Loan)	Mar 2001

Football League: 2-0. FAC: 0-0. FLC: 0-0. Others: 0-0. Total: 2-0.

Wimbledon	(Loan)	Sep 2001
Watford	(Loan)	Jan 2002

Wayne joined the club on a loan deal on the transfer deadline day. Unfortunately he suffered injuries in only his second match for Q.P.R. so returned to Portman Road.
Debut: 24. 3.2001 v. Burnley (A). 1-2. Div. 1.

BROWN William Young

(I.R.) Mid 5' 10" 12st 5lbs
b. South Inch in June 1889

Kettering Town	1909
Q.P.R.	May 1910

Southern League: 6-2. FAC: 0-0. FLC: 0-0. Others: 0-0.
Total: 6-2.

Chelsea	Jul 1911
Bristol City	Nov 1913
Swansea Town	Sep 1919
Portsmouth	1921
Northampton Town	1922

Billy was a regular scorer at Kettering but at Q.P.R. it all seemed to dry up. On being transferred to Chelsea he was so bad in one match that the crowd booed him off the field of play. At Bristol things improved and during the Great War of 1914/18 he won a medal for bravery when he was wounded in action. Billy fought his way back to fitness and played for Northampton Town until he retired.
Debut: 4.3.1911 v. Brighton & H. A. (H). 0-0. SLDiv. 1.

BROWNING Robert Ernest

(I.L.) Mid 5' 10" 11st 11lbs
b. Kettering, Northamptonshire in July 1889
Kettering Town

Q.P.R.	May 1910

Southern League: 51-20. FAC: 3-0. FLC: 0-0. Others: 0-0.
Total: 54-20.

Southampton	Feb 1913
Brentford	May 1913

The Sports Echo described Bob as a clever forward with an accurate shot. This was so until he received an injury from which he never recovered, losing his place in the first team, he played just eight times in the championship side. Southampton hoped that a change would help him but within a few months he was back in London playing for Brentford.
Debut: 8.10.1910 v. Luton Town (H). 3-3. SLDiv. 1.

BRUCE Paul Mark

Mid 5' 11" 12st 0lbs
b. Lambeth, London 18. 2.1978
Q.P.R.
Football League: 5-1. FAC 1-0. FLC: 0-0. Others: 0-0.
Total: 6-1.

Cambridge United	(Loan)	1999
Q.P.R.		Aug 1999

Football League: 32-2. FAC: 4-0. FLC: 2-0. Others: 1-0.
Total: 39-2.

Dagenham & Redbridge	Jul 2002

Paul usually plays on the left hand side of midfield and has added defence to his style of play. He was one of 15 players to be released in 2001. However, Paul survived another season at Q.P.R., and in 2002 was transferred to Dagenham & Redbridge.
Debut: 17. 1.1998 v. Tranmere Rovers (H). 0-0. Div. 1.

BUBB Alvin Ryan

Striker 5' 6" 10st 7lbs
b. Paddington, London 11.10.1980

Q.P.R.	Nov 1998

Football League: 1-0. FAC: 0-0. FLC: 0-0. Others: 0-0.
Total: 1-0.

Bristol Rovers	Aug 2001
Slough Town	Nov 2002

Alvin preferred to play on the right hand side of the pitch. He shares the distinction of having the shortest career with Q.P.R., at nine minutes! Along with 15 other players, he was released at the end of the 2001/02 season.
Debut: 6. 5.2001 v. Wolverhampton W. (A). 1-1. Div.1.

BULL Albert

(L.H.) Mid. 5' 6" 10st 10lbs
b. Derby, Derbyshire in 1875

Gravesend United	1899
Reading	1900
Q.P.R.	1903

Southern League: 13-1. FAC: 2-0. FLC: 0-0. Others: 0-0.
Total: 15-1.

New Brompton	1905
Brentford	1906

Bert was small in stature but big in heart, with a strong tackle he was a useful addition to any team. Mainly a reserve at Q.P.R., but at Reading he was well liked and received a benefit before he left the club.
Debut: 19. 9.1909 v. Tottenham H. (H). 2-0. SLDiv. 1.

BURGESS Daniel

(I.R.) Mid 5' 8" 11st 4lbs
b. Goldenhill, Staffordshire 23.10.1896

Goldenhill Wanderers	
The Army	
Port Vale	Dec 1918
Arsenal	May 1919
West Ham United	Jun 1922
Aberdare Athletic	1924
Q.P.R.	1925

Football League: 46-9. FAC: 4-0. FLC: 0-0. Others: 0-0.
Total: 50-9.

Sittingbourne	1927
Dartford	
Sheppey United	

On his demobilisation from the Royal Artillery at the end of the Great War, Dan came to the notice of the Arsenal while he was playing for Port Vale. His scoring rate while with Arsenal was phenomenal, 50 goals in 100 matches for the reserves. However, Dan couldn't turn it on in the senior squad. At Q.P.R. the side ended the season bottom of the table in 1926, yet he still managed to score eight goals.
Debut: 29. 8.1925 v. Gillingham (A). 0-3. Div. 3. (S).

BURGESS Oliver D.

Central Mid 5' 10" 11st 7lbs
b. Bracknell, Buckinghamshire 12.10.1981

Q.P.R.	2000

Football League: 14-1. FAC: 3-0. FLC: 0-0. Others: 1-0.
Total: 17-1.

Northampton Town	2003

A promising defender who suffered a ligament injury in only his fourth match for the club. This resulted in Oliver missing the rest of the season, and since has only made rare appearances.
Debut: 7. 4.2001 v. Blackburn Rovers (H). 1-3. Div. 1.

BURKE Steven James

(O.L.) Wing 5' 10" 11st 7lbs
b. Nottingham 29. 9.1960

Nottingham Forest		Mar 1978
Q.P.R.	(£125,000)	Sep 1979

Football League: 67-5. FAC: 3-0. FLC: 7-0. Others: 0-0.
Total: 77-5.

Millwall	(Loan)	Oct 1983
Notts County	(Loan)	Oct 1984
Lincoln City	(Loan)	Aug 1985
Brentford	(Loan)	Mar 1986
Doncaster Rovers		Aug 1986
Stockport County	(Loan)	Oct 1987
Sheepshed Charterhouse		
Grantham Town		

Honours: English Youth International.

Steve attracted a large fee back in 1978, bearing in mind that he hadn't played a senior match for Nottingham Forest. Full of promise when he arrived at Loftus Road, he ended his football days being loaned out to all and sundry until hiswithdrawal from football.
Debut: 8. 9.1979 v. Fulham (H). 3-0. Div. 2.

BURNHAM John Robert

(L.H.) Def 5' 11" 12st 8lbs
b. Sunderland in 1896

Sunderland Comrades	
Brighton & Hove Albion	Mar 1920
Q.P.R.	Aug 1921

Football League: 31-0. FAC: 2-0. FLC: 0-0. Others: 0-0.
Total: 33-0.

Durham City	Jul 1923
West Stanley	1924
Durham City	1927
Jarrow	1929

John was drafted into the side after Mick O'Brien moved to centre half. Burnham was a big, burley player who could fit into any defensive position.
Debut: 26.11.1921 v. Brighton & H.A. (H). 3-0. Div.3 (S)

BURNS John Charles

(I.R.) Mid 5' 10" 11st 7lbs
b. Fulham, London 27.11.1906

Crypto Athletic	
Q.P.R.	1928

Football League: 117-29. FAC: 8-5. FLC: 0-0. Others: 0-0.
Total: 125-34.

Brentford	1931
Leyton	

Honours: Middlesex County schoolboy cap. The Rest v. England. 12 English Amateur caps. 3rd Div. (South) Championship medal. 2nd Div. Championship medal. F.A. Amateur Cup winners medal. F.A.Amateur Cup runners-up medal.

A very fine all round sportsman, who excelled at boxing, tennis and football. John was a headmaster who represented his country at football on the amateur field.
Debut: 14. 1.1928 v. Southend United (H). 3-2. Div.3(S)

BURRIDGE John

Goal 5' 11" 11st 0lbs
b. Workington 3.12.1951

Workington		Dec 1969
Blackpool		Apl 1971
Aston Villa		Sep 1975
Southend United	(Loan)	Jan 1978
Crystal Palace		Mar 1978
Q.P.R.		Dec 1980

Football League: 39-0. Fac: 2-0. FLC: 4-0. Others: 0-0.
Total: 45-0.

Wolverhampton Wanderers		Aug 1982
Derby County	(Loan)	Sep 1984
Sheffield United		Oct 1984
Southampton		Aug 1987
Newcastle United		Oct 1989
Hibernian		May1991
Scarborough		Oct 1993
Lincoln City		Dec 1993
Enfield		Feb1994
Aberdeen		Mar1994
Dumbarton		Oct1994
Falkirk		Nov1994
Manchester City		Dec 1994
Notts County		Aug 1995
Witton Albion		Oct1995
Darlington		Nov 1995
Grimsby Town		Dec 1995
Gateshead		Jan 1996
Northampton Town		Jan 1996
Queen of the South		Mar 1996
Blyth Spartans		Aug 1996
Scarborough		Dec 1996
Blyth Spartans		Aug 1997

Honours: Anglo Italian Cup winners medal. 2nd Div. Championship medal. 2nd Div. runners-up medal. League Cup winners medal. Scottish Cup winners medal.

A great character who was a fitness fanatic. John had a very quick reaction to any situation that was in store for him, which obviously made him a good pro. Over 700 appearances were made by Burridge throughout his career, which saw him play for a multitude of clubs both sides of the border.

Debut: 26.12.1980 v. West Ham United (H).3-0. Div. 2.

BUSBY Martyn G

Mid 6' 1" 12st 5lbs
b. Slough, Buckinghamshire 24. 5.1953

Q.P.R.		Jul 1970

Football League: 80-6. FAC: 1-0. FLC: 10-0. Others: 1-0.
Total: 92-6.

Portsmouth		Feb 1976
Notts County		Oct 1976
Q.P.R.		Sep 1977

Football League: 66-11. FAC: 6-3. FLC: 0-0. Others: 0-0.
Total: 72-14.

Burnley	(Loan)	Feb 1980

Honours: England youth cap. 2nd Div. runners-up medal.

Martyn was an effective member of the senior squad throughout the seventies, except for an 18 month period in the middle of it. He retired in 1980 after receiving a severe injury. Later going into pub management but soon after became the manager of Beaconsfield United F.C.

Debut: 18. 4.1970 v. Leicester City (A). 1-2. Div. 2.

BUSBY Walter

(O.L.) Wing 5' 5" 11st 3lbs
b. Wellingborough, Northamptonshire in 1882

Wellingborough Britons	
Wellingborough	1898
Q.P.R.	1902

Southern League: 14-3. FAC: 1-0. FLC: 0-0. Others: 0-0.
Total: 15-3.

Woolwich Arsenal	1903
Leyton	1905

Honours: Represented the United League and the North Hants. League. North Hants cup medal. United League championship medal. South Eastern League championship medal. London League championship medal.

Walter was noted in the Athletic News, as a very useful and sterling player, a fast and direct winger who was just as good as a centre forward, however his small stature was against him in the early years of football.

Debut: 3. 9.1902 v. Wellingborough (H).2-0. SLDiv.1.

BUTLER Ernest

(O.R.) Wing 5' 6" 10st 6lbs
b. Stillington, County Durham 17. 6.1896

Ebbw Vale	
Q.P.R.	1922

Football League: 34-0. FAC: 1-0. FLC: 0-0. Others: 0-0.
Total: 35-0.

Hartlepool United	1924
Durham City	1927

The fact that Ernie could play on both wings lengthened his career at Q.P.R. However, when the club ended the season bottom of the league in 1924 he was one of those that were released at the end of the season.

Debut: 7.10.1922 v. Swindon Town (H).0-2. Div.3(S).

C

BUTTERWORTH Herbert

(W.H.) Mid 5' 6" 11st 4lbs
b. Unsworth, Manchester 1. 1.1885

Unsworth Parish Church		
P.N.E.		Sep 1904
Barrow		1906
Oldham Athletic		Sep 1908
Q.P.R.		Aug 1910

Southern League: 40-0. FAC: 1-0. FLC: 0-0. Others: 0-0. Total: 41-0.

Millwall		1912

Honours: 2nd Div. runners-up medal. Southern League championship medal.

Bert was noted as a wholehearted player who could fill both wing half positions when necessary and ended his days coaching in Holland after the 1914/18 war.

Debut: 26.11.1910 v. Crystal Palace (A) 1-2. SLDiv.1.

BYRNE John Frederick

For 6' 0" 12st 4lbs
b. Manchester 1. 2.1961

York City		Feb 1979
Q.P.R.	(£100,000)	Oct 1984

Football League: 126-30. FAC: 9-2. FLC: 13-4. Others: 1-0. Total: 149-36

Le Harve, France	(£175,000)	May 1988
Brighton & Hove Albion	(£120,000)	Sep 1990
Sunderland	(£225,000)	Oct 1991
Millwall	(£250,000)	Oct 1992
Brighton & Hove Albion	(Loan)	1993
Oxford United	(£50,000)	Nov 1993
Brighton & Hove Albion		Feb 1995
Crawley Town		Aug 1996
Shoreham		Mar 1997

Honours: 23 caps for the Rep. of Ireland. 4th Div. Championship medal. 2 League Cup runners-up medals.

John was recommended to the York City boss by a taxi driver who spotted him playing in a Manchester park. A naturally gifted player who impressed with his fine ball control. He won the first of his 23 caps with Q.P.R. (His father being born in Ireland). He became the top scorer at Le Harve until he broke a leg. At Sunderland John became a huge success when he scored in every round of the 1992 F.A. Cup except the final.

Debut: 27.10.1984 v. Norwich City (A). 0-2. Div.1.

CABLE Thomas Harry

(CH) CD 5'10" 11st 0lbs
b. Barking, Essex 27.11.1900d. Southend 23. 5.1986

Barking		
Clapton		1924
Q.P.R.		Nov 1925

Football League: 18-2. FAC: 0-0. FLC: 0-0. Others: 0-0. Total: 18-2.

Middlesex Wanderers		1926
Leyton		1927
Tottenham Hotspur		Jul 1928
Southampton		Sep 1932
Kettering Town		

Honours: 1 English Amateur Cap. The Rest v. England. 4 amateur cup winners medals.

Tommy was a hard tackling, uncompromising player who kept his amateur status until he joined Spurs. At the end of his career he became the Kettering Town player/manager, later on the Leyton manager and in 1950 the Grays Athletic boss.

Debut: 25.12.1925 v. Charlton Athletic (H).2-2. Div.3(S).

CAESAR Gus Cassius

(R.B) Def 6' 0" 12st 7lbs
b. Tottenham, London 5. 3.1966

Araenal		Feb 1984
Q.P.R.	(Loan)	Nov 1990

Football League: 5-0. FAC: 0-0. FLC: 0-0. Others: 0-0. Total: 5-0.

Cambridge United		Jul 1991
Bristol City		Sep 1991
Airdrie		Jan 1992
Colchester United		Aug 1994

Honours: 3 U21 caps for England. League Cup runners-up medal. Makita Tournament winners medal. Charity Shield runners-up medal. Football Combination championship medal. Scottish F.A. Cup runners-up medal.

Gus was (perhaps unfairly) never forgiven for making a mistake in the Arsenal v. Luton Town League Cup Final at Wembley which led to the Hatters equaliser and left his club under a dark cloud. He was loaned to Q.P.R. with the option to buy but had the propensity for making errors under pressure so his transfer was never completed.

Debut: 1.12.1990 v. Manchester City (A).1-2. Div. 1.

CAIN Thomas

(H.B.) Def 5' 8" 11st 0lbs
b. Ealing, Middlesex

Q.P.R.	1919

Southern League: 6-0. FAC: 0-0. FLC: 0-0. Others: 0-0.
Total: 6-0.

Brentford	1924

A reserve who was used as a substitute for Archie Mitchell and sometimes stood in for Broster. He was also a reserve at Brentford where he stayed until 1926.
Debut: 22. 3.1920 v. Luton Town (A).1-2. SLDiv. 1.

CAMERON James

(L.H.) Def 5' 6" 10st 7lbs
b. Inverness, Scotland
Mitchum Athletic
Hearts of Midlothian

Q.P.R.	1923

Football League: 24-0. FAC: 1-0. FLC: 0-0. Others: 0-0.
Total: 25-0.
Indiana Flooring, U.S.A.
New York Nationals, U.S.A.
New York Giants, U.S.A.

Twelve players were recruited at the beginning of the season of which Jimmy was one, eight others appeared in the senior squad. By the end of the season, six players had gone to pastures new, including Jimmy, who had moved to the States.
Debut: 25. 8.1923 v. Brentford (H). 1-0. Div. 3. (S).

CAMERON Kenneth

(I.F.) Mid 5' 9" 11st 2lbs
b. Hamilton, Scotland in 1905
Park Head F.C. (Glasgow)

P.N.E.	May 1926
Middlesbrough	Mar 1929
Bolton Wanderers	Oct 1933
Hull City	Jun 1935
Q.P.R.	Aug 1936

Football League: 8-1. FAC: 0-0. FLC: 0-0. Others: 0-0.
Total: 8-1.
Rotherham United

Ken was the substitute for Alex James when he was at P.N.E. However,, at Q.P.R. ten years later he seemed to be a player of fitful brilliance who never seemed to carry it off.
Debut: 29. 8.1936 v. Bristol City (A). 2-3. Div. 3 (S).

CAMERON Robert

(I.L.) Mid 5' 8" 11st 0lbs
b. Greenock, Scotland 23.11.1932
Port Glasgow Rangers

Q.P.R.	Jun 1950

Football League:256-54. FAC: 19-3. FLC: 0-0. Others: 4-0.
Total:279-57.

Leeds United	Jul 1959
Gravesend & Northfleet	Jul 1962
Southend United	Oct 1963
Adamstown, Australia	1964

Honours: Scottish schoolboy caps. Represented the Army during his National Service. London F.A. v. Basle. London Challenge Cup winners medal.

Bobby played the game with a somewhat casual attitude this made him appear almost too nonchalant., however, this was when he was at his most dangerous. He would demand the ball at every opportunity and almost run the match on his own. Bobby first came to the fore in the 1952/53 season when he made 34 Football League appearances. He finallt became a long-serving player at Loftus Road, with nearly 300 first team gamesto his credit in his nine year period at the club. After a further three years, at Leeds United, he dropped down into non-League football, and emigrated in 1964 to Australia where he finished his playing career.
Debut: 13. 1.1951 v. Coventry City (H). 3-1. Div.2.

CAMPBELL Charles J.

(C.F.) Striker
b. Blackburn, Lancashire in 1903
Pembroke Dock
Q.P.R. 1925
Football League: 4-1. FAC: 0-0. FLC: 0-0. Others: 0-0.
Total: 4-1.
Reading

Charlie scored his only League goal for Q.P.R. against Reading and that is probably why they bought him, however he only ever played one match for the Berkshire side, at left half.
Debut: 29. 8.1925 v. Gillingham (A). 0-3. Div.3 (S).

CAMPBELL Dougauld

(O.R.) Wing 5' 0" 11st 6lbs
b. Kirkintilloch, Scotland 14.12.1922

Q.P.R.		Mar 1948

Football League: 0-0. FAC: 1-0. FLC: 0-0. Others: 0-0.
Total: 1-0.

Crewe Alexandria		July 1949
Barrow		Aug 1950
Grimsby Town	(£500)	Oct 1951
Peterborough United		1952

Doug started as an amateur at Q.P.R. and turned pro. in 1948. He made just a single appearance for the club in an F.A. Cup replay at Huddersfield, the side losing 5-0.
Debut: 8.1.1949 v. Huddersfield T.(A).0-5.FAC. 3rd Rd.

CANNON George Frank

(I.R.) Mid 5' 9" 11st 11lbs
b. Ware, Hertfordshire 8.11.1855 d. France Feb 1916

Hitchin Town	1900
Q.P.R.	1907

Southern League: 27-0. FAC: 0-0. FLC: 0-0. Others: 2-1.
Total: 29-10.

West Ham United	1909
New Brompton	1910
Tooting	
Fulham	
Brentford	
Port Vale	1911

Honours: Represented Hertfordshire in numerous county matches and won several gold medals with Hitchin Town. Southern League Championship medal. Staffordshire Cup winners medal. Birmingham Cup winners medal.

Frank began his football career at the age of fifteen with Hitchin Town in 1900, and worked as a solicitor's clerk. He continued in that capacity after turning professional with Q.P.R. in 1907.

Frank was a dashing player, plus a fine dribbler, with a blistering shot. Sadly he was one of the many footballers to lose his life on the Western Front during the Great War of 1914 to 1918.
Debut: 29. 2.1908 v. Millwall Athletic (A) 0-0. SLDiv. 1.

CAPE John Phillips

(O.R.) Wing 5' 8" 11st 0lbs
b. Carlisle, Cumberland 16.11.1910
d. 6. 6.1994 St. Johns School, Carlisle
Penrith

Carlisle United		May 1929
Newcastle United	(£1,750)	Jan 1930
Manchester United	(£2,000)	Jan 1934
Q.P.R.		Jun 1937

Football League: 61-12: FAC: 3-1. FLC: 0-0. Others: 1-0.
Total: 65-13.

Carlisle United	1939
Scarborough	1946
Carlisle United	Oct 1946

Honours: 2nd Div. championship medal.

John captained his school at both football and rugby before joining his home town club Carlisle United at the age of 17. Moving to Newcastle United for what was a hefty fee in those days, Carlisle used the money to construct a roof on the Brunton Park stand. Johnny Cape was a very fast winger with the ball at his feet and very direct, he also had a powerful shot. Manchester United bought him after John had scored a hat-trick in a 7-4 victory at St. James Park. He moved to Loftus Road in 1937, and during the 2nd World War he worked as an electrician while continuing to play football. He finished his career back at Carlisle, and resided in his home town for the rest of his life, after retiring from the game in 1947.
Debut: 28. 8.1937 v. Brighton & H.A. (H). 2-1. Div.3(S)

CAREY Peter Richard

Def
b. Barking, Essex 14. 4.1933
Barking

Clapton Orient	Oct 1957
Q.P.R.	Jul 1960

Football League: 15-1. FAC: 1-0. FLC: 1-0. Others: 0-0.
Total: 17-1.

Colchester United	Nov 1960
Aldershot	Aug 1961
Dover	1962

Honours: Represented Essex F.A.

A play anywhere utility player that followed Alec Stock from Orient to Q.P.R. in the early sixties. After his playing days were over, he managed a number of non-League sides, including Walthamstow Avenue in the early 1970s.
Debut: 20. 8.1960 v. Bournemouth & B.A. 0-1. Div.3.

CARLISLE Clarke

Def. 6' 1" 12st 7lbs
b. Preston, Lancashire 14.10.1979
Blackpool Aug 1997
Q.P.R. May 2000
Football League: 65-5. FAC: 5-0. FLC: 3-0. Others: 0-0.
Total: 73-5

Honours: 3 England U21 Caps.

A strong central defender with good pace, and able to read the game. Clarke became a favourite of the Loftus Road faithful after producing some fine performances. He suffered a ligament injury halfway through the 2000/01 season which prevented further appearances and a long layoff, but he came back to record a near ever-present record for 2002/03. In 2002, Clarke was adjudged to be 'Britain's Brainiest Footballer' in a TV programme run by ITV.
Debut: 12. 8.2000 v. Birmingham City. 0-0. Div. 1.

CARR William Patterson

(R.B.) Def 5' 9" 12st 0lbs
b. Cambois, Cumberland 6.11.1901 d.1990
Seaton Delaval
Derby County 1925
Q.P.R. 1935
Football League: 28-0. FAC: 0-0. FLC: 0-0. Others: 0-0.
Total: 28-0.
Barrow 1937

Honours: 1st Div. runners-up medal.

A very experienced full back who was past his prime (aged 35 years) when he joined the club, nevertheless Bill played with a high degree of defensive knowledge, on either flank.
Debut: 31. 8.1935 v. Millwall (H). 2-3. Div. 3. (S).

CHALLIS Trevor Michael

Def 5' 8" 11st 0lbs
b. Paddington, London 23.10.1975
Q.P.R. Jul 1994
Football League: 13-0. FAC: 2-0. FLC: 0-0. Others: 0-0.
Total: 15-0.
Bristol Rovers 1998
Exeter City 2003

Honours: England U21 captain.

Trevor, was noted for his strength in the tackle, and he earned praise for his measured distribution and willingness to get forward. But after four years, and only a handful of Q.P.R. appearances he moved to the west country.
Debut: 19.11.1995 v. Coventry City (H).1-1. PL.

CHANDLER Arthur Clarence Hillier

(C.F.) Striker 5' 8" 11st 7lbs
b. Paddington, London 27.11.1895 d.18. 6.1984
Handley Page
Hampstead Town
Q.P.R. Sep 1920
Football League: 78-16. FAC: 8-2. FLC: 0-0. Others: 0-0.
Total: 86-18.
Leicester City Jun 1923
Notts County Jun 1935
Leicester City 1936

Honours: 2 caps for the Rest v. England. The North v. South. F.A. tour of South Africa. 2nd Div. championship medal. 1st Div. runners-up medal. Football League v. Scottish League.

Arthur was a legend throughout the city of Leicester for his prodigious goalscoring, notching 273 goals in 419 matches. A hard and courageous player with a dynamic shot. Chandler was feared by all defenders alike, yet at the same time he was always admired for his fair play. But unfortunately he somewhat lost his goalscoring touch after his transer to Q.P.R.
Debut: 1. 1.1921 v. Crystal Palace (A). 0-0. Div. 3.

CHANNING Justin Andrew

(R.B.) Def 5' 11" 11st 7lbs
b. Reading, Buckinghamshire 19.11.1968
Q.P.R. Aug 1986
Football League: 55-5. FAC: 3-0. FLC: 4-0. Others: 5-0.
Total: 67-5.
Bristol Rovers (Loan) Oct 1993
Bristol Rovers Jan 1994
Leyton Orient Jul 1996
Slough Town Aug 1998

Honours: England Youth & U20 caps.

Graduating through the apprentice ranks, he made his first team debut at the age of 17. Justin was a versatile player who could fill-in at full back, midfield or wing forward. He was a hard worker both on and off the ball and was blessed with a powerful shot. With his contract at an end at Leyton Orient, he was released in 1998 and he moved in to non-League football.
Debut: 1.11.1986 v. Luton Town (A). 0-1. Div. 1.

CHAPMAN Reginald F. J.
(C.H.) CD
b. Shepherds Bush 7. 9.1921 d. Seaford, Sussex 4.7.1992
Q.P.R. 1940
Football League: 93-3. FAC: 4-0. FLC: 0-0. Others: 0-0.
Total: 97-3.
Ashford Town
Tunbridge Wells

Honours: 3rd Div. (South) Championship medal.

A loyal club player who filled the centre half spot with natural ability. Reg joined the club in 1940 and played a few matches during the war, turning part time pro in 1946 and so keeping his job as an accountant. The hostilities robbed him of his early Football League playing years, but he remained with Q.P.R. for six post-war seasons. Never an automatic choice in the first team he nonetheless notched up nearly 100 appearances for the club before dropping down to non-League level.
Debut: 14. 9.1946 v. Reading (H). 2-0. Div.3 (S).

CHARLES Jeremy Melfyn
(C.F.) Striker 6' 1" 13st 11lbs
b. Swansea, Wales 26. 9.1959
Dynevor school

Swansea City		Jan 1977
Q.P.R.	(£100,000)	Nov 1983

Football League: 12-5. FAC: 1-0. FLC: 0-0. Others: 0-0.
Total: 13-5.

Oxford United	(£100,000)	Feb 1985

Honours: 3 Welsh youth caps. 3 U21 caps. 19 full caps for Wales. League Cup winners medal. 2 Welsh cup winners medal and Championship medals with Swansea City.

A famous name in Welsh soccer. The son of Mel and the nephew of the legendry John Charles, Jeremy was a member of the Swansea City side that rose from the 4th Division to the 1st in 4 years. He was forever plagued by injuries at Q.P.R. and lasted at Loftus Road for just 18 months.
Debut: 10.12.1983 v. W.B.A. (A). 2-1. Div. 1.

CHARLES Lee
Striker 5' 11" 12st 4lbs
b. Hillingdon, Middlesex 20. 1.1971

Yeading		1985
Chertsey Town		1994
Q.P.R.	(£67,500)	Aug 1995

Football League: 16-1. FAC: 0-0. FLC: 1-0. Others: 0-0.
Total: 17-1.

Barnet	(Loan)	Sep 1995
Cambridge United	(Loan)	Feb 1998
Hayes		1998
Nuneaton Borough		1999
Aldershot Town		Jul 2002

Honours: England Semi-professional International.

The scorer of 45 goals for Chertsey Town, the reason why such a high fee was paid for him. Lee was a confident, speedy forward, with a good first touch on the ball, but he was released in the summer of 1998 for personal reasons. He has since become a regular goalscorer once more in non-League football.
Debut: 25.11.1995 v. West Ham United (A). 0-1. PL.

CHARLESWORTH George W.
(O.R) Wing 5' 10" 12st 10lbs
b. Bristol 29.11.1901 d. 1965
Hanham United
Dings Villa
St. Silas
Barton Hill Sports
St. Phillips Adult school

Bristol Rovers	May 1921
Q.P.R.	May 1926

Football League: 23-3. FAC: 0-0. FLC: 0-0. Others: 0-0.
Total: 23-3.

Kettering Town	Jul 1927
Crystal Palace	Mar 1929
Kettering Town	May 1933

George an outside right joined Kettering Town from Q.P.R. when the legendry Eddie Hapgood was just starting out on his career. Eventually, after a famous F.A. cup run, over half the Kettering team, including Charlesworth, was snapped up by Crystal Palace, he had scored 40 goals in 105 matches for Kettering Town.
Debut: 4.9.1926 v. Coventry City (H). 1-1. Div. 3 (S).

CHARLTON William

(C.F.) Striker
b. South Stoneham 4. 6.1912
Winchester
Oxford University

Southampton	Dec 1931
Hull City	1934
Wimbledon	Aug 1935
Q.P.R.	1936

Football League: 20-10. FAC: 1-0. FLC: 0-0. Others: 0-0.
Total: 21-10.

Barnet	1939
Leyton	1939
Fulham	1939

Honours: 4 Amateur International caps. Played twice for the Oxford blues. Played for the Corinthians and the Middlesex Wanderers.

Bill was a gifted amateur of the old school who turned out for the club while he was at college. After the conflict of World War 2 he became the headmaster of a London school and lived in Barnes.
Debut: 19.12.1936 v. Bristol Rovers (A). 1-1. Div. 3 (S)

CHEETHAM Thomas Miles

(C.F.) Striker 5' 10" 11st 8lbs
b. Byker, Newcastle-upon-Tyne 11.10.1910 d. 1993
Byker
Royal Artillery in India

Q.P.R.		Aug 1935

Football League:115-81. FAC:10-10. FLC: 0-0. Others: 4-1.
Total:129-92.

Brentford	(£5,000)	Feb 1939
Lincoln City	(£500)	Oct 1945

Honours: Represented the army in India. Played in an England trial match.

A scoring sensation who exploded on to the scene in 1935. Tommy broke the club scoring record in his first season. After being sold to Brentford in 1939 he was soon called-up into the army, being on the reserve list. Wounded at Dunkirk in 1940, Tommy was rescued and continued his football career during and after the 2nd World War. In September 1949, he became the coach to Willesden F.C. (a Q.P.R. nursery side).
Debut: 4. 9.1935 v. Brighton & H.A. (A). 1-1. Div. 3 (S).

CHESTER Albert

(O.R.) Wing
b. Hexham, Northumberland
Wingate Albion

P.N.E.	1910
Croydon Common	1912
Q.P.R.	1921

Southern League: 1-0. FAC: 0-0. FLC: 0-0. Others: 0-0.
Total: 1-0.

Turning out just once for Q.P.R., Bert had played for most London clubs in the 1st World War period, during which time Croydon Common closed down.
Debut: 15.11.1919 v. Brighton & H.A. (A).3-2. SLDiv.1.

CHIVERS Gary Paul Steven

Def 5' 11" 13st 1lb
b. Stockwell, London 15. 5.1960

Chelsea		Jul 1978
Swansea City		Aug 1983
Q.P.R.		Feb 1984

Football League: 60-0. FAC: 2-0. FLC: 6–0. Others: 1-0.
Total: 69-0.

Watford		Sep 1987
Brighton & Hove Albion	(£40,000)	Mar 1988
Lyn, Norway		May 1993
AFC Bournemouth		Nov 1993
Stamco		Jan 1995
Worthing		Sep 1996

Honours: Represented the London schools. 3rd Div. runners-up medal.

Joined Chelsea at the age of 18, however, five years later when Gary went to Swansea, injuries prevented him from playing. Arriving at Q.P.R., Chivers showed that he could play right across the back four when required to do so. At Brighton he finished up as captain before later taking over the player/manager job at Worthing. Later hebecame a chauffeur with the hope of eventually becoming a taxi driver.
Debut: 7.11.1984 v. Partizan, Belgrade (A).0-4.UEFA Cup. Rd. 2. 2nd Leg.

CHRISTIE David
(I.F.) Mid 5' 7" 11st 4lbs
b. Forfar, Scotland in 1867
Forfar Athletic
Stoke 1889
Dresden United 1894
Q.P.R. 1900
Southern League: 10-1. FAC: 1-0. FLC: 0-0. Others: 0-0.
Total: 11-1.
Kensal Rise United 1904

David was an experienced Scot who covered for Frank Downing whenever he was out of the side. Despite his age, he was still playing at 37!
Debut: 1. 9.1900 v. Bristol Rovers (A). 1-2. SLDiv. 1.

CINI Joseph
(O.R.) Wing
b. Malta
Floriana, Malta
Q.P.R. 1959
Football League: 7-1. FAC: 0-0. FLC: 0-0. Others: 0-0.
Total: 7-1.

Honours: Maltese International.

Joe was the first Maltese player to make the grade in the English League, remaining an amateur throughout the season he was at Loftus Road.
Debut: 22. 8.1959 v. Swindon Town (H). 2-0. Div. 3.

CLARK Clive
(O.L.) Striker 5' 7" 10st 6lbs
b. Leeds, Yorkshire 14.12.1940
Harahills & Leeds City schools
Asley Rd. Methodists
Huddersfield Town
Leeds United Jan 1958
Q.P.R. Aug 1958
Football League: 58-7. FAC: 3-0. FLC: 2-0. Others: 0-0.
Total: 63-7.
W.B.A. (£17,000) Jan 1961
Q.P.R. (£70,000) Jun 1969
Football League: 8-1. FAC: 0-0. FLC: 2-0. Others: 0-0.
Total: 10-1.
P.N.E. (£25,000) Jan 1970
Southport Jul 1973
Telford United 1974
Washington Diplomats, U.S.A. 1974
Dallas Tornadoes, U.S.A.
Philadelfia Fury, U.S.A.
Skegness Town 1976

Honours: English U23 cap. F.A. Cup winners medal. League Cup runners-up medal. 3rd Div. championship medal.

Clive was a fast, direct and courageous winger, who was a supreme goalscorer. The son of a professional boxer he was the first player to score in every round of the League Cup. Ironically it was Clive who scored West Brom's two goals against Q.P.R. in the 1967 League Cup final. Clark retired from playing after sustaining a groin injury in the U.S.A. Although he did some coaching, he worked in the building industry in Lytham for a time, before moving to Filey.
Debut: 6. 9.1958 v. Bournemouth & B.A.(A).0-2. Div. 3.

CLARK William
(C.F.) Striker 6' 0" 13st 0lbs
b. Larkhall, Scotland 25. 2.1932
Petershill
Q.P.R. 1954
Football League: 95-32: FAC: 1-0. FLC: 0-0. Others: 0-0.
Total: 96-32.
Berwick Rangers 1956

Billy's deft touches and subtle flicks made him the ideal partner for Bobby Cameron. Unnoticed interchanging between the two of them confused the opposing defence and brought the side plenty of goals. Despite a near ever-present, his time at Loftus Road was limited to around two years, for never having really settled in London, he was homesick, and he moved back to Scotland, to Berwich Rangers.
Debut: 6. 2.1954 v. Shrewsbury Town (H).0-0. Div.3 (S).

CLARKE Charles
(I.R.) Mid
b. Fleet, Lincolnshire d.1943
Q.P.R. 1936
Football League: 6-0. FAC: 0-0. FLC: 0-0. Others: 0-0.
Total: 6-0.
Luton Town 1938

Charlie was a reserve, filling in at inside right, before an exchange deal, for R.F.Stevens, took him to Luton Town. Sadly Charlie Clarke was killed on active service during the 2nd World War.
Debut: 21.1.1937 v. Brighton & H.A.(H).2-3. Div.3 (S).

CLARKE Colin John
(C.F.) Striker 6' 0" 13st 6lbs
b. Newry, Northen Ireland 30.10.1962

Ipswich Town		Oct 1980
Peterborough United		Jun 1981
Gillingham	(Loan)	Mar 1984
Tranmere Rovers		Jul 1984
AFC Bournemouth	(£22,500)	Jul 1985
Southampton	(£400,000)	Jul 1986
AFC Bournemouth	(Loan)	Dec 1988
Q.P.R.	(£750,000)	Mar 1989

Football League: 46-11. FAC: 7-2. FLC: 3-1. Others: 0-0. Total: 56-14.

Portsmouth	(£450,000)	May 1990

Honours: 39 caps for Northern Ireland.

Rejection by Bobby Robson, the manager of Ipswich Town, and a free transfer from Peterborough United did nothing to suggest the young Irishman had a rosy future, however, in 1986 he became a World Cup hero with many European clubs wishing to sign him. At Loftus Road, Colin became a very popular player and the supporters were very sad to see him transferred to Portsmouth. In retirement he decided on a career in catering and went on to run a pub with a restaurant in a village near Newbury, Berkshire.
Debut: 11. 3.1989 v. Newcastle United (A).2-1. Div. 1.

CLARKE Frank James

(C.F.) Striker 6' 0" 11st 0lbs
b. Willenhall, Staffordshire 15. 7.1942

St. Giles, Willenhall		1960
Shrewsbury Town		Nov 1961
Q.P.R.	(£35,000)	Feb 1968

Football League: 67-17. FAC: 4-2. FLC: 5-5. Others: 0-0. Total: 76-24.

Ipwich Town	(£38,000)	Mar 1970
Carlisle United		Aug 1973

Honours: 2nd Div. runners-up medal.

An Alec Stock acquisition during the 1968 promotion season. Frank was a hard working and unselfish player who liked to supply his team mates with deft passes and little side flicks. He was the brother of Alan Clarke, the Leeds United and England striker of the 1970s. Frank continued playing football until 1977.
Debut: 24. 2.1968 v. Bolton Wanderers (A). 1-1. Div.2.

CLARKE George B.

(O.L.) Wing 5' 9" 11st 9lbs
b. Bolsover, Derbyshire 24. 7.1900 d. 11. 2.1977

Nottingham Royal		
Welbeck Colliery		
Mansfield Town		1921
Aston Villa	(£350)	Dec 1922
Crystal Palace		Jul 1925
Q.P.R.		Jul 1933

Football League: 15-6. FAC: 0-0. FLC: 0-0: Others: 1-0. Total: 16-6.

Folkstone		1934

Honours:Mansfield Hospital cup winners medal. 2 3rd Div. (South) runners-up medals.

George was a fast and tricky winger, who attracted a lot of interest in his younger days. Aston Villa snapped him up as a cover for Arthur Dorrell but he was called upon just once in six years. Clarke showed his value at Crystal Palace, (who got him on a free transfer), by scoring 100 goals in 300 matches in 8 seasons.
Debut: 26. 8.1933 v. Brighton & H.A.(H).2-0. Div.3 (S).

CLAYTON Horace Leonard

(I.R.) Mid
b. Hackney, London 4. 7.1898 d.1985
Q.P.R. 1920
Football League: 6-1. FAC: 0-0. FLC: 0-0. Others: 0-0. Total: 6-1.

Horace was a reserve and usually played in the side when Jimmy Birch was absent.
Debut: 17. 3.1921 v. Plymouth Argyle (H).4-0. Div. 3.

CLAYTON Lewis

(W.H.) Mid 5' 8" 11st 2lbs
b. Royston, Yorkshire 7. 6.1924

Monkton Colliery	
Barnsley	
Carlisle United	Sep 1946
Barnsley	Jun 1947
Q.P.R.	Aug 1950

Football League: 91-5. FAC: 2-0. FLC: 0-0. Others: 0-0. Total: 93-5.

Bournemouth & Boscombe Athletic	May 1955
Swindon Town	Jun 1957

Lewis was noted as an organiser rather than a destroyer. A dour but dependable half back who could play on both sides of the park. He had a career at Loftus Road that lasted five years, during which time he notched up a creditable 91 League games.
Debut: 9. 9.1950 v. Coventry City (A). 0-3. Div. 2.

CLEMENT David
RWB 6' 0" 12st 5lbs
b. Battersea, London 2. 2.1948
d.Putney,London31. 3.1982

Q.P.R. Jul 1965
Football League:407-21. FAC: 29-2. FLC: 34-3. Others: 6-1. Total:476-27.

Bolton Wanderers (£170,000) Jun 1979
Fulham 1980
Wimbledon 1981

Honours: Youth caps. 5 England caps. 2 2nd Div. runners-upmedals. 1st Div. runners-up medal.

Dave was a keen and dedicated player who possessed a great amount of stamina and was as strong as a bull in the tackle. His distribution was excellent when he moved up-field with the attack, yet he was a fairly rare goalscorer. He signed for Q.P.R as a 17 year old, and made five appearances for England during his time at Loftus Road. During a career that lasted fourteen years he notched up over 400 appearances, which included two ever-present seasons in the League, in 1970/71 and the following year. Yet after such valuable service, and aged 31, he was valued at £170,000 by Bolton Wanderers. His son, Neil played for Chelsea but made his name at West Brom. where he was noted for his long range free kicks. Tragically, Dave was found stabbed to death in his father-in-law's flat in Putney, at the age of 34.
Debut: 8. 4.1967 v. Scunthorpe United (H). 5-1. Div. 3.

CLIPSHAM
(H.B.) Mid
b.
Wandsworth
Q.P.R. 1902
Southern League: 2-0. FAC: 1-0. FLC: 0-0. Others: 0-0. Total: 3-0.

Clipsham played for Wandsworth before he moved to Q.P.R. but that is all is known of this player whose further details are lost in the mists of time.
Debut: 1.11.1902 v. Luton Town (H). 0-3. F.A.Cup

CLUTTERBUCK Henry James
Goal 5' 10" 12st 4lbs
b. Wheatenhurst, Gloucestershire in 1873 d.19.12.1948
Hereford Thistle
Small Heath May 1897
Q.P.R. May 1899
Southern League: 56-0. FAC: 14-0. FLC: 0-0. Others: 0-0. Total: 70-0.
Grimsby Town May 1901
Chesterfield Jul 1902
New Brompton 1903
Fulham Aug 1904

Clutterbuck started his career at the same time and in the some team as the Sharpe brothers, one of whom was destined to represent England at both cricket and football. Henry became the Rangers' first professional goalkeeper and although he was rather short for a man who stood between the sticks, he made up for this with with his physique and a sound cool agility. He did not miss a competitive match in the two years he was with the club. He retired in 1905 at the age of 32.
Debut: 9.9.1899 v. Tottenham Hot. (A). 0-1. SLDiv.1.

COCHRANE Justin Vincent
Mid 6' 0" 11st 8lbs
b. Hackney, London 26. 1.1982
Q.P.R. Jul 1999
Hayes 2002
Football League: 1-0. FAC: 0-0. FLC: 0-0. Others: 0-0. Total: 1-0.

A member of the successful Q.P.R. U19 team., Justin was a promising player who had the misfortune to receive a harsh red card just 17 minutes after coming on in his first senior match. Released in the Summer of 2002 he was signed by Hayes F.C. (He moved to Crewe Alexandra for a five figure fee in July 2003)
Debut: 28. 4.2001 v. Stockport County (H).0-3. Div. 1.

COCKBURN William Old

(C.H.) CD 6' 0" 12st 0lbs
b. Willington Quay, Northumberland in 1899
d.27.12.1958 Rosehill

F.C., Newcastle	
Stockport County	May 1921
Liverpool	May 1924
Q.P.R.	Jul 1928

Football League: 57-0. FAC: 5-0. FLC: 0-0. Others: 0-0. Total: 62-0.

Swindon Town	Jul 1930

Bill was a gritty player who was coming to the end of his career when he moved to Rangers. At Liverpool he took over from Wadsworth after he was transferred to Bristol City. Cockburn was a player with an excellent disposition and he finished his career at Swindon Town.
Debut: 25. 8.1928 v. Torquay United (A).4-3. Div.3 (S).

COCKELL David J.

(R.H.) Def
b. Ashford, Middlesex 1. 2.1939
Hounslow Town

Q.P.R.	1960

Football League: 9-0. FAC: 1-0. FLC: 0-0. Others: 0-0. Total: 10-0.

Crawley Town	1962

Dave was the substitute for either Angell or Keen, therefore he rarely got a look in. He opted to spend the rest of his footballing career in the non-League football scene.
Debut: 19.11.1960 v. Shrewsbury Town (H).1-1. Div.3.

COGGINS William Herbert

Goal 5' 11" 11st 8lbs
b. Bristol 16. 9.1901 d. Somerset 7. 7.1958

Whitehall		
Victoria Albion		
Bristol St. Georges		
Bristol City		Dec 1925
Everton	(£2,000)	Mar 1930
Q.P.R.		1935

Football League: 6-0. FAC: 0-0. FLC: 0-0. Others: 0-0. Total: 6-0.

Bath City	1936

Honours: 3rd Div. (South) championship medal. 2nd Div. championship medal.

Billy played six matches for Q.P.R. when the regular goalkeeper, Bill Mason, was injured. Coggins had played nearly 200 matches for Bristol City and over 50 for Everton. He retired to his native Bristol and died at West Town, Somerset aged 57.
Debut: 28.12.1935 v. Millwall (A). 0-2. Div. 3. (S).

COLE John E.

(R.B.) Def
b. Wales

Hereford Thistle	
Bristol St. Georges	
Gainsborough Trinity	1899
Q.P.R.	1900

Southern League: 1-0. FAC: 0-0. FLC: 0-0. Others: 0-0. Total: 1-0.

John came from the same stable as Henry Clutterbuck the goalkeeper. However, he stayed just a short time at the club, playing in the first match of the season.
Debut: 1. 9.1900 v. Bristol Rovers (A). 1-2. SLDiv. 1.

COLGAN Walter

(R.B.) Def
b. Castleford, Yorkshire 3. 4.1937
Ashley Road F.C.

Q.P.R.	1954

Football League: 3-0. FAC: 0-0. FLC: 0-0. Others: 0-0. Total: 3-0.

A regular defender in the London Combination reserve side. Walter was a replacement for Pat Woods, so he was only rarely called upon to play in the side as the regular player was very seldom injured.
Debut: 28.12.1957 v. Southend United (H).1-1. Div.3(S).

COLLIER John C.

(R.H.) Def 5' 9" 11st 10lbs
b. Dysart, Scotland 1. 2.1897 d. 28.12.40

Victoria Hawthorn Boys	
Denbeith Star	
Inverkeithing United	
Raith Rovers	1919
Hull City	Jul 1920
Q.P.R.	Jul 1926

Football League: 36 -1. FAC: 1-0. FLC: 0-0. Others: 0-0. Total: 37-1.

York City	1928

This canny Scot played with vigour and dash, being a hard tackler who always commanded respect from the opposition. In 1928 he was appointed player/ manager of the York City club, who were at the time playing in the Midland League. However, in only his second match, John broke his ankle and so ended the playing part of his contract. Nevertheless he continued to manage the side until they were elected into the Football League. He left at the end of the season to become a publican, only to return to York in 1933 to take up the manager's job again.

In March 1937 he announced that he was giving up the job to go into business with one of his brothers. Ill health overcame him suddenly and he died at the early age of 43.
Debut: 28. 8.1926 v.Crystal Palace (A).1-2. Div. 3. (S).

COLLINS Harry

Goal 6' 0" 11st 12lbs
b. Wynlaton, County Down, Ireland in 1876
Newcastle Juniors of Science & Art
Rendle
Birtley
Hebburn Argyle

Burnley	1900
Q.P.R.	1901

Southern League:115-0. FAC: 6-0. FLC: 0-0. Others: 0-0. Total:121-0.

Everton	1905

The Athletic News wrote of Harry "*He is a quick and clever custodian*" . On his transfer to Q.P.R. Harry was elected club captain of the Latimer Road side. His stay lasted four seasons during which time he was more or less a regular in the first team.
Debut: 7. 9.1901 v. Watford (H). 0-1. SLDiv.1.

COLLINS James Henry

(I.R.) Mid 5' 8" 12st 3lbs
b. Bermondsey, London 30. 1.1911 d. 10. 7.1983
Tooting & Mitcham

Q.P.R.	1931

Football League: 22-4. FAC: 0-0. FLC: 0-0. Others: 0-0. Total: 22-4.
Tunbridge Wells Rangers

Rochdale	Sep 1933
Stockport County	May 1934
Walsall	May 1935
Liverpool	Jan 1936
Cardiff City	May 1937

Honours: Welsh Cup runners-up medal.

A muscular player, Jimmy was strong and adaptable who played for several clubs during the thirties. He also played for Swindon Town and Aberman during the 2nd World War.
Debut: 7.11.1931 v. Luton Town (H). 3-1. Div. 3 (S).

COLLINS John W.

(I.L.) Mid 5' 9" 10st 10lbs
b. Chiswick 10. 8.1942
Acton, Brentford & Chiswick schools

Q.P.R.		Aug 1959

Football League:218-46. FAC:15-6. FLC: 6-4. Others: 0-0. Total:239-56.

Oldham Athletic	(£9,000)	Oct 1966
Reading	(£7,000)	Aug 1967
Luton Town	(£10,000)	Aug 1969
Cambridge United	(£6,000)	Feb 1971

John displayed a terrific amount of stamina as well as having a flair for scoring important goals. At one time he completed an unusual hat-trick against Hull City, all the goals being scored with his head. A local boy he was signed by Rangers as a seventeen year old in 1959, and his seven year career at Loftus Road encompassed over 200 games and 56 first team goals. In October 1966 he moved North to Boundary Park where his goalscoring continued and included netting six in a match for Oldham Athletic, just two days after joining them from Q.P.R. in a friendly game versus the Swiss club FC Thun. He also had an excellent time at Reading where he managed 29 goals in 96 matches and finished as the Reading top scorer in 1969. John returned to Loftus Road in the early seventies to become a member of the coaching staff.
Debut: 30. 4.1960 v. Barnsley (H). 1-0. Div.3.

COLVIN Robert

(O.R.) Wing 5' 5" 10st 0lbs
b. Dumfries, Scotland 5.12.1876

Liverpool	1897
Glossop North End	1898
New Brighton Tower	1899
Luton Town	1901
Q.P.R.	1902

Southern League: 11-0. FAC: 0-0. FLC: 0-0. Others: 0-0. Total: 11-0.

Swindon Town	1903
Carlisle United	1905

A tiny and experienced winger who proved he was skilful during the club's early days. Apparently Bob suffered from ill health while he was at Q.P.R. so he was allowed to recuperate in Scotland and the club sacked him the following season, however, this didn't deter him from carrying on playing elsewhere.
Debut: 3. 9.1902 v. Wellingborough (H).2-0. SLDiv. 1.

CONEY Dean Henry

(C.F.) Striker 6' 0" 12st 6lbs
b. Dagenham, Essex 18. 9.1963
Erkinwald school
Lopndon & Essex Boys

Fulham		May 1981
QP.R.	(£200,000)	Jun 1987

Football League: 48-7. FAC: 5-0. FLC: 6-0. Others: 3-2. Total: 62-9.

Norwich City	(£350,000)	May 1989
Ernest Borel, Hong Kong		
Farnborough Town		

Honours: 4 England caps at U21 level.

Dean made his league debut at the age of 17 while he was at Fulham and manager Trevor Francis secured his transfer. However, Coney remained disappointed with the style of play at Q.P.R. Being basically a front man he was told to play midfield by Trevor Francis. So when the offer came to sign for Norwich City he jumped at the chance '*to play for a footballing side*'.
Debut: 15. 8.1987 v. West Ham United (A).3-0. Div. 1.

CONNER Robert

(O.L.) Wing 5' 7" 11st 7lbs
b. Newcastle in 1913

Q.P.R.	1935

Football League: 5-0. FAC: 0-0. FLC: 0-0. Others: 1-0. Total: 6-0.

Yeovil & Petters	1936

Bob played just a handful of matches during the 1935-6 season, and he was one of the players released at the end of that campaign.
Debut: 26.11.1935 v. Brighton & H.A. (A). 1-5. Div.3 (S)

CONNOLLY Karl Andrew

Mid 5' 10" 11st 2lbs
b. Prescot, Lancashire 9. 2.1970
Napoli (A Sunday league side)

Wrexham	May 1991
Q.P.R.	May 2000

Football League: 73-12. FAC: 6-0. FLC: 1-0. Others: 2-0. Total: 82-12.

Honours: Welsh Cup winners medal.

Karl was on Tranmere Rovers books as a schoolboy but was not offered an apprenticeship. He continued to play for the ' Prentonians ' on a casual basis while still working in a chip shop! He then drifted into local football playing for the 'Rockies', in the St. Helens Combination, and also Napoli in the Warrington Sunday League. He eventually signed for Wrexham in May 1991, and Q.P.R. a year later. Karl is an an attacking midfield player creating numerous opportunities for the front men, through his ability to hold on to the ball and beat defenders. He was, however, never a true regular in the first team after his initial season (Moved to Swansea City August 2003)
Debut: 12. 8.2000 v. Birmingham City (H). 0-0. Div. 1.

COOPER Gary J.

Mid. 5' 8" 11st 3lbs
b. Hammersmith, London 20.11.1965

Q.P.R	Jun 1983

Football League: 1-0. FAC: 0-0. FLC: 2-0. Others: 1-0. Total: 4-0.

Brentford	(Loan)	Sep 1985
Torquay United		
Fisher Athletic		Feb 1986
Barnet		
Maidstone United		Mar 1989
Peterborough United		Mar 1991
Birmingham City		Dec 1993
Welling United		Aug 1996
Kingstonian		Apl 1997

Honours: England Youth caps. 3 England U17 caps. AutoWindscreen Shield winners medal. 2nd Div. Championship medal.

After his Q.P.R. days he was converted into a very consistent defender playing at left back.
Debut: 2. 3.1985 v. Norwich City (H). 2-2. Div. 1.

CORBETT Walter Samuel

(R.B.) Def
b. Wellington, Shropshire 26.11.1880
d. Birmingham 1955

Vicarage Road School
King Edward V1 Grammar School
Thornhill F.C.
Ashbury Richmond
Headingly F.C.
Soho Villa
Bournbrook
Aston Villa Jun 1904
Birmingham City Jul 1907
Q.P.R. Sep 1907
Southern League: 1-0. FAC: 0-0. FLC: 0-0. Others: 0-0.
Total: 1-0.
Wellington Town Apl 1911
Wolverhampton Old Church 1913

Honours: 18 English Amateur caps. 3 English professional caps. Great Britain Olympic Gold Medal for soccer. Captain of the Birmingham & District Juniors v. Scotland on 3 occasions. Represented an Amateur/Professional X1 on a continental tour.

Walter was the manager of an export house in the Midlands, this took him all over the world, and he spoke several languages. He suffered from polio as a lad and always carried a handkerchief in his withered left hand. The Sports Argus wrote about this great full back in 1906, saying that, " *He was one of the most gentlemanly players one could hope to meet*". Walter was a wonderful footballer who it was rumoured, never did a dirty trick or ever conceded a penalty on the field of play. He had a fine turn of speed and showed infinite resource.
Debut: 7. 9.1907 v. New Brompton (H). 2-2. SLDiv. 1.

COWAN James

(C.H.) CD 5' 6" 12st 3lbs
b. Jamestown, Scotland 17.10.1868d. Scotland 12.12.1918
Bonhill School
Vale of Leven
Aston Villa Aug 1889
Q.P.R. Dec 1906
Southern League: 1-1. FAC: 0-0. FLC: 0-0. Others: 0-0.
Total: 1-1.

Honours: 3 Scottish caps. 2 F.A.Cup winners medals. 5 League championship medals. A runners-up medal.

Jimmy was an untiring and energetic tackler and the mainstay of the famous Villa defence throughout the 1890s. As a centre half he was of immense value to the club, being undismayed and uncomplaining after the hardest of matches.

Known as the prince of half backs Cowen was a shrewd tactician, surprisingly quick and certainly one of the all time greats who eventually became the first manager of Q.P.R. Under his management the club won two Southern League titles. In 1896, Jimmy entered the famous Powderhall Sprint Handicap, doing so under an assumed name, winning the race and collecting £80 prize money. However, he was later fined four weeks pay by a furious Villa committee.
Debut: 16.12.1905 v. Northampton T. (H).6-1. SLDiv. 1.

COWARD William C.

(O.L.) Wing 5' 6" 10st 4lbs
b. Windsor, Buckinghamshire
Windsor & Eton
Wycombe 1926
Q.P.R. 1927
Football League:126-22. FAC: 12-4. FLC: 0-0. Others: 0-0.
Total:138-26.
Walsall 1932
Yeovil & Petters

Billy was a neat and tricky player who joined the club mid-season, and scored in his first two matches for the Rangers. He turned porfessional on his transfer from Wycombe Wanderers, and was a regular first team player during his four plus years. For a winger scored a reasonable number of goals. In 1932, Billy he was transferred to Walsall along with the goalkeeper Cunningham.
Debut: 31. 3.1928 v. Torquay United (H).2-3. Div.3 (S).

COWIE Andrew

(O.L.) Wing 5' 6" 10st 11lbs.
b. Lockee, Scotland in 1879
Dundee Harp
Thames Ironworks 1897
Gravesend United 1898
Manchester City 1899
Q.P.R. 1899
Southern League: 11-2. FAC: 5-0. FLC: 0-0. Others: 0-0.
Total: 11-2.
Woolwich Arsenal 1900

Andy was a member of the Q.P.R. side that defeated Brighton United 6-0 in their very first Southern League fixture. He scored a hat-trick in the match. However, it was deleted from the record books, on account of the later demise of their opponents.
Debut: 9. 9.1989 v. Tottenham Hot. (A). 0-1. SLDiv.1.

CRAWFORD Gavin

(R.H.) Def 5' 9" 12st 0lbs
b. Galston, Scotland in 1867 d. in March 1955

Ash Lea F.C., Scotland	
Fairfield Rangers, Glasgow	1887
Sheffield United	1890
Woolwich Arsenal	1891
Millwall Athletic	1898
Q.P.R.	1899

Southern League: 24-1. FAC: 9-0. FLC: 0-0. Others: 0-0. Total: 33-1.

Gavin was the ex captain of Arsenal and he immediately became the skipper of Q.P.R. Retiring in 1899 he later became the groundsman at the Valley, Charlton, keeping his job until 1947.
Debut: 9. 9.1899 v. Tottenham Hot. (A). 0-1. SLDiv.1.

CRAWFORD John Forsyth

(Wing) Striker 5' 2" 8st 6lbs
b. Jarrow, County Durham 26. 9.1896 d. 27. 9.1975

Jarrow Celtic		
Palmers Works, Jarrow		
Jarrow Town		
Hull City		Dec 1919
Chelsea	(£3,000)	May 1923
Q.P.R.		May 1934

Football League: 53-15. FAC: 2-1. FLC: 0-0. Others: 4-2. Total: 59-18.

Honours: 1 England cap.

Known as 'Jackie', he was a tricky little winger with intricate footwork, who could cross the ball with either foot and would shoot at goal on numerous occasions during a match. Jackie came to Loftus Road in the role of player/coach and stayed until the outbreak of World War Two. Upon leaving the club, Crawford, worked in a munitions factory in Essex and remained there until after the hostilities had ceased, becoming the part time coach of Maldon Town.
Debut: 25. 8.1934 v. Swindon Town (A).1-3. Div.3 (S).

CRIBB Stanley Roy

(O.L.) Wing 5' 8" 11st 0lbs
b. Gosport, Hamshire 11. 5.1905 d. Gosport 13. 1.1989

Grove Road School, Gosport		
Elson Saint Thomas		
Gosport Athletic		1923
Southampton		Sep 1924
West Ham United	(£500)	May 1930
Q.P.R.		Jun 1931

Football League: 28-12. FAC: 4-6. FLC: 0-0. Others: 0-0. Total: 32-18.

Cardiff City	Jul 1932

Honours: County representative before his 17th birthday.

Stan was a very fast moving winger who became a solid penalty taker. After six years at Southampton he was transferred to West Ham United but he never made an appearance for them and after a year he moved to Q.P.R. When his playing days were over he continued to be involved in football by helping with the formation of Gosport Borough F.C. and became their manager from 1944 until 1967. He then scouted for the Saints until he died in 1989.
Debut: 29. 8.1931 v. Brentford (A). 0-1. Div. 3. (S).

CRICKSON Gerry E.

(R.H.) Def
b. Dover, Kent 21. 9.1934

Q.P.R.	Sep 1951

Football League: 5-0. FAC: 1-0. FLC: 0-0. Others: 0-0. Total: 6-0.

Dover	1956

Honours: English School and Youth International.

Gerry played just six matches in four years for the Q.P.R. first eleven, before opting to return to his hosme side Dover.
Debut: 6. 4.1953 v.Millwall (H). 1-3. Div. 3. (S).

CROMPTON Norman

(C.H.) CD 5' 10" 11st 10lbs
b. Farnworth, Lancashire in 1905

Little Hulton United	
Denbeigh United	May 1925
Oldham Athletic	May 1926
Q.P.R.	May 1928

Football League: 1-0. FAC: 0-0. FLC: 0-0. Others: 0-0. Total: 1-0.

Horwich RMI	
Darwin	May 1931
Lancaster Town	1936
Rosendale United	Jun 1936
Wigan Athletic	Jan 1937

In 1932 at Denbeigh he scored 18 goals including 13 penalties from centre half while he was captain of the side. However, it was at Darwin later in his career that Norman was to become famous, as captain of the side that lost to Arsenal, 11-1 in the F.A.Cup at Highbury in 1932
Debut: 3. 5.1928 v. Norwich City (H). 0-0. Div. 3. (S).

CROSS John

(L.H.) Def 5' 11" 11st 7lbs
b. Scotland in 1879

Wishaw Rovers	1898
Third Lanark	1899
Q.P.R.	1904

Southern League: 23-0. FAC: 1-0. FLC: 0-0. Others: 0-0.
Total: 24-0.

Third Lanark	1905

The 1903 edition of 'Men Famous in Football' wrote of John that "*He is brilliant in defence and attack, he has good resources and a fine command of the ball, he places it well to his forwards*".
Debut: 5. 9.1903 v. Brentford (H). 1-0. SLDiv. 1.

CROSS William

(O.R.) Wing 5' 7" 10st 7lbs
b. Scotland in 1883

Wishaw Hearts	
Cambuslang Swifts	
Third Lanark	1901
Q.P.R.	1903

Southern League: 32-4. FAC: 1-0. FLC: 0-0. Others: 0-0.
Total: 33-4.

Brentford	1905

Billy was the younger brother of John. Both playing for Q.P.R. in the 1904/05 season. John returned to Scotland while Billy moved on to play for Brentford.
Debut: 10. 9.1904 v. West Ham United (A).3-1 SLDiv.1.

CROUCH Peter James

(C.F.) Striker 6' 7" 11st 12lbs.
b. Macclesfield, Lancashire 30. 1.1981

Tottenham Hotspur		Jul 1998
Q.P.R.	(£60,000)	Jul 2000

Football League: 42-10. FAC: 3-2. FLC: 2-0. Others: 0-0.
Total: 47-12

Portsmouth	(£1,000,000)	2002
Aston Villa	(£1,000,000)	2002

Honours: England youth caps.

Gerry Francis had coached this player as a junior at Spurs, where he stayed for two years. With Q.P.R., Peter quickly became a first team regular and finished the 2000/01 season as the top scorer. But he soon became a big money mover, when the giant centre forward was transferred to Portsmouth, where he showed tremendous ball control and the ability to run at and beat defenders. He was eventually sold on to Aston Villa in March, thus becoming the tallest striker in the Premiership. at that time. He scored on his debut for Villa against Newcastle, but was voted as Pompey's 'Player of the season', despite his earlier departure that season
Debut: 12. 8.2000 v. Birmingham City (H). 0-0. Div. 1.

CULKIN Nicolas James

G. 6' 2" 13st 7lbs
b. York 6. 7.1978.

York City		
Manchester United	(£250,000)	1995
Hull City	(loan)	1999
Manchester United		2000
Bristol Rovers	(loan)	2000
Manchester United		2001
Livingstone	(loan)	2001
Q.P.R.		2002

Football League: 17-0. FAC: 0-0. FLC: 0-0. Others: 0-0.

Nick is a solid young goalkeeper who possesses a good pair of hands and bears a passing resemblance to Peter Schmeichel. He never made the grade at Manchester United, and after a series of loan deals Nick eventually signed for Q.P.R. in the Summer of 2002.
Debut: 10. 8. 2002 v. Chesterfield (H). W. 3-1. Div. 2.

CUNNINGHAM Joel

Goal 6' 0" 11st 7lbs
b. Lockie, Dundee, Scotland in 1905

Logie Aberdeen	1923
Aberdeen	1924
Newport County	Jun 1925
Q.P.R.	Jun 1926

Football League:168-0. FAC: 6-0. FLC: 0-0. Others: 0-0.
Total:174-0.

Walsall	May 1932
York City	Aug 1934
Dartford	Jul 1935
Folkstone Town	1936
Dartford	1937

Not finding a permanent place in a Scottish club side, Joel decided to try south of the border and he gradually built up a reputation as being one of the best goalkeepers in the 3rd Division. Cunningham stayed six years with the club becoming a favourite of the spectators with his antics, of swinging on the cross bar like a trapeze artist and making sliding tackles on the opposing forwards. Joel kept goal for Walsall in 1933 when they knocked Arsenal out of the F.A.Cup and at Dartford he enjoyed the limelight again in 1936 when they sensationally beat Cardiff City at Ninian Park.
Debut: 30.10.1926 v. Northampton T. (H). 4-2. Div.3(S).

CUNNINGHAM Thomas E.

(C.H.) CD 6'1" 11st 3lbs
b. Bethnal Green, London 7.12.1955

Chelsea		Sep 1973
Q.P.R.		May 1975

Football League: 30-2. FAC: 3-0. FLC: 2-0. Others: 0-0.
Total: 35-0.

Wimbledon	(£45,000)	Mar 1979
Orient	(£60,000)	Sep 1981
Fisher Athletic		Jun 1987

Tommy joined Q.P.R. on a free transfer from Chelsea and was a big strong centre half who was somewhat over enthusiastic and accrued a non too impressive disciplinary record, he always gave 100% effort in a match. Becoming captain at Orient he was later chief coach, and then assistant manager at Barnet. In July 2001 he was appointed manager of Wingate & Finchley, the Ryman League club.
Debut: 2.10.1976 v. Arsenal (A).2-3. Div.1.

CURRIE Anthony William

Mid 5' 11" 12st 9lbs
b. Edgware, Middlesex 1. 1.1950

Watford		May 1967
Sheffield United	(£26,500)	Feb 1968
Leeds United	(£250,000)	Jun 1976
Q.P.R.	(£400,000)	Aug 1979

Football League: 81-5. FAC: 9-0. FLC: 8-1. Others: 0-0.
Total: 98-6.

Toronto Nationals, Canada	(£60,000)	May 1983
Chesham United		Aug 1983
Southend United		Sep 1983
Chesham United		Nov 1983
Torquay United		Mar 1984
Tranmere Rovers		Oct 1984
Dunstable Town		1985
Hendon		1986
Goole Town		Sep 1987

Honours: 3 England youth caps. 13 U23 caps. 17 full England caps. A Football League cap. 2nd Div. Championship medal. 2nd Div. runners-up medal. F.A.Cup runners-up medal.

Tony was one of the most gifted players during the 70s, he was an artist on the ball being blessed with great vison, his close ball control was equal to anyone past or present. He could strike the ball with accuracy but preferred to spray passes to colleagues with the most delectable ease and timing. Strong in possession and difficult to dispossess, he was flamboyant and arrogant.

Tony was the team captain in the 1982 F.A.Cup Final replay, and was last heard of in 1989, working as a community officer for Sheffield United.
Debut: 8. 9.1979 v. Fulham (H). 3-0. Div. 2.

DALY Wesley James Patrick

Mid 5' 9" 11st 2lbs
b. Hammersmith, London 7. 3.1984

Q.P.R.	2001

Football League: 7-0. FAC: 0-0. FLC: 0-0. Others: 0-0.
Total: 7-0.

A young midfield player who came up through the ranks at the club. Wesley has spent much of his time in the reserves, with just one first team appearance prior to the 2002/03 season.
Debut: 16. 3.2002 v. Colchester United (A).1-3. Div.2.

DAND Robert

(H.B.) Def 5' 7" 11st 0lbs
b. Ilford, Essex in 1900

Ashford	
Ilford	
Reading	1921
Q.P.R.	1924

Football League: 1-0. FAC: 0-0. FLC: 0-0. Others: 0-0.
Total: 1-0.
Margate

Honours: 1 English amateur cap.

A successful amateur career that included an England appearance against Ireland, Reggie was persuaded to give up his job as a stockbroker's clerk, to become a footballer at Reading. At Q.P.R. he reverted back to the City of London and ended up playing for Margate.
Debut: 25.12.1924 v. Norwich City (H).1-2. Div.3 (S).

DANIELS Arthur W. C.

(O.L.) Wing 5' 10" 10st 7lbs
b. Mossley, Manchester
Salford Boys Club
West Salford
Mossley

Manchester City	Feb 1921
Watford	May 1926
Q.P.R.	Jun 1930

Football League: 14-3. FAC: 0-0. FLC: 0-0. Others: 0-0.
Total: 14-3.

A fast and tricky winger, but Arthur lacked consistency and never relished rough play. He shared the wing with five others during his season at Q.P.R.
Debut: 30. 8.1930 v. Thames (H). 3-0. Div.3 (S).

DANIELS Harold Augustus George

(W.H.) Mid 5' 9" 11st 0lbs
b. Kensington, London 25. 6.1920
Kensington Sports

Q.P.R.		Oct 1943

Football League: 14-0. FAC: 5-0. FLC: 0-0. Others: 0-0.
Total: 19-0.

Brighton & Hove Albion	(£2,000)	Aug 1948
York City		Aug 1950
Dover	(£2,000)	1951

Honours: Represented The Royal Artillery during the war.

Harry was a very reliable player who was especially able to rectify slip-ups made by any members of the team. Wounded in the North African campaign he nevertheless made around seventy wartime appearances for Q.P.R.
Debut: 31. 8.1946 v. Watford (H). 2-1. Div.3 (S).

DARLINGTON Jermaine Christopher

WB 5' 7" 10st 10lbs
b. Hackney, London 11. 4.1974

Charlton Athletic		Jun 1992
Dover Athletic		Sep 1993
Hendon		Oct 1996
Aylesbury United		
Q.P.R.	(£25,000)	Mar 1999

Football League: 71-2. FAC: 6-0. FLC: 2-0. Others: 0-0.
Total: 79-2.

Wimbledon	(£200,000)	Jul 2001

Jermaine became a firm favourite with the spectators, because of his surging runs from out of defence, operating with equal effectiveness from either flank. However, after just over two years at Loftus Road, he was signed by Wimbledon during the close season of 2001 for £200,000. Jermaine is comfortable with the ball at his feet, and he fitted in to the side at both left and right-back. As he had previously played in midfield he likes to push forward and join the attack and his speed and vision make him a handful to control.
Debut: 10. 4.1999 v. W.B.A. (H). 2-1. Div. 1.

DAVIDSON Peter E.

Mid 5' 10" 11st 1lb
b. Newcastle 31.10.1956
Berwick Rangers

Q.P.R.	(£40,000)	Jul 1979

Football League: 1-0. FAC: 0-0. FLC: 0-0. Others: 0-0.
Total: 1-0.

Berwick Rangers	(£35,000)	1979

Peter joined Q.P.R. in the summer of 1979 but failed to grasp the opportunity. He soon returned to Berwick Rangers and stayed with them until 1987.
Debut: 25. 8.1979 v. Leicester City (H).1-4. Div. 2.

DAVIES Edmond

(C.F.) Striker
b. Oswestry, Shropshire 5. 6.1927

Liverpool	1947
Arsenal	Aug 1948
Q.P.R.	Apl 1950

Football League: 1-1. FAC: 0-0. FLC: 0-0. Scores: 0-0.
Total: 1-1.

Crewe Alexandria	Jul 1951
Oswestry Town	1952

Eddie scored in his only senior match for the club. But his potential was never realised at Loftus Road or elsewhere, and he finished up playing for his non-League home town club.
Debut: 27. 1.1951 v. Brentford (H). 1-1. Div. 2.

DAVIS Arthur George

(I.F.) Striker 5' 10" 11st 12lbs
b. Birmingham in July 1900 d. Birmingham 1955

Birmingham St. Georges
Evesham Town
Aston Villa Jul 1919
Q.P.R. Aug 1922
Football League: 62-21. FAC: 5-1. FLC: 0-0. Others: 0-0.
Total: 67-22.
Notts County 1924
Crystal Palace 1928
Kidderminster Harriers 1929

Arthur managed a goal on his debut and he was one of the three main scorers at the club at the time, along with Birch and Parker. Unfortunately during his time with Rangers, they had to apply for re-election to the League and this hastened his downfall.
Debut: 28. 8.1922 v. Norwich City (A).1-1.Div. 3 (S).

DAWES Ian Robert

(L.B.) Def 5' 10" 11st 10lbs
b. Croydon, Surrey 22. 2.1963
Q.P.R. Dec 1980
Football League:229-3: FAC: 8-0. FLC: 28-1. Others:5-0
Total:270-4.
Millwall (£150,000) Aug 1988
Bromley 1995

Honours: 8 England schoolboy caps. 2nd Div. Championship medal. League Cup runners-up medal.

Ian was under 18 when he signed for Rangers, and during his long career at Loftus Road, one period included 198 consecutive appearances before he missed a match through injury. This run, embraced the four seasons 1982/83 to 1985/86 when he was an ever-present in Football League matches.

He consistently put in faultless performances week after week for Q.P.R., and he was eventually transferred to Millwall. Despite 270 first team appearances for Rangers, he went on to become one of Millwall's longer serving players, consistently putting in faultless performances at either right or left back. He was equally adept whether defending of assisting the attack. At The Den he added another 258 first team games to his record. In 1995 he moved into the non-League scene, at Bromley, and the following year played for Dorking. But he soon had to retire due to a recurring knee injury. Ian later became the manager of Carshalton Athletic and coach at Charlton and Millwall, before taking over as manager of Redhill in 2002.
Debut: 27. 3.1982 v. Rotherham United (A).0-1. Div.2.

DAWSON Alexander

(O.R.) Wing
b. Glasgow, Scotland 21.10.1933
Gourock Juniors
Q.P.R. Feb 1957
Football League: 59-5. FAC: 5-2. FLC: 0-0. Others: 3-0.
Total: 67-7.
Sittingbourne 1959

Alex's best match was at Accrington where he notched two of the four goals that were scored that day. Just after this he was sacked by the then manager Taylor. His career at Loftus Road only lasted three seasons, during which time he made 67 first team appearances, including notably 33 League outings in the 1957/58 season.
Debut: 13. 4.1957 v. Brighton & H.A. (H).0-0. Div.3 (S)

DAWSON George

(L.H.) Mid
b. Glasgow, Scotland 13. 9.1930
Motherwell
Q.P.R. May 1955
Football League: 1-0. FAC: 0-0. FLC: 0-0. Others: 0-0.
Total: 1-0.

The only occasion that George played in the senior squad resulted in a 6-2 victory for the team.
Debut: 10. 3.1956 v. Colchester Utd. (H).6-2.Div.3 (S).

DAY

(C.F.) Striker
b.

Q.P.R.		1912

Football League: 4-0. FAC: 0-0. FLC: 0-0. Others: 0-0.
Total: 4-0.

The season after winning the Southern League title, an injury to the regular centre forward left the side bereft of a striker. Day was the sixth man to be tried in that position during the season.
Debut: 8. 3.1913 v. Portsmouth (H). 1-1. SLDiv 1.

DAY Christopher Nicholas

G 6'3" 13st 6lbs
b. Walthamstow, London 28. 7.1975

Tottenham Hotspur		Apl 1993
Crystal Palace	(£225,000)	Aug 1996
Watford	(£225,000)	Jul 1997
Lincoln City	(Loan)	Dec 2000
Q.P.R.		Jul 2001

Football League: 31-0. FAC: 0-0. FLC: 1-0. Others: 1-0.
Total: 18-0.

Honours: 6 England U21 caps. UEFA-U18s youth caps.

Chris quickly became a favourite of the Shepherds Bush fans after he signed from Watford. However, he unfortunately suffered a fracture of the right leg in November 2001 which kept him out of action for the rest of the season, but he made a successful comeback towards the end of 2002/03 after his long lay-off.
Debut: 11. 8.2001 v. Stoke City (H).1-0. Div. 2.

DEAN Jobey

(R.H.) Mid
b. Chesterfield 25.11.1934

Thoresby Colliery	1950
Q.P.R.	Nov 1952

Football League: 16-0. FAC: 1-0. FLC: 0-0. Others: 0-0.
Total: 17-0.

Sutton Town	1957
Bradford Park Avenue	Dec 1957

The stand-in for Petchey, who was very seldom injured, Jobey was eventually transferred to Bradford P.A., but he only became an a important reserve team man there.
Debut: 30. 8.1955 v. Brentford (A). 0-2. Div. 3 (S).

DELVE John F.

Mid 5' 7" 11st 0lbs
b. Isleworth, London 27. 9.1953

Q.P.R.		Jul 1971

Football League: 15-0. FAC: 1-0. FLC: 1-0. Others: 0-0.
Total: 17-0.

Plymouth Argyle	(£30,000)	Jul 1974
Exeter City	(£15,000)	Mar 1978
Hereford United		1983
Gloucester City		1986
Exeter City		1987
Minehead		1988

Honours: 2nd Div. runners-up medal. 3rd Div. runners-up medal.

John was a terrier-like player who was always looking for the ball and played a small part in the promotion of the club in 1973. However, he is known mainly as an Exeter City stalwart who captained them to a grand F.A. Cup run in 1981. In 1988 Delve took the job of caretaker/manager until the end of the season.
Debut: 9.12.1972 v. Luton Town (A). 2-2. Div.2.

DENNIS Mark Earle

(L.B.) Def 5' 9" 10st 8lbs
b. Streatham, London 2. 5.1961

Chelsea Boys		
Birmingham City		Aug 1978
Southampton	(£30,000)	Nov 1983
Q.P.R.	(£50,000)	May 1987

Football League: 28-0. FAC: 2-0. FLC: 2-0. Others: 3-0.
Total: 35-0.

Crystal Palace	Player + (£50,000)	Aug 1989

Honours: 8 England youth caps. 3 U21 caps. 1st Div. runners-up medal.

An exciting talented player who could send teasing centres across the goalmouth from the wing-back position. Mark had a potential talent that was never realised owing to his fiery temper. He was ordered off over a dozen times and received over seventy yellow card cautions. Nevertheless his enthusiasm made him a popular character with the Loftus Road crowd. Mark eventually became the manager of Fleet Town and later assisted at Eastleigh.
Debut: 15. 8.1987 v. West Ham United (A).3-0. Div.1.

DE ORNELAS Fernando

Mid. 6' 0" 11st 10lbs
b. Caracas, Venezuela 29. 7.1976
Deportivo, Chacao, South China
Happy Valley, Hong Kong

Crystal Palace	Sep 1999
Glasgow Celtic	Mar 2000
Q.P.R.	Oct 2001

Football League: 2-0. FAC: 0-0. FLC: 0-0. Others: 0-0. Total: 2-0.

CS Maritimo, Portugal	Nov 2001

Honours: 13 caps for Venezuela.

Fernando was a right sided midfield player who joined Q.P.R. on a monthly basis, but after just a month or so made a move to Portugal.
Debut: 27.10.2001 v. Oldham Athletic (H). 1-1. Div.2.

DEVINE John Steven

(I.R.) Striker
b. Aberdeen, Scotland
St. Rochs
Aberdeen

Q.P.R.	1938

Football League: 7-3. FAC: 0-0. FLC: 0-0. Others: 1-0. Total: 8-3.

This young player from Scotland couldn't settle in London. At the beginning of the 1939/40 season all contracts were cancelled owing to the outbreak of the 2nd World War. It is not known what happened to John from that time on.
Debut: 27. 8.1938 v. Reading (A). 4-2. Div.3. (S).

DEVINE Joseph Cassidy

(I.L.) Mid 5' 9" 10st 9lbs
b.Motherwell, Scotland 8. 9.1905.d. Chesterfield 9.5.1980
Motherwell Watsonians
Cleland Juniors
Bathgate Thistle

Burnley	(£250)	May 1925
Newcastle United	(£5,575)	Jan 1930
Sunderland	(£2,599)	Jan 1931
Q.P.R.	(£2,500)	May 1933

Football League: 57-9. FAC: 6-1. FLC: 0-0. Others: 2-0. Total: 65-10.

Birmingham City	(£2,000)	Jan 1935
Chesterfield		May 1937

Honours: 1 Football League cap.

Joe was the engine room of the side in the early thirties controlling the ball excellently and reading the game in an instant was no bother to him. He was given the captaincy of the club as soon as he arrived. After his retirement from playing football, Joe became a Scottish referee in the Highland League. Later in life he ran a successful sports outfitters shop in London.
Debut: 26. 8.1933 v. Brighton & H.A.(H).2-0. Div.3(S).

DICHIO Daniele Salvatore Ernest

Striker 6' 3" 12st 3lbs
b. Hammersmith, London 19.10.1974

Q.P.R,		May 1993

Football League: 76-20: FAC: 4-1. FLC: 6-2. Others: 0-0. Total: 86-23.

Welling United	(Loan)	1994
Barnet	(Loan)	Mar 1994
Sampdoria, Italy		1997
Lecce, Italy	(Loan)	1997
Sunderland	(£750,000)	1998
W.B.A.	(Loan)	Aug 2001
W.B.A.	(£1,250,000)	Nov 2001

Honours: England school caps. U21 cap. 1st Div. championship medal.

Tall, excellent in the air and possessing a fierce shot, that is Daniele Dichio, and always proving a handful for the marking defender. Danny scored on his Q.P.R. League debut whilst substituting for Les Ferdinand and the following weekend he appeared as a substitute against Newcastle and scored again. A local boy, Danny formed an excellent partnership with Bradley Allen in the reserves. After a few loan periods he was a big money signing for Sunderland in 1998, and in 2001, he commanded an even bigger fee when he made a move to The Hawthorns.
Debut: 29.10.1994 v. Aston Villa (H). 2-0. PL.

DIGBY Fraser Charles

G 6' 1" 13st 10lbs
b. Sheffield, Yorkshire 23. 4.1967

Manchester United		Apl 1985
Swindon Town	(£32,000)	Sep 1986
Crystal Palace		Aug 1998
Barry Town		Oct 2000
Huddersfield Town		Aug 2001
Q.P.R.		Oct 2001

Football League: 19-0: FAC: 1-0. FLC: 0-0. Other: 0-0.
Total: 20-0.

Kidderminster Harriers	Feb 2003

Honours: School & youth cap. 5 England U21 caps.

An experienced goalkeeper who was the replacement for Day, who broke his leg. Fraser was a regular in the line-up until he became an injury victim himself in February 2002. One year later he signed for Third Division club Kidderminster Harriers.
Debut: 3.11.2001 v. Notts County (A). 2-0. Div. 2.

DINES Joseph

(L.H.) Def
b. Kings Lynn, Norfolk 12. 4.1886 d.27. 9.1918

Kings Lynn	
Q.P.R.	1909

Southern League: 1-0. FAC: 0-0. FLC: 0-0. Others: 0-0.
Total: 1-0.

Kings Lynn	
Ilford	1911
Liverpool	1912
Millwall	1914

Honours: 27 England amateur caps. Olympic Gold medal.

A schoolmaster whose father was a blacksmith. Joe was reputed to be a gentleman, with mild manners and a charming character. Gaining a commission in the army, Dines travelled to all parts of the country on his duties, hence his solitary appearance for Q.P.R. and for Liverpool. Sadly, Joe was a casualty in the Great War and was killed on the western front.
Debut: 16.4.1910 v. West Ham United(H).3-3. SLDiv.1

DOBINSON Harold

(C.F.) Striker 5' 10" 12st 3lbs
b. Darlington 2. 3.1898 d. 1990

Stockton	1910
Durham City	1920
Burnley	1921
Q.P.R.	1923

Football League: 2-0. FAC: 0-0. FLC: 0-0. Others: 0-0.
Total: 2-0.

Honours: F.A. Amateur cup winners medal.

Harold was at the end of a long and successful career, and did not turn professional until after the Great War. At Q.P.R. he was a reserve and was not retained at the end of the 1923/24 season.
Debut: 20.10.1923 v. Northampton T.(A).0-3.Div.3 (S)

DONALD David Morgan

(O.L.) Wing 5' 7" 10st 0lbs
b. Coatbridge, Scotland 29.12.1878d. Derby Jan.1932

Albion Rovers		Jul 1905
Bradford Park Avenue		Jun 1908
Derby County	(£350)	Mar 1910
Chesterfield		Jun 1912
Watford	(£70)	Jun 1913
Q.P.R.		1914

Southern League: 97-10. FAC: 4-0. FLC: 0-0. Others: 0-0.
Total: 101-10.

Honours: Represented the London League v. London Combination.

Dave dominated the left wing from 1914 to 1920. A substantial fee having previously been paid for him in 1910 by Derby County, but Chesterfield got him on a free. A £100 sum had been placed on him, but there was no regulating transfers between the Football League and the Midland League, in which the Spireites then played. At 36 years old he moved to Q.P.R. but still managed over 100 appearances.
Debut: 12. 9.1914 v. Southampton (A).0-3. SL Div.1.

[DOUDOU] MBOMBO Azlana Ebele

For. 5' 5" 9st 11lbs
b. Kinshasha, Zaire 11. 9.1980

AS Monaco, France	
Q.P.R.	Aug 2001

Football League: 46-3. FAC: 1-0. FLC: 1-0. Others: 2-0.
Total: 50-3.

A speedy player, who became a favourite with the crowd having watched his wholehearted efforts during a match. With the club in administration, two supporters agreed to finance his wages, but after playing a handful of games during the 2002/03 season he was released during the Summer.
Debut: 25. 8.2001 v. Reading (H). 0-0. Div.2.

DOWIE Iain

Striker 6' 1" 13st 11lbs
b. Hatfield, Hertfordshire 9. 1.1965

Hendon		
Luton Town	(£30,000)	Dec 1988
Fulham	(Loan)	Sep 1989
West Ham United	(£480,000)	Mar 1991
Southampton	(£500,000)	Sep 1991
Crystal Palace	(£400,000)	Jan 1995
West Ham United	(£500,000)	Sep 1995
Q.P.R.		Jan 1998

Football League: 30-2. FAC: 2-0. FLC: 1-0. Others: 0-0.
Total: 33-2.

Honours: 59 caps for Northen Ireland. U21 cap. U23 cap.

Iain came to the club in 1998 in a part exchange deal for Trevor Sinclair. After playing centre half principally in the reserves he became the chief coach, and was later appointed manager of Oldham Athletic.
Debut: 31. 1.1998 v. Stockport County (A).0-2. Div.1.

DOWNING Samuel

(L.H.) Mid 5' 10" 13st 0lbs
b. Willesden, Middlesex 19.11883 d. Cuckfield Mar.1974

Willesden Green	1898
Willesden Town	1899
Park Royal	1899
West Hampstead	1899
Q.P.R.	1900

Southern League:179-22: FAC: 9-1: FLC: 0-0. Others: 2-0
Total:190-23.

Chelsea	Apl 1909
Croydon Common	1914

Honours: Southern League championship medal. 2nd Div. runners-up medal.

According to some contemporary writers, Sam lacked the pace that would have given him wider recognition, whilst others wrote that he was an artistic and constructive player who was noted for his accurate and long-range shooting. Nevertheless he was renowned for his scrupulously fair play. After his retirement from football he coached cricket at a college in Maidenhead.
Debut: 1. 9.1900 v. Bristol Rovers (A).1-2.SLDiv.1.

DOYLE Maurice

Mid 5' 8" 10st 7lbs
b. Ellesmore Port 17.10.1969

Crewe Alexandria		Jul 1988
Q.P.R.	(£120,000)	Apl 1989

Premier League: 6-0. FAC: 0-0. FLC: 0-0. Others: 0-0.
Total: 6-0.

Crewe Alexandria	(Loan)	Jan 1991
Wolverhampton Wanderers	(Loan)	
Millwall		May 1995
Shrewsbury Town		1998

Maurice had all the ingredients of a first class player, stamina, tenacity and fine ball control, yet he was never able to demonstrate these attributes in a match. Good in the air for such a small man, his worth was never realised, for amazingly he played in more than 170 reserve matches, yet was unable to make it in the first team.
Debut: 9. 2.1993 v. Ipswich Town (A).1-1. PL.

DRABBLE Frank

G 5' 10" 12st 0lbs
b. Southport, Lancashire 8. 7.1888.d. Staines 29. 7.1964

Blowick Wesleyans	
Southport YMCA	
Tottenham Hotspur	May 1909
Nottingham Forest	Jan 1911
Burnley	Dec 1911
Bradford Park Avenue	Jun 1913
Bolton Wanderers	Aug 1919
Southport	Jul 1921
Q.P.R.	Mar 1924

Football League: 2-0. FAC: 0-0. FLC: 0-0. Others: 0-0.
Total: 2-0.

A vastly experienced goalkeeper who stood between the sticks for Q.P.R. on two occasions when they were without custodians. He became an estate agent in later life, having previously had a short spell as a bookmaker. Frank was a useful cricketer playing for Southport & Birkdale Cricket club. He died of a heart attack just after his 76th birthday.
Debut: 1.3.1924 v.Bournemouth& B.A.(H).0-1. Div3(S)

DRAKE Alonzo Robson

(I.L.) Mid 5' 10" 12st 0lbs
b.Parkgate, Rotherham 16.4.1884 d.Hudd'field14 .2.1919
Parkgate F.C.

Doncaster Rovers	1902
Sheffield United	Aug 1904
Birmingham City	Dec 1907
Q.P.R.	Aug 1908

Southern League: 19-5. FAC: 1-0. FLC: 0-0. Others: 0-0.
Total: 20-5.

Huddersfield Town	1910

Honours: Represented Sheffield City v. Glasgow City.

Known as a hardworking and dashing player, embracing soccer in the winter and cricket in the summer, although Alonzo was better known as the latter . His career was blighted by ill-health which led to his untimely death at the early age of 34.
Debut: 1. 9.1908 v. West Ham United (A).0-2. SL Div.1

DREW William A.

(O.R.) Wing
b. London
Barnet

Q.P.R.	1926

Football League: 1-0. FAC: 0-0. FLC: 0-0. Others: 0-0.
Total: 1-0.

Honours: English Schoolboy International.

Bill was one of five right wingers to be tried in the first team during the 1926/27 season.
Debut: 18. 9.1926 v.Charlton Ath. (A). 0-2. Div.3 (S).

DRINKWATER Raymond

G
b. Jarrow, Co. Durham 18. 5.1931
Guildford City

Portsmouth	1955
Q.P.R.	1957

Football League:199-0. FAC:12-0. FLC: 3-0. Others:1-0.
Total:215-0.

Bath City	1963

Ray was a tall, agile and very reliable goalkeeper who stood between the sticks for some five seasons, and was the successor to Ron Springett. He was ever-present until the amateur Mike Pinner joined the club along with Alec Stock as manager. The newcomer was good enough to keep Drinkwater out of the side for almost half the season until the Pinner joined the RAF for his period in the National Service.

Ray enjoyed a career at Loftus Road which extended over six years, during which time he made well over 200 first team appearances, before he moved west to the non-League scene when he joined Bath City.
Debut: 15. 3.1958 v. Coventry City (A).1-1. Div.3(S).

DUDLEY Reginald Arthur

(R.B.) Def
b. Hemel Hempstead 3. 2.1915d. Cambridge Feb 1994
Boxmoor St. John's

Apsley	May 1934
Millwall	Dec 1934
Q.P.R.	Dec 1946

Football League: 58-0. FAC: 4-0. FLC: 0-0. Others: 0-0.
Total: 62-0.

Watford	July 1950
Dover	Aug 1951
Margate	Nov 1952

Honours: English amateur cap. 3rd Div (South) championship medal.

Reg was a player full of class who came to Loftus Road in an exchange deal with Wilf Heathcote. In November 1947 he suffered a double fracture of his leg, plus a broken nose during a match. In the summer of 1950 he was transferred to Watford for a token £200 to captain the reserves. Later in his career he was dismissed as the Hemel Hempstead Town (formerly Apsley) manager, in the light of financial irregularities in connection with which he had been acquitted previously.
Debut: 7.12.1946 v. Port Vale (H).2-0. Div.3 (S).

DUFF Hugh

(R.H.) Mid
b.

Millwall Athletic	1894
Woolwich Arsenal	Aug 1895
Millwall Athletic	1898
Woolwich Arsenal	1899
Q.P.R.	1908

Southern League: 20-0. FAC: 2-0. FLC: 0-0.Others: 0-0. Total: 22-0.

Honours: Kent League championship medal.

Hugh played over a hundred matches and scored some sixty goals for Arsenal reserves. At Q.P.R. he was the substitute for Archie Mitchell.
Debut: 7. 9.1908 v. Watford (H). 2-0. SLDiv.1.

DUFFIELD Martin John

Mid 5' 8" 11st 3lbs
b. Park Royal, Middlesex 28. 2.1964

Tottenham Hotspur		1979
Q.P.R.		Jan 1982

Football League: 1-0. FAC: 0-0. FLC: 0-0. Others: 0-0. Total: 1-0.

AFC Bournemouth	(Loan)	
Charlton Athletic	(Loan)	1984
Enfield		1985
Hendon		1988
Sutton United		1991
St. Albans City		1992

Honours: English youth cap.

Martin made his only appearance for the club on the last day of the 1982/83 season, when he came on as a substitute. He became a well known name in semi-pro football, and was last heard as a long distance lorry driver.
Debut: 14. 5.1983 v. Grimsby Town (A).1-1. Div.2.

DUGDALE James Robert

(C.H.) CD 5' 10" 11st 6lbs
b. Liverpool 15. 1.1932
Liverpool District schools
Liverpool Collegiate F.C.
Harrowby F.C.

W.B.A.	May 1950
Aston Villa	Feb 1956
Q.P.R.	Oct 1962

Football League: 10-0. FAC: 3-0. FLC: 0-0. Others: 0-0. Total: 13-0.

Honours: 3 England B caps. 1 Football League cap. 2 FACup winners medals. 1 League Cup winners medal.

Jimmy was a cool commanding centre half who kept the opposing centre forward well under control. He was troubled with a knee injury which eventually forced him to retire, whereupon he became a publican and had many public houses. Sadly he had to have his leg amputated in 1990 and was forced to retire.
Debut: 22.10.1962 v. Hull City (H).4-1. Div. 3.

DUGGAN Edward J.

(I.F.) Mid
b. West Ham, London 27. 6.1922 d.1982

Luton Town	1939
Q.P.R.	1949

Football League: 47-5. FAC: 1-0. FLC: 0-0. Others: 0-0. Total: 48-5.

Bedford Town	1952
Luton Town	1956

The best part of this player's career was lost due to the war, but during the hostilities Ted played in over 100 matches. He was used as a schemer rather than a goalscorer at Q.P.R.
Debut: 5. 2.1949 v. Grimsby Town (H). 1-2. Div. 2.

DURRANT Frederick H.

(C.F.) Striker
b. Dover, Kent 19. 6.1921

Folkstone		
Brentford		1939
Q.P.R.	(£5,000)	Sep 1946

Football League: 51-26. FAC: 2-0. FLC: 0-0. Others: 0-0. Total: 53-26.

Exeter City	Feb 1949
Dover	1950

Honours: 3rd Div.(South) championship medal.

This big, burley centre forward made the most of his size on the football pitch. Fred was the capture of manager Dave Mangnall who was without a centre forward at the time and a marked contribution was made by the newcomer for the club to clinch promotion. Another player whose career was blighted by the war, for he was a 1939 Brentford signing, but joined Rangers in 1946. In just over two years he made 53 first team appearances for Q.P.R. before moving west to Exeter City.
Debut: 28. 9.1946 v. Torquay United 0-0. Div. 3 (S).

DUTHIE John Flett

(W.H.) Def 5' 8" 11st 3lbs
b. Fraserburgh, Scot. 7. 1.1903 d. Fraserburgh 30. 9.1969

Roselee F.C.	
Fraserburgh Town	
Hartlepool United	May 1923
Clydebank	
Hartlepool United	Sep 1923
Norwich City	Aug 1924
Fraserburgh	
Q.P.R.	Sep 1927

Football League: 11-0. FAC: 0-0. FLC: 0-0. Others: 0-0.
Total: 11-0.

York City	Aug 1928
Crystal Palace	Jul 1929
York City	Oct 1930
Crewe Alexandria	Jul 1931
Aberdeen	1932
Workington	
Cardiff City	May 1933
Caerau	Aug 1934
Peterborough United	1935

A contempory writer, wrote about John, *"He is a clever player who prefers to pass the ball on the ground, however he is inclined to play the game too close."* John was reputed to be working as a herring fisherman, who was out at sea, when QPR offered him a trial in 1927.
Debut: 22.10.1927 v. Crystal Palace (A). 1-1. Div. 3. (S).

DUTTON Thomas

(I.L). Mid 5' 8" 10st 7lbs
b. Southport, Lancs. 11.11.1906 d. Rochdale 1982

Southport schools	
Southport juniors	
Chorley	
Leicester City	1932
Q.P.R.	1934

Football League: 23-6. FAC: 1-0. FLC: 0-0. Others: 2-0.
Total: 26-6.

Doncaster Rovers	June 1935
Mansfield Town	1938
Rochdale	1939

Honours: 3rd Div. (North) runners-up medal. Notts F.A. County Cup winners medal.

Tommy was predominately a left-footed player, who would roam anywhere in the middle of the park. He guested for Southport and Watford during the war, but the hostilities in effect curtailed his football playing career.
Debut: 25. 8.1934 v. Swindon Town (A). 1-3. Div. 3. (S).

DYKSTRA Sieb

G 6' 5" 14st 7lbs
b. Kerkrade, Holland 20.10.1966

Roda J.C., Kerkrade, Holland		
A.Z. Aalkmaar, Holland	(Loan)	
Haaselt K.S.C., Belgium	(Loan)	
Motherwell		1991
Q.P.R.	(£250,000)	1994

Football League: 11-0. FAC: 0-0. FLC: 1-0. Others: 0-0.
Total: 12-0.

Bristol City	(Loan)	1995
Wycombe Wanderers	(Loan)	1996
Dundee United	(£50,000)	1996

Sieb was a big money signing by Q.P.R. but remained at Loftus Road for only two years or so. Despite just a handful of first team appearances, he moved north to Scotland and became a huge favourite of the Dundee crowd. He featured in every first team match for Dundee United in 1997/98.
Debut: 22.10.1994 v. Norwich City (A).2-4. PL.

EASTOE Peter Robert

Striker 5' 9" 11st 0lbs
b. Tamworth, Staffordshire 2. 8.1953

Dorden Juniors		
Polesworth High school		
Nuneaton & District boys		
Glascote Highfield		
Warton Hatters		
Wolverhampton Wanderers		Jun 1970
Swindon Town	(£88,000)	Nov 1973
Q.P.R.	(£80,000)	Mar 1976

Football League: 72-15. FAC: 3-0. FLC: 8-5. Others: 2-0.
Total: 85-20.

Everton	(Exchange deal)	Mar 1979
W.B.A.	(Exchange deal)	Jul 1982
Leicester City	(Loan)	1983
Walsall	(Loan)	1984
Huddersfield Town	(Loan)	1984
Leicester City	(Loan)	1984
Wolverhampton Wanderers	(Loan)	1985
Sporting Farense, Portugal		1985
Atherstone Town		Aug 1988
Bridgenorth Town		1989

Honours: 8 England youth caps.

When Peter arrived at Loftus Road, he displayed intelligence and skill, unsettling most teams with his precise lay-offs, dummy-runs and neat ball control. Eastoe had the technique to shield the ball and the strength to ride his opponents tackles. Swapped with Everton's Micky Walsh in 1979, he was in turn exchanged for Andy King and £250,000 in 1982 by W.B.A.

Peter became a frequent loan signing until he moved into non-League football, and subsequently the player/manager of Alvechurch in 1991. Two years later he took on the post of assistant manager at Nuneaton Borough.
Debut: 16.10.1976 v. Manchester City (A).0-0. Div.1.

EATON Frank

(I.R.) Striker 5' 9" 11st 2lbs
b. Stockport, Lancashire 12.11.1902 d. 1979
New Mills, Debyshire
Cressbrook
Barnsley 1925
Reading (£1,750) Jun 1930
Q.P.R. Jul 1933
Football League: 15-2. FAC: 2-0. FLC: 0-0. Others: 2-0. Total: 19-2.

Frank was a long-striding, slim forward, who once scored five goals for Barnsley in a League match in 1927. He was unfortunate to receive a severe injury in a Third Division South game at Torquay in September 1933, and although he played a few more matches, Eaton decided to retire at the end of that season.
Debut: 26. 8.1933 v. Brighton & H.A. (H). 2-0. Div.3 (S)

EDGLEY Harold Horace

(O.L.) Wing 5' 10" 11st 6lbs
b. Crewe in January 1892d. Nottingham in March 1966
Whitechurch
Crewe Alexandria
Aston Villa June 1911
Stourbridge (Loan) 1913
Whitechurch 1914
Port Vale (Loan) 1917
Q.P.R. Aug 1921
Football League: 69-6. FAC: 6-0. FLC: 0-0. Others: 0-0. Total: 75-6.
Stockport County Aug 1923
Worcester City 1924

A useful winger, well built and surprisingly quick, Harry was at home on either flank. He had the misfortune to break his leg just three weeks before Aston Villa were due to meet Huddersfield Town in the F.A.Cup final in 1920. As he had played in all the other rounds, the club had a special medal minted for him. During his two seasons at Q.P.R., Harry was a regular in the first team, before his move north to Stockport County in 1923. He finally retired in 1927, and later became a director of Notts County.
Debut: 27. 8.1921 v. Swindon Town (H).0-0. Div.3 (S).

EDWARDS Albert

(H.B.) Def 5' 7" 11st 0lbs
b. d. in World War 1914/18
Aston Villa
Swindon Town 1901
Q.P.R. 1903
Southern League: 17-1. FAC: 0-0. FLC: 0-0. Others: 0-0. Total: 17-1.
Bristol City 1912
Newport County 1913

Bert was a defender of undoubted ability, frail but very cultured. He had a deceptive raking stride and sound positional sense. Sadly he was a casualty of the Great War of 1914/18.
Debut: 29.11.1902 v.Northampton T.(H).0-0.SL Div.1.

EDWARDS John

(L.B.) Def 5' 9" 12st 7lbs
b. Staffordshire in 1875
Port Vale Feb 1894
Stockport County Nov 1894
Port Vale Jan 1896
Grays United 1896
Q.P.R. 1901
Southern League: 28-2. FAC: 1-0. FLC: 0-0. Others: 0-0. Total: 29-2.
Plymouth Argyle 1903

John was a strong but somewhat erratic player who had a tremendous and honest attitude to the game, with a liking to going forward with the attack.
Debut: 3. 9.1902 v. Wellingborough T.(H).2-0.SL Div.1.

EDWARDS Joseph H.

(O.R.) Wing
b.
Q.P.R. 1925
Football League: 3-0. FAC: 0-0. FLC: 0-0. Others: 0-0. Total: 3-0.

Joe was one of seven wingers to be tried in the side during the 1926/27 season but to no avail. This was the second time that the club had to apply for re-election.
Debut: 2.4.1926v.Bournemouth& B.A.(H).2-2. Div.3(S)

EGGLETON James Arthur Edward

(C.H.) CD 6' 0" 12st 0lbs
b. Heston, Middlesex 29. 8.1897d. Hillingdon 13. 1.1963.

Army Football		
Slough		
Charlton Athletic		Jan 1922
Watford		Dec 1923
Lincoln City		
Q.P.R.	(£500)	Oct 1926

Football League: 42-0. FAC: 1-0. FLC: 0-0. Others: 0-0. Total: 43-0.

Honours: Represented Middlesex & London schools. 13 caps for the Army. 2 London Challenge Cup winners medals.

Jimmy was a strong tackling centre half until he was very badly injured in a match which prevented him ever playing again. His promising start in professional football extended over only approximately two seasons. Nevertheless he did stay at the club for another thirty years as a trusted backroom man in many spheres, including trainer, scout and confidant.
Debut: 27.12.1926 v. Watford (A).2-1. Div.3 (S).

ELSEY Karl W.

Mid 5' 10" 11st 6lbs
b. Swansea, Wales 20.11.1958

Pembrook Borough		1978
Swansea City		1978
Q.P.R.		Jan 1979

Football League: 7-0. FAC: 0-0. FLC: 0-0. Others: 0-0. Total: 7-0.

Newport County		Aug 1980
Cardiff City		Sep 1983
Gillingham		Jun 1985
Reading	(Player exchange)	Aug 1988
Maidstone United	(£20,000)	Jul 1989
Gillingham		Aug 1991
Sittingbourne		Mar 1992
Braintree Town		Dec 1993
Ashford Town		Feb 1994
Hastings Town		Mar 1994
Faversham Town		Sep 1994
Margate		Oct 1994
Ramsgate		Mar 1996
Chatham		Apl 1996
Lordswood		Feb 1997

The son of a Swansea Town professional, Karl was a tough tackling defender or a solid midfield man but whatever role he played he proved himself to be a versatile player of ability. However, he did have a tendency to be inconsistent. Elsey was a relatively late starter, taking up the game at the age of 17, preferring fishing as a sport. Signing for Q.P.R. after just one Combination match, he moved from the Welsh League to the English First Division in four months.
Debut: 24. 3.1979 v. W.B.A. (A). 1-2. Div. 1.

EMBLETON Sidney W.

(O.R.) Wing
b. Poplar, London

Walthamstow Avenue	
Q.P.R.	1930

Football League: 2-0. FAC: 0-0. FLC: 0-0. Others: 0-0. Total: 2-0.

One of the many amateurs drafted into the side during the period between the two World Wars. Sid was the substitute to Coward during this period.
Debut: 7. 3.1931 v. Brentford (H). 3-1. Div. 3. (S).

EMMERSON George Arthur Heads

(O.R.) Wing 5' 8" 10st 7lbs
b.Bishop Aukland 15.5.1906d.Melton Mowbray 6.12.66

Jarrow	
Middlesbrough	1928
Cardiff City	1930
Q.P.R.	1933

Football League: 52-13. FAC: 5-3. FLC: 0-0. Others: 3-0. Total: 60-16.

Rochdale	1936
Tunbridge Wells Rangers	1936
Gillingham	Mar 1937

Honours: 3 Durham County Amateur Badges. Welsh senior cup winners medal.

Emmerson was a fast and tricky winger from Cardiff City, who had come to Loftus Road in an exchange

deal with another winger named Marcroft. George had a fabulous season with the club until he was injured in April 1934.
Debut: 26. 8.1933 v.Brighton & H.A.(H).2-0. Div.3(S).

EVANS Bernard

(C.F.) Striker 6' 1" 13st 6lbs
b. Chester, Cheshire 4. 1.1937

Saltney Juniors		
Wrexham		Aug 1954
Q.P.R.	(£2,000)	Nov 1960

Football League: 78-35. FAC: 4-4. FLC: 2-0. Others: 0-0. Total: 84-39.

Oxford United	(£5,500)	Dec 1962
Tranmere Rovers		Oct 1963
Crewe Alexandria		Jul 1964
Guildford City		Aug 1965
Hastings United		Mar 1966
Rhyl		Sep 1966
Caernarvon		Nov 1966

Honours: Welsh Cup winners medal.

Bernard started his Football League career at Wrexham where as a 17 year old he made an impressive start by scoring in 27 seconds from the kick-off. He was a big hefty centre forward, recommended to Alec Stock by the chief scout in Wales. However, his League career ended in 1964 while he was playing for Crewe, when he received a bad injury. In 1966 Bernard set-up an industrial cleaning business in Chester.
Debut: 19.11.1960 v. Shrewsbury Town (H).1-1. Div.3.

EVANS Charles

(I.F.) Mid
b. Luton, Bedfordshire
Q.P.R. 1929
Football League: 1-0. FAC: 0-0. FLC: 0-0. Others: 0-0. Total: 1-0.

A reserve who turned out for the senior squad on just one occasion in the absence of J.C.Burns.
Debut: 1. 2.1930 v. Southend United (H).2-5. Div.3(S).

EVANS Ian Peter

(C.H.) CD 6' 2" 11st 2lbs
b. Egham, Surrey 30. 1.1952
Q.P.R. Jan 1970
Football League: 39-2. FAC: 4-0. FLC: 3-0. Others: 0-0. Total: 46-2.

Crystal Palace	(£40,000+player)	Sep 1974
Barnsley	(£80,000)	Dec 1979
Exeter City	(Loan)	Aug 1983
Cambridge United	(Loan)	1983

Honours: 2 Welsh U23 caps. 13 full Welsh caps. 2nd Div. runners-up medal. 3rd Div. runners-up medal.

A dominating figure at the heart of the Q.P.R. defence in the early 1970s. Ian was a tall slim defender who was particularly accomplished in the air. Unfortunately he was struck down by a severe injury in October 1977 which kept him out of the game for two years. He was made coach at Barnsley in September 1981 but was relieved of the post in August 1983. After that Ian became assistant manager to Steve Coppell at Crystal Palace until February 1989 when he succeeded Terry Yorath as manager at Swansea City, which lasted until March 1990. Ian became the reserve team coach at Millwall, and was the assistant manager to Mick McCarthy's Republic of Ireland side.
Debut: 6. 4.1971 v.Sheffield Wednesday(H).1-0. Div.2.

EVANS J. Lloyd

(O.R.) Wing
b.
Q.P.R. 1904
Southern League: 1-0. FAC: 0-0. FLC: 0-0. Others: 0-0. Total: 1-0.

Fulham	1905
Brentford	1907
Croydon Common	1908
West Norwood	1909
Southend United	1910

Just one of seven wingers to be tried during the 1904/05 season.
Debut: 25. 2.1905 v. Millwall (H).1-1. SLDiv.1.

EVANS Rhys Karl

G 6' 1" 12st 2lbs
b. Swindon, Wiltshire 27. 1.1982

Chelsea		Feb 1999
Bristol Rovers	(Loan)	Feb 2000
Q.P.R.	(Loan)	Nov 2001

Football League: 11-0. FAC: 0-0. FLC: 0-0. Others: 0-0. Total: 11-0.
Leyton Orient Aug 2002

Honours: England school & youth caps.

Rhys was originally signed as the reserve team goalkeeper, but he came into the picture when Fraser Digby was injured and hence stepped up into the first team. He then moved across London to Leyton Orient where he made a handful of first team appearances during the 2002/03 season. (Signed for Swindon Town August 2003)
Debut: 26. 2.2002 v. Wigan Athletic (H). 1-1. Div.2.

EVANS Roger

(C.F.) Striker
b.Bangor,Wales 17.11.1879d. Swanage,Dorset 25. 4.1974

Ilford	1898
Clapton	1900
Q.P.R.	1901

Southern League: 1-0. FAC: 0-0. FLC: 0-0. Others: 0-0. Total: 1-0.

London Welsh	
Southern United	1904

Honours: Represented Middlesex & London. Won London Challenge Cup winners medals in 1901,2,3 and 4. Capped for Wales in 1902.

Roger was an amateur, an ex-public schoolboy and was taught his serious football at Ilford. He was the subject of an approach by Liverpool in November 1899 which caused outrage among the Essex club's fans. The Liverpool officials were reported to the F.A. and found guilty of an illegal approach and the secretary, John McKenna was suspended for a month. Roger's work as an insurance manager made demands on his time but during 1904, Evans signed for Baron Von Rieffenstein's new club, Southern United, who hoped to challenge the best clubs in the south, but in the end nothing came of the idea. Roger remained on Clapton's books.
Debut: 15. 3.1902 v. Bristol Rovers(H). 0-0.SL Div.1.

EVANS William

(I.R.) Mid 5' 7" 10st 8lbs
b. Llansaintffraid, Wales

Newtown F.C.	
Old St. Stephens	
Shepherds Bush	
Q.P.R.	1897
Shepherds Bush	1898
Q.P.R.	1899

Southern League: 9-3: FAC: 4-3. FLC: 0-0. Others: 0-0. Total: 13-6.

Lincoln City	1900

Honours: Represented London & Middlesex.

His business took him to London regularly and it was there that Bill played most of his football. He retired in 1901 due to a serious injury he sustained whilst playing for Lincoln City.
Debut: 7.10.1899 v. Bristol City (A). 3-5.SLDiv. 1.

EVANS William B.

(R.B.) Def 5' 10" 12st 0lbs
b. Llanigloes, Wales

Everton	1919
Swansea Town	1919
Southend United	1921
Q.P.R.	1924

Football League: 17-0. FAC: 0-0. FLC: 0-0. Others: 0-0. Total: 17-0.

'Billy B.' was the least famous of the three Evans' players who were on the books of Southend United at the time. The other two were Jimmy who represented Wales and moved on to Burnley, whilst Tommy came from Rotherham County.
Debut: 20. 9.1924 v. Swansea Town (H).0-0. Div.3(S).

FALCO Mark Peter

Striker 6' 0" 12st 0lbs
b. Hackney, London 22.10.1960

Hackney schools		
Middlesex schools		
Tottenham Hotspur		Jul 1978
Chelsea	(Loan)	Nov 1982
Watford	(£300,000)	Oct 1986
Glasgow Rangers	(£300,000)	Jul 1987
Q.P.R.	(£350,000)	Jan 1988

Football League: 87-27. FAC: 10-2. FLC: 6-4. Others:3-0. Total:106-33.

Millwall	(£135,000)	Aug 1991
Enfield		Nov 1992
Worthing		Nov 1992
Hitching Town		Mar 1996

Honours: 4 England youth caps. UEFA cup winners medal.

Tall with a strapping physic, Mark appeared to be somewhat cumbersome and lacking in pace but when he ran on to a through-ball it took a good man to stop his surge on goal. A constant menace in the air with a fearless attitude, Mark was effective at retaining the ball and too frequently he took the knocks, but contributed the legwork that paved his side's way to goal. He retired in 1992, having sustained a nasty injury. Mark continued in the semi-pro game and was still playing in 1996 when he was turning-out for Worthing as player/ manager.
Debut: 5.12.1987 v. Manchester United (H).0-2. Div.1.

FALLON Peter D.

(L.H.) Def
b. Dublin, Eire 19.10.1922

Shelbourne	1941
Dundulk	1945
Exeter City	1947
Q.P.R.	1953

Football League: 1-0. FAC: 0-0. FLC: 0-0. Others: 0-0.
Total: 1-0.

Peter was the brother of the League of Ireland player Willie Fallon. On being demobbed from the R.A.F., he joined Exeter City and turned out for them in over 100 matches. At Loftus Road, Peter was mainly used for training the youngsters.
Debut: 19.9.1953 v.Shrewsbury Town (A).1-1. Div.3(S)

FARMER Alexander

(WH) Mid 5' 11" 12st 0lbs
b. Lochgelly, Scotland 9.10.1908

Kettering Town	
Nottingham Forest	1930
Leicester City	
Kettering Town	1930
Yeovil Town	1932
Q.P.R.	1933

Football League: 81-10. FAC: 4-2. FLC: 0-0. Others: 8-0.
Total: 93-12.

Alex was known as a utility player, for although his main position was at centre half, he could also play at wing half or inside forward, and either left or right. Eventually he was taken on the training staff, staying on the payroll of the club until well into the fifties.
Debut: 3.2.1934 v. Torquay United (A).1-1. Div.3(S).

FARROW Desmond A.

(LH) Def. 5' 8" 10st 2lbs
b.Peterborough, Cambs. 11. 2.1926.

Leicester City	
Q.P.R.	1944

Football League:118-7. FAC:3-0. FLC:0- 0. Others:0-0.
Total:121-7.

Stoke City	(£4,000 + Player) Oct 1952
Peterborough United	1956

Des was a fine left footed player who could defend with notable ability. A wartime signing, he played over 120 senior matches for the Rangers up to 1952. Then, one of the first moves taken by Jack Taylor when he took over the manager's job from Dave Mangnall, was to sell Farrow for a good sum to Stoke City plus a player.

The replacement was once the substitute for Stanley Matthews at the Victoria Ground, but as things transpired the deal was a complete failure on both sides.
Debut: 9.10.1948. v . Brentford (H). 2-0. Div. 2.

FAULKNER Robert

(O.R.) Wing 5' 9" 11st 0lbs
b. Paisley, Glasgow, Scotland

Glasgow St. Athony's	
Maryhill, Glasgow	
Blackburn Rovers	1919
Q.P.R.	1921

Football League: 50-1. FAC: 2-0. FLC: 0-0. Others: 0-0.
Total: 52-1.

South Shields	1922
Toronto Clarkes	
Philadelphia Field Club	
Providence Clam Diggers	
Toronto Irish	1924

Honours: 3 caps for Canada.

Robert was a very fast winger who could 'centre the ball on a sixpence'. However, he had much more success in Canada where he played three times for that country against the U.S.A. in 1925.
Debut: 28. 8.1920 v. Watford (H). 1-2. Div.3.

FENWICK Harrison

(H.B.) Def 5' 8" 11st 0lbs
b. Ashington, Co. Durham in October 1900

Shildon Colliery

Q.P.R.	1924

Football League: 19-0. FAC: 0-0. FLC: 0-0. Others: 0-0. Total: 19-0.

Harrison worked in the coal mines before he decided to go south after the 1st World War. Q.P.R. signed him for a season, where he played in any of the three halfback positions.
Debut: 4.12.1924 v. Merthyr Town (H).1-1. Div.3 (S).

FENWICK Terrence William

Def 5' 10" 10st 11lbs
b. Seaham, Co. Durham 17.11.1959

Crystal Palace		Dec 1976
Q.P.R.	(£110,000)	Dec 1980

Football League:256-33. FAC:18-6. FLC:29-6.Others:5-0. Total:308-45.

Tottenham Hotspur	(£550,000)	Dec 1987
Leicester City	(Loan)	1990
Swindon Town		1993

Honours: England youth caps. 11 U21 caps. 20 senior caps. 2 2nd Div. Championship winners medals. F.A. Cup runners-up medal. League cup runners-up medal.

Capable of playing in any defensive or midfield slots, Terry was probably one of the best defenders the club has ever possessed, and made many of his England appearances whilst with the club. Terry's versatility saw him playing full back, in central defence, in midfield, and in a continental style sweeper's role, at Spurs, where his ability to read the game and his confidence on the ball was used to good effect. He was at Loftus Road for eight seasons, during which time he appeared in over 300 senior games. Normally a first team regular, his least number of seasonal League matches totalled 21, in 1986/87. He followed his manager, Terry Venables, from Crystal Palace to Q.P.R. in 1980 where he played in over 300 matches. Terry broke his leg in 1989 and then his ankle in 1991, which virtually ended his career. Moving to Swindon Town in 1993 he then took the job of player/manager of Portsmouth in 1994, which lasted until 1998.
Debut: 19.12.1980 v. Bolton Wanderers (A).2-1. Div.2.

FERDINAND Leslie

Striker 5' 11" 13st 5lbs
b. Acton, Middlesex 18.12.1966
Hayes

Q.P.R.	(£15,000)	Mar 1987

Football League:162-80. FAC: 7-3: FLC: 13-7. Others:1-0 Total:183-90

Brentford	(Loan)	Mar 1988
Besiktas, Turkey	(Loan)	1988
Newcastle United	(£6,000,000)	Jun 1995
Tottenham Hotspur	(£6,000,000)	Aug 1997
West Ham United		Jan 2003

Honours: England B cap. 17 full English caps. Football League Cup winners medal. Turkish cup winners medal.

It was some years before Les made his mark at Q.P.R. Signed from just down the road at Hayes, he cost a reasonable fee for a non-League player (some sources incorrectly quote £30,000), but made only a handful of appearances in his first three seasons at Loftus Road.

During this time, two loan periods included a month at Brentford, whose fans considered that he would never make the grade! But Les gradually found a regular spot in the Rangers' First/Premier Division team, and after eight seasons he had become a highly sought after player. Nicknamed 'Sir Les' by the Q.P.R. fans, he adopted this title for his autobiography. A fine centre forward with great heading abilities and a sizzling shot to go with it. Les spreads his play wide before getting into position himself for a cross into the middle. His power and pace make him difficult to contain. A record £6m. transfer fee took him to Newcastle United for two years before the same sum brought him back to London, and Spurs. 2001/02 was undoubtably his best season at White Hart Lane, where he looked lean, sharp and athletic, and instilled a real threat into the attack. Les was consistently the team's most formidable player and netted a total of 15 goals in all competitions. He also developed a fine partnership with Teddy Sheringham. In January 2003 he made another move, this time to West Ham and became a near regular in the latter part of that season. (Moved to Leicester City in August 2003)
Debut: 20. 4.1987 v. Coventry City (A).1-4. Div. 1.

FEREDAY Wayne

Mid 5' 9" 11st 8lbs
b. Warley, Yorkshire 16. 6.1963

Q.P.R.		1980

Football League:196-21:FAC:14-0. FLC:29-3. Others:5-1. Total:244-25.

Newcastle United	(£400,000)	1989
AFC Bournemouth	(£150,000)	1990
W.B.A.	(£60,000)	1991
Cardiff City		1994
Merthyr Tydfil		1995
Telford United		1995

Honours: 5 U21 caps. Football League appearance.

Lithe and extremely fast, Wayne was one of the fastest players on the circuit and was probably at his best on the left wing. He was easily able to take on defenders and get in a dangerous cross. It was during 1980/81, his first season, that Wayne made a name for himself by scoring twice on his Football League debut. After nine seasons, and playing in 244 competitive matches for Q.P.R. he headed north before teaming-up with his ex-manager, Jim Smith, at Newcastle. Further moves brought him back south and to the midlands, before he finally joined the non-League scene in 1995. He moved to Poole, Dorset later that year.
Debut: 19. 8.1980 v. Bristol Rovers (H).4-0. Div.2.

FERGUSON Christopher

(I.R.) Mid 5' 6" 10st 12lbs
b. Kirkconnel, Dumfries & Galloway, Scotland

Chelsea	Oct 1927
Q.P.R.	May 1930

Football League: 15-1. FAC: 0-0. FLC: 0-0. Others: 0-0. Total: 15-1.

Wrexham	Jul 1931
Guildford City	1932
Post Office Engineers	Aug 1934

Chris was the younger brother of Bill who played full back for Chelsea in the early 1920s, and turned out mainly for the reserves at Stamford Bridge. Another brother,Pearson, played for Carlisle United.
Debut: 13.3.1930 v. Brighton & H.A.(H).4-1. Div.3 (S).

FERGUSON J.

(O.R.)
b.

Q.P.R.	1909

Southern League: 2-0. FAC 0-0. FLC: 0-0. Others: 0-0 Total: 2-0

A player who made just two appearances for Q.P.R. He never played a Southern League match, for both of his games were in the FA Cup, at West Ham and in the replay.
Debut: 19.2.1910 v. West Ham Utd.(A) 1-1. FAC 3rd.

FERGUSON Michael Kevin

Mid 5' 10" 11st 4lb
b. Burnley, Lancashire 9. 3.1943
Burnley schools

Plymouth Argyle		Mar 1959
Accrington Stanley		Jul 1960
Blackburn Rovers	(£2,500)	Mar 1962
Aston Villa	(£50,000)	May 1968
Q.P.R.	(£15,000)	Nov 1969

Football League: 68-2: FAC: 6-1. FLC: 3-0. Others: 0-0.
Total: 77-3.

Cambridge United	Jul 1973
Rochdale	Jul 1974
Los Angeles Aztecs (U.S.A.)	1975
Halifax Town	Dec 1976

Mike was a well built, strong running player, who would beat an opponant, wait for him to recover and beat him all over again. Unfortunately he had a very tempermental nature which brought about many altercations on the pitch. He was capable of playing full back, midfield or orthodox winger. His wide football career saw him initially travelling throughout the country, which started at Plymouth, and included Accrington Stanley (he was with the club when they dropped out of the League). His stay at Loftus Road lasted four years before he was on his travels again. Whilst at Rochdale he spent the Summer in the U.S.A., and late in 1975 went to manage IA Akranes in Iceland. He then coached Rossendale, briefly made a comeback as a player, with Halifax, before returning to Rochdale as manager, but was fired when the club were relegated from Division Three. After coaching around the world he managed Enfield for a time in 1989. Later living in Burnley Mike acts as a players agent and attends many matches for the England managment.
Debut: 22.11.1969 v. Leicester City(H). 1-1. Div. 2.

FIDLER Joseph Edward

(L.B.) Def 5' 9" 11st 12lbs
b. Sheffield, Yorkshire in 1885

Sheffield United	1904
Fulham	1905
Q.P.R.	1906

Southern League:172-0. FAC: 11-0. FLC: 0-0. Others: 2-0
Total:185-0.

Woolwich Arsenal	Feb 1913
Port Vale	1914

Honours: Played for the Southern League v. Scottish League. Southern League championship medal.

A strong, tough, stalwart defender, who was one of the old school, who had a long and successful period at Q.P.R.

After seven years and nearly 200 games for the Rangers, he moved across London, and played in the last thirteen League matches for Woolwich Arsenal in the 1913/14 season. Another move was soon made, to the Potteries where he started off as a regular first team player at left back, but then lost his position to the newly signed England International Bob Benson. In 1915, and unable to gain a place in the Port Vale team he decided to join the army.
Debut: 29. 9.1906 v. Clapton Orient (A). 0-3. SL Div.1.

FIDLER Thomas G.

(C.F.) Striker
b. Hounslow, Middlesex 4. 9.1933
Hounslow Town

Q.P.R.	1954

Football League: 12-2. FAC: 2-2. FLC: 0-0. Others: 0-0.
Total: 14-4.

Dover	1955

Tommy was the reserve striker to Willie Clark, and was released by manager Taylor at the end of the 1954/55 season.
Debut: 24. 8.1954 v. Southend United (A).2-2. Div.3 (S)

FIELD William H.

G 5' 11" 12st 5lbs
b. Oxford, Oxfordshire
Oxford City

Q.P.R.	1923

Football League: 29-0. FAC: 0-0. FLC: 0-0. Others: 0-0.
Total: 29-0.

Bill became the No.1 goalkeeper when Les Hill left the club. However, he reverted back to the reserves when Hebden arrived and Billy Hill was 'given his cards' after the club had to apply for re-election in 1926.
Debut: 19. 1.1924 v. Brighton & H.A.(H).1-0. Div.3 (S).

FILLERY Michael C.

Mid 5' 10" 11st 2lbs
b. Mitcham, Surrey 17. 9.1960
Merton schools
Sutton United

Chelsea		Aug 1978
Q.P.R.	(£200,000)	Aug 1983

Football League: 97-9. FAC: 5-0. FLC: 11-1. Others: 4-0. Total:117-10.

Portsmouth		Jul 1987
Oldham Athletic	(£30,000)	Oct 1990
Millwall	(Loan)	Mar 1991
Torquay United	(Loan)	1991

Honours: Schoolboy International. 7 English youth caps.

Mike was a highly talented and stylish player who always appeared casual and disinterested in the match. Despite nearly 100 League games over a four year period, he somehow lacked the consistency and application to do justice to himself. After several moves around the Football League, in 1991 he moved to Crawley Town as the assistant manager.
Debut: 27. 8.1983 v. Manchester United (A).1-3. Div.1.

FINCH Robert J.

(R.B.) Def 5' 9" 11st 0lbs
b. Camberwell, London 24. 8.1948.d. South Africa 1978

Q.P.R.	1967

Football League: 5-0. FAC: 0-0. FLC: 0-0. Others: 0-0. Total: 5-0.

Durham City, South Africa	1970

Bobby actually wrote a letter to the club asking for a trial and by April 1968 he was in the senior squad covering for Dave Clement. In 1970 Bobby emigrated to South Africa.
Debut: 16. 4.1968 v. Cardiff City (A).0-1. Div. 2.

FINNEY Charles William Thomas

(C.F.) Striker 5' 9" 10st 6lbs
b. Stoke-on-Trent 5. 9.1931
Edensor youth club
Crewe Alexandria

Stoke City	May 1949
Birmingham City	Nov 1955
Q.P.R.	May 1957

Football League: 10-1. FAC: 0-0. FLC: 0-0. Others: 0-0. Total: 10-1.

Crewe Alexandria	Jul 1958
Rochdale	Sep 1959
Macclesfield Town	
Cheltenham Town	

Charlie caused something of a sensation on his debut in the Football League, scoring at Old Trafford for Stoke City, in what was described as a 'perfect left foot shot'. He was capable of playing in any of the inside forward positions but could not turn it on at Loftus Road.
Debut: 24. 8.1957 v. Brentford (H).1-0. Div.3 (S).

FITZGERALD Brian Maurice

Mid 5' 9" 12st 2lbs
b. Perivale, Middlesex 23.10.1983

Q.P.R.	Oct 2000

Football League: 1-0. FAC: 0-0. FLC: 0-0. Others: 0-0. Total: 1-0.

Honours: Rep. of Ireland youth caps.

Following several good performances in the reserves, Brian made his senior debut as a substitute in 2002. But he never made the grade at Loftus Road and was released during the close season of 2003.
Debut: 12. 1.2002 v. Bury (H).3-0. Div.2.

FITZGERALD Michael Alfred

(I.L.) Striker
b. Conisbrough, Yorkshire 25. 1.1911d. Brighton in 1981
Denaby United

Reading	1934
Q.P.R.	1936

Football League: 94-43. FAC: 5-7. FLC: 0-0. Others: 4-2. Total:103-52.

Aldershot	1946
Tonbridge	1948

Just one of the legendary goalscorers that have turned out for the club. Mike headed the scoring list in 1937 and 1938 (scoring 17 goals on both occasions, plus another 9 in the 1938/39 season). Undoubtably the 1939 to 1946 period badly disrupted his football career, as it did so many other players in their prime. During the 2nd World War he volunteered to serve in submarines, and remained there until 1946. When the war ended he joined Aldershot and played another 60 odd matches for the Shots. He ended his playing days at non-League Tonbridge, having joined them in 1948.
Debut: 7.11.1936 v. Newport County (A).2-1. Div.3(S)

FLANAGAN Michael Anthony

Mid 5' 10" 12st 4lbs
b. Ilford, Essex 9.11.1952

Tottenham Hotspur		
Charlton Athletic		Aug 1971
New England Tea Men, U.S.A.		1978
Crystal Palace	(£650,000)	Aug 1979
Q.P.R.	(£150,000)	Aug 1980

Football League: 78-20. FAC: 12-0. FLC: 3-2. Others:0-0
Total: 93-22.

Charlton Athletic	(£50,000)	Jan 1984
Cambridge United		Sep 1986
Charlton Athletic		Oct 1987
Billericay Town		1990
Margate		Oct 1991
Billericay Town		1992

Honours: 3 England amateur youth caps. 2 England B caps. F.A. Youth cup winners medal. F.A.Cup runners-up medal. 2nd Div. championship medal.

The transfer fee between Charlton Athletic and Crystal Palace was a record deal between London clubs at that time when Mike switched bewteen the two. He was a fiery character who had an exquisite left foot shot, and teamed up with Clive Allen in what became known as the 'Flanagan & Allen Show'; between them they scored some sixty goals in four years. Mike returned to Charlton (twice) before moving down to football at non-League level.
Debut: 19.12.1980 v. Bolton Wanderers (A).2-1. Div.2.

FLEMING Mark J.

Def 5' 9" 10st 11lbs
b. Hammersmith, London 11. 8.1969

Q.P.R.	1987

Football League: 3-0. FAC: 1-0. FLC: 0-0. Others: 1-0.
Total: 5-0.

Brentford	1989
Farnborough	1991
Woking	1992
Aylesbury United	
Staines Town	1995

Honours: England Youth International. Southern Flood-light Junior cup medal.

Mark played as a defender at Loftus Road but was turned into a midfield player at his last club. A keen sportsman, embracing golf, tennis and swimming.
Debut: 27. 2.1988 v. Wimbledon (H). 1-0. Div.1.

FLETCHER Jack

(I.L.) Striker 5' 8" 11st 5lbs
b.

Reading	1903
West Ham United	1904
Q.P.R.	1905

Southern League: 38-13. FAC: 3-0. FLC: 0-0. Others: 0-0.
Total: 41-13.

Fulham	1907

Not a lot is known about this player, except that he scored a hat-trick against Northampton Town in Nov. 1906.
Debut: 23.12.1905 v. Bristol Rovers (A).1-2. SL Div.1.

FLETCHER Jack

(I.F.) Mid 5' 8" 11st 5lbs
b. Tyne Docks, South Shields in 1910

Portsmouth	1929
Chopwell Institute	
Aldershot	
Guildford City	
Bournemouth & Boscombe Athletic	1933
Q.P.R.	1935

Football League: 21-0. FAC: 0-0. FLC: 0-0. Others: 0-0.
Total: 21-0.

Clapton Orient	1937
Southampton	1938
Barrow	1938
Winchester City	

As soon as Billy Birrell took over at Q.P.R. he snapped up Fletcher from Bournemouth. Birrell wanted a play-maker and he certainly found one in Jack, as it turned out that he became the engine-room of the attack. Although he didn't score any goals himself he laid on quite few on for Cheetham. The Rangers rose from the middle of the table in 1935 to 4th in 1936.
Debut: 4. 9.1935 v. Brighton & H.A.1-1. Div. 3. (S).

FOLEY Dominic Joseph

Striker 6' 1" 12st 8lbs
b. Cork, Eire 7. 7.1976

St. James' Gate		
Wolverhampton Wanderers	(£35,000)	Aug 1995
Watford	(Loan)	Feb 1998
Notts County	(Loan)	Dec 1998
Lincoln City	(Loan)	Jan 1999
Ethnikos, Greece	(Loan)	Jan 1999
Watford		Jun 1999
Q.P.R.	(Loan)	Oct 2001

Football League: 1-0. FAC: 0-0. FLC: 0-0. Others: 0-0.
Total: 1-0.

Swindon Town	(Loan)	Jan 2002
Q.P.R.	(Loan)	Mar 2002

Football League: 4-1. FAC: 0-0. FLC: 0-0. Others: 0-0. Total: 4-1.

Southend United	(Loan)	Feb 2003
Oxford United	(Loan)	Mar 2003

Honours: 6 caps for the Rep. of Ireland. 8 U21 caps.

Dominic played Gaelic football before he turned to soccer and scored a hat-trick on his debut for Ethnikos. His first loan period at Q.P.R. was curtailed by a torn ligament, but in the second spell he scored on his debut. His fairly short playing career in England was punctuated with short loan periods both before and after his time at Loftus Road.
Debut: 27.10.2001 v. Oldham Athletic (H).1-1. Div.2.

FORBES Terrell

Def 6' 0" 12st 8lbs
b. Southwark, London 17. 8.1981

West Ham United		Jul 1999
AFC Bournemouth	(Loan)	Sep 1999
Q.P.R.		Jul 2001

Football League: 82-0. FAC: 3-0. FLC: 2-0. Others: 1-0. Total: 88-0.

Honours: FA Youth Cup.

A right sided defender with a liking to join in with the attack, Terrell soon became another favourite of the Loftus Road crowd. With his runs down the right wing invariably followed by the delivery of a good cross, Terrell was voted 'Player of the Year' by one of the club's supporters' associations for 2001/2. His first two seasons at Loftus Road saw him as a near ever-present yet he had still to score a goal for the team.
Debut: 11. 8.2001 v. Stoke City (H). 1-0. Div. 2.

FORD Ewart L.

Mid
b. Bedworth, Near Nuneaton in 1910.
Hinckley

Q.P.R.	1924

Football League: 55-4. FAC: 9-0. FLC: 0-0. Others: 0-0. Total: 64-4.

Merthyr Town	1926

A regular on the left flank until manager Bob Hewison arrived at Loftus Road. Spottiswood was bought from Swansea Town to replace Ford and Ewart was transferred to Merthyr Town at the end of the season.
Debut: 30. 8.1924 v. Newport County (A).0-0. Div.3(S)

FORTUNE James J.

(O.L.) Wing
b. Dublin, Eire in 1890
Shelbourne

Distillery	1910
Leeds City	1911
Shelbourne	1912
Barrow	
Q.P.R.	1913

Southern League: 8-0. FAC: 5-0. FLC: 0-0. Others: 0-0. Total: 13-0.

Bristol Rovers	1914

The Irishman was a reserve wherever he went. At Q.P.R. he stood in for Ben Ives.
Debut: 11.10.1913 v.Plymouth Argyle(H).0-0.SL Div.1

FOSTER Cyril James

(R.H.) Def 5' 8" 10st 7lbs
b. Aylesbury, Buckinghamshire in 1903

Aylesbury
Wycombe Wanderers 1924
Watford Sep 1925
Q.P.R. Jun 1928
Football League: 5-0. FAC: 0-0. FLC: 0-0. Others: 0-0.
Total: 5-0.

Cyril usually played at half back and he had a vigorous style of play but was used mainly as a reserve.
Debut: 20.10.1928 v. Bournemouth.(H).0-0.Div 3 (S).

FOX George F.

(O.L.) Wing
b.
City Old Boys
Q.P.R. 1916
Southern League: 8-0. FAC: 0-0. FLC: 0-0. Others: 0-0.
Total: 8-0.

Not a lot is known about George, but he did make over 200 appearances scoring some 29 goals during the 1st World War.
Debut: 27. 9.1919 v. Gillingham (A).1-0. SLDiv.1.

FOX T. S.

(L.B.) Def
b. 1904
Q.P.R. 1905
Southern League: 1-0. FAC: 0-0. FLC: 0-0. Others: 0-0.
Total: 1-0.

Honours: F.A.Amateur Cup runners-up medal.

Fox was still an amateur when he turned out for Q.P.R. in his only match for the club.
Debut: 11. 4.1906 v. Fulham (A).0-1. SLDiv.1.

FOXALL Abraham

(O.L) Wing
b. Sheffield, Yorkshire in 1874
Gainsborough Trinity 1897
Liverpool 1899
Q.P.R. 1900
Southern League: 27-2. FAC: 4-2. FLC: 0-0. Others: 0-0.
Total: 31-4.
Woolwich Arsenal 1901
Kettering 1902
Gainsborough Trinity 1903

Abe was the mainstay in the Q.P.R. forward line in the early days of the Southern League. He missed just one match during the entire season.
Debut: 8. 9.1900 v. Bristol Rovers (A).1-2. SL Div.1.

FRANCIS George E.

(C.F.) Striker 5' 9" 12st 0lbs
b. Acton, Middlesex 4. 2.1934
Brentford Jan 1953
Q.P.R. May 1961
Football League: 2-1. FAC: 0-0. FLC: 1-2. Others: 0-0.
Total: 3-3.
Brentford Oct 1961
Gillingham (£4,000) Aug 1962

In George's short stay at Loftus Road, he scored three goals in three matches, but he found in difficult to settle at the club. He was the typical centre forward of his day, quick and opportunistic. At Brentford he was known as one half of 'The Terrible Twins', the other half being Jim Towers who also moved over to Q.P.R.
Debut: 13. 9.1961 v. Crystal Palace (H).5-2. FLC.Rnd.1.

FRANCIS Gerald Charles

Mid 5' 10" 10st 8lbs
b. Chiswick, Middlesex 6.12.1951
Q.P.R. Jun 1969
Football League:295-61. FAC: 18-0. FLC: 21-5.
Others: 1-2. Total:335-68.
Crystal Palace (£150,000) Jul 1979
Q.P.R. Feb 1981
Football League:21-4. FAC: 0-0. FLC: 0-0. Others: 0-0.
Total: 21-4.
Coventry City (£150,000) Feb 1982
Exeter City Aug 1983
Cardiff City Sep 1984
Swansea City Oct 1984
Portsmouth Nov 1984
Wimbledon 1985
Bristol Rovers Sep 1985

Honours: 6 England U23 caps. 12 full caps (8 as captain). 2nd Div. runners-up medal. 1st Div. runners-up medal. 3rd Div. championship medal as manager. Leyland Daf runners-up medal as manager.

The son of Roy Francis, a reserve team player who used to play for Brentford, Gerry made his League debut at the age of 17 years. He was a midfield player of dash and quality who would have won many more caps had he not been injured, but he is the only Q.P.R. player to captain England whilst at Loftus Road. Gerry's first of two periods at Loftus Road lasted 10 years and took in nearly 300 League games. He was valued at £150,000 by Crystal Palace, but returned to Q.P.R. less than two yares later, and after only 20 plus League games he was on the move again, this time to Coventry City, and another £150,000 fee! Frequent moves followed in the next few years before he finally hung his boots up after a playing career that had spanned a notable 16 years. Gerry has had a wide managerial career, which began at Exeter City, then at Bristol Rovers, on to Q.P.R. in 1991, Spurs in 1994, then - as in his playing days - he returned to Q.P.R. in 1998 until 2001. He then managed Bristol Rovers again for a short period.
Debut: 29. 3.1969 v. Liverpool (H).1-2. Div.1.

FRANCIS Trevor John

Striker 5' 10" 11st 7lbs
b. Plymouth, Devon 19. 4.1954
Emesettle youth club
Plymouth boys

Birmingham City		Jun 1971
Detroit Express, U.S.A.		May 1978
Nottingham Forest	(£975,000)	Feb 1979
Detroit Express, U.S.A.		Jun 1979
Manchester City	(£1,200,000)	Sep 1981
Sampdoria, Italy	(£800,000)	Jul 1982
Atlanta, U.S.A.	(£900,000)	Jul 1986
Glasgow Rangers		Aug 1987
Q.P.R.		Mar 1988

Football League: 32-12. FAC: 1-0. FLC: 8-3. Others: 1-0. Total: 42-15.

Sheffield Wednesday	Jan 1990

Honours: England youth caps. 5 U23 caps. 52 senior caps. 2 2nd Div. runners-up medals. European Cup winners medal. 2 League Cup runners-up medals. Italian Cup winners medal. Scottish League Cup winners medal.

Trevor had acceleration and style in tight situations and was very dangerous around the penalty box. Intricate ball control, powerful shooting and amazing self confidence was his trade-mark. The first sixteen year old to score four goals in a League match and the first £1,000,000 footballer.

Trevor had an unhappy spell as the player/manager of Q.P.R. However, his career took a huge upturn when he took the same post at Sheffield Wednesday, for they reached two domestic Cup Finals and finished in a respectable position in the League. As manager of Birmingham City he failed to gain any trophies and moved on to take charge of Crystal Palace.
Debut: 26. 3.1988 v. Portsmouth (A). 1-0. Div.1.

FREEMAN Benjamin

(L.H.) Mid 5' 11" 11st 7lbs
b. Small Heath, Birmingham in 1878

Small Heath	1897
Grays United	1899
Q.P.R.	1901

Southern League: 51-1. FAC: 2-0. FLC: 0-0. Others: 0-0. Total: 53-1.

Ben was an ex-soldier who served in the Warwickshire Regiment and was invalided out in 1897. He took up football and was signed by Small Heath. Unable to get a game with the senior squad he was transferred to Grays United and it was from there that Q.P.R secured him.
Debut: 7. 9.1901 v. Watford (H). 0-1. SLDiv.1.

FRY Robert P.

G
b. Pontypridd, Wales 29. 6.1935

Crystal Palace	1955
Bath City	1956
Q.P.R.	1957

Football League: 1-0. FAC: 0-0. FLC: 0-0. Others: 1-0. Total: 2-0.

Bexleyheath & Welling	1958

Bob's actual first team debut came in the Southern Professional Floodlight Cup, a competition which could be considered as a forerunner to, even though regionalised, the League Cup.
Debut: 6.11.1957 v.Reading (A).2-5. 1st Rnd(Replay).

FURLONG Paul Anthony

Striker 6' 0" 13st 8lbs
b. Wood Green, London 1.10.1968
Enfield

Coventry City	(£130,000)	Jun 1991
Watford	(£250,000)	Jun 1992
Chelsea	(£2,300,000)	May 1994
Birmingham City	(£1,500,000)	Jul 1996
Q.P.R.	(Loan)	Aug 2000

Football League: 3-1. FAC: 0-0. FLC: 0-0. Others: 0-0. Total: 3-1.

Birmingham City Mar 2001
Sheffield United (Loan) Feb 2002
Q.P.R. Aug 2002
Football League: 35-14 FAC: 1-0. FLC: 0-0. Others: 1-0. Total: 37-14.

A big, strong striker who holds the ball up well and shoots with power and accuracy. Paul unfortunately injured the tendon to his patella (knee), which led to the premature end of his loan period. After a return to Birmingham City and then a further loan period, he signed permanently for Q.P.R., and became a near ever-present during the 2002/03 season.
Debut: 20. 8.2000 v. Crystal Palace (A).1-1. Div.1.

GALLEN Kevin Andrew

Striker 5' 11" 12st 10lbs
b. Chiswick, Middlesex 21. 9.1975
Q.P.R. Sep 1992
Football/Premier League:171-36. FAC: 8-2. FLC: 12-2. Others: 0-0. Total:191-40.
Huddersfield Town Aug 2000
Barnsley Jul 2001
Q.P.R. Nov 2001
Football League: 70-20. FAC: 1-0. FLC: 1-0. Others: 0-0. Total: 72-20.

Honours: England school & youth caps. 4 U21 caps.

Kevin had a phenominal scoring rate as a youth player when he netted 126 goals in two seasons, which even surpassed the earlier record of Jimmy Greaves. Kevin became a strong, quick and natural striker with a hard shot. He was with Q.P.R.initially, from a 17 year old, for eight years, and appeared in nearly 200 senior matches. He then moved to Huddersfield under the Bosman ruling. But he was plagued by injuries, and similarly at Barnsley, before manager Steve Parkin brought him back to Q.P.R., where he was a near ever-present during 2002/03
Debut: 20. 8.1994 v. Manchester United (A).0-2. PL.

GARDNER Andrew

(O.L.) Wing 5' 8" 11st 7lbs
b. Milton, Glasgow, Scotland 17. 4.1877
Kilbarchan Victoria
Kilbarchan
Clyde 1895
Grimsby Town May 1901
Newcastle United Sep 1902
Bolton Wanderers May 1903
Brighton & Hove Albion 1904
Q.P.R. 1905
Southern League: 5-0. FAC: 0-0. FLC: 0-0. Others: 0-0. Total: 5-0.
Carlisle United 1907
St. Johnston Apl 1908
Carlisle United Jan 1909

Andy was a fleet-footed sharp-shooter but it didn't happen at Q.P.R. He finished up as a left wing reserve player, although once he played at half back.
Debut: 2. 9.1905 v. New Brompton (H).4-0. SLDiv.1

GARDNER William

(I.F.) Mid 5' 7" 12st 0lbs
b. Langley Moor, Durham 7. 6.1993
Bishop Aukland 1915
Derby County Aug 1920
Spennymoor United 1921
Q.P.R. Mar 1923
Football League: 2-0. FAC: 0-0. FLC: 0-0. Others: 0-0. Total: 2-0.
Ashington Jul 1923
Grimsby Town Oct 1925
Darlington 1927
Torquay United Jun 1928
York City Jul 1929
Crewe Alexandria Jul 1931
Rochdale Sep 1932

Honours: 2 England amateur caps. Amateur cup runners-up medal. Represented the North Eastern League.

Wally was a top class forward who was much sought after by the big clubs. Chunky and powerful he played in all three inside forward berths, and he certainly turned it on after leaving Q.P.R., scoring some 80 goals in 150 matches. In 1933 Wally retired from football to help run the family business.
Debut: 7. 4.1923 v. Merthyr Town (H).1-1. Div.3 (S).

GAUL W.

(C.F.) Striker
b.
Q.P.R. 1912
Southern League: 14-7. FAC: 0-0. FLC: 0-0. Others: 0-0.
Total: 14-7.

It is known that this man was an amateur and joined the 'Footballers Battalion' during the latter part of 1914. Nothing else is known about him except that he was the sixth centre forward to be tried during his single season.
Debut: 21.12.1912 v. Crystal Palace (H). 2-0. SL Div. 1.

GAYLARD Hugh H.

(R.B.) Defender
b.
Uxbridge 1897
Q.P.R. 1899
Southern League: 4-0. FAC: 3-0. FLC: 0-0. Others: 0-0.
Total: 7-0.

Hugh was an amateur who regularly played for Uxbridge but turned-out for Q.P.R. when the usual right back was unable to play.
Debut: 16.12.1899 v. Bristol Rovers (H). 3-0. SL Div. 1.

GIBBONS John William

(C.F.) Striker
b. Charlton, London 8. 4.1925
Dartford
Q.P.R. Dec 1947
Football League: 8-2. FAC: 0-0. FLC:0-0. Others: 0-0.
Total: 8-2.
Ipswich Town May 1949
Tottenham Hotspur Mar 1950

George Smith, who was the captain of Q.P.R. during their championship season of 1947/48, became the manager of Ipswich Town upon retirement from playing, and John was his first capture on the transfer market as a manager The centre forward was unsuccessful at Portman Road and he ended his career coaching the youngsters at White Hart Lane.
Debut: 23.10.1948 v. West Ham United (H). 2-1. Div. 2.

GIBBS Derek William

(W.H.) Def 5' 10" 11st 7lbs
b. Fulham, London 22.12.1934
Chelsea Apl 1954
Leyton Orient Nov 1960
Q.P.R. Aug 1963
Football League: 27-0. FAC: 2-0. FLC: 0-0. Others: 0-0.
Total: 29-0.
Romford 1965

Alec Stock who had acquired Gibbs' services for Leyton Orient in 1960 had been so keen to sign him for Q.P.R. that he had forgotten to register him before he played. The club was fined £40 for this misdemeanour. Derek was a dependable player who could be, and was, utilised in any position.
Debut: 24. 8.1964 v. Oldham Athletic (A).1-2. Div.3.

GILBERG Harold

(I.F.) Mid 5' 7" 11st 2lbs
b. Tottenham, London 27. 6.1923.d. Torquay 16. 9.1994
Tottenham schools
Tottenham Hotspur May 1939
Walthamstow Avenue 1942
Northfleet United 1943
Tottenham Hotspur 1944
Q.P.R. Aug 1951
Football League: 66-12. FAC: 4-0. FLC: 0-0. Others: 0-0.
Total: 70-12.
Brighton & Hove Albion Dec 1952

His father played for Tunbridge Wells Rangers but Harry was taken on by the Spurs ground staff as a 14 year old in 1937 while still at school. He served the club's junior team for five years and made his first team debut in a wartime fixture. However, in the ten years he was at the club, Harry played just 16 times. During the war, Warrant Officer Gilberg served with Lancaster bombers and completed more than 30 operational flights. After his transfer to Q.P.R. he settled into a fine partnership with Bert Addinall and continued with it at Brighton & Hove Albion where they were both transferred together. Harry suffered from repeated knee problems, which brought about his enforced retirement in 1956. He lived in Broxbourne, Herts. But whilst on holiday in Torquay in 1994, he suddenly collapsed and died.
Debut: 18. 8.1951 v. West Ham United (H). 2-0. Div. 2.

GILFILLAN John E.

(G) 6' 0" 12st 0lbs
b. Townhill, Cowdenbeath, Scotland 29. 9.1896
d. Portsmouth, Hants. 2. 1.1976

Inverkeithing United
Heart of Midlothian 1921
East Fife (Loan) 1927
Portsmouth 1928
Q.P.R. 1937
Football League: 21-0. FAC: 2-0. FLC: 0-0. Others: 0-0.
Total: 23-0.

Honours: Scottish Cup runners-up medal. 2 F.A.Cup runners-up medalds.

John, who is something of a legend in Portsmouth, kept goal at Q.P.R. in 1937 at the age of 41, sharing the No.1 spot with Billy Mason. John's grandson Steve Mills, carried on the tradition and kept goal for Southampton from 1972 until 1976. John died in St. Mary's Hospital, Portsmouth in 1976.
Debut: 16.10.1937 v. Reading (A). 0-1. Div. 3. (S).

GILHOOLEY Michael

(C.H.) CD 6' 0" 12st 11lbs
b. Glencraig, Fife, Scotland 26.11.1896
Glencraig Celtic
Celtic Nov 1913
Vale of Leven
Abercorn
Clydebank 1915
Hull City (£2,500) Jul 1920
Sunderland (£5,250) Mar 1922
Bradford City May 1925
Q.P.R. May 1927

Football League: 9-0. FAC: 0-0. FLC: 0-0. Others: 0-0.
Total: 9-0.
Troon Athletic Feb 1929

Honours: 1 cap for Scotland.

An outstanding talented central defender, Mike was signed by Celtic at the age of 16. He was so dominating in the air at Hull City that he earned the nickname of 'Rubberneck' among his colleagues and spectators alike. Mike's next club, Sunderland, broke the transfer record to secure him. However, dogged by injuries which undoubtedly prevented him enjoying a longer period of success he arrived at Q.P.R. but was only to play a few matches.
Debut: 27. 8.1927 v. Newport County (H).4-2. Div.3(S).

GILLARD Ian Terrance

(L.B.) Def 6' 0" 13st 5lbs
b. Hammersmith, London 9.10.1950
Pathfinders club, Slough
Q.P.R. Oct 1968
Football League:408-9. FAC: 36-1. FLC: 33-1. Others: 8-0.
Total:485-11.
Aldershot Jun 1982

Honours: 5 England caps at U23 level. 3 full England caps. 1st Div. runners-up medal. F.A.Cup runners-up medal.

Ian was a strong and flexible defender who on the ball was confident at going forward with the attack and constructive as well. He joined Q.P.R. as a sixteen year old apprentice, making his first team debut at 18. He began to carve out a regular place in the team during the 1969/70 season. Ian eventually made the third most appearances in the club's history, over a period of almost fourteen years. In nearly five hundred matches he filled the left back position magnificently, and scored several fine goals, a memorable one being a 30 yard drive from a Stan Bowles free kick in the League Cup at Southend United. His last appearance for the club was, fittingly, the F.A.Cup final replay in 1982. He then moved to Aldershot, initially as player coach, before hanging up his boots in 1986.
Debut: 23.11.1968 v. Notts Forest (H). 2-1. Div. 1.

GILLESPIE J.

(R.B.) Def
b. Scotland in 1886
Third Lanark
Q.P.R. 1908
Southern League: 1-0. FAC: 0-0. FLC: 0-0. Others: 0-0.
Total: 1-0.

Gillespie appeared just once in the side when John McDonald was absent.
Debut: 5.12.1908 v. Millwall (H). 2-2. SLDiv. 1.

GILMORE Henry Patrick

(L.H.) Def 5' 11" 12st 0lbs
b. West Hartlepool, Co. Durham in 1913

Shotton Colliery Welfare	
Hull City	Dec 1934
Mansfield Town	Jul 1935
Bournemouth & Boscombe Athletic	1936
Runcorn	Feb 1937
Q.P.R.	May 1937

Football League: 6-0. FAC: 1-0. FLC: 0-0. Others: 3-0. Total: 10-0.

Hull City	May 1939

At Q.P.R. he stood in for Dickie March on several occasions. Although Pat was at Hull City twice, he never appeared in a League or cup match for them, although on the second occasion he played in the wartime league.
Debut: 24.12.1938 v. Reading (H). 2-2. Div.3 (S).

GITTINS Alfred G.

(I.L.) Striker 5' 9" 11st 4lbs
b. Manchester in July 1886

Atherton Church House	
Adlington	
Bolton Wanderers	
Blackpool	
Lutom Town	1906
Q.P.R.	1907

Southern League: 42-17. FAC: 2-0. FLC: 0-0. Others: 2-0. Total: 46-17.

Aston Villa	1908
Croydon Common	1909
Fulham	1910
Portsmouth	Dec 1910
Partick Thistle	

Honours: Southern League Championship medal.

Alf was recognised as one of the most dangerous men in the country at going forward. Nowhere at his other clubs was he so successful at scoring goals, finishing as top marksman in the club's first championship winning season.
Debut: 2.9.1907 v.Tottenham Hotspur (H).3-3.SLDiv.1.

GIVENS Daniel Joseph

Striker 5' 11" 11st 2lbs
b. Dublin, Eire 9. 8.1949

Dublin Rangers		1964
Manchester United		Sep 1965
Luton Town	(£15,000)	Apl 1970
Q.P.R.	(£40,000)	Jul 1972

Football League:242-77. FAC: 24-10. FLC: 20-6. Others: 8-7.
Total:294-100.

Birmingham City	(£165,000)	Aug 1978
AFC Bournemouth	(Loan)	1980
Sheffield United		Mar 1981
Xamax, Switzerland		Jun 1981

Honours: 56 Eire International caps. 2nd Div. runners-up medal. 1st Div. runners-up medal. 2nd Div. promotion medal. Swiss league championship medal.

Despite his given name of 'Daniel', he has always been known as'Don' in the football world. The son of a champion jockey hurdler, Don was a potent, intelligent and dangerous finisher and an aggressive, mobile front-runner. He won the first of his many international caps three months before his debut for Manchester United.

Don topped the goalscorers list for Q.P.R. on four separate occasions and was the leading marksman when the club achieved their best ever League place in 1976. Don played for several clubs both before and after his six years with Q.P.R. At Manchester United he made only five first team appearances before his first move, to Luton Town for a moderate fee. He finished his playing career in Switzerland, playing for Xamax for six years, winning a championship medal (the club's first such victory), before becoming the club coach. Currently he is the Eire under 21 team manager.
Debut: 12. 8.1972 v. Swindon Town (A). 2-2. Div. 2.

GLOVER Allan Richard

Mid 5' 9" 11st 2lbs
b. Staines, Middlesex 21.10.1950
Windsor C/E school
London & Middlesex schools

Q.P.R.		Mar 1968

Football League: 6-0. FAC: 1-0. FLC: 0-0. Others: 0-0. Total: 7-0.

W.B.A.	(£70,000)	Jun 1969
Southend United	(Loan)	Jan 1976
Brentford		Oct 1976
Leyton Orient		Mar 1977
Brentford		Nov 1978
Staines		1980

Allen joined W.B.A. in a deal involving Clive Clark returning to Loftus Road. A clever and witty winger-cum-midfielder who was unlucky enough to receive a bad ankle injury in 1974 which halted his career and he subsequently never shrugged off the injury. His loan spell at Southend United was the shortest on record, for it lasted all of thirty seconds, before he was carried off injured.
Debut: 11. 1.1969 v. West Ham United (H). 1-1. Div. 1.

GODDARD George

(C.F.) Striker 5' 10" 11st 7lbs
b. Gomshall, Surrey 20.12.1903d. 24. 3.1987

Redhill	1924
Q.P.R.	1926

Football League:243-174. FAC: 16-12. FLC: 0-0. Others: 0-0. Total:259-186.

Wolverhampton Wanderers	1933
Sunderland	1934
Southend United	1936

Honours: 1 county cap as an amateur.

George is the club's top goalscorer by far, leading the list of Loftus Road centre forwards, and it is highly unlikely that his total will ever be exceeded. A butcher by trade, although at the time of his signing for Q.P.R., he worked in a bus garage. He signed for the club after scoring over 200 goals in two years for Redhill. George was the Q.P.R. top marksman for seven consecutive years, and he headed the Third Division Southern section scoring list in 1930 with 39. Although he played in less then twenty matches for Wolves, he scored a dozen goals in that brief spell, all of them coming in the 1933/4 season. On his retirement from football he took over a butcher's shop in the centre of London and later ran a successful café. George died in 1987 at Kingston-upon- Thames.
Debut: 11. 9.1926 v. Brentford (A). 2-4. Div. 3. (S).

GODDARD Paul

Striker 5' 8" 11st 8lbs
b. Harlington, Middlesex 12.10.1959

Q.P.R.		Jul 1977

Football League: 70-23. FAC: 0-0. FLC: 5-0. Others: 0-0. Total: 75-23.

West Ham United	(£800,000)	Aug 1980
Newcastle United	(£415,000)	Nov 1986
Derby County	(£425,000)	Jul 1988
Millwall	(£800,000)	Dec 1989
Ipswich Town		Feb 1991

Honours: 8 England U21 caps. 1 England B cap. 1 full cap. 2nd Div. championship medal. League Cup runners-up medal. Football League championship medal.

Paul was not a tall powerful centre forward in the traditional sense but a small man who knew how to control and shield the ball. He had a poachers instinct in front of goal and a willingness to play for the team. Paul won his only cap for his country when he came on as a substitute and scored. After his playing days were over he became coach to Ipswich Town in May 1994, caretaker manager in December of the same year, and finally became assistant coach in 1995. Currently he is a member of the backroom staff at West Ham.
Debut: 11. 4.1978 v. Arsenal (H). 2-1. Div. 1.

GOFTON George

(C.F.) Striker
b. Hartlepool 28. 2.1912

Newcastle United	1931
Q.P.R.	1932

Football League: 7-8. FAC: 4-0. FLC: 0-0. Others: 0-0.
Total: 11-8.

George was just one of four centre forwards to be tried in the senior squad during the season. This was the period when the club moved to the White City and Archie Mitchell took over as manager, and who experimented with two centre forwards. Goddard was the main striker along with Gofton between October and December. Collins was then tried in place of Gofton between January and March and finally Blackman came into the side until the seasons end. Mitchell was sacked in May 1933 and Gofton stayed with the club for another two years but he never played first team football again.
Debut: 22.10.1932 v. Coventry City (H). 3-3. Div.3 (S).

GOLDIE William

(C.F.) Striker
b. Scotland

Q.P.R.	1900

Southern League: 5-1. FAC: 4-2. FLC: 0-0. Others: 0-0.
Total: 9-3.

Goldie followed Bedingfield, after the latter was snapped up by Portsmouth at the end of the previous season. It was a long time before a striker with the quality of Sam was to grace the colours of the club.
Debut: 8. 9.1900 v. Swindon Town (H). 7-1. SL Div.1.

GOLDING Norman James

(O.R.) Wing
b. Southwark, London 23. 1.1937

Crystal Palace	Jul 1959
Tonbridge	1959
Q.P.R.	Aug 1959

Football League: 30-6. FAC: 1-0. FLC: 0-0. Others: 1-0.
Total: 32-6.

Kettering Town	1961

One of Alec Stock's first signings for Q.P.R. Norman shared the outside right spot with Pat Kerrins. Astonishingly he scored five goals in his first five matches.
Debut: 14. 9.1959 v. York City (H). 0-0. Div. 3.

GOODIER Edward

(C.H.) CD 6' 1" 12st 8lbs
b. Farnworth, Lancs. 15.10.1902d. Farnworth, 4.11.1967

Brookhouse United	
Huddersfield Town	May 1922
Lancaster Town	
Oldham Athletic	May 1925
Q.P.R.	Nov 1931

Football League:139-2. FAC: 13-0. FLC: 0-0. Others: 4-0.
Total:156-2.

Watford	Jun 1935
Crewe Alexandra	Jun 1936
Rochdale	1937

Ted left Oldham Athletic because of a disagreement over a benefit payment and both he and Adlam joined Q.P.R. for a combined fee of £1,500. When Goodier arrived at the club, this tall, elegant player started as a wing half but after a season he was turned into a successful centre half. After five seasons he was transferred to Watford for a fee plus a player. The following year he was introduced to managerial duties during which he served Rochdale for five years. During the 2nd World War he became the caretaker/manager of Birmingham City and in June 1952 took over the managers job at Wigan Athletic. Finally he ended up as the manager of Oldham Athletic from May 1956 until June 1958.
Debut: 14.11.1931 v. Cardiff City (A). 4-0. Div. 3 (S).

GOODMAN William R.

(C.H.) CD
b. Islington, London in 1894

Margate	
Tufnell Park	1921
Northfleet	1922
Q.P.R.	1923

Football League: 1-0. FAC: 0-0. FLC: 0-0. Others: 0-0.
Total: 1-0.

Goodman was signed originally as a centre half but he made just a single appearance for Q.P.R. on the left wing, in a rare victory during the season of the clubs first re-election year.
Debut: 18. 4.1924 v. Norwich City (H). 2-1. Div. 3. (S).

GOODRIDGE Gregory St. Clair

(O L.) Mid 5' 6" 10st 2lbs
b. Barbados 10. 7.1971
Lambada, St. Vincent

Torquay United		Mar 1994
Q.P.R.	(£350,000)	Aug 1995

Premier League: 7-1. FAC: 1-0. FLC: 1-0. Others: 0-0. Total: 9-1.

Bristol City	(£50,000)	Aug 1996
Cheltenham Town	(Loan)	Feb 2001
Bristol City	(Loan)	Sep 2001
Torquay United		Dec 2001

Honours: Barbados International.

Greg a skilful and exciting winger with a tremendously long throw-in. The captain of the Barbados International side, he never played a full match for Q.P.R. always coming on as a substitute. Predominately a left sided player who likes to run full backs ragged.
Debut: 14.10.1995 v. Newcastle United (H). 2-3. PL.

GOUGH Claude William McKinley

(L.H.) Def
b. South Cerney, Gloustershire 17.10.1901.d. 16. 5.1963
South Cerney
Cirencester Town
Llandrindrod Wells

Swansea Town	1920
Coventry City	1921
Swansea Town	1922
Bristol Rovers	
Clapton Orient	1926
Q.P.R.	1926

Football League: 19-0. FAC: 0-0. FLC: 0-0. Others: 0-0. Total: 19-0.

Torquay United	June 1927
Clapton Orient	Aug 1928
Canterbury Waverley	May 1929
Park Royal	Oct 1933
Ealing Celtic	Dec 1935

Much was expected of him as a youngster, but it never materialised. He was given an extended run in the side but his form was sporadic and he was released at the end of the 1926/27 season.
Debut: 28. 8.1926 v. Crystal Palace (A). 1-2. Div. 3. (S).

GOULD Harry L.

G
b. London
Metropolitan Police

Q.P.R.	1920

Football League: 2-0. FAC: 0-0. FLC: 0-0. Others: 0-0. Total: 2-0.

A policeman who was an amateur goalkeeper and filled in when the other regulars were out injured.
Debut: 26. 3.1921 v. Newport County (H). 2-0. Div. 3.

GRAHAM Malcolm

(I.L.) Striker
b. Hall Green, Wakefield, Yorkshire 26. 1.1934
Crigglestone

Barnsley	Apl 1953
Bristol City	May 1959
Leyton Orient	Jun 1960
Q.P.R.	Jul 1963

Football League: 21-7. FAC: 1-1. FLC: 1-0. Others: 0-0. Total: 23-8.

Barnsley	Jul 1964
Buxton	1965
Alfreton Town	

Honours: 2nd Div. runners-up medal.

Mal was a short and bustling forward. Some spectators loved him, some disliked him. Some talked of his, 'Puskas-like left foot'. Alec Stock acquired him from his old club, Leyton Orient, however, he was the second choice at all his other clubs.
Debut: 24. 8.1963 v. Oldham Athletic (A). 1-2. Div. 3.

GRAHAM Mark Roland

Mid 5' 7" 10st 8lbs
b. Newry, Nrth. Ireland 24.10.1974

Q.P.R.	May 1993

Premier League: 18-1. FAC: 2-0. FLC: 3-0. Others: 0-0. Total: 23-1.

Cambridge United	Aug 1999
Glentoran, N.I.	1999
Stevenage Borough	2000
Aldershot Town	2000
Billericay Town	Feb 2003
Canvey Island	Apr 2003
St.Albans City	Jun 2003

Honours: School, Youth and B level for N. Ireland.

Mark, after a lengthy period at Q.P.R., soon moved out of League football and became settled at the non-League level where he moved around quite frequently. He signed for Billericay (in February 2003) along with his brother, and former Q.P.R. player, Richard.
Debut: 20. 8.1994 v. Manchester United (A). 0-2. PL.

GRAHAM Richard Stephen

Mid 5' 8" 10st 6lbs
b. Newry, Nrth. Ireland 5. 8.1979

Q.P.R.	Aug 1996

Football League: 2-0. FAC: 0-0. FLC: 0-0. Others: 0-0. Total: 2-0.

Chesham United	Aug 2002
Billericay Town	Feb 2003

Honours: Youth and 2 U21 caps for N.Ireland.

Richard is the younger brother of Mark and he can perform equally as well, either on the wing or in the central midfield. He was given a free transfer in the summer of 2002, when he moved to Chaesham United, and the following february, along with his brother signed on for Billericay Town.
Debut: 29. 9.1998 v. Wolverhampton W. (A).2-1. Div.1.

GRANT George M.

(R.H.) Mid
b. Plumstead, London in 1891

Woolwich Westley Guild	
Northumberland Oddfellows	
Dartford Invictor	
Woolwich Arsenal	1910
Millwall Athletic	1919
Q.P.R.	1920

Football League: 69-1. FAC: 3-0. FLC: 0-0. Others: 0-0. Total: 72-1.

Northfleet	1922

Honours: London Challenge Cup runners-up medal.

George was an ever-present in the Q.P.R. team in thier first Football League season. He played in 54 League games for Arsenal from 1913 to 1915.
Debut: 28. 8.1920 v. Watford (H). 1-2. Div. 3.

GRAY Andrew A.

Mid 5' 11" 13st 3lbs
b. Brixton, London 22. 2.1964

Lambeth schools		
Corinthian Casuals		Oct 1982
Dulwich Hamlet		Jun 1984
Crystal Palace	(£2,000)	Nov 1984
Aston Villa	(£150,000)	Nov 1987
Q.P.R.	(£400,000)	Feb 1989

Football League: 11-2. FAC: 0-0. FLC: 0-0. Others: 0-0. Total: 11-2.

Crystal Palace	(£500,000)	Aug 1989
Tottenham Hotspur	(Loan)	1992
Swindon Town	(Loan)	1992
Tottenham Hotspur	(£900,000)	Jun 1992
Marbella, Spain		1994
Falkirk		1995

Honours: 1 full England cap. 2 England U21 caps. 2nd Div. runners-up medal.

Andy was a forceful player, with a good all round technique that encompassed a fierce shot and a long throw in. He was a hard working, muscular midfielder who was a late entry into the professional ranks.
Debut: 4. 2.1989 v. Millwall (H). 1-2. Div. 1.

GRAY Thomas

(O.R.) Wing 5' 7" 11st 6lbs
b. Grimsby, Lincolnshire in 1876

Gainsborough Trinity	1898
New Brompton	1899
Q.P.R.	1900

Southern League: 28-8. FAC: 4-2. FLC: 0-0. Others: 0-0. Total: 32-10.

Bury	1901

Tommy was noted in the "Football Chat" magazine as a sharp forward who was not afraid of being in a scrimmage. Ever-present in his only season with the club, he was a firm favourite with the crowd.
Debut: 1.9.1900 v. Bristol Rovers (A). 1-2. SLDiv. 1.

GREEN Thomas

(C.F.) Striker 5' 8" 11st 7lbs
b. Rock Ferry, Cheshire 25.11.1883

Liverpool		1901
Swindon Town		1903
Stockport County		1904
Middlesbrough	(£300)	Feb 1905
Q.P.R.		1906

Southern League: 37-2. FAC: 2-0. FLC: 0-0. Others: 0-0. Total: 39-2.

Stockport County	1907
Exeter City	1909
P.N.E.	1910

Honours: Lancashire Combination championship medal.

Tommy was a very fast forward with a furious shot from either foot. Outside right was his natural position but he preferred to play at centre forward.
Debut: 1. 9.1906 v. Luton Town (A). 1-1. SLDiv. 1.

GREER William H. O.

(I.F.) Mid
b. County Derry, Ireland
Highland Light Infantry

Dunfermline	1903
Clyde	1904
Belfast Distillery	1905
Dumbarton	1907
Q.P.R.	1908

Southern League: 32-7. FAC: 2-0. FLC: 0-0. Others: 0-0.
Total: 34-7.

Honours: 3 Irish International caps.

Bill was one of the first player's to win a cap for his country whilst with Q.P.R. He played the game with terrific zest and a terrier-like attitude.
Debut: 25.12.1908 v. Norwich City (H). 2-2. SLDiv. 1.

GREGORY Clarence

(O.L.) Wing
b. Willinghall, Warwickshire
Willington Town

Sunderland	1920
Q.P.R.	1922

Football League: 24-1. FAC: 0-0. FLC: 0-0. Others: 0-0.
Total: 24-1

Yeovil & Petters	1923

Clarence joined Q.P.R. to be with his brother Jack but he only stayed with the club for one season, before stepping down to non-League level.
Debut: 26. 8.1922 v. Watford (H). 1-2. Div. 3. (S).

GREGORY John (Jack)

(I.F.) Mid
b. Willinghall, Warwichshire
Willinghall Swifts

Q.P.R.	1912

Southern/Football League:199-44. FAC: 12-4. FLC: 0-0.
Others: 0-0. Total:211-48.

Yeovil & Petters	1923

Jack was - presumably the older - brother of Clarence, who came to the notice of the club while he was playing for Willenhall Swifts in the Birmingham League, where he was selected to play in a Junior International match against Scotland. He scored nineteen goals for Willenhall in 1912 before the Ranger's signed him.

Jack played for Q.P.R. for ten years making over a century of appearances in wartime football and together with his peacetime games he totalled over 300. Together with his brother Clarence, the pair played together at Q.P.R. for one season, before moving into non-League football in 1923, and another brother played for W.B.A.
Debut: 7.12.1912 v. Watford (H). 2-0. SLDiv. 1.

GREGORY John Charles

Mid 6' 1" 11st 5lbs
b. Scunthorpe, Lincolnshire 11. 5.1954

Northampton Town		May 1972
Aston Villa	(£40,000)	Jun 1977
Brighton & Hove Albion	(£250,000)	Jul 1979
Q.P.R.	(£300,000)	Jun 1981

Football League:161-36. FAC: 9-1. FLC: 16-4. Others: 4-1.
Total:190-42.

Derby County	(£100,000)	Nov 1985
Portsmouth		1988
Plymouth Argyle		1990
Bolton Wanderers		1990

Honours: 6 England caps. F.A.Cup runners-up medal. 2 2nd Div championship medals.

The son of a professional footballer, John was a highly versatile player who brought a good deal of experience to the young Loftus Road starlets. Gregory had a proper 'apprenticeship' in football, after appearing in approximately 350 matches before he came to Q.P.R. in 1981. A Terry Venables buy, John spent four years at Loftus Road, appearing in the losing F.A.Cup final against Spurs in 1982, and he was ever-present in the team that won the 2nd Division title in 1982/3.

John also appeared for England during his Loftus Road period. He was a neat passer of the ball, able to dictate the tempo of the game and had a lot of stamina. He was an elegant type of player, upright and controlled and an uncompromising tackler who would get 'stuck-in'. After his playing days were over he took up coaching at Portsmouth, followed the manager's job, but this ended with dismissal twelve months later. John worked with Brian Little at Leicester City and accompanied him to Aston Villa in 1994. He was appointed manager of Wycombe Wanderers in 1996, and then the same at Aston Villa in 1998, followed by the Derby County hot seat in 2002.
Debut: 29. 9.1981 v. Wrexham (A). 3-1. Div. 2.

GRETTON Thomas

G 6' 0" 12st 0lbs
b. Walsall, Staffs.
Wolverhampton United
Q.P.R. 1929
Football League: 4-0: FAC: 0-0. FLC: 0-0. Others: 0-0. Total: 4-0.
Walsall 1930

Tom was the reserve team goalkeeper at all of his three clubs. At Q.P.R. he deputised for Jock Cunningham who was injured at the time but was released at the end of the season.
Debut: 7.12.1929 v. Swindon Town (A). 2-2. Div. 3. (S)

GRIFFITHS Leroy

Striker 5' 11" 13st 5lbs
b. London 30.12.1976
Corinthian Casuals
Hampton & Richmond Borough
Q.P.R. (£40,000) May 2001
Football League: 36-3. FAC: 1-0. FLC: 0-0. Others: 0-0. Total: 37-3.
Farnborough Town (Loan) Sep 2002
Margate (Loan) Nov 2002

A striker who can also play in a wide position. Leroy was noted by the fans after scoring a spectacular goal against Chelsea in a pre-season Friendly in August 2001. He featured regularly in the senior squad in the 2001/02 season, but only made a few appearances the next, and negotiated a termination of his contract during the Summer of 2003. (Signed permanently by Farnborough Town in August 2003)
Debut: 11. 8.2001 v. Stoke City (H). 1-0. Div. 2.

GRIMSDELL Ernest Frederick

(L.B.) Def 6' 1" 12st 10lbs
b. Watford, Herts in 1892.d. Bushy, Herts in Sept 1947
St. Stephens Apl 1909
Watford Sep 1909
Watford Orient
Reading Feb 1913
Watford 1913
St. Albans City 1914
Q.P.R. Aug 1920
Football League: 20-0. FAC: 1-0. FLC: 0-0. Others: 0-0. Total: 21-0.
Guildford United Aug 1921
Q.P.R. Jun 1922
Football League: 2-0. FAC: 0-0. FLC: 0-0. Others: 0-0. Total: 2-0.
Chatham Aug 1923
Dartford Mar 1927

Honours: 2 England amateur caps. Represented the Army v. Royal Navy and the F.A. v. Cambridge University.

An accomplished full back who turned professional at Q.P.R. (he had a famous brother, Arthur, who played for 'Spurs). Unfortunately Ernie was so badly injured in the 1922/23 season that he subsequently took up refereeing and became a Football League lineman.
Debut: 4. 9.1920 v. Watford (A). 2-0. Div. 3.

GULLAN Stanley K.

G 5' 10" 12st 2lbs
b. Edinburgh, Scotland 26. 1.1926 d. 1999
Dumbarton
Clyde
Q.P.R. Jul 1949
Football League: 48-0. FAC: 0-0. FLC: 0-0. Others: 0-0. Total: 48-0.
Tunbridge Wells
Berwick Rangers
Third Lanark
Montrose
Stenhousemuir

Stan was solid in frame and a very good shot stopper. Barry Hugman's A-Z of Players Records gives his birth place as Edinburgh, while Rothman's Annual for 2000/1 gives it as Southend, Essex. Stan was a civil servant who apparently played most of his football in Scotland.
Debut: 6. 9.1950 v. Bury (A). 1-0. Div. 2.

GUY-WATSON H.
G
b.
Paddington
Q.P.R. 1905
Southern League: 1-0. FAC: 0-0. FLC: 0-0. Others: 0-0.
Total: 1-0.

An amateur who played in the very last match of the 1905/06 season, during which Q.P.R. tried no fewer than five 'keepers.
Debut: 28. 4.1906 v. Bristol Rovers (H). 7-0. SLDiv. 1.

HAGGAN John
(C.H.) CD
b. Chester-le-Street, Durham 16.12.1896 d. 1982
Tyneside Junior club
Sunderland 1919
Q.P.R. 1919
Southern League: 1-0. FAC: 0-0. FLC: 0-0. Others: 0-0.
Total: 1-0.
Brentford May 1922
Preston Colliery

John replaced Archie Mitchell in the side, the latter being absent from the senior squad on the very last day of the season.
Debut: 26. 4.1920 v. Southend United (A). 2-2.SL Div.1

HALEY William Thomas
(I.F.) Mid 5' 8" 10st 8lbs
b. Woolwich, London 16. 2.1904d. Rochester 20. 1.1960
Bostall Heath
Charlton Athletic May 1924
Derby County Feb 1925
Dartford (Loan) Jul 1927
Fulham Jun 1928
Q.P.R. May 1931
Football League: 17-5. FAC: 0-0. FLC: 0-0. Others: 0-0.
Total: 17-5.
Dartford 1932
Sheppey United Aug 1935

Bill was in dispute with Charlton Athletic and it took around one year before he was paid the wages owing him. For his transfer, Derby County paid £1,000 plus the gate receipts of a match between the two clubs played at the Valley during the 1926/27 season. He scored on his debut for Q.P.R. but Billy soon left the professional football scene at the age of 27 to concentrate on running a sweetshop in Woolwich, until 1933. He left the district to take over a public house in Sheerness called ('The Goat'), later he kept licensed premises in Edenbridge.

At the time of his death he was the proprietor of 'The Gore Court Arms' in Sittingbourne.
Debut: 31. 8.1931 v. Bristol Rovers (A). 1-1 Div. 3 (S)

HALL Ernest W.
(L.B.) Def 6' 1" 12st 10lbs
b. Barndale, Nr. Coventry
Bedworth Town 1930
Q.P.R 1931
Football League: 61-0. FAC: 9-0. FLC: 0-0. Others: 0-0.
Total: 70-0.
Chester 1933

Ernie was a big, tough defender who formerly worked in an iron foundry before signing for Q.P.R. He finally left for Chester F.C. and turned out for them in over a hundred matches, until the start of the 2nd World War, becoming the assistant trainer and finally trainer.
Debut: 9.10.1931 v Swindon T. (H).1-2.Div.3 (S).

HAMILTON John Eley
(O.R.) Wing
b. Nottingham 23. 1.1902 d. Nottingham 16. 1.1980
Heanor Athletic
Wellbeck Colliery 1920
Watford Jun 1921
Sutton Town Jul 1922
Blackpool May 1924
Q.P.R. Jun 1926
Football League: 10-0. FAC: 0-0. FLC: 0-0. Others: 0-0.
Total: 10-0.
Sutton Town Apl 1927
Loughborough Corinthians

After playing under a pseudonym and scoring twice in a benefit match in March 1921, John joined Watford. He only played two matches however, before moving north to Blackpool. At Q.P.R. he was one of five wingers to be tried in 1926 and he was never able to impress.
Debut: 28. 8.1926 v. Crystal Palace (A). 1-2. Div.3 (S).

HAMILTON John Haggarty
(O.R.) Wing 5' 6" 11st 0lbs
b. Glasgow, Scotland in 1880
Scotia Thistle
Cambuslang 1895
Hibernian
Sunderland 1896
Burton Swifts 1898
Gainsborough Trinity 1900
Millwall 1901

Q.P.R. 1902
Southern League: 47-3. FAC: 3-0. FLC: 0-0. Others: 0-0. Total: 50-3.
West Ham United 1904

In common with many others, John travelled the soccer circuit in those early football days. Along with John Blackwood, he was transferred to West Ham United just before Boxing Day 1904. It was to no avail however, for the Hammers lost their next four matches, although Blackwood did at least get on the scoresheet.
Debut: 3. 9.1902 v. Wellingborough (H). 2-0.SL Div.1.

HAMILTON William R.

Striker 6' 1" 12st 0lbs
b. Belfast, Nth. Ireland 9. 5.1957
Linfield
Q.P.R. (£25,000) Apl 1978
Football League: 12-2. FAC: 1-0. FLC: 0-0. Others: 0-0. Total: 13-2.
Burnley (£55,000) Nov 1979
Oxford United Aug 1984
Limerick

Honours: 41 Northern Ireland International caps. 1 U21 cap. Cup & League double of Nth. Ireland. 3rd Div. championship medal. 2nd Div. championship medal.

Billy was capped at full level within a month of his arrival at Loftus Road but he was not at the club very long before being transferred to Burnley. He was not the quickest of forwards from a standing start but nevertheless a tireless campaigner who never stopped running, but Clive Allen was the preferred striker. Hamilton played over 250 matches for Burnley in a little under five years and upon retirement he took over the managership of Limerick in 1988, followed by the same job at Distillery in 1991.
Debut: 2.12.1978 v. Bolton Wanderers (H). 1-3. Div.1.

HAMMOND Joseph Henry

(O.R.). Wing 5' 10" 11st 0lbs
b. West Ham, London in 1909
London Paper Mills
Leytonstone 1933
Q.P.R. 1934
Football League: 18-6. FAC: 1-0. FLC: 0-0. Others: 2-1. Total: 21-7.

Joe came to prominence with his works team, the London Paper Mills, who won their League in the 1932/33 season, and he was instantly signed by Leytonstone. At Q.P.R., he remained an effective reserve to Emmerson, however, with the arrival of manager Billy Birrell to the club, Joe was soon released.
Debut: 14. 4.1934 v. Southend United (A).2-0. Div.3(S)

HANDFORD Thomas W.

(O.L.) Wing
b.
Q.P.R. 1894
Burton Wanderers 1895
Bury 1898
Q.P.R. 1900
Southern League: 3-0. FAC: 0-0. FLC: 0-0. Others: 0-0. Total: 3-0.

Honours: London Cup winners medal.

Tommy played for the club before they turned pro. but kept his amateur status throughout his career. In retirement he became a referee and he was prominent in the minor leagues throughout England, as well as acting as an occasional Football League linesman.
Debut: 14. 9.1901 v. Tottenham Hot. (A). 0-2. SL Div. 1.

HANNAH James

(O.L.) Wing
b. Glasgow, Scotland
Third Lanark
Sunderland Albion 1890
Sunderland Jan 1891
Third Lanark May 1897
Q.P.R. 1899
Southern League: 17-2: FAC: 3-0. FLC: 0-0. Others: 0-0. Total: 20-2.

Honours: 1 Scottish International cap. 1 Scottish Cup Winners medal. 3 Football League championship medals.

Jimmy was a fine dribbler and wily wingman, he could play in any frontline position and knew exactly when to part with the ball.
Debut: 25.11.1999 v.Sheppey (A). 1-3. SLDiv. 1.

HARKOUK Rachid

For. 6' 0" 12st 5lbs
b. Chelsea, London 19. 5.1956

Feltham		
Crystal Palace		Jun 1976
Q.P.R.	(£100,000)	Jun 1978

Football League: 20-3. FAC: 1-0. FLC: 3-0. Others: 0-0. Total: 24-3.

Notts County	(£50,000)	Jun 1980

Honours: Algerian International. 2nd Div. runners-up medal.

After only a modest number of appearances for Q.P.R., Rachid moved onto Notts County where he made over 150 appearances, until injury forced him to retire.
Debut: 26. 8.1978 v. Notts Forest (H). 0-0. Div.1.

HARPER Lee Charles Phillip

G. 6' 1" 13st 11lbs
b. Chelsea, London 30.10.1971

Eltham Town		
Sittingbourne		1993
Arsenal	(£150,000)	Jun 1994
Q.P.R.	(£125,000)	Jul 1997

Football League:118-0: FAC: 4-0. FLC: 9-0. Others: 0-0. Total:131-0.

Walsall	Jul 2001
Northampton Town	Jul 2002

A shot stopper who commands the penalty area with assurance. This earned him the runner-up spot in the supporters "Player of the Year" award in 1999/2000. A well built goalkeeper who shared the top spot with Tony Roberts, but then lost it to Ludek Miklosko. However, when the latter was injured Lee took his chance and never looked back. He was released in the summer of 2001 after four years at Loftus Road, during which time he made over 130 first team appearances. He was unable to command a regular first team place at First Division Walsall and moved on to Northampton after a year, where he has been more successful.
Debut: 9. 8.1997 v. Ipswich Town (H). 0-0. Div. 1.

HARRIS Allan J.

(L.B.) Def 5' 8" 10st 7lbs
b. Hackney, London 28.12.1942

Chelsea		Jun 1960
Coventry City	(£35,000)	Nov 1964
Chelsea	(£45,000)	May 1966
Q.P.R.	(£30,000)	Jul 1967

Football League: 94-0. FAC: 1-0. FLC: 3-0. Others: 0-0. Total: 98-0.

Plymouth Argyle	Mar 1971
Cambridge United	Jul 1973

Honours: 3 England school caps. England youth caps. F.A.Cup runners-up medal.

Allan was sold to Coventry City without playing a match for Chelsea. When he was transferred back to them in 1966, he played alongside his brother Ron, before moving onto Q.P.R. After his playing days were over he became assistant manager to Terry Venables at Crystal Palace, Q.P.R., Spurs and Barcelona, eventually becoming manager himself at the Spanish club.
Debut: 10. 8.1967 v. Portsmouth (A). 1-1. Div. 2.

HARRIS Bernard

(F.B.) Def 5' 9" 11st 0lbs
b. Sheffield, Yorkshire 14. 3.1901

Gainsborough Trinity	1920
Rotherham County	1922
Sheffield United	1924
Luton Town	1928
Q.P.R.	1929

Football League: 60-0. FAC: 7-0. FLC: 0-0. Others: 0-0. Total: 67-0.

Llanelly	
Swindon Town	1933
Margate	

Bernard was a very useful defender for he could operate at right or left back. Although playing for several other clubs during a reasonable length Football League career, it was with Q.P.R. that he spent the longest period.
Debut: 31. 8.1929 v. Crystal Palace (A). 1-1. Div. 3 (S).

HARRIS George T.

(L.H.) Mid 5' 9" 11st 10lbs
b. High Wycombe in 1898

Wycombe Wanderers	1920
Southend United	1921
Notts County	1922
Q.P.R.	1924

Football League: 38-0. FAC: 5-0. FLC: 0-0. Others: 0-0. Total: 43-0.

Fulham	1926

George was a reserve player wherever he went, except at Q.P.R. where he had a two year stint in the senior squad. At his final League club, Fulham, he scored the only goal of his professional career.
Debut: 10. 9.1924 v. Watford (A). 0-1. Div. 3. (S).

HARRIS Neil

(C.F) Striker
b. Glasgow, Scotland 9. 2.1920

Swansea Town	1938
Southampton	1939
Q.P.R.	1946

Football League: 1-1. FAC: 1-1. FLC: 0-0. Others: 0-0. Total: 2-2.

On the 4th December 1946, Neil scored in his debut match for Q.P.R. Three days later he was on the goalscorers list again, only this time he cracked his head against a goal post, knocking himself unconscious, fracturing his skull and breaking his pelvis in the process. He never played competitive football again. On his recovery, Neil was made assistant to Dave Mangnall, however, with the leaving of the manager, he moved back to Wales to run an import/export business.
Debut: 4.12.1946 v. Poole T. (A). 6-0.F.A.Cup 1st R(R)

HARRISON James H.

(C.F.) Striker
b. Hammersmith, London 31. 7.1928
Willesden

Q.P.R.	1952

Football League: 6-1. FAC: 0-0. FLC: 0-0. Others: 0-0. Total: 6-1.

Spotted by a scout playing football on Wormwood Scrubs. Jimmy was given an extended trial, first for Willesden (the Q.P.R. nursery side), and then for the senior squad. He was not retained at the end of the 1952/53 season.
Debut: 3. 1.1953 v. Coventry City (A).0-2. Div.3 (S).

HART Ernest

(I.L.) Mid
b. Huddersfield, Yorkshire
Folkstone

Q.P.R.	1922

Football League: 5-2. FAC: 0-0. FLC: 0-0. Others: 0-0. Total: 5-2.

Guildford United	1923

Ernie occasionally come into the 1922/23 side to replace Arthur Chandler when he was out injured. The following season, he left to play for Guildford United (later named City).
Debut: 4.11.1922 v. Aberdare Athletic (A). 0-0. Div.3 (S)

HART George

(R.H.) Mid
b. Gosforth, Northumberland
Bedlington Colliery Welfare

Q.P.R.	1923

Football League: 6-1. FAC: 0-0. FLC: 0-0. Others: 0-0. Total: 6-1.

Durham City	1925

George was a reserve, filling in at either wing half or inside left for two seasons. The club finished bottom of the Division at the end of his first season, yet he was one of the lucky one's to be retained for another campaign.
Debut: 27.10.1923 v. Northampton T. (H).3-2. Div.3(S).

HARTBURN John H.

(O.L.) Wing 5' 2" 10st 4lbs
b. Houghton-le-spring, Durham 20.12.1920
Bishop Aukland

Yeovil Town		1945
Q.P.R		Mar 1947

Football League: 58-11. FAC: 6-2. FLC: 0-0. Others: 0-0. Total: 64-13.

Watford	(£1,000)	Sep 1949
Millwall	(£2,500)	Mar 1951
Leyton Orient		Jun 1954
Yiewsley		
Guildford		Jul 1958

Honours: 2 3rd Div. (South) Championship medals.

Johnny was a very fast, tiny winger, who came with the full recommendation of Alec Stock, his manager at Yeovil Town.

He could centre the ball "on a sixpence" and had one of the deadliest shots in the 3rd Division. At Leyton Orient he hit one of the fastest hat-tricks in the history of the game, by scoring all three in three minutes. On his retirement from playing, Johnny spent four years as the commercial manager at Leyton Orient. He then had a further nine years in the same capacity at Fulham, and finally spent five years as the secretary of Barnet F.C., before retiring in 1987.
Debut: 23. 8.1947 v. Norwich City (H).3-1. Div.3 (S).

HARTWELL Ambrose Walter

(C.H.) CD 5' 11" 12st 7lbs
b. Exeter, Devon 26. 6.1883

Budleigh Town schools	
Erdington	
Feltham	
Redditch Excelsior	
Erdington	
Birmingham City	Aug 1901
Bradford Park Avenue	Jun 1908
Q.P.R.	Aug 1909

Southern League: 57-2. FAC: 7-0. FLC:0-0. Others: 0-0. Total: 64-2.

Kidderminster Harriers	1911
Shrewsbury Town	

Honours: Represented the Southern League v. the Football League on 2 occasions.

Regarded as a *"good man"* and a *"thorough trier"* to have in the team. Ambrose was renowned for his prodigious kicking, it was once said that he fired a penalty shot clear out of the ground!
Debut: 1. 9.1909 v. Watford (H). 4-3. SLDiv. 1.

HASTY Patrick Joseph

(C.F.) Striker
b. Belfast, Nth. Ireland 17.3.1932

Tooting & Mitchum	1956
Leyton Orient	Jul 1958
Q.P.R.	Oct 1959

Football League: 1-0. FAC: 0-0. FLC: 0-0. Others: 0-0. Total: 1-0.

Tooting & Mitchum	1960
Aldershot	Mar 1961
Guildford	1962

Honours: Northern Ireland Amateur International cap.

Paddy made just one appearance turning out for Q.P.R. on the last day of the 1959/60 season.
Debut: 4. 5.1960 v. Wrexham (A). 1-1. Div. 3.

HATELEY Mark Wayne

Striker 6' 1" 11st 7lbs
b. Liverpool 7. 11.1961

Coventry City		Dec 1978
Detroit Express, U.S.A.	(Loan)	1980
Portsmouth	(£190,000)	Jun 1983
AC Milan, Italy	(£915,000)	Jun 1984
Monaco, France		1987
Glasgow Rangers	(£500,000)	Jul 1990
Q.P.R.	(£1,500,000)	Nov 1995

Premier/ Football League: 27-3. FAC: 5-2. FLC: 1-0. Others: 1-0. Total: 34-5.

Leeds United	(Loan)	Aug 1996
Glasgow Rangers	(£300,000)	Mar 1997
Hull City		Aug 1997
Ross County		1999

Honours: 7 England youth caps. 10 U21 caps. 32 full caps. 5 Scottish championship medals. 1 runners-up medal. 3 Scottish Cup medals. 3 Scottish League Cup medals. 1 French championship medal.

The son of the ex Liverpool player, Tony Hateley, Mark had been groomed for England stardom. Q.P.R. chased him in 1983 along with Portsmouth, but the latter club won his signature. The nickname of 'Attilla' was born in Italy, during his debut for AC Milan when he was sent off. He scored five goals early on in his career and his headwork was reminiscent of his father. After injuries and lost form, things started to come together with the Rangers - Glasgow version - as Mark hammered in 113 goals in 220 matches. However, at his next club, Q.P.R., he was a great disappointment, as he was at Hull City, both as player and manager, and he was sacked in 1999.
Debut: 29.11.1995 v. Aston Villa (A).1-1.FLCup 4th Rd.

HATTON Cyril

(I.L.) Striker 5' 8" 11st 0lbs
b. Grantham, Lincs. 14. 9.1918 d. Grantham 3. 7.1987

Nottingham Corinthians		
Grantham Co-op		
Notts County		Jul 1936
Q.P.R.	(£1,000+Player)	Apl 1946

Football League:162-64. FAC: 15-7. FLC: 0-0. Others: 0-0. Total:177-71.

Chesterfield	Jun 1953
Grantham Town	May 1954

Honours: 3rd Div. (South) championship medal. 3rd Div.(South) runners-up medal.

Cyril was a schemer and scorer of goals who was at the heart of the 1949 championship side. The general of the team he was an excellent servant of the club for seven years.

Hatton was introduced to Q.P.R. during the war years and when normal football resumed he was exchanged for goalkeeper Harry Brown plus a small transfer fee. His last post was that of player/manager plus secretary of Grantham Town. He later bought a shop and became a newsagent in his home town.
Debut: 31. 8.1946 v. Watford (H). 2-1. Div. 3 (S).

HAWKINS Bertram W.

(C.F.) Striker
b. Bristol 29. 9.1923

De Veys F.C.		
Bristol Rovers		Aug 1947
Bristol City		May 1949
Bath City	(Loan)	1950
West Ham United		Sep 1951
Q.P.R.		Jun 1953

Football League: 8-3. FAC: 0-0. FLC: 0-0. Others: 0-0.
Total: 8-3.

Cheltenham Town	1954

Bert enjoyed a brief but spectacular spell at Upton Park, but it came to an end at Q.P.R. He started with a pre-season injury in a practice match, and after three matches and one goal, he sustained another injury. Without a reserve centre forward, manager Jack Taylor was put on the spot. After four weeks Hawkins rejoined the squad but his return did not solve the centre forward problem. During the 1954 close season he was transferred to Cheltenham Town.
Debut: 19. 8.1953 v. Brighton & H.A.(H). 1-2. Div.3 (S).

HAWLEY Frederick W.

(C.H.) CD 5' 10" 12st 0lbs
b. Alverston, Derbyshire 27. 8.1890 d. 1954

Derby Midland		
Ripley Athletic		
Sheffield United	(£70)	1912
Coventry City	(£350)	May 1919
Birmingham City	(£250)	Jan 1920
Swindon Town		May 1920
Bristol City		Mar 1923
Brighton & Hove Albion	(£350)	Jun 1925
Q.P.R.		May 1926

Football League: 29-1. FAC: 0-0. FLC: 0-0. Others: 0-0.
Total: 29-1.

Loughborough Corintians	Apl 1928

Fred was a well built pivot who entered professional football with Sheffield United before the 1st World War. During hostilities he worked in a munitions factory guesting for various clubs, notably Coventry City, Birmingham City, Derby County and both Nottingham teams.
Debut: 28. 8.1926 v. Crystal Palace (A). 1-2. Div.3 (S).

HAYWOOD Adam B.

(I.R.) Mid 5' 5" 10st 10lbs
b. Burton-on-Trent 23. 3.1875 d. 1932

Anslow Gate School	
Burton Ivanhoe	
Swadlincote	
Burton Wanderers	1891
Woolwich Arsenal	1896
Glossop North End	1899
Q.P.R.	1899

Southern League: 17-3. FAC: 10-6. FLC: 0-0. Others: 0-0.
Total: 27-9.

New Brompton	1900
Wolverhampton Wanderers	1901
W.B.A.	1905
Blackpool	1907
Crystal Palace	1908

Honours: Represented the United League v. Thames & Medway Combination. Represented the North v. South.

A much travelled player who not only played in all the forward positions but right and left half as well. Adam had all the qualities that these positions demanded, and had a keen eye for half a chance, plus a fierce shot, and could rough it with the biggest and strongest in the game. Haywood became the Crystal Palace player/coach and then retired from the game in 1912.
Debut: 9. 9.1899 v. Tottenham H. (A). 0-1. SLDiv. 1.

HAZELL Anthony Phillip

Def 5' 9" 12st 7lbs
b. High Wycombe 19. 9.1947

Q.P.R.	Oct 1964

Football League:369-4. FAC: 18-0. FLC: 28-1. Others: 0-0. Total:416-5.

Millwall	Dec 1974
Crystal Palace	Nov 1978
Charlton Athletic	Sep 1979

Honours: 5 England youth caps. 3rd Div. Championship medal. League Cup winners medal. 2 Div. 2 runners-up medals.

A loyal and dedicated defender who was both solid and skilful. Tony was a fast and skilful defender who added steel to the Ranger's defence and was a hard ball-winner. Tony joined the club at 15 years of age, and gave outstanding service to Q.P.R. over a period of ten years, during which time he made no less than 416 first team appearances. His least number of League games was during his final season at Loftus Road (12), but on four occasions he made over 40, being ever-present three times and missing just one match in the 1972/73 season. Remarkably he was on the playing staff of Millwall, Crystal Palace and Charlton Athletic when they each won promotion. After three years at the Valley, he retired from football and became an Insurance salesman, before working for B.T.

Debut: 3.10.1964 v. Gillingham (A). 2-2. Div.3.

HAZELL Robert Joseph

CD 6' 1" 14st 7lbs
b. Kingston, Jamaica 14. 6.1949

Wolverhampton Wanderers		May 1977
Q.P.R.	(£240,000)	Sep 1979

Football League:106-8. FAC: 6-1. FLC: 11-0. Others: 0-0. Total:123-9.

Leicester City	(£100,000)	Sep 1983
Kilfa AIK, Sweden	(Loan)	May 1985
Wolverhampton Wanderers	(Loan)	Sep 1985
Luton Town	(Trial)	Aug 1986
Leeds United	(Trial)	Oct 1986
Reading	(Trial)	Nov 1986
Port Vale		Dec 1986

Honours: 2 England youth caps. 1 U21 cap. 1 B cap. 2nd Div. championship medal. F.A.Cup runners-up medal.

For such a big man, Bob's delicate control of the ball during a match was a surprise. Generally regarded as his best performance for the Rangers was in the 1982 FA Cup semi-final when he nullified the effects of West Brom's Cyrille Regis. Bob was very popular with the spectators at Loftus Road but unfortunately he had a disagreement off the pitch over training tactics and his contract was annulled after four years at Loftus Road. The same thing happened at Leicester and he was again transferred. Bob's final club, Port Vale, released him when he fell victim to a back injury in January 1989, and he was given a free transfer in June that year. Hazell moved to Walsall, and started working for the Birmingham Social Services in 1999.

Debut: 5. 9.1979 v. Bradford City (A).2-0. FL Cup.

HEATH William J.

Def
b. Stepney, London 26. 6.1920
Q.P.R. Sep 1945
Football League: 96-3. FAC: 5-0. FLC: 0-0. Others: 0-0. Total:101-3.

Although Bill played in many positions, he was noted mainly as a defender. During the war years he played in any position he was asked to and therefore became known, in modern terms, as a utility player. Bill carried out each task with a certain aplomb and was the first reserve for whoever was injured.
Debut: 14. 9.1946 v. Reading (H). 2-0. Div. 3 (S).

HEATHCOTE Wilfred

(C.F.) Striker
b. Hemsworth, Nr. Dewsbury 29. 6.1911
Millwall 1942
Q.P.R. 1943
Football League: 5-1. FAC: 0-0. FLC: 0-0. Others: 0-0. Total: 5-1.
Millwall 1946

Wilf was a school teacher by profession who played football for a hobby. He was a great favourite of the spectators and became the top scorer for Q.P.R. during the war years, scoring some 90 goals in approximately 105 appearances. Wilf also played many wartime representative matches, in a goalscoring role. He moved on to Millwall at the end of the war in exchange for Reg Dudley, but soon faded out of League football.
Debut: 31. 8.1946 v. Watford (H). 2-1. Div. 3. (S).

HEBDEN George Horace Robert

G 5' 10" 12st 2lbs
b. West Ham, London 2. 6.1900d. Leicester 16. 8.1973
Clapton
Barking Town
Leicester City May 1920
Q.P.R. May 1925
Football League: 59-0. FAC: 4-0. FLC: 0-0. Others: 0-0. Total: 63-0.
Gillingham May 1927
Q.P.R. Nov 1929
Football League: 1-0. FAC: 0-0. FLC: 0-0. Others: 0-0. Total: 1-0.

Honours: 2 schoolboy caps.

George's future was severely jeopardised by wartime service during his teens. He was first in the Royal Navy and then in the Merchant Marines, and reported as being torpedoed on four occasions. After the 1st World War he was elevated from London amateur football to the professional level with Leicester City. By 1922 he had made the senior squad with a string of instinctively fearless performances. His sojourn at Q.P.R. was not so good, with the club having to apply for re-election. When he retired, in 1930, he initially ran his own garage business in Ilford, Essex.
Debut: 29. 8.1925 v. Gillingham (A). 0-3. Div.3. (S).

HEINOLA Antti Juhani

(L.B.) Def 5' 10" 12st 6lbs
b. Helsinki, Finland 20. 3.1973
HJK Helsinki, Finland
Emmem, Germany
Heracles, Holland
Q.P.R. (£150,000) Jan 1998
Football League: 34-0. FAC: 1-0. FLC: 3-0. Others: 0-0. Total: 38-0.

Honours: 8 senior caps for Finland plus U21 caps.

Antti had good pace going forward while remaining sound at the back. A fractured cheekbone and a serious head injury in the second half of 1998/99 put paid to the rest of the season and he struggled to win his place back in the senior squad. Suddenly, in 2001, Antti announced his retirement from the game and returned to Finland to study for an Economics degree at Helsinki University.
Debut: 24. 1.1998 v. Notts Forest (H). 0-1. Div. 1.

HELLAWELL Michael Stephen

(O.R.) Wing
b. Keighley, Yorkshire 30. 6.1938
Salts F.C.
Huddersfield Town Jul 1954
Q.P.R. Aug 1955
Football League: 45-7. FAC: 3-1. FLC: 2-0. Others: 0-0. Total: 50-8.
Birmingham City (Exchange deal) May 1957
Sunderland (£27,500) Jan 1965
Huddersfield Town (£1,500) Sep 1966
Peterborough United Dec 1968
Broomsgrove Rovers Aug 1969

Honours: 2 England caps. Fairs Cup runners-up medal. Football League Cup winners medal. Represented a Div. 3. X1.

A red haired winger with an astonishing turn of speed over the first 20 to 25 yards. Mike Hellawell was also a fine cricketer and played a match for Warwickshire. At Q.P.R. he was exchanged for Bill Finney, another winger. When retirement came in May 1971, he set himself up in business, running a shop in his home town of Keighley.
Debut: 25. 2.1956 v. Exeter City (H). 1-0. Div.3 (S).

HERRERA Roberto

(L.B.) Def. 5' 7" 10st 6lbs
b. Torbay, Devon 12. 6.1970

Q.P.R.		Mar 1988

Football League: 6-0. FAC: 0-0. FLC: 3-0. Others: 2-0.
Total: 11-0.

Torquay United	(Loan)	Mar 1992
Torquay United	(Loan)	Oct 1992
Fulham		Oct 1993
Torquay United	(£30,000)	Aug 1998
Leyton Orient		Oct 2001
Merthyr Tidfil		2002

Roberto is a flamboyant character whose pace and control made him a firm favourite of the crowd at his various clubs. An unusual Q.P.R. post-war sequence that Roberto holds is the 145 reserve matches that he played for the club, second only in number to Maurice Doyle.

Debut: 14. 1.1989 v. Wimbledon (A). 0-1. Div. 1.

HIGGINS Alexander John

Mid 5' 9" 11st 6lbs
b. Sheffield, Yorkshire 22. 7.1981

Sheffield Wednesday	Nov 1998
Q.P.R.	Mar 2001

Football League: 1-0. FAC: 0-0. FLC: 0-0. Others: 0-0.
Total: 1-0.

Chester City	Nov 2001
Stalybridge Celtic	Mar 2002
Boston United	Nov 2002

Played in the last nine minutes of the last game of the 2000/01 season at Molineux. This being the only Q.P.R. appearance makes his the second shortest career with the club. Became out of contract that summer and was released.

Debut: 6. 5.2001 v. Wolverhampton W. (A).1-1. Div.1.

HIGGINS Dennis

(R.B.) Def
b.

Q.P.R.	1913

Southern League: 26-0. FAC: 4-0. FLC: 0-0. Others: 0-0.
Total: 30-0.

Honours: Represented the South v. the North.

Dennis was an amateur who joined the "Sportsmen Battalion" during the 1st World War, and became a captain. Unfortunately he was so badly injured at Ypres, in Flanders, that he never played again.

Debut: 21. 3.1913 v. Reading (A). 0-1. SLDiv. 1.

HIGGINS Ronald Valentine

(C.F.) Striker
b. Silvertown, East Ham, London 14. 2.1923

Green & Siley Weir Works	
Leyton Orient	1949
Tonbridge	1950
Brighton & Hove Albion	Dec 1951
Q.P.R.	Jan 1953

Football League: 3-1. FAC: 0-0. FLC: 0-0. Others: 0-0.
Total: 3-1.

Sittingbourne	1953
Canterbury City	1954

Ron was a fitter in a London shipyard and was a part time professional, who was part of the deal that took Addinall and Gilberg to Brighton. Developing into a prolific goalscorer at Tonbridge, in 1951, he became the subject of many clubs fighting for his signature. Ron didn't enjoy the best of luck at any of his Football League clubs and soon returned to the non-League scene.

Debut: 28. 2.1953 v. Brighton & H.A. (H).3-3.Div.3 (S).

HILL Charles John

(L.H.) Mid
b. Cardiff, Wales 6. 9.1918 d. December 1998

Cardiff City	Jun 1938
Torquay United	Jul 1947
Q.P.R.	Mar 1949

Football League: 21-1. FAC: 0-0. FLC: 0-0. Others: 0-0.
Total: 21-1.

Swindon Town	Sep 1950
Barry Town	

Charlie, nicknamed 'midge', was such of small stature that he was lost when played as a centre forward, nevertheless he scored his goal from this position. His time was during the period of the 'utility player'.

Debut: 2. 4.1949 v. W.B.A. (A). 1-1. Div. 2.

HILL Gordon Alexander

(O.L.) Wing 5' 7" 10st 12lbs
b. Sunbury, Mddx. 1. 4.1954

Ashford youth club		
Q.P.R.	(Trial)	
Southend United	(Trial)	
Slough Town		
Southall		
Millwall		Jan 1973
Chicago Sting, U.S.A.		Apl 1975
Manchester United	(£70,000)	Nov 1975
Derby County	(£250,000)	Apl 1978
Q.P.R.	(£175,000)	Nov 1979

Football League: 14-1. FAC: 1-0. FLC: 1-0. Others: 0-0.
Total: 16-1.

Montreal Manic, Canada	Apl 1981
Chicago Sting, U.S.A.	May 1982
New York Arrows, U.S.A.	
Kansas Comets, U.S.A.	
Tacoma Stars, U.S.A.	
HJK Helsinki, Finland	
Twenty Enschede, Holland	
AFC Bournemouth (Trial)	
Northwich Victoria (Caretaker/Manager)	1986
Stafford Rangers	Aug 1987
Northwich Victoria(Player/Manager)	1988
Radcliff Borough	Mar 1990

Honours: England amateur cap. Youth, U23, England B. 6 full England caps. FA.Cup runners-up medal. F.A.Cup winners medal.

At home on either wing he was tricky, fast and possessed a shot that was like a thunderbolt. Rejected by Q.P.R. in the early sixties for refusing to get his hair cut, the club had to pay a substantial sum to acquire him in the late seventies. Gordon was something of a flamboyant character and temperamental. Tommy Docherty bought him on three occasions, first when manager of Manchester United, then Derby County, and lastly at Loftus Road for a short period. Gordon was last heard of living and working in Tampa, Florida, as a tennis and football coach.

Debut: 1.12.1979 v. Cambridge United (A).1-2. Div. 2.

HILL Joseph

(I.R.) Mid

b. Sheffield, Yorkshire in 1906

Leeds United	1927
Torquay United	Jan 1929
Mansfield Town	1930
Newark Town	1931
Barnsley	Feb 1932
Q.P.R.	1932

Football League: 15-1. FAC: 1-0. FLC: 0-0. Others: 0-0. Total: 16-1.

Stockport County	1933
Walsall	1938

Honours: Notts senior cup winners medal. 3rd Div. (North) Cup winners medal. 3rd Div. (North) League championship medal.

Joe had the ability to find space and was a clever dribbler, possessing a truly splendid shot. He enjoyed the most successful period of his career at Stockport County where he hit a hat trick on his debut for the club in that famous 13-0 thrashing of Halifax Town. When Joe retired from football he worked as an assistant to a bookmaker in Yorkshire for many years.

Debut: 1. 9.1932 v. Aldershot (H). 2-2. Div. 3. (S).

HILL Leonard G.

G 5' 11" 12st 0lbs

b. Islington, London 15. 2.1899 d. Southend 1979

Cranley Rovers	
Southend United	1919
Q.P.R.	1920

Football League:162-0. FAC: 14-0. FLC: 0-0. Others: 0-0. Total:176-0.

Southampton	Jun 1925
Rochdale	Jun 1926
Lincoln City	Jul 1927
Grays Thurrock United	Jul 1929

Honours: League v. The Army. F.A.X1 v. Oxford University.

A survivor of the Great War, Hill cheated death on a couple of occasions before he was invalided out of the army with a suspected fractured skull. Len then embarked on a somewhat safer occupation, that of a goalkeeper, proving to be a fine and reliable custodian. On his retirement from football, in 1930, he worked as a cricket coach at Watford Grammar school, and in 1933 he was reported to be coaching at the Hercules sports club in Utrecht, Holland.

Debut: 4. 9.1920 v. Watford (A). 2-0. Div. 3.

HILL William L.

(O.R.) Wing
b. Uxbridge, Mddx. 9. 6.1930
Uxbridge
Q.P.R. 1951
Football League: 10-1. FAC: 1-0. FLC: 0-0. Others: 0-0.
Total: 11-1.
Ramsgate 1952

William's one season at Q.P.R. was that when they were relegated from the 2nd Division to the 3rd Division (South). Billy seemed to excel in the reserves but couldn't seem to pull it off in the senior squad. He was released at the end of the season.
Debut: 1.12.1951 v. Leicester City (A) 0-4 Div.2.

HIRST Henry

(H.B.) Mid 5' 8" 11st 7lbs
b. Horbury, Yorkshire 24.10.1899
Rotherham County
P.N.E. Aug 1923
Q.P.R. May 1925
Football League: 26-0. FAC: 4-1. FLC: 0-0. Others: 0-0.
Total: 30-1.
Charlton Athletic Jun 1926
Thames Association 1927

At Q.P.R. Henry had the longest spell of first team football than at any of his other clubs. He filled in at centre half as well as at wing half during the club's seond re-election season.
Debut: 5. 9.1925 v. Merthyr Town (H). 1-1. Div.3. (S).

HITCH Alfred

(C.H.) CD 5' 8" 11st 3lbs
b. Walsall, Staffs. In 1878 d. Uxbridge in 1962
Walsall Unity
Walsall Oct 1897
Wellington Town Jan 1898
Thames Ironworks Sep 1898
Grays United Dec 1898
Q.P.R. May 1899
Southern League: 49-4. FAC: 12-3. FLC: 0-0. Others: 0-0.
Total: 61-7.
Notts Forest May 1901
Q.P.R. May 1902
Southern League:118-13. FAC: 4-0. FLC:0-0. Others: 0-0.
Total:122-13.
Watford May 1906

Honours: North v. South England trial match.

Alf was a very astute and clever player who in the days when heading the ball was classed as 'not fashionable', and was noted in the football paper of the time, Bells Weekly, as a, *"Greatly gifted player when heading the ball out of defence."*

The England selectors took note of him, however, honours eluded him, probably because of his unconventional style of playing the game. With his retirement from football he opened a tobacconist shop in St. Albans, which he had for many years.
Debut: 7.10.1899 v. Bristol City (A). 3-5. SLDiv. 1.

HITCHCOCK Ernest

(C.F.) Striker
b.
Aston Villa 1906
Q.P.R. 1907
Southern League:2-2. FAC: 0-0. FAC: 0-0. Others: 0-0.
Total: 2-2.
Manchester City 1908

Ernie played and scored in the opening two matches of the 1907/08 season, but never played again! The arrival of Walker put paid to that, for the newcomer made the position his own.
Debut: 2. 9.1907 v. Tottenham Hot. (H). 3-3. SLDiv. 1.

HODGE Steven Brian

Mid 5' 7" 10st 3lbs
b. Nottingham 25.10.1962
Nottingham & District schools
Notts County boys
Nottingham Forest Oct 1980
Aston Villa (£450,000) Aug 1985
Tottenham Hotspur (£650,000) Dec 1986
Nottingham Forest (£550,000) Aug 1988
Leeds United (£900,000) Jul 1991
Derby County (Loan) Aug 1994
Q.P.R. (£300,000) Oct 1994
Premier League: 15-0. FAC: 1-0. FLC: 0-0. Others: 0-0.
Total: 16-0.
Watford Dec 1995

Honours: 24 England caps. 8 U21 caps. 2 League Cup winners medals. F.A.Cup winners medal. 1st Div. championship medal.

Steve was a left sided defensive midfield player who had a strikers instinct around the penalty area. He had a fierce shot and the gift of slipping away from defenders.
Debut: 29.10.1994 v.Aston Villa (H). 2-0. PL.

HOLD Oscar

(C.F.) Striker 5' 9" 11st 0lbs
b. Carlton, Barnsley 19.10.1918
Regent Street Congregational
Denaby United
Manchester United 'A'

Barnsley		Aug 1937
Aldershot		Apl 1939
Norwich City		Mar 1946
Notts County	(£6,000)	Oct 1948
Chelmsford City		Aug 1949
Everton		Feb 1950
Q.P.R.		Feb 1952

Football League: 5-1. FAC: 0-0. FLC: 0-0. Others: 0-0. Total: 5-1.

March Town		Jul 1953

Oscar had a delicate one touch style of play which was his hallmark. Although he was known more as a manager and a coach in his later, football life. When his playing days were over he became the manager of March Town, then Gainsborough Trinity and finally Wisbech Town. In 1960 Oscar became the F.A. coach in Nigeria, then the manager of Cambridge City a year later. The following year he took over the managership of Doncaster Rovers, and in 1964 the same at Fenerbache, Instanbul, followed by coach to Ankara the following year. His next job was that of coach to the National Sporting Club, Jeddah in1967, followed by the same role at Apollon, Cyprus in 1972. Oscar also coached in Kuwait in 1974 and finally in Apollon, Cyprus, again, in 1982. He was last heard of living in retirement in Cyprus.
Debut: 8. 3.1952 v. Southampton (H). 2-1. Div. 2.

HOLLINS John William

(R.H.) Mid 5' 8" 11st 7lbs
b. Guildford, Surrey 16. 7.1946
Guildford schools
Guildford Junior football

Chelsea		Jul 1963
Q.P.R.	(£80,000)	Jun 1975

Football League:151-6. FAC: 11-1. FLC: 13-0. Others: 8-0 Total:183-7.

Arsenal	(£40,000)	Jul 1979
Chelsea	As the player coach	Jun 1983

Honours: 8 England youth caps. 4 Football league caps. 6 B caps. 12 U23 caps. 1 England senior cap. F.A.Cup winners medal. F.A.Cup runners-up medal. League Cup runner-up medal. European Cup winners medal. European Cup runners-up medal. F.A.Charity Shield runners-up medal. 2nd Div. Championship medal.

John came from a family of four brothers, three of whom played League football, as did his father and grandfather. His brother Dave was a Welsh International and his father played in goal for Stoke City and Wolves. John was an outstanding attacking winghalf whose running, tackling and passing was always crisp. A totally dedicated player who would always give 100% in whatever match he was playing in. In 1985, he became the manager of Chelsea until 1988. In 1995 he became the reserve team coach at Q.P.R. until taking on the manager's job at Swansea in 1998.
Debut: 16. 8.1975 v. Liverpool (H). 2-0. Div. 1.

HOLLOWAY Ian Scott

Mid 5' 7" 10st 0lbs
b. Kingswood, Gloucestershire 12. 3.1963
Northavon boys

Bristol Rovers		Mar 1981
Wimbledon	(£35,000)	Jul 1985
Brentford	(£25,000)	Mar 1986
Torquay United	(Loan)	Jan 1987
Bristol Rovers	(£10,000)	Aug 1987
Q.P.R.	(£230,000)	Aug 1991

Football League:147-4. FAC: 8-1. FLC: 13-0. Others: 2-0. Total:170-5.

Honours: 3rd Div. championship medal. Leyland Daf Trophy runners-up medal.

The son of Bill Holloway, a well respected local amateur footballer, young 'Olly ' broke into the Bristol Rover's side during the 1983 season. He was never far from the centre of the action and his enthusiasm and commitment caused much interest from elsewhere. Eventually, Ian was tempted to Loftus Road and rejoined Gerry Francis at Q.P.R., where he played alongside a number of former Bristol Rovers team-mates including Dennis Bailey, Gary Penrice, Devon White and Steve Yates. Ian was a grafter with an aggressive tackle and he was also a good distributer of the ball. Holloway became the manager of Bristol Rovers in 1996, before following Gerry Francis as manager at Q.P.R. in February 2001. Ian is a great credit to his profession, on and off the field, and remains one of the club's most popular of former players. There can be no finer example for any young player to emulate than that of Ian Holloway.
Debut: 17. 9.1991 v. Arsenal (A). 1-1. Div. 1.

HOOPER Harold

(R.B.) Def 5' 8" 12st 0lbs
b. Brierley Hill 18. 8.1900

Brierley Hill Alliance	
Southampton	May 1921
Leicester City	May 1924
Q.P.R.	May 1926

Football League: 16-0. FAC: 0-0. FLC: 0-0. Others: 0-0.
Total: 16-0.

A dour and resolute defender who was mainly a reserve wherever he went. Harold was the cousin of Charlie Roberts, the Manchester United and England defender.
Debut: 28. 8.1926 v. Crystal Palace (A) 1-2. Div. 3. (S).

HOTEN Ralph Vincent

(I.L.) Mid 5' 11" 12st 4lbs
b. Pinxton, Notts. 27.12.1896d.Wellingborough 1. 2.1978

Pinxton F.C.	
Notts County	1918
Portsmouth	1920
Luton Town	1922
Northampton Town	1924
Q.P.R.	1930

Football League: 9-4. FAC: 0-0. FLC: 0-0. Others: 0-0.
Total: 9-4.

Honours: Represented the Southern League v. the Welsh League

A respected, good, all round Third Division player who spent his last football days at Q.P.R. Ralph scored on his debut for the club and in his last match.
Debut: 30. 8.1930 v. Thames Ass. (H).3-0. Div. 3 (S).

HOWE Ernest James

(C.H.) CD 6' 3" 12st 12lbs
b. Chiswick, Mddx. 15. 2.1953

Crystal Palace		
Croydon Amateurs		
Hounslow		
Fulham		Oct 1973
Q.P.R.	(£50,000)	Dec 1977

Football League: 89-3. FAC: 12-3. FLC: 5-0. Others: 0-0.
Total:106-6.

Portsmouth	(£50,000)	Jun 1982

Ernie was one of the first players to have his transfer fee set by a tribunal, being valued at £50,000, which was far below Fulham's estimation. Portsmouth also paid a £50,000 transfer fee for his signature. He was an excellent header of the ball and very tricky on the ground, whilst memorable goals were scored by him from set pieces. Injury forced him prematurely into coaching, initially at Wokingham. Later Ernie joined Farnham Town and then Woking, before becoming the Basingstoke manager in 1994.
Debut: 17.12.1977 v. Liverpool (A). 0-1. Div. 1.

HOWE Harold G.

(O.L.) Wing 5' 6" 11st 2lbs
b. Hemel Hempstead 9. 4.1906 d. 1976

Watford	
Q.P.R.	1929

Football League: 68-13. FAC: 6-1. FLC: 0-0. Others: 0-0.
Total: 74-14.

Crystal Palace	May 1933
Rochdale	1934
Dartford	1935

Harold was a left footed player with a phenomenal shot. Plucked out of the Watford reserve team and sharing the left wing spot with about half-a-dozen others, he helped the club to 3rd position in the League.
Debut: 19.10.1929 v. Clapton Orient (H). 1-1. Div.3 (S).

HOWES Arthur

G 5' 11" 13st 0lbs
b. Leicester in 1876

Leicester Waverley		
Leicester Fosse		Sep 1896
Reading		Nov 1897
Lincoln City	(Trial)	Mar 1898
Leicester Fosse		Sep 1898
Brighton United		Sep 1899
Dumbarton		1900
Dundee		1901
Brighton & Hove Albion		Sep 1902
Q.P.R.		1904

Football League: 49-0. FAC: 4-0. FLC: 0-0. Others: 0-0.
Total: 53-0.

Alert and agile, Arthur was usually the reserve to the first team keepers, Collins and then Kingsley. Finally, on earning the role as first choice 'keeper, he was so severely injured that he never played in a first class game again.
Debut: 12.11.1904 v. Luton Town (A). 1-1. SLDiv. 1.

HUCKER Peter I.

G 6' 4" 13st 0lbs
b. Hampstead, London 28.10.1959
London & District schools

Q.P.R.		Jul 1977

Football League:160-0. FAC: 11-0. FLC: 12-0. Others: 4-0. Total:187-0.

Cambridge United	(Loan)	1978
Oxford United		Feb 1987
W.B.A.	(Loan)	Jan 1988
Manchester United	(Loan)	1988
Millwall		1989
Aldershot		1990
AFC Bournemouth		1991
Farnborough Town		1991
Enfield		1992

Honours: 2 England U21 caps. 2nd Div. championship medal. FACup runners-up medal.

Early in his career, at Q.P.R., he found his way blocked, in turn by Phil Parkes, Derek Richardson and Chris Woods. But Peter finally made his League debut in the last game of the 1980/81 season. Named 'Man of the Match' in the Cup Final of 1982, he won two England U-21 caps as an over-aged player in 1984. A sound and solid goalkeeper who was ever-present in the Q.P.R. side from January 2nd 1982 until September 21st 1985, apart for one FACup match.

After several loan periods and other brief moves, he switched to the non-League circuit, in 1991, and three years later moved away from football and into the Dairy business.
Debut: 2. 5.1981 v. Shrewsbury Town (A). 3-3. Div. 2.

HUDSON Stanley R.

(O.L.) Wing
b. Fulham, London 10. 2.1923. d. 1951

Q.P.R.	1948

Football League: 22-7. FAC: 1-0. FLC: 0-0. Others: 0-0. Total: 23-7.

A fast and tricky winger who by his direct play and shooting became the darling of the fans. Sadly he died prematurely at the age of 28.
Debut: 10. 9.1948 v. Brentford (H). 2-0. Div. 2.

HUMPHREYS Percy

(I.L.) Mid 5' 7" 12st 6lbs
b. Cambridge 3.12.1880 d. Stepney, London 13.4.1959
Cambridge St. Marys
Cambridgeshire

Q.P.R.		May 1900

Southern League: 27-9. FAC: 4-3. FLC: 0-0. Others: 0-0. Total: 31-12.

Notts County		Jul 1901
Leicester Fosse		Jun 1907
Chelsea	(£350)	Feb 1908
Tottenham Hotspur		Dec 1909
Leicester Fosse		Oct 1911
West Hartlepool		1913
Norwich City		

Honours: 1 England cap. 1 Football League cap.

A strongly built player described as full of class and dash. Percy, a probing and thrustful forward with a dexterous dribble and a dangerous shot. At the beginning of the 1st World War, he was due to take up an appointment as a player/coach with a Swiss club. However, this role didn't materialise, so he returned to England and played just three games as an adieu to the senior game, with Norwich City in 1915. Percy's death was registered as suicide.
Debut: 8. 9.1900 v. Swindon Town (H). 7-1. SLDiv. 1.

HUNT Ronald G.

(C.H.) CD 5'11" 11st 10lbs
b. Paddington, London 19.12.1945
West Ham United
Reading

Q.P.R.	Mar 1963

Football League:219-1. FAC: 14-0. FLC: 22-0. Others: 0-0. Total:255-1.

Honours: League Cup winners medal. 3rd Div. championship medal. 2 2nd Div. runners-up medals.

Ron was a ground staff boy with West Ham United and later, after moving to Slough, in Buckinghamshire, he joined Reading F.C. He was recommended to Q.P.R. by Dave Dorman of the Pathfinders club, in Slough, a nursery team for young talent. Ron turned out to be a loyal club man and a very fine central defender, and his time at Loftus Road spanned ten years during which time he made over 250 first team appearances. A knee injury shortened his career and he retired in 1973. Ron Hunt is probably best remembered for his foray into the West Brom penalty area towards the end of the League Cup final in 1967. Following his collision with the Albion goalkeeper, the ball ran loose to Mark Lazarus who netted that famous winning goal.
Debut: 28.12.1964 v. Bristol Rovers (H). 3-1. Div. 3.

HURRELL William P.

(I.F.) Mid
b. Dundee, Scotland 28. 1.1920
Raith Rovers
Millwall Jan 1946
Q.P.R. Jul 1953
Football League: 6-1. FAC: 3-2. FLC: 0-0. Others: 0-0
Total: 9-3.
Tunbridge Wells 1954

Bill came to Q.P.R. as a stop gap, being 33 years old and at the end of his career. He played mostly in the reserves and filled in, in the senior squad, when injuries required. He was a skilful and tricky player.
Debut: 16. 9.1953 v. Southampton (H). 1-3. Div. 3 (S).

HURST William

(C.F.) Striker
b. Newcastle
Walker Celtic
Derby County 1922
Q.P.R. 1924
Football League: 8-4. FAC: 0-0. FLC: 0-0. Others: 0-0.
Total: 8-4.

Bill was a reserve centre forward and scored two goals on his debut for the club. After such a bright start he gradually faded from the picture and left at the same time as manager, Ned Liddell, during the 1924 close season.
Debut: 7. 3.1925 v. Luton Town (H). 3-1. Div. 3. (S).

IMPEY Andrew Rodney

RWB 5' 8" 11st 2lbs
b. Hammersmith, London 13. 9.1971
Yeading
Q.P.R. (£35,000) Jun 1990
Football League:187-13. FAC: 10-1. FLC: 16-3. Others: 2-1.
Total:215-18.
West Ham United (£1,300,000) Sep 1997
Leicester City (£1,600,000) Nov 1998

Honours: England U21 cap.

Andy, is an outstandingly good player, reflected in the transfer fees that he has twice commanded, who is aggressive, strong and very quick, and able to play on either flank. He was popular with the fans being voted the 'Player of the year' in 1995. He was a fairly regular first team player for five of his six playing seasons at Loftus Road.

During the 1992/93 season he missed appearing in just one League match (including one as substitute). Andy moved on to West Ham in 1997, after a toe injury delayed his transfer, for a £1m plus fee, but after only 25 League matches soon became a Leicester City player, at an even higher cost.
Debut: 23.10.1991 v. Norwich City (A).2-1.2nd Rd.FMC

INGHAM Anthony

(L.B.) Def 5' 10" 11st 5lbs
b. Harrogate, Yorkshire 18.12.1925
Harrogate school
Harrogate Town

Leeds United		Apl 1947
Q.P.R.	(£5,000)	Jun 1950

Football League:514-3. FAC: 30-0. FLC: 4-0. Others: 7-0. Total:555-3.

Honours: Represented the 3rd Div. (South) v. 3rd Div. (North).

Tony turned out to be arguably the best buy that manager Mangnall bought for the club. He turned out to be a fine captain and a first class defender who became a favourite of the crowd at Loftus Road. Tony was ever-present from February 25th 1956 until September 17th 1961, a total of 274 matches, and played in the senior squad from 1950 until 1963. With his 514 League matches, and a staggering 555 matches in total he comfortably holds the club record for the most appearances. With Q.P.R. as a player he played League football for 13 seasons, during which time his least number of appearances was 'only' 17 in 1951/52.

Tony made his last Q.P.R. appearance in 1963, playing in 41 League matches that season and epitomizing the term 'one club' man (despite his earlier time at Leeds United for three years or so and just three League appearances). Apart from his activities on the pitch he also served the club as that of commercial manager, when his playing days were over, and for a short period acted as club secretary. He finally became a director of the club.
Debut: 25.11.1950 v. Doncaster Rovers (H). 1-2. Div. 2.

IORFA Dominic

For 6' 1" 12st 12lbs
b. Lagos, Nigeria 1.10.1968
Royal Antwerp, Holland

Q.P.R.	(£145,000)	Mar 1990

Football League: 8-0. FAC: 0-0. FLC: 1-0. Others: 0-0. Total: 9-0.

Galatasaray, Turkey		Dec 1991
Peterborough United		Oct 1992
Southend United	(£15,000)	Aug 1994
Falkirk		Jan 1995

Honours: 3 Nigerian caps.

A tall, gangly, Nigerian International who failed to make any impression at the club. Dominic was released and moved onto several clubs on free transfers.
Debut: 5. 5.1990 v. Wimbledon (H). 2-3. Div. 1.

IVES Benjamin

(O.L.) Wing
b. Tottenham, London in 1889
Page Green Old Boys
Romford
Tufnell Park

Tottenham Hotspur	Sep 1908
Exeter City	1912
Q.P.R.	1913

Southern League: 36-3. FAC: 0-0. FLC: 0-0. Others: 0-0. Total: 36-3.

Clapton Orient	1919
Ton Pentre	Aug 1920

Ben made a promising start to his career with the club by scoring two goals on his debut. However, he soon appears to have faded from the team completely.
Debut: 19. 4.1913 v. Merthyr Tydfil (H). SLDiv. 1.

J

IVES George H.
(O.R.) Wing
b. Barton, Lincolnshire
Brentford
Q.P.R. 1937
Football League: 0-0. FAC: 0-0. FLC: 0-0. Others: 1-0.
Total: 1-0.

George played just one match for the club and that was in the 3rd Round of the Division 3 (South) Cup.
Debut: 1. 3.1938 v. Watford (H). 2-3. Div. 3. (S) Cup.

JACKMAN V.
(O.L.) Wing
b.
Q.P.R. 1912
Southern League: 3-0. FAC: 0-0. FLC: 0-0. Others: 0-0.
Total: 3-0.

Jackman used to fill in when a player was absent from the team.
Debut: 21. 3.1913 v. Reading (A). 0-1. SLDiv. 1.

JACKS George Charles
(I.L.) Mid 5' 6" 10st 8lbs
b. Stepney, London 14. 3.1946
East London schoolboys
West Ham United
Q.P.R. Jan 1964
Football League: 1-0. FAC: 0-0. FLC: 0-0. Others: 0-0.
Total: 1-0.
Millwall Jul 1965
Gillingham Jul 1972
Gravesend & Northfleet Jul 1976
Barking Jul 1981
Canterbury City Mar 1982

Honours: 3rd Div. runners-up medal. 4th Div. runners-up medal.

George was a tireless player with boundless energy who became a footballer of some repute. He was given a free transfer by Q.P.R. and was quickly snapped up by Millwall where manager Benny Fenton developed Jacks into a first class midfield man-to-man marker. He went on to work for the 'Kent Messenger' group and still lives locally.
Debut: 24. 4.1965 v. Exeter City (H). 0-0. Div. 3.

JACKSON Matthew Alan
(R.B.) Def 6' 1" 12st 12lbs
b. Leeds, Yorkshire 19.10.1971
Luton Town Jul 1990
P.N.E. (Loan) Mar 1991
Everton (£600,000) Oct 1991
Charlton Athletic (Loan) Mar 1996
Q.P.R. (Loan) Aug 1996
Football League: 7-0. FAC: 0-0. FLC: 0-0. Others: 0-0.
Total: 7-0.
Birmingham City (Loan) Oct 1996
Norwich City (£450,000) Dec 1996
Wigan Athletic Oct 2001

Honours: English Schools International. 10 U21 caps. FACup winners medal.

Matt is a polished defender, renowned for his excellent positional play and composure under pressure. He is comfortable on the ball and strikes it well. Q.P.R. tried to sign him permanently, but couldn't agree a fee, and Norwich City snapped him up, where he subsequently became team captain.
Debut: 23. 8.1996 v. Portsmouth (A). 2-1. Div. 1.

JAMES Leighton
(O.L.) Wing 5' 9" 12st 6lbs
b. Llwchwyr, Wales 16. 2.1953
Gowerton & Penyrheo schools
Swansea schoolboys
Burnley Feb 1970
Derby County (£140,000) Oct 1975
Q.P.R. (£180,000) Oct 1977
Football League: 28-4. FAC: 5-2. FLC: 0-0. Others: 0-0.
Total: 33-6.
Burnley (£165,000) Sep 1978
Swansea City (£130,000) May 1980
Sunderland Jan 1983
Bury Aug 1984
Newport County Aug 1985
Burnley Jul 1986

Honours: 12 Welsh youth caps. 7 U23 caps. 54 full Welsh caps. 2nd Div. championship medal. FA Charity Shield winners medal. Texaco Cup runners-up medal. Anglo Scottish Cup winners medal. Sherpa Van Trophy runners-up medal.

Leighton had tremendous ability, pace, two good feet, a teasing centre and an eye for a goal. He was one of the youngest players to gain full international honours, being 18 years and 238 days old when he won his first cap. In 1987 he became the manager of the Burnley youth team, the Bradford City coach in 1990 and in the same year the manager of Gainsborough Trinity. In 1993 the Morecombe managership followed, then the same job at Netherfield in 1995. In the same year he managed Darwin as well asIlkeston Town. He now owns and runs a sweet shop in Burnley, while he helps out at the local junior club - Burnley Bank Hall.
Debut: 29.10.1977 v. W.B.A. (H). 2-1. Div. 1.

JAMES Norman Leslie

(C.H.) CD 6' 2" 13st 0lbs
b. Bootle, Lancashire 25. 3.1908 d. October 1985
Bootle, St. James
Braby's Athletic
Liverpool 1929
Bradford City 1933
Q.P.R. 1936
Football League: 68-1. FAC: 5-0. FLC: 0-0. Others: 3-0.
Total: 76-21.

At Liverpool Norman was the reserve for Bradshaw and showed fine promise when he appeared. He didn't make it as a first team player at Bradford City, but at Q.P.R. he was the centre of a very fine defence put together by Billy Birrell. The team challenged strongly for promotion in 1938 and nearly made it.
Debut: 31.10.1936 v. Gillingham (H). 0-1. Div. 3. (S).

JAMES Robert Mark

Mid 5' 11" 13st 11lbs
b. Gorseinon, Wales 23. 3.1957 d. Llanelli, 19. 2.1998
Bishop Vaughan school
Swansea schoolboys
Swansea City
Arsenal (Loan)
Swansea City Apl 1973
Stoke City (£160,000) Jul 1983
Q.P.R. (£1,00,000) Oct 1984
Football League: 87-4. FAC: 5-1. FLC: 9-0. Others: 0-0.
Total:101-5.
Leicester City Jun 1987
Swansea City Jan 1988
Bradford City Aug 1990
Cardiff City Aug 1992

Honours: 11 Welsh youth caps. 3 U21 caps. 47 full caps for Wales. 4 Welsh Cup winners medals. League Cup runners-up medal. 4th Div. promotion medal. 3rd Div. promotion medal. 2nd Div. promotion medal.

A barrel-chested midfield player who was turned into a defender by Q.P.R., Robbie's enthusiasm and pace led him to prompt the attack with subtle balls from out of defence. After playing for Cardiff City he managed non-League Merthyr before returning to playing with Barry Town. He then went on to manage Weston-Super-Mare and finally Llanelli. Robbie finally took over the managership of a notable Swansea city centre public house, before his untimely death in 1998.
Debut: 17.11.1984 v. Arsenal (A). 0-1. Div. 1.

JEANNE Leon Charles

Mid 5' 8" 10st 10lbs
b. Cardiff, Wales 17.11.1980
Q.P.R. Nov 1997
Football League: 12-0. FAC: 0-0. FLC: 0-0. Others: 0-0.
Total: 12-0.
Cardiff City Jul 2001
Port Talbot Town
Barry Town Jan 2003

Honours: Youth caps for Wales. 8 U21 caps. Welsh Cup winners medal.

Early in his career, Leon showed among other things that he is a very pacey player. Not only very fast but also able to play as a wide front man. Somewhat undisciplined, he was released and signed up by Cardiff City in the Summer of 2001, but he failed to make his mark there and drifted into non-League football.
Debut: 20. 2.1999 v. Watford (H). 1-2. Div. 1.

JEFFERIES M.

G
b. Bristol
Aberdare Athletic
Q.P.R. 1913
Southern League: 1-0. FAC: 0-0. FLC: 0-0. Others: 0-0.
Total: 1-0.

He made just a single appearance for Q.P.R. in their early Park Royal days.
Debut: 27.9.1913 v. West Ham United (H). 2-2. SLDiv.1.

JEFFERSON Arthur

(L.B.) Def 5' 8" 13st 6lbs
b. Goldthorpe, Yorkshire 14.12.1916 d. 1997
Goldthorpe Working Mens club.
Peterborough United 1934
Q.P.R. Feb 1936
Football League:211-1. FAC: 23-0. FLC: 0-0. Others: 5-0.
Total:239-1.
Aldershot Mar 1950

Honours: 3rd Div. (South) runners-up medal. 3rd Div. (South) championship medal.

After impressive displays in the reserves, Arthur, who had been with Peterborough United, accepted a contract - and so began his long association with the club. He was a fearless character for whom personal safety counted little when the interests of his side were at stake. He suffered a broken collarbone and in the first match after recovery suffered concussion. In his initial season with Q.P.R. a broken leg resulted in three months absence. He had a cartilage removed and a few seasons later, suffered a broken arm.

Arthur was a favourite of the spectators at Loftus Road, a good old fashioned full back was how he can be described. He was an expert at the sliding tackle, (which is not allowed in the modern game) and an expert at the first time volley. After leaving Rangers he notched-up another 180 matches for Aldershot. On retiring from football, at the age of 36 years, he, along with team-mate Bert Smith opened a fish and chip shop near Loftus Road.
Debut: 31. 8.1936 v.Millwall (A). 0-2. Div. 3 (S).

JOBSON John Thomas

(C.H.) CD
b. Hebburn, Durham 8. 8.1903
Washington Colliery

Plymout Argyle	1922
Hartlepool United	1924
Stockport County	Jun 1927
Q.P.R.	Jun 1932

Football League: 4-0. FAC: 0-0. FLC: 0-0. Others: 0-0. Total: 4-0.

Gateshead	1933

Honours: 2 3rd Div. runners-up medals.

Jack (as he was known) was a very experienced player who was used as a reserve at Q.P.R. At Hartlepool he was the mainstay of their defence for three years and at Stockport for a further five. Jobson was a totally committed player who could be relied upon until the final whistle of every match.
Debut: 27. 8.1932 v. Brentford (H). 2-3. Div. 3. (S).

JOHN Reginald

(R.H.) Mid 5' 10" 11st 0lbs
b. Aberdare, Wales 27. 7.1899
Aberdare Athletic

Q.P.R.	Aug 1920

Football League:131-1. FAC: 14-0. FLC: 0-0. Others: 0-0. Total:145- 1.

Charlton Athletic	Jul 1926
Folkstone	Aug 1927

Reg was a strong, fast and determined tackler who had sound defensive qualities. After a six year spell of fairly regular first team football at Q.P.R., where he notched up over 140 first team games, Reg failed to make a big impact in his one season with Charlton Athletic, when he played just six senior matches. During his time at the Valley he was the victim of a case of mistaken identity, when it was reported that John had been booked for misconduct in a reserve match. However, the manager informed the F.A. that he had not been cautioned or even spoken to by the referee and that the player who actually offended was someone else! He played in all three half back positions before his move to Folkestone in August 1927.
Debut: 6.11.1920. v. Southampton (A). 2-2. Div. 3.

JOHNS Nicholas Paul

G 6' 2" 11st 5lbs
b. Bristol 8. 6.1957
Minehead

Millwall	(£2,000)	Feb 1976
Tampa Bay Rowdies, U.S.A.	(£150,000)	1977
Sheffield United	(Loan)	Sep 1978
Charlton Athletic	(£135,000)	Dec 1978
Q.P.R.	(£40,000)	Dec 1987

Football League: 10-6. FAC: 3-0. FLC: 2-0. Others: 1-0. Total: 16-0.

Maidstone United	(Loan)	Oct 1989
Maidstone United		Mar 1990

Honours: 2nd Div. runners-up medal.

Nicky was on accasions an outstandingly brilliant goalkeeper who played throughout the eighties for Charlton Athletic, and Q.P.R. bought him as the reserve to their regular keeper, David Seaman. Johns was last heard of as being employed as a Football-in-the-Community officer based at Crystal Palace.
Debut: 21.12.1987 v. Reading (H). 1-3. FMC. Rd. 1.

JOHNSON Henry Edward

(C.F) Striker 5' 7" 11st 6lbs
b. Birmingham in 1897

The Army
Coventry City Sep 1919
Darlaston (Loan) 1920
Southampton Apl 1921
Q.P.R. Feb 1924
Football League: 50-15. FAC: 5-0. FLC: 0-0. Others: 0-0.
Total: 55-15.
Cradley Heath 1926

Honours: Junior International. British Army representative.

Harry was secured on a free transfer by Southampton where he started well but faded badly. On arriving at Q.P.R. he played through the two re-election campaigns before finally leaving in 1926.
Debut: 16. 2.1924 v. Reading (H). 1-4. Div. 3. (S).

JOHNSON John Henry

(I.L.) Mid 5' 8" 11st 6lbs
b. Bristol 25. 5.1897 d. 1974
Fry's
Swindon Town
Q.P.R. 1927
Football League: 18-7. FAC: 1-1. FLC: 0-0. Others: 0-0.
Total: 19-8.

John was the usual substitute for Goddard whenever the latter was injured. He scored in his first two matches, so he was tried as a twin centre forward, alongside Goddard, however, this plan failed completely.
Debut: 3. 9.1927 v. Swindon Town (A). 2-0. Div.3 (S).

JONES Charles H.

(I.F.) Mid 5' 10" 11st 7lbs
b. Swansea, Wales in 1911
Northend
Q.P.R. 1932
Football League: 16-0. FAC: 0-0. FLC: 0-0. Others: 0-0.
Total: 16-0.

Charlie was used as a replacement for George Rounce whenever George was out of the side, injured, or otherwise.
Debut: 10. 9.1932 v. Crystal Palace (H). 2-1.Div. 3. (S).

JONES Vincent Peter

Mid 6' 0" 11st 12lbs
b. Watford, Herts 5. 1.1965
Wealdstone
Wimbledon (£10,000) Nov 1986
Leeds United (£650,000) Jun 1989
Sheffield United (£700,000) Sep 1990
Chelsea (£575,000) Aug 1991
Wimbledon (£700,000) Sep 1992
Q.P.R. (£500,000) Mar 1998
Football League: 7-1. FAC: 0-0. FLC: 0-0. Others: 0-0.
Total: 7-1.

Honours: 9 caps for Wales. FACup winners medal. 2nd Div. championship medal.

A midfield player who was a great motivator on the field and hated to lose. Vinny always gave 100% effort and was well known for his intimidatory style. He was a transfer deadline signing and was brought into the team as the player/coach. Jones was well known for his dangerous set pieces and long throw-ins. He now has many interests outside football, including that of film star, and appearing in television game and chat shows.
Debut: 28. 3.1998 v. Huddersfield Town (A). 1-1. Div.1.

JORDAN Frank

(O.R.) Wing
b.
Q.P.R. 1899
Southern League: 2-0. FAC: 0-0. FLC: 0-0. Others: 0-0.
Total: 2-0.

A reserve tean player, Frank had been a member of the club in its formative years.
Debut: 14. 9.1901 v. Tottenham H. (A). 0-2. SLDiv. 1.

JORDAN Harry

(O.R.) Wing
b.
Watford St. Mary's
Watford
Q.P.R. Jun 1899
Southern League: 1-0. FAC: 1-0. FLC: 0-0. Others: 0-0.
Total: 2-0.
Watford Oct 1901

He was the brother of Frank, and the pair turned pro. at Q.P.R. Harry had been an amateur at Watford.
Debut: 7.10.1899 v. Bristol City (A). 3-5. SLDiv. 1.

KEECH William

(W.H.) Mid 5' 9" 12st 7lbs
b. Irthlingborough, Northamptonshire in 1872
Wellingborough
Barnsley St. Peters Sep 1894
Liverpool Oct 1895
Barnsley Apl 1897
Blackpool Feb 1898
Leicester Fosse Feb 1899
Loughborough 1899

Q.P.R. Aug 1899
Southern League 55-3. FAC: 14-3. FLC: 0-0. Others: 0-0. Total: 69-6
Brentford May 1902
Kensal Rise 1904

Honours: Northamptonshire County representative. Sheffield & Hallomshire Cup winners medal. Represented the Southern League.

By all accounts William was a very good athlete, winning three handicaps and numerous boxing titles. He was also the holder of the Royal Humane Society's gold medal. Football-wise he was a very good midfield man whose brother Ben played for Q.P.R. also, but in the reserves. After retirement William came back to the club as a member of the training staff.
Debut: 9. 9.1899 v. Tottenham H. (A). 0-1. SLDiv. 1.

KEEN James Frederick

(O.R.) Wing 5' 7" 10st 6lbs
b. Newcastle 25.11.1897 d. 1980
Walker Celtic
Bristol City Apl 1920
Newcastle United May 1922
Q.P.R. May 1923
Football League: 31-0. FAC: 1-0. FLC: 0-0. Others: 0-0. Total: 32-0.
Hull City Jul 1924
Darlington 1925
Wigan Borough 1926

A product of the Welbeck Road school in Newcastle's East-End, Jimmy could play on both wings, however, speed was the major asset of his game for he was a professional sprinter of some repute and held many titles. Jimmy was not retained at the end of the 1923/24 season and later returned to the Newcastle area to play in minor football.
Debut: 25. 8.1923 v. Brentford (H). 1-0. Div.3. (S).

KEEN Michael Thomas

(R.H.) Mid 6' 1" 11st 8lbs
b. High Wycombe 19. 3.1940
Q.P.R. Jun 1958
Football League:393-39. FAC: 25-2. FLC: 21-3. Others: 0-0. Total:439-44.
Luton Town Jan 1969
Watford Jun 1972

Honours: 2nd Div. runners-up medal. League Cup wiiners medal. 3rd Div. runners-up medal. Isthmian League championship medal as the manager.

As a tall, stylish all round wing half he captained the side to a unique double, of League Cup winners & 3rd Division champions, in 1967. Mike was a tough, skilful, no compromise wing half of the old fashioned school, he was perceptive and also a strong tackler and was ever-present from 16th March 1963 until 14th September 1968. His time in the first team at Loftus Road extended over ten season, that of 1964/65 being the most successful so far as goals were concerned, when he notched up a very creditable 13 in League matches. After turning out for Watford on over a hundred occasions he became manager in 1973, then the same at Northampton Town in 1978. Mike had retired as a player after making a career total of 664 League appearances, half-way through his spell as the Watford manager, when the club dropped into the Fourth Division. However he did lead Wycombe Wanderers to the Isthmian League championship. Five years later, in 1985, he became the boss of Marlow, and in 1995 the same at Flackwell Heath. Mike later took up coaching one night a week at the West Ham school of excellence in Slough.
Debut: 7. 9.1959 v. York City (A). 1-2. Div. 3.

KEETCH Robert

CD 5' 10" 11st 7lbs
b. Tottenham, London 25.10.1941 d. 29. 6.1996
West Ham United
Fulham Apl 1959
Q.P.R. Nov 1966
Football League: 52-0. FAC: 2-0. FLC: 2-0. Others: 0-0. Total: 56-0.

Honours: 2nd Div. runners-up medal.

Bobby was a typical footballer of the swinging sixties after the abolition of the maximum wage. A somewhat paradoxical character off the pitch but very tough and uncompromising on it. He would arrive at the ground, more often than not in a Rolls Royce wearing a pinstripe suit and a fob-watch in his waist-coat pocket. However, he was a star in the middle of the defence and played a big part in the rise of the club from the 3rd to the 1st Divisions in successive seasons. He retired at the age of 27, in 1968, to spend more time with his business. This involved flying all over the world, buying and selling.. Bobbie died of a stroke in 1996.
Debut: 11. 3.1967 v. Peterborough Utd. (H). 0-0. Div. 3.

KELLARD Thomas

(I.F.) Mid 5' 9" 10st 4lbs
b. Oldham, Lancashire in 1905

Chamber Colliery	
Glossop	
Hurst	
Oldham Athletic	Nov 1926
Q.P.R.	May 1928

Football League: 5-1. FAC: 0-0. FLC: 0-0. Others: 0-0. Total: 5-1.

Burton Town	Aug 1929
Hurst	Sep 1929
Mossley	1931
Stalybridge Celtic	1934
Ashton United	1937

A first class reserve who won many honours in the lower leagues of professional football. Tom was a keen sprinter in his younger days and he was a regular scorer in the reserve team, however, he was rarely in line for a first team place. Tom came to the club from Oldham Athletic, along with Norman Crompton.
Debut: 25.12.1928 v. Swindon Town (H). 4-2. Div. 3 (S)

KELLY Edward Patrick

Mid 5' 7" 12st 0lbs
b. Glasgow, Scotland 7. 2.1951

Possilpark YMCA		
Arsenal		Feb 1968
Q.P.R.	(£80,000)	Sep 1976

Football League: 28-1. FAC: 0-0. FLC: 3-0. Others: 2-0. Total: 33-1.

Leicester City	(£50,000)	Jul 1977
Notts County		Jul 1980
AFC Bournemouth		Aug 1981
Leicester City		Dec 1981
Kettering Town		Mar 1983
Melton Town		1984
Torquay United		Oct 1984
Saltash United		1985

Honours: 5 Scottish youth caps. 3 U23 caps. Combination Cup winners medal. 2 Combination League winners medals. London Challenge Cup winners medal. European Fairs Cup winners medal. League Championship winners medal. FACup winners medal. League runners-up medal. 2nd Div. championship medal.

Eddie had been the captain of Arsenal in the early seventies but at Q.P.R., although he was tough in the tackle and gave the impression of strength and skill, he seemed to lack a certain pace. He left after a season and thereafter changed clubs constantly. Eddie became the manager of Barnstable in 1995, before moving into the double glazing industry in Paignton, Devon.
Debut: 11. 9.1976 v. Aston Villa (H). 2-1. Div. 1.

KELLY Michael John

G. 6' 0" 12st 7lbs
b. Northampton 18.10.1942

Islington Boys		
Chelsea Juniors		1959
Wimbledon		1960
Q.P.R.	(£3,000)	Mar 1966

Football League: 54-0. FAC: 4-0. FLC: 5-0. Others: 0-0. Total: 63-0.

Birmingham City	(£18,000)	Aug 1970
Minnesota Kicks, U.S.A.		1976

Honours: 3 English Amateur caps. FA amateur cup winners medal. 2 Isthmanian League championship medals. 2nd Div. runners-up medal.

Mike was a highly efficient goalkeeper who had turned out in over 200 matches for Wimbledon as an amateur before turning professional at Q.P.R. Apt to communicate (in a loud voice) with defenders during the course of a match, he had the unusual pre-match ritual of kicking the base of both goal-posts and touching the crossbar in the centre before the start of every match. In 1976 he became the manager of the Minnesota Kicks in the U.S.A. A year later he was in charge of Plymouth Argyle and then the Fulham assistant manager in 1978. This was followed by becoming the Crystal Palace coach in 1981, then a year later the same at Portsmouth, followed by W.B.A. in 1983. In 1985 he was given the job at the FA school of Excellence as chief coach, then the England goalkeeping coach in 1987. Mike was last heard of at Liverpool in 1991 - as the coach!
Debut: 29. 8.1967 v. Bristol City (H). 3-1. Div. 2.

KELLY William Brian

(C.F.) Striker
b. Isleworth, London 25. 9.1937
Dover

Q.P.R.	Nov 1958

Football League: 6-0. FAC: 0-0. FLC: 0-0. Others: 0-0.
Total: 6-0.
Bexleyheath & Wells

Bill was one of seven players to be tried during the 1958/59 season in an effort to cure the centre forward problem. All were failures until George Whitelaw came along the following season.
Debut: 13.12.1958 v. Swindon Town (A). 0-2. Div. 3.

KENNEDY Mark

(O.L.) Wing 5' 11" 11st 9lbs
b. Dublin, Eire 15. 5.1976

Millwall		May 1992
Liverpool	(£1,500,000)	Mar 1995
Q.P.R.	(Loan)	Jan 1998

Football League: 8-2. FAC: 0-0. FLC: 0-0. Others: 0-0.
Total: 8-2.

Wimbledon	(£1,750,000)	Mar 1998
Manchester City	(£1,000,000)	Jul 1999
Wolverhampton Wanderers	(£1,800,000)	Jul 2001

Honours: 34 Republic of Ireland International caps. Youth caps School caps and 7 caps at U21 level.

Mark, is a highly talented left footed player who was on loan to Q.P.R. with a view to a permanent transfer, but the deal fell through.
Debut: 31. 1.1998 v. Stockport County (A). 0-2. Div. 1.

KERR Andrew

(C.F.) Striker 5' 8" 11st 7lbs
b. Falkirk, Scotland in 1900
Ardrosson Winton Rovers

Luton Town	1923
Reading	May 1925
Q.P.R.	Mar 1926

Football League: 2-0. FAC: 0-0. FLC: 0-0. Others: 0-0.
Total: 2-0.

Andrew was successful at Luton Town and Reading where he topped the reserve team goalscorers, but he couldn't pull it off at Q.P.R.
Debut: 20. 3.1926 v. Crystal Palace (H). 1-3. Div. 3. (S).

KERRINS Patrick Michael

(C.F.) Striker 5' 11" 11st 2lbs
b. Fulham, London 13. 9. 1936

Q.P.R.	Dec 1953

Football League:146-30. FAC: 9-0. FLC: 0-0. Others: 2-1.
Total:157-31.

Crystal Palace	Jun 1960
Southend United	Jul 1961
Romford	Aug 1962

Pat was a product of the juniors. He was very fast and could play on either wing as well as at centre forward. When he first appeared as a striker it must have seemed to all and sundry at the club that this problem position had been solved, for he scored five goals in four matches. He was given an extended run leading the attack the following season but to no avail. However, he effectively kept the club in the 3rd Division when the regional Leagues were split to form the new 3rd and 4th Divisions in 1958. At this time he scored another crucial five goals in four late season matches from the centre forward position. Pat ended his days as a half back at Romford.
Debut: 13. 2.1954 v. Exeter City (A). 0-0. Div. 3. (S).

KERSLAKE David

Mid 5' 8" 11st 0lbs
b. Stepney, London 19. 6.1966

Q.P.R.	Jun 1983

Football League: 58-6. FAC: 4-0. FLC: 8-4. Others: 4-0.
Total: 74-10.

Swindon Town	(£110,000)	Nov 1989
Leeds United	(£500,000)	Mar 1993
Tottenham Hotspur	(£450,000)	Sep 1993
Swindon Town	(Loan)	Nov 1996
Charlton Athletic		Aug 1997
Ipswich Town		Aug 1997
Wycombe Wanderers	(Loan)	Dec 1997
Swindon Town		Mar 1998

Honours: 10 English school caps. 29 Youth caps. 3 U17 youth caps. 1 U21 cap. 2nd Div. play off medal.

David was a very good midfield player, who at the time was the most capped Youth International. He was later turned into a defender although he was happier going forward. Although at Loftus Road for over six years, he only made 74 appearances in the senior squad, but was snapped up by Swindon Town for a sizeable fee, which was considerably increased when he subsequently moved on. He ended his career back at Swindon Town in 2000.
Debut: 19. 4.1985 v. Newcastle United (A). 0-1. Div. 1.

KING Andrew Edward

Mid 5' 9" 10st 13lbs
b. Luton, Bedfordshire 14. 8.1956
Luton & Dunstable schools
Bedfordshire boys
Stopsley youths

Tottenham Hotspur	(Trial)	1971
Luton Town		Jul 1974
Everton		Apl 1976
Q.P.R.	(£425,000)	Sep 1980

Football League: 30-9. FAC: 2-0. FLC: 1-0. Others: 0-0. Total: 33-9.

W.B.A.	(£400,000)	Sep 1981
Everton		Jul 1982
SC Cambuur, Holland		Jan 1984
Wolverhampton Wanderers		Jan 1985
Orebro, Sweden	(Loan)	1985
Luton Town		Dec 1985
Aldershot		Aug 1986
Aylesbury		1988

Honours: 2 England U21 caps. League Cup final runners-up medal. 4th Div. promotion medal.

Andy was a hugely gifted player but at the same time an erratic and inconsistent one. Yet if he had harnessed his undoubted talent with a degree of self discipline, he would almost certainly have gone on to full England honours. His masterful control and deft distribution was on show, yet he never really fitted into the set-up as one would have liked, so he left the club. His most notable achievement at Q.P.R. was to score the first ever goal on the Loftus Road artifical pitch! He became the Waterford player manager in 1988, before playing for Southport a year later. He then took over the managership at Mansfield Town in 1993.
Debut: 20. 9.1980 v. Sheffield Wed. (A). 0-1. Div. 2.

KING A.

For
b.

Darwin	1894
Q.P.R.	1911

Southern League: 3-0. FAC: 1-0. FLC: 0-0. Others: 0-0. Total: 4-0.

Nothing is known about this player, except that he played most of his games in the reserve team.
Debut: 26.12.1911 v. Crystal Palace (A). 0-3. SLDiv. 1.

KING Arthur

For
b.

Willesden	1899
Gainsborough Trinity	1900
Q.P.R.	1901

Southern League: 21-2. FAC: 1-0. FLC: 0-0. Others: 22-2. Total: 22-2.

Arthur took over the centre forward position when the regular player, Millar, was injured in 1902. However, he played the majority of his matches at outside right.
Debut: 7. 9.1901 v. Watford (H). 0-1. SLDiv. 1.

KING R

(I.R.) Mid
b.

Q.P.R.	1908

Southern League: 3-0. FAC: 0-0. FLC: 0-0. Others: 0-0. Total: 3-0.

A reserve player who was briefly tried unsuccessfully, in the first team.
Debut: 21.11.1908 v. Swindon Town (A). 1-3. SL Div. 1.

KINGSLEY Matthew

G 5' 11" 14st 5lbs
b. Turton, Lancashire in 1876 d. 27. 3.1960
Edgeworth

Blackburn Rovers	1893
Turton	
Darwen	1896
Newcastle United	Apl 1898
West Ham United	May 1904
Q.P.R.	1905

Southern League: 20-0. FAC: 0-0. FLC: 0-0. Others: 0-0. Total: 20-0.

Rochdale	1907
Barrow	

Honours: 1 England cap. 3 Football League caps.

Matt was a reliable goalkeeper who usually fisted the ball away instead of catching it, so as not to be bundled into the net as was the practice in those far off days. He also had the habit of continually swinging his arms to and fro as he was waiting for action. He was sacked by West Ham United in 1904 following a fracas on the pitch with Herbert Lyon of Brighton, when the ex-England goalkeeper kicked him. The crowd spilled onto the pitch, ugly scenes developed, before Kingsley was sent off, and Lyon was carried off to the dressing room for treatment.
Debut: 2. 9.1905 v. New Brompton (H). 4-0. SLDiv. 1.

KIWOMYA Christopher Mark

Striker 5' 9" 11st 2lbs
b. Huddersfield, Yorkshire 2.12.1969

Ipswich Town		Mar 1987
Arsenal	(£1,500,000)	Jan 1995
Le Havre	(Loan)	Aug 1997
Selanger, Malaysia	(Loan)	Oct 1997
Q.P.R.		Aug 1998

Football League: 86-25: FAC: 5-3. FLC: 5-2. Others: 0-0.
Total: 96-30.

Aalborg, Denmark	Jul 2001
Grimsby Town	Mar 2002

Honours: 2nd Div. championship medal. European Cup Winners Cup runners-up medal.

Much of Chris' career was spent at Ipswich, until he was signed by Arsenal for a large fee. But he was unable to justify the expenditure and after less than two years and only a few appearances for the Gunners he was loaned out. He finally signed on a free transfer for Rangers and spent three years at Loftus Road. A swift-footed striker Chris can play on the left hand side of the field or in a central role, and is able to get behind defences without breaking the off-side rule. After nearly 100 appearances he moved on, first to Le Havre (France) and then to Grimsby Town.
Debut: 29. 8.1998 v. Bury (H). 0-0. Div. 1.

KNIGHT Frederick C.

(C.F.) Striker
b.
Botwell Mission

Q.P.R.	1921

Football League: 2-1. FAC: 0-0. FLC: 0-0. Others: 0-0.
Total: 2-1.

Fred stood in for the centre forward J.W.Smith when he was injured, and scored on his debut. However, he was never heard of again.
Debut: 12.11.1921 v. Aberdare Ath. (H). 1-0. Div. 3. (S).

KNOWLES Frank

(C.D.) CD 5' 11" 11st 12lbs
b. Hyde, Cheshire in 1891

Hyde F. C.	
Stalybridge Celtic	1911
Skelmersdale United	
Manchester United	Dec 1911
Hartlepool United	1919
Manchester City	Oct 1919
Stalybridge Celtic	1920
Ashington	Aug 1921
Stockport County	May 1922
Newport County	Jun 1923
Q.P.R.	Feb 1924

Football League: 35-0. FAC: 5-0. FLC: 0-0. Others: 0-0.
Total: 40- 0

Aston National	Aug 1926
Macclefield	Oct 1926

Frank proved himself at Manchester United by being the stand-in for the great Charlie Roberts and he was first choice whenever he was absent. Frank had a very fortunate escape in 1912, when he was one of six passengers in a car, which crashed and overturned near Rudyard Lake in Staffordshire. Two of the passengers were killed instantly but Knowles escaped with no more than a severe shaking. During the First World War, Frank, guested for Hyde, Arsenal & Oldham Athletic, but at Q.P.R. he could not stop the club from having to seek re-election for the first time in their history.
Debut: 23. 2.1924 v. Reading (A). 0-4. Div. 3 (S).

KNOWLES Joseph

(R.B.) Def 5' 6" 11st 6lbs
b. Monkwearmouth, Sunderland in 1872

Monkwearmouth	1892
Sunderland	1895
Tottenham Hotspur	May 1897
South Shields	1898
Q.P.R.	1899

Southern League: 22-0. FAC: 7-0. FLC: 0-0. Others: 0-0.
Total: 29-0.

Joe was noted as a safe and sturdy player, as well as a brilliant defender. He was one of the first players to join Q.P.R. when they embraced professionalism and was a good capture for the fledgling club in their first season in the Southern League.
Debut: 9. 9.1899 v. Tottenham H. (A). 0-1. SLDiv. 1.

KOEJOE Samuel

Striker 6' 1" 12st 2lbs
b. Paramaribo, Surinam 17. 8.1974
Lustenau, Austria
DWV Amsterdam, Holland
Salzberg, Austria
Q.P.R. (£250,000) Nov 1999
Football League: 34-3. FAC: 5-0. FLC: 3-0. Others: 0-0. Total: 42-3.
Stoke City (Trial)
Northampton Town (Trial)
Lustenau, Austria 2002

Sammy was a big, bustling striker with good pace who's contract was cancelled by mutual agreement at the end of August 2002.
Debut: 4.12.1999 v. Huddersfield T. (A). 0-1. Div.1.

KULCSAR George

Mid 6' 2" 13st 4lbs
b. Budapest, Hungary 12. 8.1967
Canberra City, Australia
Budapest, St. George, Hungary
Royal Antwerp, Belgium
Bradford City (£100,000) Mar 1997
Q.P.R. (£250,000) Dec 1997
Football League: 56-1. FAC: 2-0. FLC: 2-0. Others: 0-0. Total: 60-1.

Honours: 3 Australian caps.

Ray Harford's first buy during the short period he was with the club as manager. George never seemed to stop running, and was a strong ball winning player with control over the centre of the park. His single goal for the club was a valuable one, for it was one of six scored at Crystal Palace in May 1969, which saved the Rangers from relegation. He was released from his contract by mutual consent in May 2001.
Debut: 21.12.1997 v. Bradford City (H). 1-0. Div. 1.

LANE Harry William

Def 5' 11" 11st 4lbs
b. Stoney Stanton, Leicestershire 23.10.1894
Hinckley United Oct 1911
Nottingham Forest 1912
Notts County 1913
Sutton Town 1914
West Ham United 1919
Charlton Athletic May 1921
Q.P.R. Jul 1922
Football League: 5-0. FAC: 0-0. FLC: 0-0. Others: 0-0. Total: 5-0.

Harry was a school teacher by profession, and therefore an amateur and mainly a reserve at his various clubs. During the Great War he served in the Army and the Air Force. He was a versatile player appearing in defence or attack, but at Q.P.R. he was used mainly as a defender.
Debut: 4.11.1922 v. Aberdare Athletic (A). 0-0. Div.3 (S)

LANGFORD Walter

(I.L.) Mid 5' 9" 11st 8lbs
b. Wolverhampton 24. 3.1905d. Wolverhampton ?. 1.1996
Sunbeam Motor Works Ltd. 1924
Wellington Town
Leicester City May 1928
Q.P.R. Aug 1933
Football League: 11-0. FAC: 1-0. FLC: 0-0. Others: 1-0. Total: 13-0.
Wellington Town Jul 1935
Kidderminster Harriers

Walter was a reserve who stood in for the captain of the side, Joe Devine, he could also fill in at half back and did so during his time at Loftus Road. Walter was one of the first signings of manager Mick O'Brien and was part of a very good side put together by him.
Debut: 9. 9.1933 v. Luton Town (H). 2-1. Div.3. (S).

LANGLEY E. James

(L.B.) Def 5' 10" 11st 12lbs
b. Kilburn, London 7. 2.1929
Yiewsley
Hounslow
Uxbridge
Hayes
Brentford 1946
Guildford City 1949
Leeds United Jun 1952
Brightom & Hove Abion Jul 1953
Fulham Feb 1957
Q.P.R. Jul 1965
Football League: 87-8. FAC: 8-1. FLC: 10-1. Others: 0-0. Total:105-10.
Hillingdon Borough Sep 1967

Honours: 3 England caps. 1 Football League cap. 3 B caps. 4 caps for the FA X1. Went on the tour of the West Indies and South Africa. 2nd Div runners-up medal. Championship medal. League Cup winners medal.

Jim became the favourite of the Loftus Road crowd with his wholeheartedness and tough but legal tackling. He was always noted for his fairness in the game, and was given license to roam the field.

L

Jim would use a wide range of tricks, such as a bicycle-kick, the overhead-kick, he had an enormous throw-in and his sliding tackle, were all superb. Jim played in over 50 matches during the successful 1966/67 campaign, including the League Cup final. At Hillingdon Borough, as player/manager, he made another trip to Wembley, when he took his team in 1971 to the F.A.Challenge Trophy final.
Debut: 21. 8.1965 v. Brentford (A). 1-6. Div. 3.

LANGLEY Richard Barrington Michael

Mid 5' 10" 11st 4lbs
b. Harlesden, London 27.12.1979

Q.P.R.		Dec 1996

Football League: 133-18. FAC: 2-0. FLC: 1-1. Others: 1-0. Total:147-19.

Honours: England youth. 6 caps for Jamaica.

A central midfield player from the Q.P.R. youth academy who could pass, shoot, tackle and play his way out of tight situations, rather than hoofing the ball up the pitch. A lot of injuries have passed Richard's way, including a broken hand, keyhole surgery on his knee, a kidney and a cartilage operation. Richard made around 100 appearances at Loftus Road in over five years, however, during the 2002/03 he was a big influence in the side, when he missed few games during the season. Crucial goals, including a hat-trick helped to ensure Q.P.R. a promotion play-off place that season.
Debut: 31.10.1998 v. Swindon Town (A). 1-3. Div. 1.

LANGLEY Thomas W.

(C.F.) Striker 5' 11" 10st 7lbs
b. Lambeth, London 8. 2.1958

Chelsea		Apl 1975
Q.P.R.	(£425,000)	Aug 1980

Football League: 25-8. FAC: 0-0. FLC: 3-1. Others: 0-0. Total: 28-9.

Crystal Palace	(£200,000)	Mar 1981
AEK Athens, Greece		1983
Coventry City		Mar 1984
Wolverhampton Wanderers		Jul 1984
Aldershot	(Loan)	Mar 1985
Hong Kong, China		1985
Aldershot		Aug 1986
Exeter City		Jul 1988
Slough Town		1989
Aylesbury United		1991
Staines Town		1991
St. Albans City		1991
Basingstoke Town		1991
Wokingham Town		1992

Honours: England schoolboy caps. 8 youth caps. 1 U21 cap. 3 'B' caps.

Associated with Chelsea at the age of ten years old, Tommy played for the Colts team at the age of twelve. He made his Football League debut at the age of sixteen and he was a fast and totally committed player who showed his enthusiasm throughout the match.
Debut: 28. 3.1980 v. Swansea City (H). 0-0. Div. 2.

LARGE Frank

(C.F.) Striker 5' 10" 13st 2lbs
b. Leeds, Yorkshire 26. 1.1940

Holbeck Loco		
British Railways		
Halifax Town		Jun 1959
Q.P.R.	(£7,500)	Jun 1962

Football League: 18-5. FAC: 3-2. FLC: 1-0. Others: 0-0. Total: 22-7.

Northampton Town	(£8,500)	Mar 1963
Swindon Town	(£10,000)	Mar 1964
Carlisle United	(£6,500)	Mar 1964
Oldham Athletic	(£6,000)	Dec 1965
Northampton Town	(£15,000)	Dec 1966
Leicester City	(£20,000)	Nov 1967
Fulham		Jun 1968
Northampton Town		Aug 1969
Chesterfield	(£6,000)	Nov 1972
Baltimore Comets, U.S.A.		Apl 1974
Kettering Town		Sep 1974

Honours: 2 3rd Div. Championship medals.

A bustling centre forward who could terrify goalkeepers just by looking in their direction, Frank scored a career total of 209 goals in 569 competitive matches. He was an Alec Stock acquisition, but it was Northampton Town that seemed to get the best out of him. After less than a year at Loftus Road he made frequent moves, and after his retirement from the game he became a charge hand in a factory in Northampton. In the mid-1980s he moved to County Mayo, Ireland, to run a bed and breakfast business combined with working on a nearby estate as a handyman/gamekeeper.
Debut: 18.8.1962 v. Brighton & H.A. (H). 2-2. Div. 3.

LAW Brian John

CD 6' 2" 13st 12lbs
b. Merthyr Tidfil, Wales 1. 1.1970
Q.P.R. Aug 1987
Football League: 20-0. FAC: 3-0. FLC: 3-0. Others: 1-0. Total: 27-0.
Wolverhampton Wanderers(£134,000) Dec 1994
Millwall Jul 1997

Honours: School & youth caps for Wales. 2 U21 caps. 1 full Welsh cap.

A powerful youngster who was very quick, but Brian was forced to retire in 1992 with foot ligament injuries. He embarked on a back-packing holiday around the world and when he returned he resurrected his career with Wolves, who put him through a rigorous trial which lasted a month. After two and a half years, Brian was transferred to Millwall, where he became captain of the side until 2000 when he was released from his contract.
Debut: 23.4.1988 v. Sheffield Wed. (H). 1-1. Div. 1.

LAW R.

(O.R.) Wing
b.
Q.P.R. 1910
Southern League: 1-0. FAC: 0-0. FLC: 0-0. Others: 0-0. Total: 1-0.

A young trialist who played for the senior squad in the last match of the 1910/11 season.
Debut: 29.4.1911 v. Plymouth Argyle (H).1-0. SLDiv. 1.

LAW William Daniel

(O.L.) Wing 5' 7" 11st 7lbs
b. Pleck, Walsall in March 1882 d.1952
Wolverhampton Road school, Pleck
Rushall Olympic
Walsall 1903
Scarborough
Doncaster Rovers Jun 1904
W.B.A. May 1905
Watford Jun 1906
Q.P.R. May 1908
Southern League: 4-1. FAC: 1-0. FLC: 0-0. Others: 0-0. Total: 5-1.
Glossop North End 1909

A clever little winger who could centre the ball with accuracy while on the run. Billy was used as a reserve to the first choice winger and captain Billy Barnes, and retired from football in 1914.
Debut: 16. 9.1908 v. Watford (A). 0-0. SLDiv. 1.

LAY Peter J.

(C.H.) CD
b. Stratford, London 4.12.1931
Nottingham Forest Apl 1953
Q.P.R. Jul 1956
Football League: 1-0. FAC: 0-0. FLC: 0-0. Others: 0-0. Total: 1-0.
Kings Lynn 1958

Peter arrived at Loftus Road, and stayed for two years. But the the consistency and freedom from injury of the regular centre half, Keith Rutter ensured that Peter was never able to make his mark in the side.
Debut: 26.12.1956 v.Crystal Palace (H). 4-2. Div.3 (S).

LAZARUS Mark

(O.R.) Wing 5' 8" 11st 3lbs
b. Stepney, London 5.12.1938

Dagenham		
Barking		
Leyton Orient		Nov 1957
Q.P.R.	(£3,000)	Sep 1960

Football League: 37-19. FAC: 2-0. FLC: 3-1. Others: 0-0. Total: 42-20.

Wolverhampton Wanderers	(£27,500)	Sep 1961
Q.P.R.	(£15,000)	Feb 1962

Football League: 81-28. FAC: 6-1. FLC: 1-0. Others: 0-0. Total: 88-29.

Brentford	(Exchange deal)	Jan 1964
Q.P.R.	(£10,000)	Nov 1965

Football League: 88-29. FAC: 6-2. FLC: 11-4. Others: 0-0. Total:105-35.

Crystal Palace	(£10,000)	Nov 1967
Leyton Orient		Oct 1969
Folkestone Town		
Rainham Town		

Honours: League Cup winners medal. Two 2nd Div. runners-up medals. 3rd Div. Championship medal.

Mark was one of a family of eight brothers plus five sisters, and he was a former boxer who was unbeaten in ten fights. Two of his brothers, Harry and Lew Lazar, were also famous in the 'ring'. A powerfully built player, he had been on the books of Fulham as an amateur, before being taken in hand by Leyton Orient. Mark made his debut for the 'O's; in the London Challenge Cup match v. Charlton Athletic, scoring two brilliant goals, and he signed professional forms in November 1957. He was noted as being very fast and aggressive, by Alec Stock, who watched him on several occasions before eventually signing him.

Mark became a big favourite of the crowd at Loftus Road. However, after just one season he became a big money signing for Wolves, but was back at Loftus Road four months later. In 1964 he agreed to a move to Brentford where he was equally popular during his near two year stay. Mark made a second return to Q.P.R., and in two years added another 105 games to produce a grand total of 235 with 84 goals. In 12 years of League football, Mark notched up a total of 134 goals in 442 League appearances. He has the distinction of being the only Q.P.R.player to score a winning goal at Wembley Stadium. He went on to run his own transport business in Romford, Essex.

Debut: 17. 9.1960 v. Colchester United (A). 1-0. Div. 3.

LEABURN Carl Winston

(C.F.) Striker 6' 3" 13st 0lbs
b. Lewisham, London 30. 3.1969

Charlton Athletic		Apl 1987
Northampton Town	(Loan)	Mar 1990
Wimbledon	(£300,000)	Jan 1998
Charlton Athletic	(Trial)	2001
Wycombe wanderers	(Trial)	2001
Leyton Orient	(Trial)	2001
Q.P.R.		2002

Football League: 1-0. FAC: 0-0. FLC: 0-0. Others: 0-0. Total: 1-0.

Grays Athletic		Feb 2003

Carl created a new club record, when he had the shortest first team career for Q.P.R., with just a three minute appearance!

Debut: 5. 1.2002 v. Reading (A). 0-1. Div. 2.

LEACH James M.

(L.H.) Def 5' 10" 11st 8lbs
b. Spennymore, Cty. Durham in July 1890 d. 1951

Newcastle St. Wilfred's	1908
Spennymore United	1910
Spen Black & White	1911
Aston Villa	Aug 1912
Q.P.R.	Jul 1922

Football League: 1-0. FAC: 0-0. FLC: 0-0. Others: 0-0. Total: 1-0.

Jim was an excellent player, who was brainy, witty, always looked confident on the ball, and always seemed to have plenty of time in which to manoeuvre. Unfortunately a very bad injury kept him out of the side for the whole of the 1919/20 season, which forced him to miss the Aston Villa Cup Final v. Huddersfield Town. Jim retired from football in 1923 after leading the reserves at Loftus Road.

Debut: 26. 8.1922 v. Watford (H). 1-2. Div. 3. (S).

LEACH Michael J. C.

Mid 6' 0" 12st 0lbs
b. Hackney, London 16. 1.1947
Walthamstow schoolboys
West Ham United
Q.P.R. Feb 1964
Football League:313-61. FAC: 23-3. FLC: 19-6. Others: 6-0. Total:361-70.
Detroit, U.S.A. 1978
Cambridge United Sep 1978
Leatherhead 1980

Honours: 2 England youth caps. 2 2nd Div. runners-up medals.

Mike could always be relied on to give 100% effort in a match and was one of the many debutants to have scored in their opening match. Some of the crowd did not appreciate his running off the ball, as he never appeared to be moving fast but in this he was deceptive. It wasn't until his fifth season at Loftus Road that Mike became more or less a regular in the first team. Alec Stock brought Mike into the team for the last five matches of the 1967/8 season, and this inclusion proved to be a master stroke. For during this period Mike struck-up an instant relationship with Rodney Marsh and he scored three goals in five matches as Rangers clinched a place in the 1st Division. Mike's a stay at Q.P.R. was to last 14 years in total, when over 300 League matches were played. Mike moved out to the U.S.A. in 1978, but soon returned and played for Cambridge United, until moving into the non-League world.
Debut: 26. 2.1965 v. Colchester United (H). 5-0. Div. 3.

LEARY Stuart Edward

(C.F.) Striker 5' 9" 10st 9lbs
b. Cape Town, South Africa 30. 4.1933 d. August 1988
Clyde F.C.
Charlton Athletic Feb 1950
Q.P.R. Dec 1962
Football League: 94-29. FAC: 7-3: FLC: 3-0. Others: 0-0. Total:104-32.

Stuart's movement off the ball was superb and his shooting was excellent, he was a very good opportunist and a shrewd distributer of the ball. His services were in demand all year round, for cricket was his other sport. Stuart accumulated 16,000 runs and took 140 wickets at an average of 33.67 for Kent. He retired from football in 1966 and died on Table Mountain, South Africa in 1988, his body being discovered on the 23rd August; Stuart had been missing for five days.
Debut: 15.12.1962 v. Brighton & H.A. (A). 2-2. Div. 3.

LEATHER John

G 6' 0" 11st 10lbs
b. in 1875
Macclesfield Swifts 1893
Macclesfield
Woolwich Arsenal 1896
Q.P.R. 1898
Southern League: 2-0. FAC: 0-0. FLC: 0-0. Others: 0-0. Total: 2-0.

Jack was a reserve to the other goalkeepers at Arsenal as well as at Q.P.R. He played in eight League and two FA Cup matches as well as 58 reserve matches for the Gunners.
Debut: 26. 3.1904 v. Wellingborough (H). 3-0. SLDiv.1.

LEE Samuel

Mid 5' 7" 10st 2lbs
b. Liverpool 7. 2.1959
Merseyside schools
Liverpool Apl 1979
Q.P.R. (£200,000) Aug 1986
Football League: 30-0. FAC: 3-1. FLC: 2-0. Others: 0-0. Total: 35-1.
Osasuna, Spain (£200,000) Jul 1987
Southampton Jan 1990
Bolton Wanderers Oct 1990

Honours: 7 English youth caps. 6 U21 caps. 14 England caps. 2 European Cup winners medals. 3 Div.1 championship medals. 4 Football League Cup winners medals.

Sammy was the original 'super-sub', at Liverpool, a fine all round player and a complete midfield dynamo. He was an enthusiastic and strong runner, who was solid in the tackle and a fine distributer of the ball. All his honours were won whilst with Liverpool.
Debut: 30. 8.1986 v. Aston Villa (H). 1-0. Div. 1.

LEGGE Albert Edward

(I.R.) Mid 5' 7" 10st 4lbs
b. Hednesford, Walsall 19. 1.1901 d. July 1988
Prestwood Road school
Lewisham Athletic, Wolverhampton
Wolverhampton Wanderers 1923
Gillingham Jun 1928
Charlton Athletic May 1929
Q.P.R. Jun 1930
Football League: 9-1. FAC: 0-0. FLC: 0-0. Others: 0-0.
Total: 9-1.
Wellington Town
Hednesford
Cradley Heath

Honours: 3rd Div. (North) championship medal.

The son of a coalminer, Bert was a hard working and reliable inside right who played the game until he was 38 years old. With retirement came the almost inevitable pub management, in Heathtown and Wolverhamton, followed by a job for the Goodyear Tyre Company until he reached pensionable age. At the time of his death he was resident in Wednesfield and died in New Cross Hospital.
Debut: 30. 8.1930 v. Thames Ass.. (H). 3-0. Div. 3. (S).

LEIGH Thomas

(F.B.) Defender 5' 8" 11st 3lbs
b. Hollins, Nr. Bury in 1888
Haslingdon F.C. 1904
Oldham Athletic 1906
Fulham 1907
Q.P.R. 1910
Southern League: 4-0. FAC: 0-0. FLC: 0-0. Others: 0-0.
Total: 4-0.
Croydon Common 1911

Honours: Held 7 league & cup medals.

Tommy is described in contemporary sources as, "*a dandy who was both bold and vigorous, and very fast.*" He was also noted for his hard and low clearances. Tommy won many prizes for cycling, swimming, and at football where he could play on either flank, thereby being a reserve for both full backs.
Debut: 19.11.1910 v. Bristol Rovers (H). 1-2. SLDiv. 1.

LENNON Alexander Victor

(I.L.) Mid
b. Glasgow, Scotland 23.10.1925
Rotherham United Nov 1944
Q.P.R. Jan 1947
Football League: 1-0. FAC: 0-0. FLC: 0-0. Others: 0-0.
Total: 1-0.
Mansfield Town Feb 1949

A surfeit of inside forwards at Loftus Road led to the free transfer of this player to Mansfield Town. Alex played just three matches for them before they too released him.
Debut: 4.12.1948 v Coventry City (H). 0-3. Div. 2.

LENNOX Stuart

(R.H.) Def
b. Scotland
Q.P.R. 1900
Southern League: 11-0. FAC: 0-0. FLC: 0-0. Others: 0-0.
Total: 11-0.
Morton 1903

Stuart was a typical Scottish player plying his trade south of the border. He was kept as a reserve at Q.P.R. and stood in as substitute for Keech when he was out of the side.
Debut: 29.12.1900 v. Reading (H). 0-0. SLDiv. 1.

LEWIS Dudley Reginald James

(C.F.) Striker 5, 11" 12st 0lbs
b. Kensington, London 19.11.1909 d. Bath 24. 4.1987
London Junior football
Q.P.R. 1929
Football League: 1-0. FAC: 0-0. FLC: 0-0. Others: 0-0.
Total: 1-0.
Bristol Rovers Jul 1932
Exeter City May 1934
Bath City
Newport County Aug 1935
Milford United May 1936

Dudley was still an amateur when he played for Q.P.R., scoring a goal on his debut, and didn't sign pro. forms until a few weeks later. During the 1931/32 season he appeared in twenty reserve team matches and scored five goals.
Debut: 2.5.1931v. Bournemouth & B.A.(H).3-0. Div.3(S)

LEWIS James William

(I.R.) Mid 5' 9" 12st 0lbs

b. Hackney, London 2.12.1905		d. March 1976
London junior football		
Walthamstow Avenue		1929
Q.P.R.		1931

Football League: 11-4. FAC: 0-0. FLC: 0-0. Others: 0-0. Total: 11-4.

Walthamstow Avenue	1932

Honours: 13 English amateur caps. Member of a tour to South Africa winning 2 caps. Full England wartime cap as a substitute 3 Athenian League championship medals.

Jim Lewis senior was the leading amateur of his day and Q.P.R. engaged him to play in their team in the 1931/32 season at the White City Stadium (just up the road from Loftus Road, where the reserve team played). Lewis had scored over 300 goals in his career and was a sound player in most aspects of the game, being able to seize a scoring opportunity at a moment's notice. But the hopes of the player and the club came to nothing when the team ended the season in 13th place in the Division.

Debut: 29. 8.1931 v. Brentford (A). 0-1. Div. 3 (S).

LILLIE John

(L.B.) Def 5' 9" 12st 0lbs

b. Newcastle

Liverpool	1921
Q.P.R.	1924

Football League: 3-0. FAC: 0-0. FLC: 0-0. Others: 0-0. Total: 3-0.

Clapton Orient	1925
Blyth Spartans	Aug 1926
New Brighton	Oct 1926

John was a member of the reserve squad at Liverpool before he moved to Q.P.R., staying for a season before he moved to East London.

Debut: 30. 8.1924 v. Newport County (A). 0-0. Div.3 (S).

LINIGHAN Andrew

CD 6' 3" 13st 10lbs

b. Hartlepool 18.12.1962

Hartlepool United		Sep 1980
Leeds United	(£20,000)	May 1984
Oldham Athletic	(£65,000)	Jan 1986
Norwich City	(£350,000)	Mar 1988
Arsenal	(£250,000)	Jul 1990
Crystal Palace	(£150,000)	Jan 1997
Q.P.R.	(Loan)	Mar 1999

Football League: 7-0. FAC: 0-0. FLC: 0-0. Others: 0-0. Total: 7-0.

Oxford United	Oct 2000
St. Albans City	2001

Honours: 4 England B caps. Div. 1 championship medal. Football League Cup winners medal. F.A.Cup winners medal. European Cup winners medal.

Andrew was born into a footballing family, for his father played for Lincoln City and Darlington, while his brothers, Brian and David, played for Bury and Mansfield Town respectively.

Debut: 5. 4.1999 v. Ipswich Town (A). 1-3. Div. 1.

LINTOTT Evelyn Henry

(H.B.) Def 5' 9" 12st 4lbs

b. Goldaming, Surrey 2.11.1883		d. July 1918
King Edward V1 Grammar school		
St. Lukes training collage, Exeter		
Woking		
Surrey County		
Plymouth Argyle		1906
Q.P.R.		1907

Southern League: 31-1. FAC: 2-0. FLC: 0-0. Others: 2-0. Total: 35-1.

Bradford City	(£1,000)	Nov 1908
Leeds City		Jun 1912

Honours: 7 full English caps. 5 England amateur caps. Southern League championship medal. 1 Football League cap.

A schoolmaster by profession, he stayed an amateur throughout his career. Lintott was noted at the time as a player that followed in the foot steps of Needham and Forrest. A contemporary of the time wrote '*He was a vigorous and clever player, tackling and passing with fine judgement*'. Evelyn was the club's first ever full international, when he played for England in February 1908. For a time he was the chairman of the Players Union, however, he resigned from the post in 1911. Like so many others he volunteered to serve in the army in the 1914/18 conflict and served in the Light Infantry as a subaltern on the Somme in Flanders, where he lost his life.

Debut: 7. 9.1907 v. New Brompton (H). 2-2. SLDiv. 1.

LISBIE Kevin Anthony

Striker 5' 8" 10st 7lbs

b. Hackney, London 17.10.1978

Charlton Athletic		May 1996
Gillingham	(Loan)	Mar 1999
Reading	(Loan)	Nov 1999
Q.P.R.	(Loan)	Dec 2000

Football League: 2-0. FAC: 0-0. FLC: 0-0. Others: 0-0. Total: 2-0.

Charlton Athletic	Jan 2001

Honours: English youth caps. 2 caps Jamaica..

Kevin, a very fast and skilful on the ball and able to play as a central striker or on the wing, was on loan at Loftus Road for a short petriod.
Debut: 2.12.2000 v. Sheffield Wed. (A). 2-5. Div. 1.

LOCK Herbert

G 5' 8" 12st 0lbs
b. Southampton 22. 1.1887 d. Southampton 16. 3.1957
St. Marys Guild

Southampton	1907
Glasgow Rangers	1909
Q.P.R.	Aug 1921

Football League: 6-0. FAC: 0-0. FLC: 0-0. Others: 0-0.
Total: 6-0.

Southampton	Sep 1922
Bournemouth & Boscombe Athletic	Jan 1924

By all accounts, Bert was a daring and acrobatic 'keeper who was noted for his uncanny anticipation when he was facing penalty kicks. In the days when the goalkeeper had to stand still on the goal-line, he would pace up and down rather like a caged lion and eventually position himself slightly off centre. The penalty taker would invariably shoot towards the larger gap and Bert, anticipating correctly, would make the save. On retirement he settled in his home town of Southampton and worked as a carpenter and joiner for the South Western Railways.
Debut: 12.11.1921 v. Aberdare Ath. (H). 1-0. Div. 3. (S).

LOCKE Leslie C.

(I.L.) Mid.
b. Perth, Scotland 24. 1.1934
Bromley

Q.P.R.	May 1956

Football League: 76-24. FAC: 3-2. FLC: 0-0. Others: 3-3.
Total: 82-29

Guildford City	1960

Honours: Scottish Amateur International.

Les helped in no small part to ensure Rangers' Third Division survival. The top eleven clubs of each Division (North and South) were to form the new Third. Q.P.R. just managed it with fifty points, and by finishing in tenth place. During this period Les notched up another four goals to end the season with thirteen, the second highest scorer. His stay at Loftus Road only lasted four seasons, and in 1960 he drifted into non-League football.
Debut: 27. 8. 1956 v. Plymouth Argyle (H). 3-0. Div.3(S).

LOFTHOUSE James

(O.L.) Wing 5' 6" 11st 4lbs
b. St. Helens, Lancashire 24. 3.1898
Cabbage Hall F.C.
St. Helens Recreation
Stalybridge Celtic

Reading	May 1913
Sheffield Wednesday	Jul 1920
Rotherham County	Feb 1923
Bristol Rovers	Dec 1923
Q.P.R.	May 1926

Football League: 80-27. FAC: 1-0. FLC: 0-0. Others: 0-0.
Total: 81-27.

Aldershot	Aug 1928
G.P.O. Reading	Sep 1934

A short, stocky winger who was both tricky and very fast. Jimmy possessed an excellent shot. He was very experienced, having played during the 1914/18 conflict for Manchester United and was ever-present for Q.P.R. in the 1926/27 season. After retirement he worked and played for the G.P.O.
Debut: 28. 8.1926 v. Crystal Palace (A). 1-2. Div. 3 (S).

LOGAN W.

(F.B.) Def 5' 8" 11st 6lbs
b. Scotland in 1885
Vale of Leven

Q.P.R.	1909

Southern League: 7-0. FAC: 0-0. FLC: 0-0. Others: 0-0.
Total: 7-0.

A reserve defender who stood in for any injuries or absentees at full back during the 1909/10 season. He could play at either right or left back.
Debut: 1. 9.1909 v. Watford (H). 4-3. SLDiv. 1.

LONEY Basil (Reverend)

(R.B.) Def
b.
Darlington Grammar school
St. James, Stockton
Middlesbrough

Stockton	1911
Q.P.R.	1914

Southern League: 1-0. FAC: 0-0. FLC: 0-0. Others: 0-0.
Total: 1-0.

Durham University	1915

Honours: F.A.Amateur cup winners medals.

The Reverend Basil played for Q.P.R. on one solitary occasion, when he was passing through London!
Debut: 24. 4.1915 v. Crystal Palace (H). 3-2. SLDiv. 1.

LONGBOTTOM Arthur

(I.L.) Striker 5' 8" 10st 12lbs
b. Leeds, Yorkshire 30. 1.1933
Methley United

Q.P.R.		Mar 1954

Football League:201-62. FAC: 11-4. FLC: 0-0. Others: 3-1. Total:215-67.

Port Vale	(£2,000)	May 1961
Millwall	(£2,000)	Jan 1963
Oxford United	(£1,500)	Aug 1963
Colchester United		Oct 1964
Scarborough		1965

Arthur had a touch of mischief in his play, which endeared him to many supporters. He kept his hair close cropped and later changed his surname to Langley (some say in order not be ridiculed when he moved to Millwall!). He equalled the feats of Addinall and Smith by heading the goalscorers for three years running from 1956/57 to 1958/59. Yet strangely, apart from this 'purple' patch, his scoring was infrequent, for in his other four seasons at Q.P.R. he could manage only 11 League goals in total. During his nine years at Loftus Road he made over 200 first team appearances. In 1963, Arthur was transferred to Millwall together with Jim Towers, but neither made any impact, and Arthur moved on to Oxford United less than a year later. Two further short periods followed before he dropped down to non-League football.
Debut: 12. 3.1955 v. Leyton Orient (A). 0-3. Div. 3. (S).

LOWE Henry Pratt

(I.L.) Striker 5' 7" 11st 0lbs
b. Keetle, Fife, Scotland 24. 2.1907
d.Calne, Wilts. Oct 1988

St. Andrews United	Aug 1928
Watford	Mar 1929
Q.P.R.	Jun 1935

Football League:161-40. FAC: 10-0. FLC: 0-0. Others: 0-0. Total:171-40.

Guildford City	1939

Q.P.R. definitely got the better of the exchange deal when they brought Harry Lowe to Loftus Road and let Ted Goodier go to Watford. In one match for the Vicarage Road side, he scored a goal, but also failed with a penalty, on his wedding day, in a 4-1 victory over Swindon Town Harry was a direct inside forward who had a powerful long range shot in his right foot, and he made over 160 Football League appearances during his four years at Loftus Road. Shortly after moving to Guildford City, war broke out and so effectively cutting short his playing career. He became a successful Chelsea scout in 1943, then in 1945 took the manager's job at Guildford City. In 1947 he became the Bournemouth manager and the same position followed at Yeovil Town in 1951. In 1954 he was scouting for Watford, and finally became the Cheshunt manager in 1955.
Debut: 31. 8.1935 v. Millwall (H). 2-3. Div. 3 (S).

LOWE O.

(L.B.) Def
b.
Q.P.R.
Southern League: 2-0. FAC: 0-0. FLC: 0-0. Others: 0-0. Total: 2-0.

Replaced regular left back Fidler for the last two Southern League games of the 1907/08 season.
Debut: 25.4.1908 v.Southampton (A). 2-5. SLDiv. 1.

LOWE W.

(I.L.) Mid
b.
Q.P.R.
Southern League: 1-0. FAC: 0-0. FLC: 0-0. Others: 0-0. Total: 1-0.

This player stood in just once for the injured Jack Gregory when he was out of the team.
Debut: 8.11.1919 v. Millwall (H). 1-2. SLDiv.1.

M

LUMSDON Francis L.

(O.R.) Wing
b. Sunderland
Castletown

Huddersfield Town	Oct 1933
Q.P.R.	Apl 1935

Football League: 38-8. FAC: 1-0. FLC: 0-0. Others: 0-0. Total: 39-8.

Burnley	Mar 1937

Frank was a very fast and tricky winger whose best match by far was that against Cardiff City at Loftus Road, when he scored a hat-trick in a 5-1 victory for Q.P.R.
Debut: 29. 9.1935 v. Swindon Town (A). 2-2. Div.3 (S).

LYON Frank H.

(F.B.) Def 5' 8" 11st 3lbs
b. Crewe, Cheshire 23. 9.1879

Stockport County	1895
Crewe Alexandria	1900
Stoke	Oct 1901
Watford	Aug 1902
Q.P.R.	1903

Southern League: 56-0. FAC: 4-0. FLC: 0-0. Others: 0-0. Total: 60-0.

Chelsea	Mar 1907
Crewe Alexandra	May 1908

Honours: Played for Cheshire v. Lancashire. 2 Cheshire senior cup medals plus a runners-up medal. Southern professionals v. the Amateurs. In the Ilford side that toured Denmark. He was also with Chelsea when they toured Holland.

Frank established the reputation for his exceptional pace by being a competitive sprinter and held many trophies. Injury forced his early retirement from the game. He later opened a business in Crewe.
Debut: 24.10.1903 v. Fulham (A). 2-2. SLDiv. 1.

MACDONALD John

(O.R.) Wing 5' 10"
b. England

Glasgow Ashfield	1894
Newcastle United	Oct 1895
Lincoln City	Nov 1899
St. Mirren	1900
Q.P.R.	1908

Southern League: 18-0. FAC: 2-0. FLC: 0-0. Others: 0-0. Total: 20-0.

Inverness	1909

Honours: 2 Scottish junior caps.

Although John was born in England, he first played for the Scottish junior side Glasgow Ashfield. (n.b. Some contemporary publications spell his name as McDonald but this spelling is incorrect)
Debut: 1.9.1908 v. West Ham United (A). 0-2. SLDiv. 1.

MADDIX Daniel Shawn

CD 5' 11" 12st 2lbs
b. Ashford 11.10.1967

Tottenham Hotspur		Jul 1985
Southend United	(Loan)	Nov 1986
Q.P.R.		Jul 1987

Football/Premier League:292-13: FAC: 23-2. FLC: 28-3. Others: 5-0. Total:348-18.

Sheffield Wednesday	Jul 2001

Honours: 2 caps for Jamaica

Danny is a tough defender who has the ability to mark a man out of a match. He became the most popular player at the club, both with the supporters and with his fellow players. Danny suffered a serious foot injury which kept him out of the side for a long spell, but made a comeback as a substitute on the opening day of the 1994/95 season at Old Trafford. Then, in 2000, a knee injury meant another long lay-off. He never made a successful return to the Q.P.R. squad, adding just one League appearance, to a previous impressive record. His 14 years at Loftus Road saw him play in nearly 350 first team matches for the Rangers, during which time he scored a modest18 goals.

In the Summer of 2001, he moved up north, and in a strange twist of fate it was to the club that he had made his debut against 14 years earlier. After adding 61 Football League appearances to his record he was released by the Blades in the Summer of 2003. (Joined Barnet)
Debut: 28.11.1987 v. Sheffield Wed. (A). 1-3. Div. 1.

MAGUIRE Gavin Terence

CD 5' 10" 11st 8lbs
b. Hammersmith, London 24.11.1967

Q.P.R.		Oct 1985

Football League: 40-0. FAC: 6-0. FLC: 3-0. Others: 0-0.
Total: 49-0.

Portsmouth	(£225,000)	Jan 1989
Newcastle United	(Loan)	Oct 1991
Millwall	(£115,000)	Mar 1993
Scarborough	(Loan)	1994
U.S.A.		1995

Honours: 7 caps for Wales. 1 B cap.

A hard, uncompromising defender, who had undoubted skills and was adept at creating attacks by long and accurate passes out of defence. Gavin's mother came from the Rhondda and his father came from Ireland, so he was eligible for any one of the three home countries. He chose Wales.
Debut: 27.12.1986 v. Oxford United (A). 1-0. Div. 1.

MAHONEY-JOHNSON Michael Anthony

Striker 5' 10" 12st 0lbs
b. Paddington, London 6.11.1976

Q.P.R.		Apl 1995

Football League: 3-0. FAC: 0-0. FLC: 0-0. Others: 0-0.
Total: 3-0.

Wycombe Wanderers	(Loan)	Aug 1996
Brighton & Hove Albion	(Loan)	Feb 1998
Aylesbury		1999

A striker who has pace and has been given a couple of chances to prove himself but has failed to do so. Mike was given a free transfer.
Debut: 2.10.1996 v. Port Vale (H). 1-2. Div. 1.

MALCOLM Andrew

(R.H.) Mid 5' 9" 11st 4lbs
b. East Ham, London 4.5.1953
Romford school

West Han United		Jul 1950
Chelsea	(£12,000)	Nov 1961
Q.P.R.	(£12,000)	Oct 1962

Football League: 84-5. FAC: 8-1. FLC: 2-0. Others: 0-0.
Total: 94-6.

Apollen, South Africa	Jun 1965
Port Elizabeth, South Africa	1966
Brentwood Town	1967

Honours: Schoolboy & Youth International. 1 Football League cap. 2nd Div. championship medal.

Andy was a wholehearted player who would give his all on the field of play during a match. His serious expression during it, earned him the nickname of smiler. When his playing career was finished he worked for Lyons (on the ice cream side) until 1977. Andy then became a public house manager in Maldon, then later in Latchendon. In 1986 he emigrated to South Africa.
Debut: 22.10.1962 v. Hull City (H). 4-1. Div. 2.

MALLETT Joseph

(I.R.) Mid 5' 7" 11st 0lbs
b. Gateshead 8. 1.1916
St. Cuthbert's school
Dunston Colliery Welfare

Charlton Athletic		Nov 1935
Q.P.R.	(Loan)	1937

Football League: 29-4. FAC: 2-0. FLC: 0-0. Others: 1-0.
Total: 32-4.

Charlton Athletic		May 1938
Q.P.R.	(£800)	Feb 1939

Football League: 41-7. FAC: 5-2. FLC: 0-0. Others: 1-0.
Total: 47-9.

Southampton	(£5,000)	Feb 1947
Clapton Orient		Jul 1953

Joe was a very classy player, a true midfield general who could command the play with subtle touches and deft passes from a defensive position. He had two spells at Q.P.R., both before the war, during which time he notched up a total of 79 first team appearances. After the hostilities he commanded a large transfer fee when he moved to Southampton, despite being aged 31 at the time. In fact he was still playing, for Nottingham Forest reserves, at the age of 43 in 1959. He became the Birmingham City coach in 1964 then the manager one year later. Joe went to Greece in 1970 to coach Panionios, but five years later he was in the U.S.A. coaching New York Cosmos, Washington Diplomats in 1979 and finally San Jose Earthquakes in 1982. He returned to England a year later to become chief scout at Southampton. On his retirement, Joe moved to St. Leonards, Sussex.
Debut: 23.10.1937 v. Crystal Palace (H). 1-0. Div. 3. (S).

MANCINI Terence John

(C.H.) CD 6' 0" 12st 0lbs
b. Camden Town, London 4.10.1942

Fulham		
Watford		Jul 1961
Port Elizabeth, South Africa		Apl 1966
Leyton Orient		Nov 1967
Q.P.R.	(£20,000)	Oct 1971
Football League: 94-3. FAC: 12-2. FLC: 5-0. Others: 0-0. Total:111-5.		
Arsenal	(£20,000)	Oct 1974
Aldershot		Sep 1976
Los Angeles Aztecs, U.S.A.		1977

Honours: 5 caps for Eire. 2nd Div. runners-up medal. South African League championship medal. 3rd Div. championship medal.

Terry had an Italian father and an Irish mother and came from a family more renowned for their prowess in the boxing ring than on the football pitch. He was a tall, unflappable, self confident player, solid in the air but somewhat erratic on the ground, he knew his limitations and played to his strengths. Terry was one of the most colourful and popular characters to turn out for the club in the early seventies and had an infectious sense of humour which was liked by spectators and players alike. Whilst with Q.P.R. he played for Eire. In retirement he became the Fulham coach and later the Luton Town assistant manager for a while. He was then involved in running a car hire business followed by a long period working for Barwood Leisure, a sports travel company, as their sports events director.
Debut: 16.10.1971 v. Sheffield Wed. (A). 0-0. Div. 2.

MANNING John Thomas

(O.R.) Wing 5' 9" 11st 12lbs
b. Boston, Lincs. in 1886

Boston Lindum	
Boston Swifts	
Boston Town	
Hull City	Apl 1905
Bradford Park Avenue	Aug 1907
Rochdale	Jun 1910
Lincoln City	Aug 1911
Rotherham County	Aug 1919
Q.P.R.	Jul 1920
Football League: 22-5. FAC: 2-0. FLC: 0-0. Other: 0-0. Total: 24-5.	
Boston Town	Jul 1921

Honours: Central League championship medal.

John was a hefty winger who could brush aside the opposition with a repertoire of tricks and tremendous acceleration, who also had a bullet like shot to boot. One contemporary writer noted in 1913, "*impervious to hard knocks, he gets through by weight alone, where lighter men would be hustled off the ball*".
Debut: 23.10.1920 v.Swansea Town (A). 3-1. Div. 3.

MARCH Richard

(R.H.) Def 5' 7" 10st 8lbs
b. Washington, Co. Durham 9.10.1908 d.1987

Crowcrook Albion	
Q.P.R.	1932
Football League:220-3. FAC: 14-0. FLC: 0-0. Others: 7-0. Total:241-3.	

Tenacity, fearlessness and willingness were the attributes of this man. Dicky was a fiery red haired stripling who was revered by the spectators for his style of play. He played for Q.P.R. until 1941/42, a total of ten seasons. He clocked-up an extra 59 wartime appearances bringing his total to 300 overall; a true one club man. During the pre-war years he was a regular in the Football League team for nine seasons. After his retirement from playing he was made catering manager at the club.
Debut: 24.12.1932 v. Torquay United (A). 1-3.Div. 3 (S).

MARCROFT Edward Hollows

(O.R.) Wing 5' 6" 10st 2lbs
b. Rochdale, Lancashire in April 1910

Bacup Borough		
Great Harwood		Jul 1930
Middlesbrough	(£200)	Dec 1931
Q.P.R.		May 1932

Football League: 29-8. FAC: 4-1. FLC: 0-0. Others: 0-0. Total: 33-9.

Cardiff City	Jun 1933
Accrington Stanley	Jul 1934
Bacup Borough	Sep 1935
Rochdale	Jul 1936
Macclesfield	1937

When Ted signed for Great Harwood, he was said to have scored 66 goals in a run of 63 matches for his previous club. This prompted Middlesbrough to sign him but despite scoring on his debut, this match proved to be his only outing for the club. However, not only was Ted a fast and tricky winger but he was an excellent piano player too, for those after match sing-a-longs!
Debut: 27. 8.1932 v. Brentford (H). 2-3. Div. 3. (S).

MARSDEN Benjamin

(R.B.) Def 5' 9" 12st 6lbs
b. Hanley, Nr. Stoke in 1898

Port Vale	1918
Q.P.R.	1920

Football League:126-6. FAC: 6-0. FLC: 0-0. Others: 0-0. Total:132-6.

Reading	Jul 1925

Ben became the backbone of the Q.P.R. defence in the early days of the 3rd Division. It was acknowledged that he had an exceptionally hard kick, so he became the penalty expert of the side, and in his 132 appearances for the first team he netted six goals. He only played two matches for Reading during the 1925/26 season after which they released him. Ben served out the rest of his football career in minor non-League football.
Debut: 27.12.1920 v. Brentford (H). 1-0. Div. **3.**

MARSH Rodney William

Striker 6' 0" 12st 6lbs
b. Hatfield, Herts. 11.10.1944

Fulham		Oct 1962
Q.P.R.	(£15,000)	Mar 1966

Football League:181-89. FAC: 9-8. FLC: 16-17. Others: 0-0. Total:206-114.

Manchester City	(£200,000)	Mar 1972
Tampa Bay Rowdies, U.S.A.	(£45,000)	1976
Fulham		Aug 1976

Honours: Young England cap. 2 U23 caps. 9 England caps. 3rd Div. championship medal. League Cup winners medal. 2nd Div. runners-up medal. League Cup runners-up medal.

At the risk of repetition, Alec Stock's most inspired buy on the transfer market was Rodney Marsh from Fulham. At the time Rodney was an out of form player who had sustained an horrendous injury in 1965 which left him partially deaf. In form he was a flamboyant individual with a bountiful amount of skill and flair. Rodney was the top player during the most successful period in the club's history, in the mid-seventies. The cry of '*Rod-nee, Rod-nee*', would reverberate from the terraces at Loftus Road during his reign at the club. Amongst his many achievements, he created a new seasonal club goalscoring record when he netted 44 in the 1966/67 season. After six seasons at Loftus Road he moved on to Manchester City for a huge fee, before making his first move to the U.S.A. In 1978 he became the general manager of Tampa Bay Rowdies.
Debut: 19. 3.1966 v. Peterborough Utd. (A).1-1. Div.3.

MASON William Sidney

G 5' 10" 11st 8lbs
b. Wimbledon 31.10.1908 d. Bognar Regis Nov 1995

Wimbledon	1926
Fulham	Sep 1928
Q.P.R.	1933

Football League:154-0. FAC: 6-0. FLC: 0-0. Others: 10-0. Total:170-0.

Honours: Represented a Surrey Amateur X1. London Challenge Cup winners medal. London Combination runners-up medal.

A former amateur player at Wimbledon, Bill then spent five years at Fulham before his move to Q.P.R. Bill was a strong, muscular goalkeeper who played for the club well into World War Two (after being given a benefit match in 1939), adding over 70 matches to his total for the club. Besides becoming a War Reserve Policeman, he then worked in a munitions factory from 1943 to 1947 before rejoining the police. He was a P.C. in the Wimbledon Division for 20 years and then worked as a security guard until his retirement in 1975.
Debut: 18. 1.1934 v. Coventry City (A). 1-0. Div.3 (S).

MASSON Donald Sandison

Mid 5' 8" 10st 12lbs
b. Banchory, Scotland 28. 8.1946

Middlesbrough		Sep 1963
Notts County	(£6,000)	Sep 1968
Q.P.R.	(£100,000)	Dec 1974

Football League:116-18. FAC: 8-1. FLC: 12-3. Others: 8-2. Total:144-24.

Derby County	(Exchange deal)	Oct 1977
Notts County		Aug 1978
Minessota Kicks, U.S.A.		1981
Bulova, Hong Kong		1982
Los Angeles Kickers, U.S.A.		1987
Kettering		

Honours: 19 Scottish caps. 4th Div. championship medal. 1ST Div. runners-up medal.

Don entered First Division football at the age of 28, in December 1974, and gave the impression that a decade had been wasted for this gifted Scottish midfield player. Don had the apparent time to find his openings and distribute with precision and style.

Don is a fine example of talent finding its own reward no matter at what level it is exposed. He was a fiercely competitive and highly creative player who became the general of the attack in the mid-seventies. After three years at Loftus Road, further moves were made before he switched to the U.S.A. After he returned from the USA he became, for a time, the player/manager of Kettering, and later ran the Gallery Hotel in Nottingham.
Debut: 14.12.1974 v. Sheffield United (H). 1-0. Div. 1.

MATTHEWS F. W.

G
b.
Hampstead Town
Q.P.R. 1913
Southern League: 2-0. FAC: 0-0. FLC: 0-0. Others: 0-0. Total: 2-0.

An amateur goalkeeper who deputised for Nicholls at the end of the 1913/14 season. Matthews successfully managed to keep a blank sheet on both occasions.
Debut: 23. 4.1914 v. Brighton & H.A. (H). 3-0. SLDiv.1.

MAYES Thomas

(I.R.) Mid
b.
Grays United
Q.P.R. 1902
Southern League: 4-0. FAC: 0-0. FLC: 0-0. Others: 0-0. Total: 4-0.

Tom was the man who turned out in different forward positions when a player was absent or injured, in the early days of the club.
Debut: 6.12.1902 v. Watford (A). 2-0. SLDiv. 1.

McADAMS William J.

(C.F.) Striker 5' 11" 11st 9lbs
b. Belfast, N. Ireland 20. 1.1934

Bainbridge Town		
Glenavon		
Distillery		
Manchester City	(£10,000)	Dec 1953
Bolton Wanderers	(£15,000)	Sep 1960
Leeds United		Dec 1961
Brentford	(£8,000)	Jul 1962
Q.P.R.	(£5,000)	Sep 1964

Football League: 33-11. FAC: 3-1. FLC: 2-0. Others: 0-0. Total: 38-12.

Barrow	(£5,000)	Jul 1966
Netherfield		

Honours: 15 Northern Ireland caps. 4th Div championship medal. 4th Div. promotion medal.

A product of the Grosvenor Secondary School, Belfast, Billy worked as an apprentice heating engineer and turned down a career with Burnley after trials. A thrustful and courageous player, he had a fine burst of speed. Billy retired from football in 1968.
Debut: 25. 9.1964 v. Hull City (H). 2-1. Div. 3.

McALLISTER William

(L.H.) Mid 5' 8" 11st 4lbs
b. Glasgow, Scotland in 1900

Renton		Aug 1919
St. Mirren		Aug 1920
St. Johnston	(Loan)	Apl 1921
Ebbw Vale		Jul 1921
Brighton & Hove Albion		Oct 1921
Middlesbrough		Feb 1925
Q.P.R.		Oct 1926

Football League: 26-1. FAC: 0-0. FLC: 0-0. Others: 0-0. Total: 26-1.

Raith Rovers	Nov 1927
Heart of Midlothian	May 1929

Honours: Represented the Southern League v. the Central League.

Billy was noted as a, '*Brilliant ball player but very temperamental*'. A story goes that when the Scotsman signed for Brighton & Hove Albion from Ebbw Vale, the club played a friendly against his former Welsh team later that season as part of the deal. However, Billy threw a clod of earth into the crowd following a dispute with a number of fans on the terraces and had to be escorted into the dressing room at the end of the match. In the course of the same evening the fans caught up with him in a local restaurant and further ugly scenes developed. Although it was trouble caused in another match, when he was sent off, which resulted in a one month suspension.
Debut: 23.10.1926 v. Millwall (A). 1-2. Div. 3. (S).

McCAIRNS Thomas

(C.F.) Striker 5' 9" 11st 10lbs
b. Dinsdale, Co. Durham 22.12.1873d. Willesden 1932

Middlesbrough Ironopolis	
Whitby	1891
Grimsby Town	Sep 1893
Bristol Rovers	May 1898
Notts County	May 1899
Lincoln City	Nov 1899
Barnsley	Jun 1901
Wellington Town	May 1902

Q.P.R.	May 1903

Southern League: 1-0. FAC: 2-0. FLC: 0-0. Others: 0-0. Total: 3-0.

Brighton & Hove Albion	Dec 1903
Southern United	May 1904
Kettering Town	1904

Honours: Northern League championship medal. Football League v. Irish League.

Tommy ended his career as a journeyman, with a whirlwind tour of nine clubs in seven years. At Grimsby Town he scored 104 goals in 154 competitive matches, including six goals in a 7-1 victory over Leicester Fosse in 1896. Although it was reported that he was slow during his time at Q.P.R. he nevertheless still possessed excellent ball control and had the knack of being in the right place at the right time. Alas he never got the chance to prove himself at the club, for he only played one match in place of Milward who was ill at the time.
Debut: 24.10.1903 v. Fulham (A). 2-2. SLDiv. 1.

McCARGILL H.

(L.H.) Mid
b.
South Shields Aderlaide

Q.P.R.	1905

Southern League: 4-0. FAC: 0-0. FLC: 0-0. Others: 0-0. Total: 4-0.

McGargill was the man that stood in for either Downing or Yenson at wing half when either of the pair were injured.
Debut: 14. 4.1906 v. Fulham (A). 0-1. SLDiv. 1.

McCARTHY Alan James

CD. 5' 11" 12st 10lbs
b. Wandsworth, London 11. 1.1972

Q.P.R.		Dec 1989

Football League: 11-0. FAC: 1-0. FLC: 0-0. Others: 1-0. Total: 13-0.

Watford	(Loan)	Nov 1993
Plymouth Argyle	(Loan)	Feb 1994
Leyton Orient	(£25,000)	Aug 1995
Boreham Wood		Aug 1997

Honours: Youth cap for England. B cap for Wales. 3 U21 caps for Wales.

A reliable defender who was comfortable on the ball and tackled strongly. Alan was one of the few players to have represented two countries in the same sport, both Wales and England. He suffered an injury just as he was to about to join Northampton Town in 1998.
Debut: 24.11.1990 v. Arsenal (H). 1-3. Div. 1.

McCARTHY Leonard Daniel

(I.R.) Mid 5' 7" 11st 6lbs
b. Caerau, Wales
Caerau Harlequins

Crystal Palace	1929
Thames Association	1930
Portsmouth	1932
Q.P.R.	Jun 1937

Football League: 22-9. FAC: 4-1. FLC: 0-0. Others: 1-1. Total: 27-11.

Honours: London Challenge Cup winners medal.

Although not making many appearances or being a prolific goalscorer for the first team, Len netted 27 goals in 30 matches when the reserve side finished in second place to Arsenal in the London Combination, and won the London Challenge Cup in 1939
Debut: 30.10.1937 v. Notts County (A). 2-2. Div. 3 (S).

McCELLAND John Bonar

(O.R.) Wing 5' 8" 10st 10lbs
b. Bradford, Yorkshire 5. 3.1935
Manchester YMCA

Manchester City		Mar 1953
Lincoln City		Sep 1958
Q.P.R.	(£14,000)	Sep 1961

Football League: 71-22. FAC: 7-1. FLC: 1-0. Others: 0-0. Total: 79-23.

Portsmouth	(£10,000)	May 1963
Newport County		Jul 1968

The son of much travelled Jimmy, of Middlesbrough fame and the younger brother of Charlie. John proved to be a consistent player who was fast, skilful and always supplied a good supply of goals during the season. He retired in 1969 having scored over 100 goals in less than 400 matches.
Debut: 23. 9.1961 v. Watford (A). 2-3. Div. 3.

McCONNELL Alexander

(L.B.) Def 5' 8" 11st 10lbs
b. Glenbuck, Scotland in 1875
Glenbuck Athletic

Everton	1895
Woolwich Arsenal	Nov 1897
Q.P.R.	Jul 1899

Southern League: 51-0. FAC: 13-0 FLC: 0-0. Others: 0-0. Total: 64-0.

Grimsby Town	May 1901

Honours: Scottish Junior International.

Alex was a full back of the highest quality and was noted by the sports writers of the day as "*A powerful kicker and a splendid tackler*."

He had a younger brother, John, who also played for Grimsby Town around the same period. When Alex's playing days were over he became the reserve team manager of Grimsby Town in 1908.
Debut: 9. 9.1899 v. Tottenham Hot. (A). 0-1. SLDiv. 1.

McCREERY David

Mid 5' 6" 10st 7lbs
b. Belfast, Northern Ireland 16. 9.1957

Manchester United		Oct 1974
Q.P.R.	(£200,000)	Aug 1979

Football League: 57-4. FAC: 2-0. FLC: 8-1. Others: 0-0. Total: 67-5.

Tulsa Roughnecks, USA	(£125,000)	Mar 1981
Newcastle United	(£80,000)	Oct 1982
Sundsvaal, Sweden		Jun 1989
Heart of Midlothian		Sep 1989
Hartlepool United		Aug 1991
Coleraine, N. Ire.		Sep 1992
Carlisle United		Sep 1992

Honours: Northern Ireland school, youth and U21 caps. 67 full caps. 2nd Div. promotion medal. FA Cup winners medal. FA Cup runners-up medal.

A Tommy Docherty signing during his second stay at Loftus Road. The 'Doc' described him as *"The bargain of the century"*. David was a strong running enthusiastic player, who possessed an endless amount of energy, he was very fiery and full of action. He was appointed the Carlisle United player/ manager in 1992, and two years later the same at Hartlepool United. A Barnet scout in 1995 and a Blyth Spartans consultant later that year followed.
Debut: 19. 9.1979 v. Bristol Rovers (H). 2-0. Div. 2.

McCULLOCH Andrew

Striker 6' 2" 13st 11lbs
b. Northampton 3. 1.1950

Tottenham Hotspur		
Walton & Hersham		
Q.P.R.		Oct 1970

Football League: 42-10. FAC: 1-0. FLC: 4-1. Others: 0-0. Total: 47-11.

Cardiff City	(£45,000)	Oct 1972
Oxford United	(£70,000)	Jul 1974
Brentford		Mar 1976
Sheffield Wednesday		Jun 1979
Crystal Palace		Aug 1983
Aldershot		Nov 1984

Honours: Scottish U23 cap. 4th Div. promotion medal. 3rd Div.promotion medal.

Andy was the team mate of Steve Perryman, when he played in the 'Spurs Metropolitan League side of the late sixties. Andy obtained a degree in Civil Engineering at the time and was still an amateur footballer who didn't turn professional until he joined Q.P.R. He was sold on to Cardiff City after two years and nearly 50 senior side outings. Andy was a brave and bighearted striker who was the son of a former Scottish centre forward.
Debut: 17.10.1970 v. Birmingham City (H). 5-2. Div.2.

McDERMOTT Andrew

Def 5' 9" 11st 3lbs
b. Sydney, Australia 24. 3.1977

Australian Institute of Sport		
Q.P.R.		Aug 1995

Football League: 6-2. FAC: 0-0. FLC: 0-0. Others: 0-0. Total: 6-2.

W.B.A.	(£400,000)	Mar 1997
Notts County		Aug 2000
Northern Spirit (Aust.)		June 2001

Honours: Australian U23.

Andy had his contract cancelled by Notts County in the summer of 2001 to allow him to return to Australia. He returned to his native Australia and signed on for the NSL club Northern Spirit at the beginning of June that year.
Debut: 14.12.1996 v. Southend United (H).4-0. Div.1.

McDONALD Alan

CD 6' 2" 12st 7lbs
b. Belfast, Northern Ireland 12.10.1963

Q.P.R.		Aug 1981
Charlton Athletic	(Loan)	Mar 1983
Q.P.R.		May 1983

Football/Premier League:402-13. FAC: 33-2. FLC: 43-3. Others: 5-0. Total:483-17.

Swindon Town		Jul 1997

Honours: Northern Ireland school & youth caps. 52 full caps. League Cup runners-up medal.

The captain of his club and country on many occasions, Alan became a vastly experienced and imposing stopper, and the joker in the team. Although he was very likable, Alan was a tough defender who was good in the air and a real threat from free kicks in the opposing penalty area. Signed as a schoolboy, it was several seaasons before he got his first team chance, having spent a loan spell at Charlton Athletic in 1983.

He played nine matches and even in those early days, he showed his poise and composure, in the centre half position that was quite incredible for a youngster of 19 years. It was reported in those early days that Charlton tried to buy him for £50,000. But Alan remained loyal to Rangers, and in the next 14 years amassed no less than 402 League games, hence making him one of the top all-time players for appearances. During his long career at Q.P.R. he made his many appearances for Northern Ireland and also played in the EUFA Cup. He was ever-present in the League in 1985/86, and on three occasions missed just three games each season. After 16 years at Loftus Road, Alan was given a free transfer, and he moved to Swindon Town in 1997. He had the unusual experience of playing in goal in one match when the Swindon 'keeper was dismissed; the game was at Q.P.R.!
Debut: 24. 9.1983 v. Wolverhampton W. (A).4-0. Div.1.

McDONALD John

(R.B.) Def 5' 10" 12st 7lbs
b. Ayr, Scotland in 1882

Arden Villa	
Ayr F.C.	
Blackburn Rovers	May 1903
Leeds City	Jul 1905
Grimsby Town	Aug 1906
Q.P.R.	1907

Southern League:182 -0. FAC: 13-0. FLC: 0-0. Others: 3-0. Total:198-0.

Honours: 2 Southern League championship medals.

John played reserve to the famous Bob Crompton, the England captain, while playing for Blackburn Rovers. Staying a couple of seasons there before he moved to Leeds City. John was described as, '*a quiet fellow who was unassuming, whose play was more solid than showy and was a useful man to have in any defence*'. He retired from playing in 1913.
Debut: 14. 9.1907 v. Tottenham Hot. (A). 2-3. SLDiv. 1.

McEWAN David

Striker 6' 0" 11st 0lbs
b. Westminster, London 2.11.1977

Dulwich Hamlet	
Tottenham Hotspur	Jan 2000
Q.P.R.	Jul 2001

Football League: 5-0. FAC: 0-0. FLC: 1-0. Others: 0-0. Total: 6-0.

Dave arrived on a six month contract in the summer of 2001 and although supposedly playing well in the reserves, he failed to impress in the seniors and he was released in January 2002.
Debut: 25. 8.2001 v. Reading (H). 0-0. Div. 2.

McEWAN Robert

(L.B.) Def 5' 10" 12st 8lbs
b. Scotland in 1881

St. Bernards	
Bury	1903
Glasgow Rangers	1904
Heart of Midlothian	
Chelsea	May 1905
Glossop North End	Aug 1906

Q.P.R. 1908
Southern League: 1-0. FAC: 0-0. FLC: 0-0. Others: 0-0.
Total: 1-0.

Honours: F.A.Cup winners medal.

Bob was used as a reserve to Joe Fidler and was called upon just once on Boxing Day 1908.
Debut: 26.12.1908 v. Southampton (A). 4-1. SLDiv. 1.

McEWAN William

(O.R.) Wing
b. Glasgow, Scotland 29. 8.1914 d. Gravesend Dec1991
Petershill

Q.P.R.	Jun 1938
Football League: 96-17. FAC: 12-3. FLC: 0-0. Others: 2-0. Total:110-20.	
Leyton Orient	Feb 1950
Gravesend & Northfleet	Jul 1951

Honours: 3rd Div. (South) championship medal.

A terrier-like winger who could strike panic into an opposing defender. Billy was on tour in Burma at the end of the war with an Army X1 and although he had lost a lot of his pace from 1939, he was nevertheless still able to reproduce his tricks. As with others, the war deprived Billy of part of his football career, and his peacetime appearances span each side of the conflict. He made 76 wartime appearances scoring 34 goals and at the age of 38 years, along with Johnny Pattison, he was tranferred to Leyton Orient to make another 21 appearances before his move to Gravesend & Northfleet.
Debut: 4. 3.1939 v. Crystal Palace (A). 1-0. Div. 3. (S).

McFLYNN Terence

Mid 5' 11" 12st 2lbs
b. Magherafelt, Northern Ireland 27. 3.1981

Q.P.R.	May 1998
Football League: 2-0. FAC: 0-0. FLC: 0-0. Others: 0-0. Total: 2-0.	
Woking	Aug 2001
Margate	Dec 2001

Honours: Northern Ireland school and youth caps. 7 U21 caps.

Terry was the captain of the Under-19 side that reached the final of the Premier League Youth Academy play-offs in 2001. Yet he was was one of fifteen players to be released by the club in the summer that year.
Debut: 28. 4.2001 v. Stockport County (H). 0-3. Div.1.

McGEE Paul G.

Striker 5' 9" 11st 7lbs
b. Sligo, Eire 19. 6.1954

Summerhill College		
Sligo Rovers		
Kidderminster Harriers		1972
Hereford United		1973
Finn Harps		1973
Sligo Rovers		1974
Toronto Mets, Canada		1975
Montreal Castors, Canada		1976
Q.P.R.		Nov 1977
Football League: 39-7. FAC: 2-0. FLC: 3-1. Others: 0-0. Total: 44-8.		
P.N.E.		Oct 1979
Burnley	(Loan)	Nov 1981
Burnley	(£25,000)	Mar 1982
Dundalk	(Loan)	Mar 1983
Sligo Rovers		1983
Shamrock Rovers		1984
Waterford		1985
Sligo Rovers		1985
Galway		1986
Haarlem, Holland	(£12,000)	1987
Galway		1987
Sligo Rovers		Nov. 1990
Derry City		1990
Sligo Rovers		Nov 1991
Athlone Town		1991
Sligo Rovers		Nov 1992
Galway United		Dec 1992
Finn Harps		Jan 1993

Honours: Youth International. 2 U21 caps. 15 caps at full level. Canadian League championship medal. 3rd Div. championship winners medal. 3 times the Irish school champions. FACup of Ireland winners medal. Football League of Ireland League championship medal.

Paul was a somewhat bubbly and confident character renowned for his speed off the mark. A much travelled striker, who remained at Loftus Road for two years - one of his longest stays! He helped his school, Summerhill College, to win the All-Ireland schools title in successive seasons netting a hat-trick in one of the finals, and made his debut for Sligo Rovers as a sixteen year old.
Debut: 19.11.1977 v. Coventry City (A). 1-4. Div. 1.

McGOVERN Brian

CD 6' 3" 12st 7lbs
b. Dublin, Eire 28. 4.1980
Cherry Orchard

Arsenal		Sep 1997
Q.P.R.	(Loan)	Dec 1999

Football League: 5-0. FAC: 0-0. FLC: 0-0. Others: 0-0. Total: 5-0.

Norwich City	(£50,000)	Jul 2000
Peterborough United		Nov 2002
St.Patricks Athletic (Ireland)		Mar 2003
Longford Town (Ireland)	(Loan)	Apr 2003

Honours: 2 U21 caps for Eire. Youth caps for Eire.

Brian was loaned-out by Arsenal in December 1999 for three months to gain experience. Good in the air and a strong tackler, he uses the ball well, especially at set pieces. Brian stayed for just a month, but left after suffering an injury.
Debut: 28.12.1999 v. Crewe Alexandria (H). 1-0. Div.1.

McGOVERN Michael John

Mid 5' 11" 12st 0lbs
b. Hayes, Middlesex 15. 2.1951
Harrow Borough

Q.P.R.		Nov 1968

Football League: 12-0. FAC: 1-0. FLC: 0-0. Others: 0-0. Total: 13-0.

Watford	(Loan)	Aug 1972
Swindon Town		Feb 1973
Aldershot	(Loan)	Mar 1975
Hillingdon Borough		Aug 1975
Hayes		Aug 1977
Southall		Jan 1986
Chalfont		Mar 1987

Mick began his apprenticeship in July 1966 at the age of 16 years. He made just 13 appearances in four and a half years at Loftus Road, but went on to a long career outside the League.
Debut: 26.12.1967 v. Plymouth Argyle (A). 1-0. Div. 2.

McGOVERN Thomas

(R.H.) Mid 5' 9" 11st 0lbs
b. Glasgow, Scotland
Halifax Town

Brentford	1918
Q.P.R.	1920

Football League: 2-0. FAC: 0-0. FLC: 0-0. Others: 0-0. Total: 2-0.

Bristol City	1924
Millwall	1924
Merthyr Town	1925
Clydebank	1926

Tom played in the first two matches of the newly formed Division 3, both defeats, and three team changes were then made, of which McGovern was one. He never played for the senior squad again.
Debut: 28. 8.1920 v. Watford (H). 1-2. Div. 3.

McGOWAN Frank

(I.L.) Striker
b.
Morpeth F.C.

Q.P.R.	1903

Southern League: 7-3. FAC: 2-0. FLC: 0-0. Others: 0-0. Total: 9-3.

Frank scored on his debut for the club and indeed netted three goals in the first three matches. However, he only played when Blackwood was out of the side, and added just four more games to his total.
Debut: 19. 9.1903 v. Tottenham Hot. (H).2-0. SLDiv. 1.

McKAY John

(O.L.) Wing
b. Port Glasgow, Scotland 27. 6.1927
Irvine F.C.

Q.P.R.	Mar 1949

Football League: 17-1. FAC: 0-0. FLC: 0-0. Others: 0-0. Total: 17-1.

Yeovil Town	1952

John was one of five tried in the outside left position in 1950. Then Ernie Shepherd arrived the next year, and that effectively put an end to the left wing problem. The club was relegated in 1952 and McKay was given a free transfer.
Debut: 19.11.1949 v. Bury (H). 1-0. Div. 2.

McKAY William

(O.R.) Wing
b. Rothsay, Scotland 10. 3.1927
Deal Town
Q.P.R. Jul 1955
Football League: 6-0. FAC: 0-0. FLC: 0-0. Others: 0-0.
Total: 6-0.
Dover 1956

Billy was a tiny winger who was tricky and shared the right wing spot with three others. In 1956 he joined Fred Durrant at Dover.
Debut: 30. 8.1955 v. Brentford (A). 0-2. Div. 3. (S).

McKENZIE Thomas

(C.F.) Striker
b. Invernass, Scotland
Petershill
Third Lanark
Sunderland 1905
Plymouth Argyle
Portsmouth
Glossop North End 1907
Q.P.R. 1908
Southern League: 9-1. FAC: 0-0. FLC: 0-0. Others: 0-0.
Total: 9-1.
Brentford

Tommy played centre forward for the opening seven matches of the season, when the team scored just three goals. That season the club had to play all their matches in mid-week and it was not until W.O.Steer was recruited that things started to improve.
Debut: 1. 9.1908 v. West Ham United (A). 0-2. SLDiv.1.

McKIE Daniel

(C.F.) Striker
b.
P.N.E. 1904
Glossop North End 1905
Chorley 1907
Q.P.R. 1910
Southern League: 68-28. FAC: 1-2. FLC: 0-0. Others: 1-0.
Total: 70-30.

A fine opportunist centre forward who could find the net with rewarding regularity. Daniel possessed a very hard shot and was the team's penalty taker. He was the club's leading goalscorer during the second championship season. Unfortunately during the following campaign, after suffering a very bad injury during the close season tour of Germany, he faded from the scene.
Debut: 12.9.1910 v. West Ham United (H). 0-2. SLDiv.1.

McKINLAY

(H.B.) Mid
b.
Q.P.R. 1901
Southern League: 4-0. FAC: 0-0. FLC: 0-0. Others: 0-0.
Total: 4-0.

McKinlay was a reserve who filled in for the likes of Seeley, Bowman, Keetch and McQueen.
Debut: 26.10.1901 v. Luton Town (A). 0-1. SLDiv. 1.

McKINNEY E.

(O.R) Wing
b.
Broom Athletic
Q.P.R. 1914
Southern League:; 2-0. FAC: 0-0. FLC: 0-0. Others: 0-0.
Total: 2-0.

This winger appeared twice in consecutive matches in place of Thompson who was injured at the time. The youngster obviously didn't impress and he was not give another chance.
Debut: 27. 2.1915 v. Gillingham (H). 3-0. SLDiv. 1.

McLARNEY P.

(R.B.) Def
b.
Q.P.R. 1905
Southern League: 8-0. FAC: 0-0. FLC: 0-0. Others: 0-0.
Total: 8-0.

McLarney replaced Lyon who had been injured during the close season. However, as soon as Lyon recovered, McLarney faded from the scene.
Debut: 2. 9.1905 v. New Brompton (H). 4-0.SLDiv. 1.

McLEAN John C.

(C.H.) CD 5' 6" 12st 7lbs
b. Port Glasgow, Scotland 22. 5.1872
Greenock Volunteers 1890
Liverpool 1894
Grimsby Town Jun 1897
Bristol City May 1898
Bristol Rovers 1902
Millwall Athletic Apl 1904
Q.P.R. May 1906
Southern League: 41-0. FAC: 1-0. FLC: 0-0. Others: 2-0.
Total: 44-0.

Honours: 2 County caps for Renfrewshire. Scottish Junior International cap. Southern League championship medal.

John arrived at the club at the end of his career with the reputation of being a hard grafter as well as fearless in the tackle. By todays standards he was short for a central defender but this was evidently not unusual for this era.
Debut: 1. 9.1906 v. Luton Town (A). 1-1. SLDiv. 1.

McLEOD George J.

(O.L.) Wing
b. Inverness, Scotland 30.11.1932

Inverness Clachnaccudin		
Luton Town		Jan 1955
Brentford	(£6,000)	Oct 1958
Q.P.R.	(£8,000 + Lazarus)	Jan 1964

Football League: 41-4. FAC: 0-0. FLC: 1-0. Others: 0-0.
Total: 42-4.

A good buy for Brentford, George remained at Griffin Park for over five years, before being sold within a part exchange deal to Q.P.R. He was at Loftus Road for little over a year before retiring in 1965. George emigrated to South Africa and around the same time Mark Lazarus returned to Loftus Road.
Debut: 17. 9.1963 v. Bristol Rovers (A). 0-0. Div. 3.

McLEOD Robert

G 6' 0"
b. Scotland
7th Scottish Rifles

Raith Rovers	1911
Newport County	1913
Q.P.R.	1914

Southern League: 38-0. FAC: 3-0. FLC: 0-0. Others: 0-0.
Total: 41-0.

Armadale	1921

Honours: Scottish cup winners medal.

Bob was noted as an outstanding goalkeeper. He saved two penalties in a match for Newport County on Xmas Day 1913 to enable them to take the points.
Debut: 1. 3.1914 v. Millwall (A). 1-3. SLDiv. 1.

McLINTOCK Francis (M.B.E.)

CD 5' 10" 11st 4lbs
b. Glasgow, Scotland 28.12.1939

Shawfield Juniors		1955
Leicester City		Jan 1957
Arsenal	(£80,000)	Oct 1964
Q.P.R.	(£20,000)	Jun 1973

Football League:127-5. FAC: 14-0. FLC: 14-1. Others: 8-0.
Total:163-6.

Honours: 9 Scottish caps. 1 U23 cap. 3 FA Cup runners-up medals. 3 League Cup winners medals. London FA Challenge Cup medal. Inter Cities Fairs Cup winners medal. League Championship medal plus FA Cup winners medal (the double). Footballer of the Year.

Frank was a natural leader of men, a very resolute and skilled player. He was transferred to Arsenal for a record fee for a wing half, it was also the highest amount that Arsenal had until then paid for a player. Even after 18 years playing experience he still commanded a transfer fee when he moved to Loftus Road. He captained the Q.P.R. side to the runners-up spot in the 1st Division (1976) and to the quarter finals of the UEFA Cup one year later. After four years with Rangers, he retired from playing in 1977, having enjoyed a career which spanned twenty years, and in which he played well over six hundred League matches.

Frank first became the Leicester City manager, then was appointed the Q.P.R. coach in 1982. The Brentford manager post followed in 1984 and finally the Millwall assistant/manager in 1988. He now runs a chain of 'Cash Converter' shops and also keeps busy as an after dinner speaker.
Debut: 22. 9.1973 v. Birmingham City (H). 2-2. Div. 1.

McMAHON Hugh J.

(O.L.) Wing 5' 10" 10st 8lbs
b. Grangetown, Yorkshire 24. 9.1909 d. in 1986

Mexborough Town		
Sheffield Wednesday		
Cowdenbeath		
Blackpool		1930
Stoke City		
Reading		Aug 1932
Mexborough Town		
Southend United		1933
Reading		Jun 1934
Q.P.R.		May 1936

Football League: 41-3. FAC: 3-1. FLC: 0-0. Others: 1-1. Total: 45-5.

Sunderland	(£3,000)	Nov 1937
Hartlepool United		1946
Rotherham United		1947

Hugh sampled football in the 1st Division as well as life in the 3rd in both North and South Divisions. Q.P.R. were lucky that he came into form at the right time, for what was known as the Bank of England club, Sunderland, paid £3,000 for him to cash-strapped Rangers. Hugh continued to play football until well after the 2nd World War.
Debut: 12. 9.1936 v.Notts County (A). 2-1. Div.3 (S).

McNAB John S.

(R.H.) Mid 6' 1" 11st 7lbs
b. Cleland, Scotland 17. 4.1895 d. 2. 1.1949

Army football	
Bellshill Athletic	
Liverpool	Nov 1919
Q.P.R.	Jun 1928

Football League: 54-2. FAC: 5-0. FLC: 0-0. Others: 0-0. Total: 59-2.

Honours: 1 Scottish cap. 2 League championship medals.

John was described as a tall, rawboned, long-legged defender who was tough in the tackle and strong in defence. With him went the reputation of being the most likely winner of most 50/50 situations. John was noted as the hard man of the 1920s, after being banned for a six week period in 1925, after having been sent off in a match. In his retirement he became a licensee in Bootle.
Debut: 25. 8.1928 v. Torquay United (A).4-3.Div.3. (S).

McNAUGHT John William

(O.R.) Wing
b.

Bourne College, Quinton	
Hounslow	
Q.P.R.	1908

Southern League: 57-5. FAC: 5-1. FLC: 0-0. Others: 1-0. Total: 63-6.

Southend United	1911
Llanelly	1914

John made his debut for the club, in the Charity Shield replay match at Stamford Bridge in place of Pentland who had moved up north to Middlesbrough. As an amateur he was signed from Hounslow, and made nearly 60 first team appearances for the Rangers over the following three years.
Debut: 29. 8.1908 v. Manchester Utd. 0-4. Charity Shield

McQUADE Terrance J.

(O.L.) Wing
b. Hackney, London 21. 2.1941

Enfield	
Millwall	Oct 1961
Q.P.R.	Jul 1963

Football League: 20-2. FAC: 3-0. FLC: 1-0. Others: 0-0. Total: 24-2.

Leyton Orient	
Millwall	Nov 1965

Honours: 4th Div. championship medal.

Alec Stock acquired this winger along with the Brady brothers in 1963, but Terry made little impression at Loftus Road, playing in only 20 League matches in the next fourteen months before he moved back across London.
Debut: 17. 9.1963 v. Bristol Rovers (A). 0-0. Div. 3.

McQUEEN Hugh

(O.L.) Wing 5' 8" 11st 7lbs
b. Harthill, Scotland 1.10.1867 d. Norwich 8. 4.1944

Benhar Sab school	
Leith Athletic	1890
Liverpool	Oct 1892
Derby County	Jul 1895
Q.P.R.	May 1901

Southern League: 26-9. FAC: 3-0. FLC: 0-0. Others: 0-0. Total: 29-9.

Gainsborough Town	Jul 1902
Fulham	Dec 1902
Hibernian	Jan 1903
Kilmarnock	Sep 1904
Norwich City	Sep 1905

Honours: Roseberry Charity cup winners medal. Edinburgh Shield winners medal. 2 FACup runners-up medals. 2nd Div. Championship winners medal.

Hugh's father was a pit manager and father to nine more boys. Hugh was the Victorian equivalent of a play-maker with his skill, courage and enthusiasm much to the fore. The speed and accuracy of his crosses gained him a fine reputation and he was voted the best player on the losing side (Derby County) in the 1898 FACup Final by the "Football Chat" magazine. He was near the end of his career when he joined Q.P.R., but moved on after a year, and continued for three more. On his retirement he acquired a newsagent's shop in Norwich which he kept until the 2nd World War.
Debut: 7. 9.1901 v. Watford (H). 0-1. SLDiv. 1.

MEAKER Michael John

Mid 5' 11" 11st 5lbs
b. Greenford, Middlesex 18. 8.1971

Q.P.R.		Feb 1990

Football/Premier League: 34-1. FAC: 3-1. FLC: 2-1. Others: 2-0. Total: 41-3.

Plymouth Argyle	(Loan)	Nov 1991
Reading	(£550,000)	Jul 1995
Bristol Rovers		Aug 1998
Swindon Town	(Loan)	Mar 2000
Plymouth Argyle		Feb 2001
Northwich Victoria		Jul 2001
Southall Town		2003

Honours: Welsh B International. 2 caps at U21 level.

Although Mike was born in England he claimed Welsh nationality on his mothers side. A tricky performer with exciting attacking skills on a good day, on others his potential remains unfulfilled.
Debut: 20.11.1990 v. Southampton (A). 0-4. L.C.Rnd.2.

MERRICK Jack

G
b. Great Barr, Scotland in 1900
Aston Villa
Q.P.R. 1919
Southern League: 38-0. FAC: 1-0. FLC: 0-0. Others: 0-0. Total: 39-0.
Birmingham City
Walsall 1921
Nuneaton Town
Manchester United

Jack was the goalkeeper who played in the team for the last season of the club's Southern League days.
Debut: 30. 8.1919 v. Bristol Rovers (A). 2-0. SLDiv. 1.

METCHICK David J.

(I.F.) Mid 5' 8" 11st 0lbs
b. Bakewell, Derbyshire 14. 8.1943

West Ham United	
Fulham	Aug 1961
Leyton Orient	Dec 1964
Peterborough United	Mar 1966
Q.P.R.	Aug 1968

Football League: 3-1. FAC: 0-0. FLC: 1-0. Others: 0-0. Total: 4-1.

Arsenal	Sep 1970
Atlanta Chiefs, USA	1971
Miami Toros	
Atlanta Apollos	
Brentford	Sep 1973
Hendon	1975
Hillingdon Borough	
Woking	

Honours: 7 England youth caps.

Dave was a highly promising midfield player who had a flair in his younger days for scoring goals. Alas he was too small for a striking role and he was played out of position on the wing. He joined Arsenal for a small fee and served the reserve side well, being a great influence on the youngsters of the day.
Debut: 5.10.1968 v. W.B.A. (A). 1-3. Div. 1.

MICKLEWHITE Gary

(O.R.) Wing 5' 7" 10st 4lbs
b. Southwark, London 21. 3.1961

Manchester United		Mar 1978
Q.P.R.		Jul 1979

Football League: 106-11. FAC: 6-1. FLC: 13-5. Others: 2-0. Total: 127-17.

Derby County	(£90,000)	Feb 1985
Gillingham		Jul 1993
Slough Town		1996

Honours: FACup runners-up medal. 2 2nd Div. championship medals. 3rd Div. promotion medal.

Gary was a hard working, energetic midfield player, who was full of class, having come from Manchester United on a free transfer. A fringe first team player, playing in about half the games, nearly six years later Derby County paid £90,000 for him and he made 112 consecutive appearances for them. Gary was used as a full back at his next, and last, Football League club, Gillingham.
Debut: 3.10.1981 v. Blackburn Rovers (H). 2-0. Div.2.

MIDDLEMISS Herbert

(O.L.) Wing 5' 10" 11st 5lbs
b. Newcastle 19.12.1888 d. Brixham, Devon 28. 6.1941
Stalybridge

Stockport County	Sep 1907
Tottenham Hotspur	Nov 1907
Q.P.R.	Jun 1920

Football League: 16-1. FAC: 0-0. FLC: 0-0. Others: 0-0.
Total: 16-1.

Honours: 4 trial matches for England. South v. North. Football League v. Southern League. 2nd Div. runners-up medal.

Bert was a very fine winger, always keen to cut inside and take a shot at goal. He joined Q.P.R. in their first season in the Football League, but by then near the end of his playing career.
Debut: 28. 8.1920 v. Watford (H). 1-2. Div.3.

MIDDLETON John

(I.R.) Mid 5' 10" 12st 6lbs
b. Sunderland 19. 4.1898
Herrington Swifts
Durham City
Lambton Star

Leicester City	May 1922
Q.P.R.	May 1925

Football League: 54-9. FAC: 0-0. FLC: 0-0. Others: 0-0.
Total: 54-9.

Aldershot	Jul 1927

Although John was an inside forward he was gradually converted into a half back. In fact he eventually became a player able to play right across the half back line, playing centre half for Aldershot until 1937. On hanging-up his boots he became the trainer/coach at the Hampshire club.
Debut: 29. 8.1925 v. Gillingham (A). 0-3. Div. 3 (S).

MIKLOSKO Ludek

G 6' 5" 14st 0lbs
b. Ostrava, Czechoslovakia 9.12.1961
Banik Ostrava

West Ham United	(£300,000)	Feb 1990
Q.P.R.	(£50,000)	Oct 1998

Football League: 57-0. FAC: 6-0. FLC: 2-0. Others: 0-0.
Total: 65-0.

Honours: 44 caps for Czechoslovakia. B.I. U23

A tall and commanding goalkeeper who was released by Q.P.R. during the Summer of 2001. After a lengthy stay at West Ham, Ludo moved across London to Loftus Road during the 1998/99 season. He began the 2000/01 season as understudy to Lee Harper before playing his first match of the season in November. Ludo retained his place until March 2001 before being dropped. After he was released, he took up the post of goalkeeping coach at West Ham United.
Debut: 3.10.1998 v. Grimsby Town (H). 1-2. Div. 1.

MILLAR Harry

(C.F.) Striker 5' 9" 12st 0lbs
b. Paisley, Renfrewshire, Scotland in 1874
Abercorn
P.N.E.

Bury	1894
Reading	1899
Sheffield Wednesday	1900
Q.P.R.	1901

Southern League: 24-7. FAC: 3-5. FLC: 0-0. Others: 0-0.
Total: 27-12.

Harry was recognised as one of the cleverest strikers in the Victorian era, although his playing career was apparently quite short. Unfortunately little has been traced in print of this player. Probably his most memorable matches for Bury were his four goals v. Crewe Alexandria in 1894 and the same tally for Stockton in the FACup in 1897. He also scored a quartet of goals for Q.P.R. in an FACup match v. West Norwood in 1901.
Debut: 7. 9.1901 v. Watford (H). 0-1. SLDiv. 1.

MILLBANK Joseph H.

(C.H.) CD
b. Edmonton, London 30. 9.1919
Wolverhampton Wanderers

Crystal Palace	Aug 1939
Q.P.R.	Jul 1948

Football League: 1-0. FAC: 0-0. FLC: 0-0. Others: 0-0.
Total: 1-0.

Gillingham	1949
Bedford Town	1950

Transferred to Crystal Palace at the beginning of the War, Joe was unlucky in that, footballwise, he was born at the wrong time. Of the 87 appearances he made for Crystal Palace only 29 were in the League, the rest being wartime matches.
Debut: 11. 9.1948 v. Barnsley (H). 2-2. Div. 2.

MILLER James

(C.F.) Striker
b. Glasgow, Scotland
Vale of Leven

Q.P.R.	1913

Southern League: 63-28. FAC: 8-3. FLC:0-0. Others: 0-0.
Total: 71-31.

Hartlepool United	1921

Jimmy was a very tough centre forward who lost the better part of his playing days whilst in the trenches at Flanders. When peace came and he returned home from France, he seemed a different person; in 1921 moved to Hartlepool where he played for the United in the North Eastern League.
Debut: 1. 9.1913 v. Swindon Town (A). 0-3. SLDiv. 1.

MILLINGTON Thomas

(R.B.) Def
b. Manchester in 1887
Pendlebury
Bury 1908
Q.P.R. 1914
Southern League: 28-0. FAC: 3-0. FLC: 0-0. Others: 0-0. Total: 31-0.

Tom turned out quite regularly for the club up to the First World War. He started out as an inside forward at Bury but settled in nicely at full back at Q.P.R. There is no trace of him after the Great War.
Debut: 1. 9.1914 v. Millwall (A). 1-3. SLDiv. 1.

MILLS Donald G.

(I.L.) Mid 5' 10" 10st 6lbs
b. Rotherham 17. 8.1928 d. Torquay in February 1994
Q.P.R. Aug 1946
Football League: 45-6. FAC: 3-3. FLC: 0-0. Others: 0-0. Total: 48-9.
Torquay United (Loan) Mar 1949
Q.P.R. Jan 1950
Football League: 31-3. FAC: 0-0. FLC: 0-0. Others: 0-0. Total: 31-3.
Cardiff City (£12,500) Feb 1951
Leeds United (£12,000) Sep 1951
Torquay United Dec 1952

Honours: Represented the 3rd Div. (South) 3 times. 3rd Div. (South) championship medal. 4th Div. promotion medal.

Spotted at the age of 16 years old playing football in a mining community in Bramley, near Rotherham, Don signed professional forms for Q.P.R. on his 17th birthday. Loaned to Torquay United because of his frailty, it was thought that a spell of sea air would help to fill out his frame. The 'Don', as he became known was so popular at the Devonshire club that they tried to buy him, and eventually they did in 1952. Don stayed there for 20 years as a player, coach and scout. Later he became a traffic warden in Torquay.
Debut: 25.9.1946v.Bournemouth&B.A.(H).3-0. Div.3 (S)

MILWARD George

(C.F.) Striker
b. Chesterfield in 1879 d. Whittington 16. 1.1909
Poolsbrook United May 1900
New Whittington Exchange Sep 1901
Chesterfield Town Jun 1902
Q.P.R. May 1903
Southern League: 46-14. FAC: 0-0. FLC:0-0. Others: 0-0. Total: 46-14.

George or Paddy as he was generally known, was a deadly finisher, well liked by spectators. Unfortunately he sustained a bad injury, which caused the onset of a serious illness from which he never recovered. Paddy returned to Chesterfield to open a tobacconist shop until his premature death at the age of 29 years.
Debut: 5. 9.1903 v. Brentford (H). 1-0. SLDiv. 1.

MITCHELL Archibald P.

(C.H.) CD 5' 8" 12st 0lbs
b. Smethwick, Staffs 15.12.1885 d. April 1949
Aston Villa 1905
Q.P.R. 1907
Southern/Football League:306-11. FAC: 24-1. FLC: 0-0. Others: 1-0. Total:331-12.
Brentford 1921

Honours: 2 Southern League championship medals. 7 Southern League caps. Represented an FA X1 & The League.

The captain who became a legend in the side, who was later to become manager, Archie was to play many matches for the club, for including wartime appearances he totalled 467, during which time he scored 22 goals.

Strong and wiry, he developed into one of the pivots in the Southern League, and being an excellent header of the ball and a good tackler, he was probably the most influential player in the early history of the Rangers. After retirement from playing, Archie became the manager of Brentford for a time, then coached on the Continent for two years. When he returned he managed Dartford in 1928. He finally embraced the job of manager at Q.P.R. in 1930.
Debut: 2. 9.1907 v. Tottenham Hot. (H). 3-3. SLDiv. 1.

MOBLEY Victor J.

(C.H.) CD 6' 0" 13st 8lbs
b. Oxford 11.10.1943

Oxford City		
Sheffield Wednesday		Sep 1961
Q.P.R.	(£55,000)	Oct 1969

Football League: 25-0. FAC: 3-0. FLC: 3-0. Others: 0-0.
Total: 31-0.

Honours: Capped by Young England. 13 caps for the U23. 1 Football League cap.

Vic must have been one of the most unluckiest players in the Football League during the middle to late sixties. First of all a poisoned foot prevented him from winning an England cap in 1964, then badly damaged ankle ligaments caused him to miss the 1966 FACup final. He was a big solid, fair haired man and was the club's bmost notable signing to that date. Shortly after joining Q.P.R. it was discovered that he suffered from osteo-arthritis in his knees. A court case ensued, in which the Rangers sued for their money back, but it was to no avail. After hanging his boots up, in 1971, he became involved in the part time management of Oxford City. In the end, however,, Vic elected to emigrate to New Zealand where he became the coach to Papatoetoe.
Debut: 4.10.1969 v. Middlesbrough (H). 4-0. Div. 2.

MOFFATT Hugh

(O.R.) Wing 5' 4" 9st 2lbs
b. Camerton, Cumberland in 1900

Arsenal	1923
Guildford United	
Luton Town	1925
Everton	1926
Oldham Athletic	1926
Walsall	1928
Q.P.R.	1929

Football League: 15-3. FAC: 0-0. FLC: 0-0. Others: 0-0.
Total: 15-3.

A tiny winger who was mainly used as a reserve to Coward. Hugh was fast and tricky and moved between quite a few clubs in the 1920s.
Debut: 31. 8.1929 v. Crystal Palace (A). 1-1. Div. 3 (S).

MOGER

G
b.

Q.P.R.	1905

Southern League: 3-0. FAC: 0-0. FLC: 0-0. Others: 0-0.
Total: 3-0.

One thing certain about Moger is that he is not the same goalkeeper that played for Manchester United, despite what some references generally state. Although detailed research has not revealed anything further about this man.
Debut: 21. 4.1906 v. Northampton T. (A). 1-1 SLDiv.1.

MOLLOY Peter

(L.H.) Mid 5' 10" 12st 0lbs
b. Haslington, Lancashire 20. 4.1904
d. St. Albans 16. 2.1993

Accrington Stanley	Jul 1930
Fulham	Dec 1931
Bristol Rovers	May 1933
Cardiff City	Feb 1934
Q.P.R.	Jul 1935

Football League: 3-0. FAC: 0-0. FLC: 0-0. Others: 0-0.
Total: 3-0.

Stockport County	Jul 1936
Carlisle United	May 1937
Bradford City	May 1938
Belfast Distillery	1943
Accrington Stanley	1944
Kettering	
Notts County	Apl 1948

Honours: Northern Ireland League X1 v. Northern Ireland Regional League. 3rd Div. (North) Cup winners medal.

A shilling each-way bet on a horse called King of Clubs changed Peter's life completely, when it won, and he ran away from home to join the Kings Royal Rifles. Pete was released after three months and found a job as a fair ground boxer before turning to professional football. Playing in the reserves wherever he went, he did manage three senior games for Q.P.R. before moving on. He performed alongside such greats as Len Shackleton during the war, and notched up over sixty wartime matches for Bradford City together with twenty six for Accrington Stanley.

Peter completed an FA coaching course in 1947, and become the manager of the Turkish national side in 1949. He once refereed a championship decider in Turkey, and abandoned the match after a sending off, and a penalty decision prompted a pitch invasion. A full apology was recieved from the Turkish FA. Turning down an offer from Chile, Peter joined Watford as their trainer in 1951 and stayed until 1992.
Debut: 14. 9.1935 v. Aldershot (H). 5-0. Div. 3. (S).

MOORE James

(I.L.) Mid 5' 8" 10st 8lbs
b. Bolden Colliery, Durham 1. 9.1891 d. Dec. 1972
Bolden Colliery Welfare
Ardsley Nelson

Barnsley	Aug 1911
Southampton	May 1919
Leeds United	May 1921
Brighton & Hove Albion	Jun 1922
Halifax Town	Sep 1923
Q.P.R.	Nov 1924

Football League: 26-5. FAC: 0-0. FLC: 0-0. Others: 0-0.
Total: 26-5.

Crewe Alexandria	Jul 1925

Honours: FACup winners medal.

Neat with his footwork and particularly clever at heading the ball, Jimmy was effectively rediscovered by Southampton in 1916 while he was helping to construct aeroplanes, being a carpenter by trade, in a boatyard in Cowes on the Isle of Wight. He guested for the Saints in several wartime matches and was persuaded to sign on a permanent basis in May 1919. Jimmy had the unfortunate distinction of being the first ever Southampton player to be sent off in a League match. After several moved he came to Q.P.R. but only stayed for part of the 1924/25 season. After a spell at Crewe, in 1927 he moved to NAC Breda, in Holland, as a coach. When he retired from the game he ran a public house for a time in Barnsley, then he purchased a greengrocery business, and after the 2nd World War he became a director of Barnsley FC.
Debut: 30. 8.1924 v. Newport County (A). 0-0. Div.3 (S).

MORALEE William Ernest

(L.H.) Mid 5' 9" 10st 10lbs
b. Crook County, Durham 3. 5.1906 d. 1967
Crook Town

Huddersfield Town	1926
Bournemouth & Boscombe Athletic	1928
Q.P.R.	June 1936

Football League: 22-0. FAC: 0-0. FLC: 0-0. Others: 1-0.
Total: 23-0.

Billy was noted as a stalwart who was both loyal as a player and as a person. He was used mainly as a reserve who substituted for Dicky March, and retired in 1938.
Debut: 23. 1.1937 v. Clapton Orient (A).0-0. Div. 3 (S).

MORGAN Ian Arthur

(O.R.) Wing 5' 8" 11st 0lbs
b. City of London 14.11.1946
Essex schools

Q.P.R.		Sep 1964

Football League:173-26. FAC: 6-1. FLC: 11-1. Others: 0-0.
Total:190-28.

Watford	(Loan)	Sep 1973
Watford	(£10,000)	Nov 1973
Barking		Mar 1976

Honours: 3rd Div. championship medal. 2nd Div. championship medal. F.A.tour of America & the Far East.

The Morgan twins on either wing were a familiar sight at Q.P.R. In his heyday Ian was a fast and skilful winger, who was very adaptable in switching from left to right during a match and would probably finish it in midfield. He was bought by his former skipper, Mike Keen, who became manager of Watford. However, Ian sustained an injury which eventually brought about the cancellation of his contract and he retired from full time football.
Debut: 25. 9.1964 v. Hull City (H). 2-1. Div. 3.

MORGAN Roger Ernest

(O.L.) Wing 5' 8" 11st 0lbs
b. City of London 14.11.1946
Essex schools

Q.P.R.		Sep 1964

Football League:180-39. FAC: 13-1. FLC: 13-4. Others: 0-0.
Total:206-44.

Tottenham Hotspur	(£110,000)	Feb 1969

Honours: 5 England youth caps. 1 U23 cap. 3rd Div. championship medal. League Cup winners medal. 2nd Div.

The career of Roger followed a close parallel course to that of his identical twin Ian. The similarity did not end there, for they were not only alike in appearance but also in style, as both were fast, tricky wingers who could cross the ball accurately or cut in for a shot. Of the two, Roger was probably regarded as slightly the better. However, the pair proved a real handful for opposing defences. In 1969, Roger signed for Spurs and made his debut for them at Loftus Road against his old club, and who included his brother in the opposition line-up! Sadly, Roger was forced into a premature retirement in the summer of 1973.

He worked for Harringay Council as a recreation officer for a time before returning to football as the West Ham Community Development Officer.
Debut: 3.10.1964 v. Gillingham (A). 2-2. Div. 3.

MORRIS Samuel

(C.H.) CD
b. Handsworth, Birmingham

Aston Villa	1906
Q.P.R.	1908

Southern League: 42-2. FAC: 2-0. FLC: 0-0. Others: 0-0. Total: 44-2.

Birmingham	1911
Bristol Rovers	
Brentford	1920
Maidstone United	

Sam was a totally dedicated player who stayed with the club for four years. Morris stood in for McLean on at least two occasions in the championship season of 1908. However,, the following season with Lintott moving to Bradford City and McLean suffering from injuries, Sam was called upon to play quite often. When Hartwell came onto the scene, Sam played mostly reserve team football.
Debut: 25. 4.1907 v. Southampton (A). 2-5. S.L.Div. 1.

MORROW Steven Joseph

Def 6' 0" 11st 6lbs
b. Belfast, Northern Ireland 2. 7.1970

Bangor		
Arsenal		May 1988
Reading	(Loan)	Jan 1991
Watford	(Loan)	Aug 1991
Reading	(Loan)	Oct 1991
Barnet	(Loan)	Mar 1992
Q.P.R.	(£500,000)	Mar 1997

Football League: 91-2. FAC: 3-0. FLC: 6-0. Others: 0-0. Total:100-2.

Peterborough United	2001
Dallas Burn U.S.A.	

Honours: FA youth cup medal. European Cup Winners medal. League Cup winners medal. Northern Ireland schoolboy caps. 3 youth caps. 3 U21 caps. B cap. 39 full caps. Football Combination championship medal. European Cup winners Cup finalists medal. European Super Cup finalist medal.

Steve turned out in the Irish League when he was 15 years of age, and won his first of his 39 caps before he had even made his debut for Arsenal. In the Gunners League Cup victory he scored his first ever goal in senior football and then broke his arm in the celebratory horseplay after the final whistle. A half million pound signing for Q.P.R. late in the 1996/97 season, he spent four years at Loftus Road, making exactly 100 first team appearances, then moved on to Peterborough, before crossing the Atlantic to play for Dallas Burn in the U.S.A. He is one of the few professionals to wear contact lenses.
Debut: 5. 4.1997 v. Bolton Wanderers (A). 1-2. Div.1.

MORTIMORE John Henry

(C.H.) CD 6' 0" 11st 9lbs
b. Farnborough 23. 9.1934

Woking		
Aldershot		
Chelsea		Aug 1957
Q.P.R.	(£8,000)	Sep 1965

Football League: 10-0. FAC: 0-0. FLC: 0-0. Others: 0-0. Total: 10-0.

Sunderland	1966

Honours: Youth caps for England. 17 Amateur caps. Football League cup winners medal. 2nd Div. runners-up medal.

John was a commanding pivot, especially in the air and becoming the star of the side. Unfortunately he left after a short spell to become the player/coach of Sunderland. In the 1970s he took over as the manager of Portsmouth and later the same position in Greece, before becoming the assistant manager of Southampton. In the 1980s John led Benfica as manager, followed by Betis, Saville and finally Belenenses of Portugal. In this role he won the Portugese League once and the Potugese Cup three times running.
Debut: 11. 9.1965 v. Reading (H). 0-2. Div. 3.

MOUGHTON Colin E.

(L.H.) Mid 6' 0" 10st 8lbs
b. Harrow, Middlesex 30.12.1947

Q.P.R.	Dec 1965

Football League: 6-0. FAC: 0-0. FLC: 0-0. Others: 0-0.
Total: 6-0.

Colchester United	Jul 1968
Bedford	1969

Colin showed promise as an apprentice but was allowed to leave for Colchester United after a two month trial. They in turn released him in the following year.
Debut: 21. 5. 1966 v. Bournemouth (h) 5-0. Div.3

MOUNTFORD George Frederick

(O.R.) Wing 5' 9" 11st 0lbs
b. Kidderminster 30. 3.1921 d. Kidderminster 14. 6.1973
Kidderminster Harriers

Stoke City	(£40)	Sep 1938
Indepentiente Santa Fe, Bogota		Jun 1950
Stoke City		Sep 1952
Q.P.R.		Oct 1952

Football League: 35-2. FAC: 3-0. FLC: 0-0. Others: 0-0.
Total: 38-2.
Hereford United
Kidderminster Harriers
Lockheed Lemington

George made occasional appearances in the Stoke City side when Stanley Matthews was unavailable. After World War Two, George kept Matthews out of the side which resulted in Stan being transferred to Blackpool in 1947. In the summer of 1950, George, along with Neil Franklin and Charlie Mitten of Manchester United, went to play their soccer in British Columbia which was then outside the domain of FIFA. Mountford became immensely popular in Bogota, where he became known as the bald arrow, and stayed for the season. On his arrival back in England he was suspended for six months without pay for playing outside of FIFA regulations. The FA fined him £250 and George was never the same again. Much resentment was felt among the spectators at Loftus Road with the swap of Des Farrow (who was much liked) with that of the renegade George Mountford. With his football career in tatters he became a GPO engineer and played minor football till the end of his playing days.
Debut: 25.10.1952 v. Crystal Palace (A). 2-4. Div.3 (S).

MUIR Ian James

For 5' 8" 10st 13lbs
b. Coventry 5. 5.1963
Calludon Castle school
Stockingford Scholars
Bedworth juniors

Q.P.R.		Sep 1980

Football League: 2-2. FAC: 0-0. FLC: 0-0. Others: 0-0.
Total: 2-2.

Burnley	(Loan)	Nov 1982
Birmingham City		Aug 1983
Brighton & Hove Albion		Feb 1984
Swindon Town	(Loan)	Jan 1985
Tranmere Rovers		Jul 1985
Birmingham City	(Loan)	1995
Darlington	(Loan)	1995
Sing Tao, Hong Kong		

Honours: England schoolboy & youth caps. 4th Div. runners-up medal. Leyland Daf Cup winners medal. 3rd Div. runners-up medal. Leyland Daf Cup runners-up medal.

Ian only played two games for Rangers, and in the first he scored his two goals for the club. His ability was badly misjudged at Loftus Road, and indeed by a string of managers throughout the country, until the summer of 1985, when Frank Worthington took him under his wing at Tranmere Rovers. He continues to be the Tranmere Rovers top aggregate goalscorer.
Debut: 25. 4.1981 v. Cambridge United (H). 5-0. Div. 2.

MUIR William M.

(O.R.) Wing
b. Ayr, Scotland 27. 8. 1925
Irvine

Q.P.R.	Feb 1949

Football League: 16-4. FAC: 0-0. FLC: 0-0. Others: 0-0.
Total: 16-4.

Torquay United	Oct 1952
Tonbridge	

A Scottish born winger who had breakneck speed down the flank and could cross the ball with some accuracy.
Debut: 3. 2.1951 v. Birmingham City (H). 2-0. Div. 2.

MURDIN Steven H.

(C.F.) Striker
b.

Q.P.R.	1925

Football League: 1-0. FAC: 0-0. FLC: 0-0. Others: 0-0.
Total: 1-0.

Steve was just one of nine centre forwards to be tried during the dismal 1925/26 season. Q.P.R. ended the campaign in Division 3 (South), bottom of the table with just 21 points, 14 points less than the next placed team Charlton Athletic.
Debut: 25. 2.1926 v. Aberdare Athletic (H).1-3.Div.3 (S).

MURPHY Daniel Thomas

Def 5' 6" 10st 8lbs
b. Southwark, London 4.12.1982

Q.P.R.	Dec 1999

Football League: 23-0. FAC: 1-0. FLC: 0-0. Others: 0-0. Total: 24-0.

Honours: Rep. of Ire. Youth.

Danny is a left-sided defender who is quick to the tackle and passes the ball well. Only a fringe player in the first team squad, by the end of the 2002/03 season he had not established a regular slot. (Signed by Swindon Town July 2003)
Debut: 26.12.2001 v. Chesterfield (A). 3-2. Div. 2.

MURPHY Neil

(C.F.) Striker
b. Ireland

Sheffield United	1901
Q.P.R.	1903

Southern League: 51-11. FAC: 2-1. FLC: 0-0. Others: 0-0. Total: 53-12.

Luton Town	1907
Gainsboborough Trinity	1908

Honours: 3 Irish International caps.

Neil was the first Q.P.R. player to be capped by Ireland. Many tributes were written about him in the local papers of the time, an example being: *"Fast and clever is Murphy the Ranger... As a forward to fans he's no stranger... Fast as a flash, then a loud thud... Bet your boots that it's 'Spud'... With his lightening-like drives that spell 'danger'."*
Debut: 26. 9.1903 v. Luton Town (A). 0-1. SLDiv. 1.

MURRAY Paul

Mid 5' 8" 10st 5lbs
b. Carlisle, Cumberland 31. 5.1976

Carlisle United		1994
Q.P.R.	(£300,000)	Mar 1996

Premier/Football League:140-7. FAC: 9-0. FLC: 8-1. Others: 0-0. Total:157-8.

Southampton	Aug 2001
Oldham Athletic	Dec 2001

Honours: England youth caps. 4 U21 caps. 1 B cap.

A highly talented left footed player who looks to be comfortable at defending or attacking. At Q.P.R. he broke his leg once and his ankle twice, hence missing much of the 2000/01 season. During a five year career at Loftus Road, Paul notched up nearly 160 first team matches, before joining Southampton. Newcastle United had also been interested, but he signed a one year contract with the Saints. However, just one substitute appearance was made for the south coast team, and a few months later he joined Oldham Athletic on a free Bosman transfer, where he met up again with manager Iain Dowie. The end of the 2002/03 season saw Paul up against his former team in the Second Division play-off semi-final.
Debut: 5. 5.1996 v. Nottingham Forest (A). 0-3. PL.

MUSSLEWHITE John

(C.H.) CD
b.
West Hampstead

Q.P.R.	1896

Southern League: 2-0. FAC: 0-0. FLC: 0-0. Others: 0-0. Total: 2-0.

John was the reserve team captain and centre half for many years, even before the club were playing in the Southern League. He filled in for Hitch in 1900 and again in 1902.
Debut: 14. 4.1900 v. Bedminster (H). 2-1. SLDiv. 1.

MUSTARD John

(O.R.) Wing 5' 8" 11st 0lbs
b. Boldon, County Durham in 1905
Boldon Colliery
Crawcrook Albion

Q.P.R.	Nov 1926

Football League: 37-4. FAC: 1-0. FLC: 0-0. Others: 0-0. Total: 38-4.

South Shields	Sep 1929
Wrexham	Jun 1930
P.N.E.	May 1932
Burnley	Mar 1933
Southend United	Dec 1933
Crewe Alexandria	Jul 1934
Wrexham	May 1935
New Brighton	Jul 1936

Honours: Welsh Cup winners medal. Welsh Cup runners-up medal.

John was described as "*handily versatile. A strong raiding winger, who carries a good shot and often uses it, as well as crossing the ball very accurately*". Discovered by Q.P.R., he was a noted sprinter and in his later career he also took a sweet penalty kick. On joining New Brighton he was immediately appointed captain, although he relinquished it shortly afterwards, stating that outside right was not a suitable position to supervise players. He retired from the game in December 1938 at the age of 33.
Debut: 11.12.1026 v. Plymouth Argyle(A).0-2. Div. 3 (S)

MYERS Colin Ernest

(I.L.) Striker 5' 11" 11st 12lbs
b. Wortley, Yorkshire in July 1894

Northfleet	
Crystal Palace	
Hickleton Plain Colliery	
Bradford City	1919
Southend United	Jul 1920
Aberdare	Jul 1921
Northampton Town	1922
Q.P.R.	1924

Football League: 17-3. FAC: 5-7. FLC: 0-0. Others: 0-0.
Total: 22-10.

Exeter City	1925
Hartlepool United	1926
Gainsborough Trinity	1927
Grantham	
Kings Lynn	

Noted as a brilliant player, Colin scored on his introduction to League football, for Bradford City, in 1919. But he was a journeyman who played for a different club virtually every season. His most successful match of all was for Q.P.R. in a Cup-tie against Clapton at Loftus Road, when he scored all four goals in a 4-4 draw.
Debut: 25.10.1924 v. Millwall (H). 0-0. Div. 3 (S).

NASH Robert G.

(L.B.) Def
b. Hammersmith, London 8. 2.1946

Q.P.R.	Feb 1964

Football League: 17-0. FAC: 1-0. FLC: 0-0. Others: 0-0.
Total: 18-0.

Exeter City	1966

Bob had just consolidated himself into the left back position, left vacant by Peter Angell's retirement, when he received an horrendous injury during a match at Scunthorpe. This paved the way for the transfer of Jim Langley to the club. Bob was transferred to Exeter City after his recuperation, but to no avail for he left the game for good during the following season.
Debut: 25. 9.1964 v. Hull City (H). 2-1. Div. 3.

NEAL Dean J.

Striker 5' 10" 12st 0lbs
b. Edmonton, London 5. 1.1961

Q.P.R.	Jan 1979

Football League: 22-8. FAC: 0-0. FLC: 1-0. Others: 0-0.
Total: 23-8.

Tulsa Roughnecks, USA		
Millwall	(£100,000)	Oct 1981
Southend United		Jan 1986
Cambridge United	(Loan)	Dec 1987
Q.P.R.	(Loan)	Jun 1988

Football League: 0-0. FAC: 0-0. FLC: 0-0. Others: 0-0.
Total: 0-0.

Fisher Athletic	Aug 1988

Honours: Football League Trophy winners medal.

There cannot be many players who have come back to their original club as a loan player. However, on his return, Dean did not play for the club even though he was a striker who had a deceptive turn plus a hard shot. He was Millwall's top goalscorer in 1983.
Debut: 18. 8.1979 v. Bristol Rovers (H). 2-0. Div. 2.

NEARY Harold Frank

(C.F.) Striker 5' 9" 12st 4lbs
b. Aldershot, Hants 6. 3.1921

Finchley	
Q.P.R.	Jul 1945

Football League: 9-6. FAC: 0-0. FLC: 0-0. Others: 0-0.
Total: 9-6.

West Ham United	(£4,000)	Jan 1947
Clapton Orient	(£2,000)	Nov 1947
Q.P.R.	(£7,500)	Oct 1949

Football League: 18-5. FAC: 1-0. FLC: 0-0. Others: 0-0.
Total: 19-5.

Millwall	(£6,000)	Aug 1950
Gravesend		May 1954

Frank played his early football in Northern Ireland during the 1940s and then turned out for Fulham in wartime matches. Q.P.R. signed him from Finchley at the beginning of the pre-war period. His incredible pace and tremendous shooting power was the feature of his game and Neary scored 23 goals in 21 matches during the 1945/46 season. At Leyton Orient he was their top marksman in 1948 and again in 1949. Frank was remembered for forcing the Bristol Rovers goalkeeper, Jack Weare, backwards into the net as he attempted to save his penalty kick. Also Archie McFeat of Torquay United was knocked unconscious when he got in the way of a Neary drive. He made a brief return to Q.P.R., before moving to Millwall, where he notched up 59 goals in 142 appearances. Frank scored a career total of 118 goals in 245 League games.
Debut: 4.9.1946v.Bournemouth & B.A.(A).1-1. Div.3 (S)

NEEDHAM David William

CD 6' 1" 12st 7lbs
b. Leicester 21. 5.1949

Blaby Old Boys	
Notts County	Jul 1966
Q.P.R.	Jun 1977

Football League: 18-3. FAC: 0-0. FLC: 2-0. Others: 0-0. Total: 20-3.

Nottingham Forest	Dec 1977
Toronto Blizzard	1982
Kettering Town	

Honours: 4th Div. championship medal. 3rd Div runners-up medal. League Championship medal. 2 League Cup medals. League Cup runners-up medal.

David was brought into the side to replace Frank McLintock but he last just six months. The team only won two games with him playing in defence and Needham never seemed to be able to fit in. He went on to become a successful businessman in Leicester.
Debut: 20. 8.1977 v. Aston Villa (H). 1-2. Div.1.

NEIL Andrew

(W.H.) Def 5' 8" 11st 0lbs
b. Crosshouse, Scotland 18.11.1892
d.Kilmarnock 14. 8.1941

Kilmarnock		1913
Clydebank		
Third Lanark		
Galston		
Stevenston United		
Brighton & Hove Albion		Dec 1920
Arsenal	(£3,000)	Mar 1924
Brighton & Hove Albion		Mar 1926
Q.P.R.		May 1927

Football League:106-1. FAC: 6-0. FLC: 0-0. Others: 0-0. Total:112-1.

Honours: London Challenge Cup runners-up medal. League Championship runners-up medal.

Andy was a slightly built character who was both skilful and dazzling with his wonderful ball control. In his first spell at the Goldstone Ground he was ever-present in the 1922/23 season which led to his transfer to Arsenal. He was to play in The Gunners best ever season in the twenties when they were First Division runners-up in 1925/26. He became the general of the Q.P.R. side, who guided the team to third position in the 3rd Division (South) in 1930. This was to be his last season, in a short but notable Q.P.R. career, during which he played over 100 League matches.
Debut: 27. 8.1927 v. Newport County (H).4-2. Div.3 (S).

NEILL Warren Anthony

(R.B.) Def 5' 10" 11st 5lbs
b. Acton, Middlesex 21.11.1962

Q.P.R.		Sep 1980

Football League:181-3. FAC: 12-1. FLC: 19-1. Others: 3-1. Total:215-6.

Portsmouth	(£110,000)	Jul 1988
Watford		1996

Honours: England schoolboy caps. FACup runners-up medal. 2nd Div. championship medal. League Cup runners-up medal.

Warren was a defender who liked to come forward with the attack whenever possible. His stay at Loftus Road lasted nearly eight years, during which time he made over 200 first team appearances. Although not established by then in the first team, he stood in for his subsequent Watford manager, Glen Roeder, who was suspended for the FA Cup Final replay, after the first game was drawn. From that time on he became a fairly regular first team player, but suffering from sciatica, he announced his retirement from the game in 1995. However, he turned out for Watford on a non-contractual basis, and made several appearances for their reserve side.
Debut: 30. 8.1980 v. Chelsea (A).1-1. Div. 2.

NELSON David

(H.B.) Def 5' 8" 11st 3lbs
b. Douglas Water, Scotland 3. 2.1918
d.in USA Sep 1988

Thistle	
Douglas Water F.C.	
St. Bernards	Aug 1935
Arsenal	May 1935
Fulham	Dec 1946
Brentford	Aug 1947
Q.P.R.	Feb 1950

Football League: 31-0. FAC: 1-0. FLC: 0-0. Others: 0-0. Total: 32-0.

Crystal Palace	Mar 1952
Ashford Town	

Honours: 3 London Combination championship medals. London Challenge Cup runners-up medal. Bath Coronation Cup winners medal.

The move to Loftus Road stunned the Brentford supporters for he had been the backbone of their defence as well as their captain. Dave was a versatile player who was equally at home in defence or attack. He played regularly throughout the war and had made over 150 appearances for Arsenal, and was part of the swap deal that brought Ronnie Rooke to Highbury just after the hostilities. In 1954 he became the Ashford Town manager and later moved to the USA.
Debut: 18. 2.1950 v. Sheffield United (H).1-3. Div. 2.

NELSON William E.

(F.B.) Def
b. Silvertown, London 20. 9.1929

West Ham United	Oct 1950
Q.P.R.	Jul 1955

Football League: 9-0. FAC: 0-0. FLC: 0-0. Others: 0-0.
Total: 9-0.
Guildford

Billy was the brother of Andy Nelson the skipper of Ipswich Town. At Q.P.R. he was used mainly as cover for Ingham and Woods.
Debut: 24. 9.1955 v. Torquay United (H). 3-1. Div.3 (S).

NEWBIGGING Alexander

(For & G) 5' 9" 11st 3lbs
b. Larkhall, Scotland. 27.12.1879
Lanark Athletic
Paisley

Abercorn	1879
Lanark United	Sep 1900
Q.P.R.	Jul 1901

Southern League: 5-0. FAC: 2-1. FLC: 0-0. Others: 0-0.
Total: 7-1.

Nottingham Forest	Oct 1901
Reading	Jul 1905
Glasgow Rangers	Jul 1906
Reading	Jul 1908
Coventry City	Jul 1909
Inverness Thistle	Feb 1911

Hounours: Scottish Junior International.

Alex played for Q.P.R. as an outfield player who scored his one goal while playing at centre forward. Later at Nottingham Forest he became a very good goalkeeper and was selected to play for his country at junior level in that position in 1906. Newbigging lived a long life for he was at the centenary celebrations of the Glasgow Rangers FC aged of 99.
Debut: 20.10.1900 v. Tottenham H. (H). 2-1.SLDiv. 1.

NEWLANDS George

(R.B) Def 5' 7" 12st 9lbs
b. Govenhill, Glasgow in 1882
Parkhead Oaklea
Parkhead Reserves
Parkhead Athletic
Vale of Clyde
Parkhead Juniors

Q.P.R.	Aug 1900

Southern League:174-1. FAC: 12-0. FLC: 0-0. Others: 0-0.
Total:186-1.

Norwich City	May 1907

Honours: Represented the London League v. the Buckinghamshire League.

George was a hard tackling, sturdy full back who was always in a position to defend his ranks and he could play in any position (except goalkeeper). In January 1909 a newspaper article gave the best summation of George: *"If he could feed his forwards as well as he tackles he would be a great defender. You can depend on finding him where the fight is keenest".* Newlands was the club captain and was proud to be so. He later joined John Bowman at Norwich City and stayed there until 1910. When his career in football was over, George returned to Scotland and became a bricklayer in Dunfermline.
Debut: 29. 9.1900 v. Kettering (A). 1-2. SLDiv.1.

NGONGE Felix Michel

Striker 6' 0" 12st 8lbs
b. Huy, Belgium 10. 1.1967
KRC Harelbeks, Belgium
Samsunspor, Turkey

Watford		Jul 1998
Huddersfield Town	(Loan)	Mar 2000
Q.P.R.	(£50,000)	Dec 2000

Football League: 13-3. FAC: 2-0. FLC: 0-0. Others: 0-0.
Total: 15-3.

Kilmarnock	July 2001

Honours: 6 caps fot the Democratic Republic of Congo.

Unable to hold down a regular place in the team at Loftus Road, Michel was released at the end of the 2001 season.
Debut: 16.12.2000 v. Nottingham Forest (H). 1-0. Div.1.

NICHOLAS Charles Brian

(R.H.) Def 5' 9" 11st 7lbs
b. Aberdare, Wales 20. 4.1933

Q.P.R.	May 1950

Football League:112-2. FAC: 7-0. FLC: 0-0. Others: 0-0.
Total:119-2.

Chelsea	(£5,000)	Jul 1955
Coventry City	(£3,000)	Feb 1958
Rugby Town		Jul 1962

Honours: English Schools International. Represented the 3rd Div. (South) v. the 3rd Div. (North).

Brian made his debut for Q.P.R. at the age of sixteen, and stayed at Loftus Road for five years, appearing in the Football League on 112 occasions. A tenacious tackler and a sound defender who proved his worth to the side in the days when substitutes were not allowed. On two separate occasions, he took over in goal when Harry Brown was injured, and he kept a clean sheet in both games.

First Division Chelsea paid a large fee for him, but after less than three years he moved on to Coventry City Despite his notable balding patch, at the age of 24 years, he gave the midland side over four years excellent service, before moving into non-League football.
Debut: 31. 8.1950 v.Notts County (A). 3-3. Div. 2.

NICHOLLS A.

G
b.
Port Glasgow
Q.P.R. 1911
Southern League: 37-0. FAC: 5-0. FLC: 0-0. Others: 0-0. Total: 42-0.

With the departure of Charlie Shaw to Celtic in the close season of 1913, Nicholls became the main custodian of the side and stayed until the end of the season.
Debut: 20. 1.1912 v. Watford (H). 1-1. SLDiv. 1.

NIXON Thomas

(R.B.) Def 6' 0" 11st 4lbs
b. Newcastle
Crawcrook Athletic
Q.P.R. 1927
Football League: 51-1. FAC: 0-0. FLC: 0-0. Others: 0-0. Total: 51- 1.
Crystal Palace
Swindon Town 1933
Barrow 1935
Felling Colliery 1937

Tom was brought into the side as a centre half (and made his debut in a record-breaking 8-0 victory), but was not discovered until the new manager, Archie Mitchell, came along in 1931 and thought he would make a very good full back. Tommy was used in that position mainly as a reserve, but with the arrival of Mick O'Brien, the next manager in 1933, Nixon was released.
Debut: 9.3.1929 v. Merthyr Town (H). 8-0 Div.3(S).

NUTT Phillip J.

Striker 5' 11" 11st 8lbs
b. Westminster, London 18. 5.1975
Q.P.R. Jul 1975
Fooball League: 4-1. FAC: 0-0. FLC: 0-0. Others: 0-0. Total: 4-1.

Phil never played a full ninety minutes in a match, always coming on as a substitute. However, in one game he made an impact by scoring the equaliser in a 1-1 draw at home to Derby County, to keep the club at the top of the First Division.
Debut: 29.11.1975 v. Stoke City (H). 3-2. Div. 1.

O'BRIEN Michael Terrance

(C.H.) CD 6' 2" 13st 7lbs
b. Kilcock, County Down 10. 8.1893 d. Uxbridge in 1940
Walker Celtic
Wallsend
Blyth Spartans
Newcastle East End
Glasgow Celtic
Brentford Nov 1914
Alloa Athletic Mar 1919
Brentford May 1919
Norwich City Aug 1919
South Shields Dec 1919
Q.P.R. May 1920
Football League: 66-3. FAC: 4-1. FLC: 0-0. Others: 0-0. Total: 70-4.
Leicester City Mar 1922
Hull City Jun 1924
Brooklyn Wanderers May 1926
Derby County Dec 1926
Walsall Jun 1928
Norwich City May 1929
Watford Jun 1931

Honours: 4 caps as captain of the Republic of Ireland. 10 caps for Northern Ireland. Football League v. The Army.

Mick's first job was as a handyman to the groundsman at St. Anthony's Cricket club near Dublin. He then became assistant groundsman to the Durham Cricket club, and didn't start playing football until he was 18 years old. He served in the army before the 1st World War, in the navy during it, (getting sunk in the battle of Jutland), and ended up with the Royal Flying Corps! In 1920 he joined Q.P.R. and won his first cap. He sampled soccer in the USA in the mid-1920s and retired from playing in 1933, when he became manager of Q.P.R., then the assistant manager of Brentford, in 1935. One year later he become the Ipswich Town manager taking them into the Football League. Tragically his wife and daughter both died before he was badly beaten-up by an ex-boxer. He bred Alsations, ran a shop in Derby and had a tobacconists shop in Norwich. Few men packed more into their 47 years than Michael O'Brien.

Debut: 26. 8.1920 v.Watford (H). 1-2. Div. 3 (S).

O'CONNER Mark Andrew

Mid 5' 7" 10st 2lbs
b. Rochford, Kent 10. 3.1963

Q.P.R.		Jun 1980

Football League: 3-0. FAC: 0-0. FLC: 0-0. Others: 0-0. Total: 3-0.

Exeter City	(Loan)	Oct 1983
Bristol Rovers	(£20,000)	Aug 1984
AFC Bournemouth	(£25,000)	Mar 1986
Gillingham	(£70,000)	Dec 1989
AFC Bournemouth		Jul 1993
Gillingham		Aug 1995

Honours: U21 cap for Eire.

Unable to find a regular place in the side, this nippy fleet-footed player was transferred to Bristol Rovers. Mark was a capable and consistent midfield player or wing back before he broke his leg in two places. He later became the youth team coach at Portsmouth.

Debut: 26.12.1981 v. Chelsea (H). 0-2. Div. 2.

O'DONNELL Dennis

For 5' 10" 10st 12lbs
b. Willington Quay, Northumberland in 1880

Willington Athletic		
Lincoln City	(£47)	Sep 1901
Sunderland	(£370)	May 1905
Q.P.R.		May 1906

Southern League: 25-7. FAC: 2-0. FLC: 0-0. Others: 0-0. Total: 27-7.

Notts County	1908
Bradford Park Avenue	Jun 1908

Dennis was a resourceful player whose accurate shooting and passing made him a favourite of the crowd. It seemed that he was an excellent prospect in the early Edwardian era but after the time he spent with Lincoln City, he seemed to be burnt out. Dennis was the elder brother of Magnas, who also played for Lincoln City.

Debut: 1. 9.1906 v. Luton Town (A). 1-1. SLDiv. 1.

OGLEY William

(L.H.) Def 5' 9" 12st 0lbs
b. Rotherham, Yorkshire in 1896

Swansea Town	Jun 1919
Porth	1921
Newport County	Apl 1922
Q.P.R.	Jul 1924

Football League: 36-2. FAC: 5-0. FLC: 0-0. Others: 0-0. Total: 41-2.

Castleford	1925
Denby United	

Billy started playing football in the army during the 1st World War. On his demob he joined Swansea Town who were at the time in the Southern League. Billy spent a year with Q.P.R. before he returned to Yorkshire.

Debut: 30. 8.1924 v. Newport County (A).0-0. Div.3 (S).

OLI Dennis Chiedozie

Striker 6' 0" 12st 4lbs
b. Newham 28. 1.1984

Q.P.R.	Oct 2001

Football League: 20-0. FAC: 1-0. FLC: 1-0. Others: 1-0. Total: 21-0.

A youngster who twice appeared as a substitute in 2001/02, but managed to command a more regular place during the following season.

Debut: 26. 2.2002 v. Wigan Athletic (H).1-1. Div. 2.

OLSEN C.

(C.H.) CD
b.

Q.P.R.	1919

Southern League: 1-0. FAC: 0-0. FLC: 0-0. Others: 0-0. Total: 1-0.

A trialist who played in place of Archie Mitchell on a single occasion.

Debut: 9. 4.1920 v. Newport County (A).0-3. SLDiv.1.

O'NEILL John Patrick

CD 6' 0" 13st 0lbs
b. Derry, Northern Ireland 11. 3.1958
Derry Athletic boys club

Leicester City		Mar 1976
Q.P.R.	(£150,000)	Jul 1987

Football League: 2-0. FAC: 0-0. FLC: 0-0. Others: 0-0. Total: 2-0.

Norwich City	(£100,000)	Dec 1987

Honours: 39 caps for Northern Ireland. U21 cap. 2nd Div. championship medal. 3rd Div. promotion medal.

An experienced, polished and cool defender who played second fiddle to Alan McDonald. He came from Leicester, but was transferred to Norwich City, at a much reduced fee, just a few months later. John was just 34 minutes into his debut match when he received an injury which was to end his career. In 1990 he spent a two year spell as the manager of League of Ireland side Finn Harps. Two years later he kept a wine and spirits shop in Derry while he was sitting on the board of Derry City. In October 1994, John won a high court action against John Fashanu and Wimbledon FC. (arising from the tackle that put him out of the game), for £70,000.
Debut: 31.10.1987 v. Norwich City (A). 1-1. Div. 1.

O'ROURKE John

Striker 5' 8" 10st 10lbs
b. Northampton 11. 2.1945
Arsenal

Chelsea		Apl 1962
Luton Town		Dec 1963
Middlesbrough		Jul 1966
Ipswich Town	(£30,000)	Feb 1968
Coventry City	(£80,000)	Nov 1969
Q.P.R.	(£70,000)	Oct 1971

Football League: 34-12. FAC: 2-0. FLC: 1-0. Others: 0-0. Total: 37-12.

AFC Bournemouth	(£35,000)	Jan 1974
Rangers, South Africa		Aug 1975

Honours: Youth International. U23 cap. 2nd Div. runners-up medal. 2nd Div. championship medal.

John was an opportunist with a fierce shot but at Loftus Road the goals dried-up. In his early days he was unable to make an impression at either Arsenal or Chelsea until he dropped down to the 4th Division to play for Luton Town. Success with them provided a springboard for better times. John later moved to live and work, running a Newsagents, in a seaside resort.
Debut: 19.10.1971 v. Luton Town (H). 1-0. Div. 2.

ORR Douglas M.

(O.L.) Wing
b. Glasgow, Scotland 8.11.1937
Hendon

Q.P.R.	Jun 1957

Football League: 5-0. FAC: 0-0. FLC: 0-0. Others: 0-0. Total: 5-0.

Hendon	1958

Honours: Scottish Amateur International.

Dougie was given a one year trial before returning to Hendon.
Debut: 16. 9.1957 v. Swindon Town (H). 2-1. Div.3 (S).

OSBORN Simon Edward

Mid 5' 10" 11st 4lbs
b. Croydon, Surrey 19. 1.1972

Crystal Palace		Jan 1990
Reading	(£90,000)	Aug 1994
Q.P.R.	(£1,100,000)	Jul 1995

Premier League: 9-1. FAC: 0-0. FLC: 2-0. Others: 0-0. Total: 11-1.

Wolverhampton Wanderers	(£1,000,000)	Dec 1995
Tranmere Rovers		Mar 2001
Port Vale		Sep 2001
Gillingham		Oct 2001

Simon was one of Ray Wilkins' first transactions on his becoming manager at Loftus Road. He was a steady and composed midfield player with fine passing ability and a good shot. Unfortunately he later suffered from knee trouble due to a flaky cartilage, but had been involved in two £1m transfers.
Debut: 19. 8.1995 v. Blackburn Rovers (A).0-1. PL.

OVENS Gilbert

(R.H.) Def
b. Bristol

Bristol Rovers	1904
Chelsea	1910
Q.P.R.	1911

Southern League:103-3. FAC: 9-1. FLC: 0-0. Others: 0-0. Total:112-4.

Although Bert didn't turn out for the Chelsea side, he nevertheless was a regular senior squad player at Q.P.R. for three years and he was in the team that won the Southern League title for the second time in 1912. He was an important member of the side and could play anywhere in defence.
Debut: 30. 9.1911. v. Exeter City (A).1-1. SLDiv. 1.

P

OVENSTONE David Guthrie

(O.L.) Wing 5' 8" 10st 12lbs
b. Coal Wynd, Scotland 17. 6.1913d. Cardiff 19. 1.1983
St. Monance Swifts

Raith Rovers	1932
Bristol Rovers	
Q.P.R.	Jun 1935

Fooball League: 15-3. FAC: 1-0. FLC: 0-0. Others: 0-0.
Total: 16-3.

Cardiff City	May 1936
Watford	Jun 1937
Southport	Nov. 1937
Barry Town	Aug 1938
Ebbw Vale	
Broughty Ex-Service	
Forthill Athletic	

Dave was in such devastating form when Cardiff City visited Loftus Road that the Welsh club snapped him up during the close season. Showing many fine touches he nevertheless found himself in the reserves for a lot of his time at Cardiff so he was released in the spring of 1937. To accommodate his wife he moved back to South Wales at the end of his career and played in non-League football, finishing as the player/manager of Ebbw Vale and working on the railway at the same time. At the time of his death from a heart attack, he was living in a Salvation Army hostel in Cardiff.
Debut: 9.11.1935 v.Bournemouth& B.A.(H).2-0. Div.3(S)

OXLEY Richard Lambert

(O.R.) Wing 5' 10" 11st 10lbs
b. Barrow-on-Furness 10. 4.1893 d. Wallsend 17. 4.1953
Wallsend

Newcastle United	(Trial)	
Accrington Stanley		May 1921
Southport		May 1922
Q.P.R.		Aug 1923

Football League: 18-0. FAC: 0-0. FLC: 0-0. Others: 0-0.
Total: 18-0.

Northampton Town	Dec 1924
Crystal Palace	Dec 1926
Durham City	
Blyth Spartans	Feb 1930

Though Dick was born in Barrow he spent much of his early life on Tyneside working in a munitions factory during the First World War. Well known as a sprinter, having won the Powderhall Handicap, Oxley was noted as a speedy winger with a sense of ball control and a happy knack of placing it on the right spot. His private life was dogged by tragedy having lost his wife in 1927 just five years after they were married. Their only son Jack died of consumption at 20 years old, in 1943, while on an Officer Cadet course, and within seven years Dick himself had died of jaundice.
Debut: 8. 9.1923 v. Swindon Town (A).0-0. Div.3 (S).

PACQUETTE Richard Francis

Striker 6' 0" 12st 7lbs
b. Paddington, London 28. 1.1983

Q.P.R.		Feb 2000

Football League: 18-2. FAC: 1-0. FLC: 1-0. Others: 1-0.
Total: 21-2.

Stevenage Borough	(Loan)	Oct 2002
Q.P.R.		Jan 2003

Football League: 14-4. FAC: 0-0. FLC: 1-0. Others: 0-0.
Total: 14-4.

A strongly built striker who substituted for Andy Thompson during 2002, and made a reasonable number of appearances during the 2002/03 season, despite a short period out on loan.
Debut: 21. 4.2001. v. Huddersfield T. (A).1-2. Div. 1.

PADULA Diego Gino Mauro.

D. 5' 9" 12st. 1lb.
b. Buenos Aires, Argentina. 11. 7.1976.
River Plate, Argentina
Huracan, Argentina
Xerez, Spain

Bristol Rovers	(Trial)	Oct 1999
Dundee United	(Trial)	
Derby County	(Trial)	
Walsall		Nov 1999
Wigan Athletic		2000
Q.P.R.		2002

Football League:23-1. FAC:1-0. FLC:0-0. Others:1-0.

A quick and skilful left back, who won several ‘Man of the match’ awards at Walsall with his determined tackling, ability in the air and readiness to move forward.
Debut: 17. 8.2002 v. Barnsley (A). 0-1. Div. 2.

PALMER Stephen Leonard

CD 6' 1" 12st 13lbs
b. Brighton, Suffolk 31. 3.1968
Cambridge University

Ipswich Town		Jan 1989
Watford	(£135,000)	Sep 1995
Q.P.R.		Jul 2001

Football League: 95-5. FAC: 3-0. FLC: 2-0. Others: 2-0.
Total: 102-5.

Honours: English schools cap.

Steve possesses height, strength and energy, and as a Cambridge Blue he captained his side in their second Varsity Match, in 1989. He went on to play Premier League football for Ipswich Town, and after a six year spell, he moved on for a similar period, to Watford. He then signed for Q.P.R. as a defender and also with a view to improving the Rangers stability in midfield. He immediately became the club captain and was the only ever-present player in the League side in 2001/02, which he repeated the following season.
Debut: 11. 8.2001 v. Stoke City (H). 1-0. Div. 2.

PAPE Andrew M.

G 6' 0" 12st 0lbs
b. Hammersmith, London 22. 3.1962
Feltham

Q.P.R.	Jul 1980

Football League: 1-0. FAC: 0-0. FLC: 0-0. Others: 0-0. Total: 1-0.

Ikast, Denmark	1980
Crystal Palace	1981
Feltham	1982
Harrow Borough	1983
Enfield	1985
Barnet	Aug 1991
Enfield	1994
Aldershot	2000

Honours: Middlesex schools & County honours. 15 semi-pro. Caps. Gola league championship medal. FA Trophy winners medal. Middlesex Senior Cup winners medal. Vauxhall Championship medal.

Andy only played once for Q.P.R., but his consistency between the sticks was valued very highly by the England semi-pro. management, and non-League clubs, that he later moved on to.
Debut: 13. 4.1980 v. Charlton Athletic (A).2-2. Div. 2.

PARKER Paul Andrew

Def 5' 7" 10st 13lbs
b. West Ham, London 4. 4.1964
Essex & Havering schoolboys

Fulham		Apl 1982
Q.P.R.	(£500,000 joint fee)	Jun 1987

Football League:125-1. FAC: 16-0. FLC: 14-0. Others: 5-0. Total:160-1.

Manchester United	(£2,000,000)	Aug 1991
Derby County		Aug 1996
Sheffield United		Nov 1996
Fulham		Jan 1997
Chelsea		Mar 1997
Farnborough		

Honours: 3 England youth caps. 8 U21 caps. 3 B caps. 19 full caps. 2 Premier League championship medals. FACup winners medal. League Cup runners-up medal.

Paul was an adaptable defender who could play at wing-back or in the centre of defence. He was also excellent in the air for such a small man and could outjump players much taller than himself. In addition what he lacked in inches was compensated with tremendous speed and astute reading of the game, he always seemed to have more time than anybody else. Parker moved from Fulham to Q.P.R. along with Dean Coney for a joint fee of £500,000. During his four years at Loftus Road he made 125 League appearances, but he really came to notice after his signing for Manchester United for £2m. Later moves took him to various clubs before becoming the manager of Chelsmford City, and later the same at Welling United.
Debut: 15. 8.1987 v. West Ham United (A). 3-0. Div.1.

PARKER Richard

(C.F.) Striker 5' 8" 11st 3lbs
b. Stockton-on-Tees 14. 9.1894
d. Stockton-on-Tees 1. 1.1969

Norton United		1913
Thornaby Corinthians		
South Bank		
Stockton		
Sunderland		Jun 1919
Coventry City	(£1,500)	Jan 1920
South Shields	(£1,000)	Oct 1920
Wallsend		1921
Q.P.R.		Jul 1922

Football League: 61-30. FAC: 5-4. FLC: 0-0. Others: 0-0. Total: 66-34.

Millwall Athletic		Jul 1924
Watford	(£1,100)	Nov 1927
Merthyr Town		1928
Tunbridge Wells Rangers		1930

Dick was a fast, clever and crafty player who preferred the ball at his feet rather than in the air. The outcome of a pass, followed by a hard sizzling shot would almost invariable culminate in a goal. Dick still holds the scoring record at Millwall with 40 goals in the 1926/27 season.
Debut: 26. 8.1922 v. Watford (H). 1-2. Div. 3. (S).

PARKES Phillip B. F.

G 6' 3" 14st 9lbs
b. Sedgley, Staffordshire 8. 8.1950

Brierly Hill		
Walsall		Jan 1968
Q.P.R.	(£15,000)	Jun 1970

Football League:344-0. FAC: 27-0. FLC: 27-0. Others: 8-0. Total:406-0.

West Ham United	(£565,000)	Feb 1979
Ipswich Town		Aug 1990

Honours: 1 England cap. B cap. U21 cap. 6 U23 caps. 2nd Div. runners-up medal. 1st Div. runners-up medal. F ACup winners medal. League Cup runners-up medal. 2nd Div. championship medal.

Rated on a par with the other great Q.P.R. goalkeepers of the past, Phil was the second for Ranger's to break the transfer record. Commanding in the air as well as the six yard box, he had lightning reflexes which made him very hard to beat. Phil would surely have won many more England caps if it hadn't been for Peter Shilton. With Q.P.R. in decline and regularly involved in relegation struggles, Phil jumped at the chance of joining West Ham United in February 1979. Parkesy set a club record of 22 clean sheets in the Hammers 1980/81 campaign.

His career spanned more than 800 League and cup games and by a statistical quirk, he made exactly 344 League appearances each for Q.P.R. and West Ham United. He moved back to Loftus Road in 1991 to become the goalkeeper coach.
Debut: 22. 8.1970 v. Leicester City (H). 1-3. Div.2.

PARKINSON Alfred A.

(I.R.) Mid
b. Camden Town, London 30. 4.1922

Q.P.R.	Sep 1943

Football League: 76-5. FAC: 3-2. FLC: 0-0. Others: 0-0. Total: 79-7.

Alf was the reserve for such players as Joe Mallett, Ivor Powell and Don Mills, and effectively became a utility player. Alf retired from the game in 1951.
Debut: 1. 3.1947 v. Norwich City (A). 1-0. Div. 3. (S).

PARSONS Derek J.

(L.H.) Mid
b. Hammersmith, London 24.10.1929

Q.P.R.	Feb 1950

Football League: 2-1. FAC: 1-0. FLC: 0-0. Others: 0-0. Total: 3-1.

Ashford Town	1953

Derek joined the club as a 19 year old in 1952, and subsequently he was allowed to leave for Ashford Town after just one season.
Debut: 8.11.1952 v. Torquay United (A). 1-1. Div.3 (S).

PATERSON John

(I.L.) Mid. 5' 9" 11st 0lbs
b. Fifeshire, Scotland in 1904
Edinburgh Emmet
Dundee in Spain FC.
Bathgate Aug 1924
Mid-Rhondda United
Q.P.R. 1925
Football League: 36-6. FAC: 0-0. FLC: 0-0. Others: 0-0. Total: 36-6.
Wellesley Juniors 1927
Bristol Rovers Feb 1928

John was one of the few players to stay with the club after the disastrous season of 1925/26. He emigrated to Canada in 1930 and played the game until he was fifty. John visited England in 1977 when he was 72 years old.
Debut: 16. 1.1926 v. Merthyr Town (A). 0-1. Div.3 (S).

PATTISON John Maurice

(O.L.) Wing
b. Glasgow, Scotland 19.12.1918
Motherwell
Q.P.R. May 1937
Football League: 92-26. FAC: 9-5. FLC: 0-0. Others: 2-0. Total:103-31.
Leyton Orient Feb 1950
Dover May 1951

Honours: 3rd Div. (South) championship medal.

John was an old fashioned type of winger, one that could turn on a sixpence, who was fast and tricky and enticed opponents to tackle him and had a sizzling shot to boot.

But like so many of his age, the war robbed him of some of his best football playing years and consequently restricted his appearances. John played a further 44 matches for Leyton Orient until 1951 before teaming up with Fred Durrent at Dover. He later coached the Queensland club in Australia.
Debut: 12. 3.1938 v. Notts County (H). 2-1. Div. 3 (S).

PEACOCK Darren

CD 6' 2"12st 6lbs
b. Bristol 3. 2.1968
Bristol City
Bristol Rovers
Newport County Feb 1986
Hereford United Mar 1989
Q.P.R. (£350,000) Dec 1990
Football League:126-6. FAC: 3-0. FLC: 12-1. Others: 2-0. Total:143-7.
Newcastle United (£2,700,000) Mar 1994
Blackburn Rovers Jul 1998
West Ham United (Loan) Sep 2000
Wolverhampton Wanderers (Loan) Oct 2000

Honours: Welsh Cup winners medal.

Darren's attempt to establish himself in the Newport County side came to an abrupt halt when a broken leg put him out of football for 18 months. He joined Hereford United when Newport County were wound up and gradually turned into a very good central defender. Late in 1990 he became a big money signing for Q.P.R., where he spent the next four years. Eventually He became the country's most expensive defender (to that time), and Newcastle's record purchase when he moved from Loftus Road to Gallowgate in 1994.

Kevin Keegan, the Newcastle United manager, had persistently sought his signature. Another move and two loan signings followed, but an injury to his neck in the League Cup tie at Fulham in the year 2000 led to his retirement from the game on medical grounds.
Debut: 23.12.1990 v. Derby County (A). 1-1. Div. 1.

PEACOCK Gavin Keith

Mid 5' 8" 11st 5lbs
b. Eltham, Kent 18.11.1967

Q.P.R.		Nov 1984

Football League: 17-1. FAC: 1-0. FLC: 0-0. Others: 0-0. Total: 18-1.

Gillingham	(Loan)	Oct 1987
Gillingham	(£40,000)	Dec 1987
AFC Bournemouth	(£250,000)	Aug 1989
Newcastle United	(£275,000)	Jan 1990
Chelsea	(£250,000)	Aug 1993
Q.P.R.	(£1,000,000)	Nov 1996

Football League:190-35. FAC: 9-3. FLC: 9-3. Others: 0-0. Total:208-41.

Charlton Athletic	(Loan)	Aug 2001

Honours: English school caps. 5 youth caps. 1st Div. champs. medal. Represented the Football League.

Gavin's ability to make threatening runs from midfield made him a potent attacking threat. Always able to fire home quality strikes from midfield when he was in a scoring position. His twisting runs and quick turns were appreciated by his various clubs. He captained the England schools side and is the son of Keith Peacock the ex-Charlton player. His appearances for Q.P.R. were rare, and so he moved on to Gillingham. Subsequent moves in the next nine years saw his value rapidly rise until he was bought for £1m. by Rangers, who had earlier released him for a relatively small fee. He gave nearly five years service in his second spell at Loftus Road, being a near ever-present during this period. After a loan spell at Charlton, he was not retained at the end of the 2001/02 season, and retired from playing.
Debut: 29.11.1986 v. Sheffield Wed. (H). 2-2. Div.1.

PEACOCK Terrence M.

(C.F.) Striker 5' 9" 11st 3lbs
b. Hull, Humberside 18. 4.1935

Hull City	Dec 1952
Q.P.R.	Aug 1956

Football League: 16-4. FAC: 1-0. FLC: 0-0. Others: 0-0. Total: 17-4.

Scarborough	Jul 1958

Terry was a wholehearted genuine player who made an impressive start to his career at Loftus Road by scoring three goals in his first three matches. However, an injury that he received proved to be long term and he was forced to retire at the age of 23.
Debut: 15.12.1956 v. Reading (H). 1-1. Div. 3 (S).

PEARSON Harold

(O.R.) Wing 5' 7" 10st 6lbs
b. Birkenhead, Liverpool in 1910
Shaftesbury boys club

Tranmere Rovers	1932
Bournemouth & Boscombe Athletic	1934
Prescott Cables	
Northwich Victoria	Jun 1936
Coventry City	Nov 1936
Q.P.R.	1938

Football League: 11-1. FAC: 3-0. FLC: 0-0. Others: 1-0. Total: 15-1.

Barrow	1939

"Tich" was regarded as a future international at Prenton Park and made his debut at the age of 17. However, he turned out to be just another journeyman, and his career was cut short by the 2nd World War.
Debut: 8.10.1938 v. Swindon Town (A).2-2. Div.3 (S).

PEARSON John A.

(I.L.) Mid
b. Isleworth, Middlesex 23. 4.1935

Brentford	Nov 1952
Q.P.R.	Jun 1958

Football League: 21-9. FAC: 0-0. FLC: 0-0. Others: 0-0. Total: 21-9.

Kettering Town	1960

Manager Jack Taylor was a fan of John Pearson but with the arrival of Alec Stock as manager, he was released and in came Brian Bedford instead. John was given a free transfer to Kettering in 1960.
Debut: 1. 9.1958 v. Tranmere Rovers (A). 0-2. Div.3.

PENNIFER H. J.

(C.F.) Striker
b.

Q.P.R.	1913

Southern League: 3-0. FAC: 0-0. FLC:0-0. Others: 0-0. Total: 3-0.

He was one of the many youngsters who stood in for centre forward Miller. Pennifer joined the army in 1914 and he was one of the many to lose his lives in the battle of the Somme.
Debut: 13.12.1913 v. Cardiff City (A). 0-3. SLDiv. 1.

PENRICE Gary Kenneth

Mid 5' 7" 10st 0lbs
b. Bristol 23. 3.1964
Bristol City schoolboys
Bristol Rovers
Mangotsfield United

Bristol Rovers		Nov 1984
Watford	(£500,000)	Nov 1989
Aston Villa	(£1,000,000)	Mar 1991
Q.P.R.	(£625,000)	Oct 1991

Football/Premier League: 82-20. FAC: 4-1. FLC: 7-2. Others: 1-0. Total: 94-23.

Watford	(£300,000)	Nov 1995
Bristol Rovers		Jul 1997

Gary was of small stature but was very tricky player, and had plenty of guile and determination. His passing was a delight to watch and his ability to read a match was excellent. Both the Bristol clubs initially rejected Gary on account of his size, however, he rejoined Rovers in 1984. After a million pound move to Aston Villa, in which he appeared in just fifteen League matches he joined Q.P.R. But in four years he only played in 82 League games before moving to Watford for a much reduced fee.
Debut: 2.11.1991 v. Aston Villa (H). 0-1. Div.1.

PENTLAND Frederick Beaconsfield

(O.R.) Wing 5' 9" 11st 11lbs
b. Wolverhampton 18. 9.1883d. Poole, Dorset 16. 3.1962
Avondale juniors
Willenhall Swifts

Small Heath		Aug 1900
Blackpool		Jun 1903
Blackburn Rovers		Oct 1903
Brentford		May 1906
Q.P.R.		May 1907

Southern League: 37-14. FAC: 2-0. FLC: 0-0. Others: 1-0. Total: 40-14.

Middlesbrough	(£350)	Jul 1908
Halifax Town		Feb 1913
Stoke City		May 1913
Halifax Town		

Honours: 5 England caps. Represented the South v. the North. Southern League championship medal.

Fred's unusual middle name stems from his father, a former Lord Mayor of Birmingham, who was an admirer of Benjamin Disraeli, the Earl of Beaconsfield. Fred was a fast and very talented winger who was tricky on the ball and could centre it with precision. Q.P.R. were lucky to acquire him at the start of their first Southern League championship. Pentland was coaching in Germany when the 1st World War broke out and he was interned for the duration, along with Steve Bloomer. A telegram received in England via the Netherlands FA stated that he was allowed to "*go about his business but he cannot leave Germany*". After the war he coached in France and spent 15 years in Spain, coaching Athletico Bilbao until the outbreak of the Spanish civil war. When Fred returned to England he joined the coaching staff at Brentford and then became manager of Barrow from January 1938 until September the next year.
Debut: 2. 9.1907 v. Tottenham H. 3-3. SLDiv.1.

PERKINS Stephen A.

Def 5' 11" 11st 0lbs
b. Stepney, London 3.10.1954

Chelsea	Nov 1971
Q.P.R.	Jun 1977

Football League: 2-0. FAC: 0-0. FLC: 0-0. Others: 0-0. Total: 2-0.

Wimbledon	Oct 1978
Wealdstone	1981

Steve was transferred along with reserve player Haverson who was also a defender.
Debut: 1. 4.1978 v. Middlesbrough (H). 1-0; Div.1.

PERRY Mark James

Def 5' 11" 12st 10lbs
b. Ealing, Middlesex 19.10.1978.

Q.P.R.	Oct 1995

Football League: 66-1. FAC: 3-0. FLC: 5-0. Other: 1-0. Total: 65-1.

Honours: Englarnd school and youth caps.

Mark is an excellent reader of the game, being comfortable on the ball and tackles and passes effectively. His normal position was on the right side of defence but he could play in a more forward midfield role when needed. Mark was given a free transfer in July 2002.
Debut: 18. 3. 2000 v. Walsall (A) 3-2 Div.1

PESCHISOLIDO Paolo (Paul) Pasquale

Striker 5' 7" 10st 12lbs
b. Scarborough, Canada 25. 5.1971
Toronto Blizzards

Birmingham City	(£25,000)	Nov 1992
Stoke City	(£400,000)	Aug 1994
Birmingham City	(£400,000)	Mar 1996
W.B.A.	(£600,000)	Jul 1996
Fulham	(£1,100,000)	Oct 1997
Q.P.R.	(Loan)	Nov 2000

Football League: 5-1. FAC: 0-0. FLC: 0-0. Others: 0-0. Total: 5-1.

Sheffield United	(Loan)	Jan 2001
Norwich City	(Loan)	Mar 2001
Sheffield United	(£150,000)	Jul 2001

Honours: 45 Canadian caps. 11 U23 caps. 2nd Div. championship medal.

Paul produces some excellent performances full of commitment, anticipation and selfless running.
Debut: 4.11.00 v. Portsmouth (H). 1-1. Div. 1.

PETCHEY George W.

(R.H.) Mid
b. Stepney, London 24. 6.1931

West Ham United	Aug 1948
Q.P.R.	Jul 1953

Football League:255-22. FAC: 16-2. FLC: 0-0. Others: 7-0. Total:278-24.

Crystal Palace	Jun 1960

Honours: 4th Div. runners-up medal. 3rd Div. runners-up medal.

George was one of the highest rated halfbacks throughout the lower divisions. A tough tackler who would give no quarter nor ask for any.

The fans at Loftus Road enjoyed his no nonsense attitude and were dismayed when he was transferred to Crystal Palace. Although he only spent seven years at Loftus Road, George chalked up nearly 300 first team appearances, and also netted 22 League goals. Later he became youth team manager and later the assistant manager of the senior squad at Selhurst Park. Then in 1971 the Orient manager's job came along, followed in 1978 by the same at Millwall. In 1984 George became the assistant manager of Brighton & Hove Albion, later becoming the Youth Development Officer until 1986.
Debut: 19. 8.1953 v. Brighton & H.A. (H). 1-2. Div.3(S).

PICKETT Thomas Alfred

G 5' 11" 12st 3lbs
b. Merthyr, Wales 5. 2.1909
Kentish Town

Q.P.R.	1929

Football League: 46-0. FAC: 6-0. FLC: 0-0. Others: 0-0. Total: 52-0.

Bristol Rovers	1932
Bristol City	1932
Yeovil & Petters United	1933

Not much is known about Pickett, except that he was the reserve to Joe Cunningham, and in 1932 he made way for Ernie Beecham. In fact Thomas' Football League career was short, and his 46 appearances for Rangers easily surpassed those that he made at the two Bristol clubs.
Debut: 16.11.1929 v. Torquay United (H). 1-1. Div.3(S).

PIDGEON Henry T.

(O.R.) Wing 5' 7" 10st 7lbs
b. Tottenham, London
Q.P.R. 1919
Southern League: 6-0. FAC: 0-0. FLC: 0-0. Others: 0-0.
Total: 6-0.

Southend United	Nov 1921
Yeovil & Petters United	Jun 1923

Henry played in the last six matches of the old Southern League.
Debut: 5. 4.1920 v. Merthyr Tidfil (H).0-0. SLDiv. 1.

PIERCE William

(R.B.) Def 5' 9" 12st 7lbs
b. Howden-on-Tyne, Durham 29.10.1907 d. 1976
Bedlington Colliery Welfare
Q.P.R. 1922
Football League:179-2. FAC: 14-1. FLC: 0-0. Others: 0-0.
Total:193-3.
Carlisle United Aug 1931

Bill was a hard tackling, never say die type of player who played for Q.P.R. throughout the twenties. At 16 years of age he made his debut, and during his eight seasons, he saw the highs and lows at Loftus Road, including, seeing the club applying for re-election, to that of finishing in third place.
Debut: 6.10.1923 v. Swansea Town (A).0-2. Div.3 (S).

PIGG William

(L.H.) Mid 5' 8" 11st 6lbs
b. High Spen, County Durham in 1897
Ashington Nov 1921
Q.P.R. Aug 1924
Football League: 21-0. FAC: 4-0. FLC: 0-0. Others: 0-0.
Total: 25-0.

Carlisle United	Jun 1926
Accrington Stanley	Jun 1930

Bill was an unrelenting tackler and was unlucky to be with the club at this period in their history. He arrived just after they had to apply for re-election and left two seasons later when they had to apply for the second time.
Debut: 7. 3.1925 v. Luton Town (H). 2-1. Div.3. (S).

PINNER Michael John

G
b. Boston, Lincolnshire 16. 2.1934
Bosten Grammar School
Wyberton Rangers
Notts County Oct 1948
Cambridge University
Pegasus

Aston Villa	May 1954
Sheffield Wednesday	Dec 1957
Q.P.R.	Jul 1959

Football League: 19-0. FAC: 2-0. FLC: 0-0. Others: 1-0.
Total: 22-0.

Manchester United	Feb 1961
Hendon F.C.	
Chelsea Casuals	
Chelsea	Oct 1961
Arsenal	
Swansea City	May 1962
Leyton Orient	Oct 1962
Belfast Distillery	Jun 1965

Honours: 4 Cambridge varsity blues. 52 England amateur caps. Represented Great Britain in the 1960 and 1964 Olympics. Represented the R.A.F.

Mike began as a 15 year old and was invited to join Aston Villa at 17. He did his National Service as a Pilot Officer and on his demob became a Solicitor. He was regarded as one of the finest amateur goalkeepers of his day. At the age of 29 he signed his first professional contract, with Leyton Orient, and played over 80 matches for them. Besides playing for the large number and variety of clubs listed he also toured with the famous Middlesex Wanderers.
Debut: 22. 8.1959 v. Swindon Town (H).2-0. Div.3.

PIZANTI David

Def 5' 10" 11st 0lbs
b. Israel 27. 5.1962
F.C. Koln
Q.P.R. 1987
Football League: 21-0. FAC: 4-1. FLC: 4-0. Others: 3-0.
Total: 32-1.

Honours: 25 caps for Israel.

David took quite awhile to acclimatise himself to the English game, however, when he did he was used mainly as a reserve or was substituted. He was released during the 1989 close season.
Debut: 17.10.1987 v. Liverpool (A). 0-4. Div. 1.

PLUMMER Christopher Scott

CD 6' 2" 12st 9lbs
b. Isleworth, London 12.10.1976
Q.P.R. Jul 1994
Premier/Football League: 62-2. FAC: 7-0. FLC: 2-0.
Others: 0-0. Total: 71-2.

Bristol Rovers	(Loan)	Nov 2002
Barnet		June 2003

Honours: England youth caps. 5 U21 caps.

Chris is a tall central defender who looks very assured on the ball. He likes to get forward in set pieces where he can cause problems for the opposing defenders. His first team appearances were fairly rare, and he missed the start of the 2001/02 season while he was recovering from a long term injury. Returning eventually to the side in November 2001, he then broke his ankle in only his second game back and was on the sideline for the remainder of the campaign. After a loan period at Bristol Rovers he returned to Q.P.R. but was not retained at the end of the 2002/03 season, and during the Summer was signed by Barnet.

Debut: 5. 5.1996 v. Nottingham Forest (A).0-3. PL.

PLUNKETT Adam E. T. B.

(L.B.) Def 5' 8" 11st 0lbs

b. Blantyre, Scotland 16. 3.1903 d. in 1992

Blantyre Celtic	
Bury	1922
Q.P.R.	Jul 1925

Football League: 15-0. FAC: 0-0. FLC: 0-0. Others: 0-0.
Total: 15-0.

Guildford United	Aug 1926
Walsall	Jun 1927
Coventry City	Jun 1928
Crystal Palace	Aug 1929
Southend United	Sep 1929
Oswestry Town	Oct 1929
Hinckley Athletic	1930
Loughborough Corinthians	Aug 1930
Rochdale	Mar 1931
Stalybridge Celtic	1932
Hinckley Athletic	1933

Adam was a nomad as far as football was concerned, for he never stayed at the same club too long. Released by Q.P.R. he later became the subject of crowd barracking during his time at Coventry.

Debut: 29. 8.1925 v. Gillingham (A). 0-3. Div. 3. (S).

POINTON William James

(C.F.) Striker

b. Hanley, Staffordshire 25.11.1920

Port Vale		Feb 1941
Q.P.R.	(£10,000)	Jan 1949

Football League: 26-6. FAC: 0-0. FLC: 0-0. Others: 0-0.
Total: 26-6.

Brentford	(Player/Exchange)	Feb 1950
Leek Town		

Perhaps Bill was a touch too delicate for a centre forward, for he was not as brash as Durrant or Addinall. However, his move to Brentford brought about an exchange deal which brought Dave Nelson to Loftus Road, much to the chagrin of the Bees supporters.

Debut: 22. 1.1949 v. Barnsley (A). 0-4. Div. 2.

POLLARD Robert

(R.B.) Def 5' 11" 11st 10lbs

b. Plattsbridge, Lancashire 25. 8.1899

Plattsbridge United	
Plank Lane	1918
Exeter City	1920
Q.P.R.	1929

Football League: 66-0. FAC: 7-0. FLC: 0-0. Others: 0-0.
Total: 73-0.

Cardiff City	Jul 1931
St. Etienne, France	

Bob was a stockily built player, who had an aggressive streak in him and was seldom beaten in the air or on the ground. For nine years he had been regarded as one of the best full backs in the third division. Eventually he went to coach in France.

Debut: 14. 9.1929 v. Northampton T. (A).1-2. Div.3 (S).

PONTING William Robert

(L.B.) Def

b. Andover Hampshire in 1872

d. Whetstone, Mddx.21. 3.1952

Andover	
Ryde	
Southampton	Mar 1897
Andover	1897
Q.P.R.	1900

Southern League: 1-0. FAC: 0-0. FLC: 0-0. Others: 0-0.
Total: 1-0.

Bill was a schoolmaster by profession and an amateur, but he left teaching to go into the insurance business in London. Later he was to become a very influential broker.
Debut: 22. 9.1900 v. Watford (H).1-0. SLDiv. 1.

POPPITT John

(R.B.) Def
b. Bedlington, Durham 20. 1.1923.
West Sleekburn
Derby County — May 1945
Q.P.R. — Sep 1950
Football League:106-0. FAC: 5-0. FLC: 0-0. Others: 0-0. Total:111-0.
Chelmsford — 1954

A very dour performer who was fast and direct when tackling for the ball. In earlier days John had been a junior athletics champion and at Derby County he was the substitute to the captain Bert Mozley. He helped Q.P.R. in 1953/54 to cope with their first season back in the 3rd Division by helping to ensure that valuable points were won in as many as fifteen draws. After four years and 111 first team appearances, he dropped down to non-League football.
Debut: 23. 9.1950 v. Birmingham City (A). 1-1.Div. 2.

POUNDER Albert William

(O.R.) Wing 6' 0" 12st 7lbs
b. Charlton, London 27. 7.1931
Harvey's Sports
Charlton Athletic — Jan 1950
Tonbridge — Oct 1950
Charlton Athletic — May 1952
Q.P.R. (£500) — Feb 1954
Football League: 53-6. FAC: 2-0. FLC: 0-0. Others: 0-0. Total: 55-6.
Sittingbourne — Jul 1957
Ramsgate — May 1960
Yeovil Town

Because Bert was a somewhat ungainly character on the right wing, his attitude and endeavours never really endeared him to the spectators. He ended his footballing days on the non-League scene becoming player/manager of Sheppey United in 1964.
Debut: 13. 2.1954 v. Exeter City (A). 0-0. Div.3 (S).

POWELL George R.

(R.B.) Def
b. Fulham, London 11.10.1924d. in 1989
Fulham
Q.P.R. — Dec 1946
Football League:145-0. FAC: 10-0. FLC: 0-0. Others: 0-0. Total:155-0.
Snowdon Colliery — 1953
Honours: 3rd Div. (South) championship medal.

George was recommended by a supporter who had seen him play in Germany during the War for the B.A.O.R. side. On being demobbed he joined the club as an amateur. In the1947/48 season's F.A. Cup run, the side beat Gillingham, Stoke City and Luton Town to reach the 6th round versus Derby County, then a power in the land. The teams drew 1-1 at Loftus Road, but at Derby the following week, Reg Allen fractured a bone in his hand a few minutes after the start and George Powell went in goal. George stayed at Loftus Road for seven years and played in 155 competitive matches, before moving to Kent to play for the Snowdon Colliery side.
Debut: 8.11.1947 v. Reading (A). 2-3. Div. 3. (S).

POWELL Ivor Verdun

(R.H.) Mid 5' 7" 11st 6lbs
b. Gilfach, Wales 5. 7.1916
Bargoed F.C.
Barnet
Q.P.R. — Sep 1937
Football League:110-2. FAC: 12-0. FLC: 0-0. Others: 2-0. Total:124-2.
Aston Villa (£17,500) — Dec 1948
Port Vale — Aug 1951
Barry Town — Dec 1951
Bradford City — Jun 1952

Honours: 8 caps for Wales plus 4 wartime appearances. 3rd Div. (South) championship medal.

Ivor was the first post-war player to be capped by his country while at the club. A tenacious, short, stocky halfback possessing a biting tackle and a very long throw-in. During World War Two he was a P.T. Instructor with the R.A.F. stationed at Blackpool and appeared for the seasiders. Ivor struck up a great friendship with Stan Matthews who was subsequently best man at his wedding. In his last war-time match for Wales, Powell broke his collar-bone and was substituted by the Englishman, Stan Mortenson. When Aston Villa secured Ivor's transfer it was the highest fee paid for a half back at that time. Injury finally put paid to his playing career in 1954, however, he remained the manager of Bradford City until the following year. Ivor became a publican in Manningham but then returned to the game as a coach for Leeds United. In 1960 he became the manager of Carlisle United and two years later took them into the 3rd Division. Later he managed Bath City and then coached in Greece, subsequently retuning to coach the university football team.
Debut: 28. 1.1939 v. Walsall (H). 3-0. Div. 3 (S).

POWELL Michael P.

(C.H.) CD 6' 2" 14st 4lbs
b. Slough, Buckinghamshire 18. 4.1933

Q.P.R.	Jan 1951

Football League:105-0. FAC: 3-0. FLC: 0-0. Others: 0-0.
Total:108-0.

Yiewsley	1959

Mike was a tall, strong, hefty defender who filled the central defender's spot in the middle fifties. He was brought into the side to replace Bill Spence, who was injured. Michael gradually made the position his own until the emergence of Keith Rutter, who became the preferred player. Although Powell was given a couple of games at centre forward he was released in 1959.
Debut: 6. 9.1952 v. Norwich City (A). 0-2. Div.3 (S).

PRICE Edward

G
b. Walsall

Walsall	
Stockport County	1909
Croydon Common	
Brentford	1912
Q.P.R.	1920

Football League: 7-0. FAC: 0-0. FLC: 0-0. Others: 0-0.
Total: 7-0.

Ted appeared as the goalkeeper in the first two matches ever played by the club in the Football League. He then stood between the sticks in April 1921 during an injury crisis, but retired from the game during the close season that followed.
Debut: 28. 8.1920 v. Watford (H). 1-2. Div. 3.

PRICE Llewellyn Percy

(O.L.) Wing 5' 9" 11st 7lbs
b.Caersws, Wales 12. 8.1898 d. in December 1969

Barmouth	
Hampstead Town	
Mansfield Town	Jun 1920
Aston Villa	Mar 1921
Notts County	Jun 1922
Q.P.R.	Jun 1928

Football League: 3-0. FAC: 0-0. FLC: 0-0. Others: 0-0.
Total: 3-0.
Grantham Town

Honours: 1 cap for Wales. 2nd Div. championship medal.

Originally Lew was an inside or centre forward until he was turned into a winger at Aston Villa. He came to Q.P.R. late into his career and played in the first three matches of the 1928/29 season.
Debut: 25. 8.1928 v.Torquay United (A). 4-3. Div.3 (S).

PRIOR Stanley John

(C.F.) Striker
b. Swindon 20.12.1910. d. Swindon 22. 6.1972

Swindon Corinthians		
Charlton Athletic		Oct 1933
Q.P.R.	(£150)	Jun 1937

Football League: 6-3. FAC: 0-0. FLC: 0-0. Others: 0-0.
Total: 6-3.

Cheltenham Town	Aug 1938

Honours: 3rd Div. (South) championship medal. 2nd Div. runners-up medal. 1st Div. runners-up medal.

When Stan hit Charlton Athletic's first ever goal in Division One it gave him the unique record of scoring the club's first goals in all three Divisions of the Football League. In minor matches he had already notched five v. Islington Corinthians and eight v. Woolwich Garrison. Having to play second fiddle to Tommy Cheetham, he was transferred to Q.P.R. for a nominal fee, but found his chances were limited there. After the 2nd World War he worked as a poultry farmer near Swindon, but at the time of his death he was a carpenter.
Debut: 15. 9.1937 v. Torquay United (A). 2-0. Div.3 (S).

PRITCHETT Keith Bernard

(L.B.) Def 5' 9" 11st 4lbs
b. Glasgow, Scotland 8.11.1953

Wolverhampton Wanderers		Apl 1972
Doncaster Rovers		Jul 1973
Q.P.R.		Jan 1975

Football League: 4-0. FAC: 0-0. FLC: 0-0. Others: 0-0. Total: 4-0.

Brentford		Jul 1976
Watford	(£4,000)	Nov 1976
Blackpool		Nov 1982
Mount Roskil, New Zealand		1986
Waitakere, New Zealand		

Honours: 2nd Div. runners-up medal. 4th Div. championship medal. 3rd Div. runners-up medal.

Keith took over from Ian Gillard when the latter filled in for David Webb. Pritchett became the national coach of New Zealand in 1996 and also a successful soccer journalist.
Debut: 31. 3.1975 v. Newcastle United (A).2-2. Div. 1.

PRYCE John

(I.R.) Mid 5' 9" 11st 10lbs
b. Renton, Dumbartonshire, Scotland 25. 1.1874

Renton	1893
Hibernian	May 1896
Glossop North End	Sep 1898
Sheffield Wednesday	Mar 1899
Q.P.R.	May 1901

Southern League: 19-2. FAC: 3-0. FLC: 0-0. Others: 0-0. Total: 22-2.

Brighton & Hove Albion	Oct 1903

Honours: Scottish Cup runners-up medal. 2 2nd Div. promotion medals.

By the time John reached the club he had lost a lot of his drive and penetration, so he never fitted well in the side. He retired in 1905.
Debut: 7. 9.1901 v. Watford (H). 0-1. SLDiv. 1.

PULLEN Henry

(L.B.) Def 5' 10" 12st 7lbs
b. Wellingbrough in 1888

Kettering Town	
Q.P.R.	1910

Southern League:168-1. FAC: 13-0. FLC: 0-0. Others: 1-0. Total:182-1

Newport County	1920
Hartlepool United	1921

Honours: Southern League Championship medal. Played for the Southern League team.

Henry was a clever two-footed left back who was a fine tackler. When he moved to Hartlepool in 1921 Henry had already played his last football match, for he was struck down with appendicitis and never did turn out for his new club.
Debut: 29. 4.1911 v. Plymouth Argyle (H).1-0. SLDiv. 1.

QUASHIE Nigel Francis

Mid 6' 0" 12st 4lbs
b. Peckham, London 20. 7.78

Q.P.R.		Aug 1995

Premier League/Football League: 57-3. FAC: 4-2. FLC: 1-0. Others: 0-0. Total: 62-5.

Nottingham Forest	(£2,500,000)	Aug 1998
Portsmouth	(£600,000)	Aug 2000

Honours: England youth caps. 4 U21 caps. 1 B cap. 1st Div. championship medal.

On his day, Nigel is a talented player with good passing ability and a powerful shot. After three years at Loftus Road, he cost Nottingham Forest an enormous fee, but only a quarter of this figure when he moved back south two years later. Since he has been with Portsmouth, Nigel's vision, tackling and first touch made him one of the better players in Portsmouth's rise to the Premiership. However many consider that Nigel still needs to find greater consistency.
Debut: 30.12.1995 v. Manchester United (A).1-2. PL.

QUIGLEY Thomas Cook

(C.F.) Striker
b. Mid-Calder, Lancashire 26. 3.1932

Barry Town	
Portsmouth	Dec 1955
Q.P.R.	Jun 1956

Football League: 16-7. FAC: 0-0. FLC: 0-0. Others: 1-0. Total: 17-7.

Worcester City	1957

Tom was one of four players to be tried in the centre forward spot during the 1956/57 season, at the start of which he scored seven goals in nine matches. However, he had trouble settling in London, so he was released at the end of the season.
Debut: 18. 8.1956 v. Reading (A). 0-1. Div. 3 (S).

QUINN Gordon P.

(I.F.) Mid 5' 11" 11st 6lbs
b. Shepherds Bush, London 11. 5.1932
Eastcote boys club.

Q.P.R.	Aug 1952

Football League: 22-1. FAC: 1-0. FLC: 0-0. Others: 0-0.
Total: 23-1.

Plymouth Argyle	Sep 1956
Tunbridge Wells	1957

Gordon was a tall, slim player, who was excellent at controlling the ball and his passing was first class, but he somehow lacked that little bit of confidence. Plymouth Argyle signed him in an attempt to take the club back into the Second Division, but Gordon lasted just one season with the club, after failing to win a permanent place in the side.
Debut: 18.10.1952 v. Newport County (H). 4-2. Div.3 (S)

RADNAGE Joseph J.

(H.B.) Mid.
b.
Reading

Q.P.R.	1909

Southern League: 3-0. FAC: 0-0. FLC: 0-0. Others: 0-0.
Total: 3-0.

Radnage is believed to have come from Reading and was a reserve player. He stood in for Hartwell and Wake.
Debut: 11. 9.1909 v. Clapton Orient (H). 2-1. SL Div. 1.

RAMSCAR Fredrick T.

(I.R.) Mid 5' 6" 9st 6lbs
b. Salford, Lancashire 24. 1.1919.
Salford boys
Manchester City
Stockport County

Wolverhampton Wanderers	Sep 1945
Q.P.R.	Oct 1947

Football League: 51-4. FAC: 6-1. FLC: 0-0. Others: 0-0.
Total: 57-5.

P.N.E.	Nov 1949
Northampton Town	Jul 1951
Millwall	Sep 1954
Peterborough United	1955

Honours: 3rd Div. (South) championship medal.

Fred made his debut in the Fooball League for Manchester City, as an amateur, during the war period but signed for Stockport County in 1943, being offered terms with Manchester United on the same day.

A smooth and classy player with a good strong shot who became the general of the side that won the 3rd Division title in 1948. When his playing days were over he went back to Northampton to take charge of the colts team and then finished up at Wellingborough in the late 1950s. Fred was last heard of living in retirement in Northampton.
Debut: 25.10.1947 v. Ipswich Town (A). 0-1.Div. 3 (S).

RAMSEY Alexander Parrott

(O.L.) Wing 5' 8"
b. Gateshead in 1899
Spen Black 'n' White
Swalwell

Newcastle United	(£100)	May 1919
Q.P.R.		Jun 1921

Football League: 6-0. FAC: 0-0. FLC: 0-0. Others: 0-0.
Total: 6-0.

Aberman Athletic	1922

Alex had been a gunner in the Machine Gun Corps in France and Egypt during World War One, and cost the Newcastle club a £100 transfer fee from Swalwell in 1919. Stan Seymour was brought in from the Scottish club, Morton, to replace him the following year and Alex was transferred to Q.P.R. Great things were expected of him but he disappointed many observers of the game, and he only made six League appearances.
Debut: 27. 8.1921 v. Swindon Town (H). 0-0.Div.3 (S).

RAMSEY C. B.

(O.R.) Wing
b.
Q.P.R. 1919
Southern League: 12-1. FAC: 0-0. FLC: 0-0. Others: 0-0. Total: 12-1.

Ramsey was just one of six outside rights to be tried during this season, which was the last in the old Southern League. None of them were retained for the following campaign.
Debut: 6.12.1919 v. Northampton T. (H).5-1. SLDiv.1.

RANCE Charles Stanley

(C.H.) CD 6' 1" 12st 4lbs
b. Bow, London 28. 2.1889
d.Chichester, Sussex 29.12.1966

West Ham Schools
London Schools
Clapton
Tottenham Hotspur Jul 1910
Derby County Mar 1921
Q.P.R. Sep 1922
Football League: 13-0. FAC: 0-0. FLC: 0-0. Others: 0-0. Total: 13-0.
Guildford United

Honours: Amateur Cup winners medal. 2nd Div. championship medal.

Charlie was an extraordinarily clever player, determined and intelligent, who always tried to be creative with his clearances out of defence. He played as an amateur for Clapton as a fifteen year old and went on to represent London & Essex County and rapidly developed into one of the best amateur central defenders in the country. A goalscoring member of the Clapton FA Amateur Cup winning team, Charlie was selected as a reserve for the England amateur team on four occasions, but when he was picked for a match against Denmark, in 1910, it was postponed because of the death of King Edward V11. At Q.P.R. his appearances were limited so he moved back to non-Leaguefootball, and was appointed manager of Guildford United in 1925. In 1930 he became coach to Wood Green.
Debut: 30. 9.1922 v. Brighton & H.A. (A).0-2. Div.3 (S).

READ Arthur

(H.B.) Mid
b. Ealing, Middlesex in 1899

Tufnell Park 1920
Q.P.R. 1921
Football League: 21-0. FAC: 0-0. FLC: 0-0. Others: 0-0. Total: 21-0.
Reading 1922

Honours: 2 England Amateur International caps. F.A.Amateur cup runners-up medal.

Arthur was rather unobtrusive yet effective at all three wing half positions. The ball was usually kept on the ground by him and passes were astutely placed. After leaving for Reading he received an injury which forced him to retire in 1923.
Debut: 27. 1.1921 v. Swindon Town (H).0-0. Div.3 (S).

READY Karl

CD 6' 1" 13st 3lbs
b. Neath, Wales 14. 8.1972
Q.P.R. Aug 1990
Premier/Football League:226-10. FAC: 8-0. FLC: 12-1. Others: 0-0. Total:246-11.
Motherwell Jul 2001
Aldershot (Loan) Sep 2002

Honours: 5 Welsh caps. 2 B caps. 5 U21 caps. School caps.

Karl is comfortable both in the air and on the ground, a first class defender who can play anywhere across the back four. He came up through the club's youth system and signed as a pro. in August 1990. He started as a right back but after injury returned as a central defender, and was an excellent foil to Alan McDonald. He stayed at Loftus Road for 11 years, but it was around five seasons before he established himself as a first team regular.

However, he was unfortunate in never being able to gain the full support of some fans, often being accused of lack of pace. During his time at Loftus Road he was one of several players to wear the captain's arm band. In the Summer of 2001 Karl was one of fifteen players to be released, and he was signed on by Motherwell. But in September 2002, he was temporarily released from his contract and journeyed back south to sign for ambitious Aldershot Town of the Ryman League. This was a coup for the Hampshire side, and Karl remained for much of the season, helping the Shots promotion to the Conference.

Debut: 9.10.1991 v. Hull City (H).5-1.R.2.League Cup.

REAY Edwin Peel

(R.B.) Def
b. Tynemouth, North Shields 5. 8.1914
North Shields
Sheffield United 1936
Q.P.R. 1937
Football League: 34-0. FAC: 1-0. FLC: 0-0. Others: 3-0. Total: 38-0.

Honours: 3rd Div. (South) championship medal.

A loyal servant to the club despite his appearances being limited in a six year period. Ted was very unfortunate that his career coincided with the 2nd World War, around which period he did tour Italy with an Army eleven led by Stan Cullis.

Debut: 2. 4.1938 v. Watford (A). 1-3. Div. 3. (S).

REED Gordon

(C.F.) Striker 5' 9" 11st 4lbs
b. Spennymore, Durham in May 1913
Shildon Colliery 1929
Spennymore United
Huddersfield Town
Everton 1931
Bristol City 1932
Newport County 1934
Q.P.R. 1935
Football League: 9-4. FAC: 0-0. FLC: 0-0. Others: 0-0. Total: 9-4.
Darlington 1936
Gateshead 1937

Gordon was a dashing centre forward who could find the net with a certain regularity. However, his main claim to fame lay outside the football world, for he was an excellent saxophonist and became the leader of one of the most famous bands in London during the late 1930s.

Debut: 25. 8.1934 v. Swindon Town (A).1-3. Div.3 (S).

REID Peter

Mid 5' 8" 10st 8lbs
b. Huyton, Lancashire 20. 6.1956
Bolton Wanderers May 1974
Everton Dec 1982
Q.P.R. Feb 1989
Football League: 29-1. FAC: 0-0. FLC: 3-0. Others: 0-0. Total: 32-1.
Manchester City Dec 1989
Southampton 1993
Notts County 1994
Bury 1994

Honours: 2nd Div. championship medal. F.A.Cup winners medal. European cup winners medal. 2 1st Div. championship medals. 13 England caps. 6 U21 caps. Voted "Player of the Year" in 1985.

A player of superb skill and vision who distributed the ball with precision and briskness. Peter rarely needed more than two touches of the ball; he would get it, move into space and demand it back, forever bringing colleagues into the game and opening up fresh avenues of attack. Peter's time at Loftus Road was towards the end of his football career, although he played for several clubs both before and after.

Debut: 11. 2.1989 v. Nottingham Forest (A).0-0. Div.1.

REVILL Edward J.

(I.R.) Striker
b. Bolsover, Nottinghamshire
Bolsover Wesleyans
Bridgeford Corinthians
Bolsover Town
Sutton Town
Chesterfield Town May 1910
Q.P.R. Aug 1911
Southern League: 62-21. FAC: 4-1. FLC: 0-0. Others: 1-1. Total: 67-23.
Chesterfield Town May 1913
Bolsover Colliery May 1914
Chesterfield 1920
Clay Cross Town
Bolsover Town
Alfreton Town 1923

Honours: Southern League championship medal.

A prolific scorer for whichever team he played for, and on the continental tour of 1912, he scored six goals versus Saabrucken/ Teddy was the eldest of three brothers, who all played for Chesterfield around this time. After his retirement from football he became a licensee at the Cross Keys Hotel in Bolsover.

Debut: 2. 9.1911 v. Plymouth Argyle (A).1-0.SLDiv.1.

RHODES Albert

(R.B.) Def
b. Dinnington, Yorkshire 29. 4.1936
Worksop Town

Q.P.R.	Dec 1954

Football League: 5-0. FAC: 0-0. FLC: 0-0. Others: 0-0.
Total: 5-0.

Tonbridge	1957

Bert was the reserve, who stood in for Woods at right back whenever he was injured or unavailable; which wasn't very often!
Debut: 14. 4.1956 v. Reading (A).1-3. Div. 3 (S).

RICHARDSON Anthony J.

(R.B.) Def
b. Southwark, London 7. 1.1932
Slough Sports club

Q.P.R.	Apl 1951

Football League: 2-0. FAC: 0-0. FLC: 0-0. Others: 0-0.
Total: 2-0.

This was the season that relegation from the 2nd Division loomed large. George Powell stood in for left back Tony Ingham, who was injured and Tony Richardson was the man to fill in at right back.
Debut: 5. 1.1952 v. Bury (H). 3-2. Div. 2.

RICHARDSON Derek W.

G 6' 1" 14st 4lbs
b. Hackney, London 13. 7.1956

Chelsea	Feb 1974
Q.P.R.	Apl 1976

Football League: 31-0. FAC: 0-0. FLC: 1-0. Others: 0-0.
Total: 32-0.

Sheffield United	Dec 1979
Coventry City	Mar 1982
Maidstone United	1982

Honours: 2 England youth caps. 2 semi-pro caps.

Derek was Phil Parkes' understudy but after the horrendous season of 1978/79, he was released.
Debut: 8. 3.1977 v. Leeds United (H).0-0. Div. 1.

RICHARDSON Stuart

(L.H.) Mid 5' 9" 11st 0lbs
b. Leeds 12. 6.1938
Methley United

Q.P.R.	Nov 1956

Football League: 1-0. FAC: 0-0. FLC: 0-0. Others: 0-0.
Total: 1-0.

Oldham Athletic	Jul 1959

Stuart received just one first team opportunity owing to the brilliant form of Peter Angell. He was therefore given a free transfer to Oldham Athletic, but unfortunately they had to apply for re-election that season, and manager Jack Rowley released him.
Debut: 3. 1.1959 v. Colchester United (A).0-3. Div.3.

RICHMOND Hugh

(C.H.) CD 5' 11" 11st 10lbs
b. Kilmarnock, Scotland 9. 3.1893

Kilbirnie Ladeside		1911
Kilmarnock		Jul 1913
Galston		May 1914
Arthurlie		Aug 1916
Leicester Fosse		Mar 1919
Nuneaton Town	(Loan)	Jan 1920
Coventry City		May 1922
Q.P.R.		May 1925

Football League: 10-0. FAC: 0-0. FLC: 0-0. Others: 0-0.
Total: 10-0.

Blyth Spartans	Jul 1926
Spennymore United	Aug 1929

Hugh served with Scottish clubs before World War One and fought with the Seaforth Highlanders during it. He joined Leicester City and was initially regarded as a goalscoring inside forward but was soon to demonstrate a natural ability at centre half. He captained the Leicester City reserve team in the Central Alliance. At Coventry City, Hugh became known as 'Rubberneck' and bagged a hat-trick of goals against Nelson in 1923. At Q.P.R. they were fighting for the second time in three years against re-election, when no less than ten centre halves were tried in the team, of which Hugh was one. The following season he was coaching at Blyth Spartans and in 1929, at Spennymore United.
Debut: 29. 8.1925 v. Gillingham (A). 0-3. Div. 3 (S).

RIDLEY John George

(R.B.) Def 5' 6" 11st 11lbs
b. Bardon Mill 19. 1.1903 d. Prudhoe 25.12.1977
Mickley

South Shields	1920
Manchester City	Sep 1927
Reading	Jun 1933
Q.P.R.	1934

Football League: 17-0. FAC: 1-0. FLC: 0-0. Others: 3-0.
Total: 21-0.

North Shields	1935

Honours: 2nd Div. championship medal.

After the departure of Warney Cresswell in 1922 from South Shields to Arsenal, John Ridley made the left back berth his own at the North-East club, once clocking up 110 consecutive appearances.
Debut: 8.12.1934 v. Brighton & H.A.(H). 1-2. FAC.

RIDYARD Alfred

(C.H.) CD 6' 3" 13st 0lbs
b. Cudworth 5. 5.1908 d. West Bromwich in 1981
Shafton & Royston schools
Hemsworth Rovers
South Kirby boys club

Barnsley		Sep 1929
W.B.A.	(£900)	Jun 1932
Q.P.R.	(£625)	Mar 1938

Football League: 28-0. FAC: 4-0. FLC: 0-0. Others: 1-0. Total: 33-0.

Honours: 3 Central League championship medals.

Tall, commanding and built like the side of a house, Alf was as tough as old boots and was regarded as a real stopper centre half. He was milking a cow on his Handsworth farm when a representative from Q.P.R. signed him on the transfer deadline day in 1938. Most of Alf's matches for the club (over 200 of them), were played during the wartime period. Retiring in 1948 he became the assistant manager and later had a spell as chief coach, before becoming the club's head scout.
Debut: 9. 4.1938 v. Gillingham (H). 2-0. Div. 3 (S).

RIVERS Walter

(R.H.) Mid 5' 11" 12st 7lbs
b. Throckley, Newcastle 8. 1.1909
Walbottle F.C.
Throckley Welfare

Gillingham	Sep 1927
Crystal Palace	Aug 1929
Q.P.R.	May 1933

Football League: 3-0. FAC: 0-0. FLC: 0-0. Others: 1-0. Total: 4-0.

Gateshead	Aug 1934
Aldershot Town	Jan 1936
Carlisle United	Jun 1936
Accrington Stanley	Oct 1936
Scarborough	Aug 1938

A miner before he started playing football, Wally spent his whole career in the two Third Divisions making over 200 appearances. He was a tall, stalwart figure who was not easily shaken off the ball, opening up the game with his impressive distribution.
Debut: 26. 8.1933 v. Brighton & H.A. (H).2-0.Div.3 (S).

ROBERTS Anthony Mark

G 6' 0" 12st 0lbs
b. Bangor, Wales 4. 8.1969
Holyhead United

Q.P.R.	Jul 1987

Premier/Football League:122-0. FAC: 11-0. FLC: 10-0. Others: 2-0. Total:145-0.

Millwall	Aug 1998
St. Albans City	June 1999
Dagenham & Redbridge	Summer 2000

Honours: Welsh youth caps. 2 U21 caps. 1 B cap. 1 Welsh caps. Welsh semi-pro caps.

Tony is a tall commanding goalkeeper, who is something of a shot stopper, with a huge kick. He spent eleven years at Q.P.R. but was not often the first team 'keeper, hence only 122 League appearances during this long period. Unfortunately he suffered a hand injury which kept him out of the game for much of 1998. However, Tony made a comeback after a period with Millwall, St. Albans City, and then with Dagenham & Redbridge in the Conference. He won his single (full) Welsh cap when he came on as substitute for Neville Southall during the World Cup qualifying game against Georgia in August 1996.
Debut: 18.11.1989 v. Arsenal (A). 0-3. Div. 1.

ROBERTS Joseph

(O.L.) Wing 5' 7" 11st 0lbs
b. Tranmere 2. 9.1900 d. Watford 9. 3.1984
Oswestry Town

Watford	Aug 1926
Q.P.R.	May 1927

Football League: 4-0. FAC: 0-0. FLC: 0-0. Others: 0-0. Total: 4-0.

York City	Aug 1928
Halifax Town	Jun 1929
Southport	Mar 1930
Clapton Orient	May 1931
Luton Town	Aug 1932
Millwall	Dec 1932
Barrow	Jul 1933
Luton Town	1934
Cardiff City	Aug 1935
Dartford	
Worcester City	Aug 1936

One of a large family, Joe was raised in Birkenhead and one of his first jobs was that of a plater and boiler-maker on the docks. A widely travelled player, appearing with no less than 14 clubs in 10 years, he was a fast and clever winger who preferred to pass than shoot.

He was also a brilliant billiards player and an excellent golfer, right into his eighties. Joe took over his father-in-law's newsagents and tobacconist shop close to the Watford ground, and ran it for many years, whilst he continued as an avid Hornets supporter.
Debut: 5.11.1927 v. Luton Town (A). 1-0. Div. 3 (S).

ROBERTS John William

(O.L.) Wing
b. Liverpool in September 1880
White Star Wanderers

Tottenham Hotspur	Dec 1899
Stockport County	Jan 1902
Grays United	Mar 1902
Brighton & Hove Albion	Jun 1902
Q.P.R.	May 1905

Southern League: 22-1. FAC: 0-0. FLC: 0-0.Others: 0-0. Total: 22-1

P.N.E.	Jun 1906

"A wonderfully clever dribbler and if his shooting were only on par with his wizard-like manipulation of the ball, he would indeed be a great player." So wrote a newspaper during his first season at Brighton. John was transferred to Q.P.R. along with Andy Gardner in May 1905, but failed to impress.
Debut: 21.10.1905 v. Norwich City (A). 0-4. SLDiv. 1.

ROBINSON John William

(I.L.) Mid 5' 8" 11st 9lbs
b. Grangetown

Middlesbrough	1920
Portsmouth	1921
Guildford United	1922
Q.P.R.	1923

Football League: 5-1. FAC: 0-0. FLC: 0-0. Others: 0-0. Total: 5-1.

John scored in his debut match for Q.P.R., but the club ended the season at the bottom of the League.
Debut: 27.10.1923 v. Northampton T. (H).3-2. Div.3 (S).

ROBINSON Michael John

Striker 6' 0" 12st 7lbs
b. Leicester 12. 7.1958
Blackpool schools
Waterloo Wanderers
Dolphinholm boys club

P.N.E.		Jul 1974
Manchester City	(£756,000)	Jul 1979
Brighton & Hove Albion	(£400,000)	Jul 1980
Liverpool	(£200,000)	Aug 1983
Q.P.R.	(£100,000)	Aug 1984

Football League: 48-5. FAC: 2-0. FLC: 8-1. Others: 0-0. Total: 58-6.

Osasuna, Spain	1987

Honours: 23 caps for Rep of Ire. 1 B cap. FACup runners-up medal. League championship medal. European Cup winners medal. League Cup runners-up medal.

Mike was an aggressive and hard working player, but injury forced him to retire from the game after two years with the Spanish club, Osasuna. However, he remained in the country and became a media star, as the co-host of the award winning T.V. football programme *" El Dia Despues"* (The Day After).
Debut: 29.12.1984 v. Stoke City (A). 2-0. Div.1.

ROEDER Glen Victor

CD 6' 1" 12st 3lbs
b. Woodford, Essex 13.12.1955
Arsenal schools

Orient		Oct 1973
Q.P.R.	(£250,000)	Aug 1978

Football League:157-17. FAC: 11-0. FLC: 13-1. Others: 0-0. Total:181-18.

Notts County	(Loan)	1983
Newcastle United	(£150,000)	Dec 1983
Watford		Jul 1989
Orient		Jan 1992
Purfleet		Oct 1992
Gillingham	(Player/manager)	Oct 1992

Honours: 6 B caps for England. FACup runners-up medal. 2nd Div. championship medal. 2nd Div. promotion medal.

The trademark of this player was to be unruffled and very cool. Glen was so elegant going forward that it seemed a pity to play him as a defender. He became the Watford manager in July 1993, and this lasted until February 1996. He became part of the England coaching staff before he joined West Ham in a similar capacity. With the shock departure of Harry Redknapp he became the caretaker manager of West Ham United. Glen was appointed manager in June 2001.
Debut: 26. 6.1978 v. Nottingham Forest (H).0-0. Div.1.

ROGERS A.

(I.R.) Mid
b.
Ealing
Q.P.R. 1907
Southern League: 32-10. FAC: 2-0. FLC: 0-0. Others: 0-0. Total: 34-10.
Bristol Rovers 1910

Very little is known about this player, except that he became the second highest goalscorer during the season., when Q.P.R. were ordered by the Southern League to play all their matches in mid-week. After two years with Bristol Rovers, Rogers had drifted out of football altogether.
Debut: 2. 9.1907 v. Tottenham H. (H). 3-3. SLDiv. 1.

ROGERS Albert J.

(I.L.) Mid
b. Manchester
Southall
Q.P.R. 1928
Football League: 12-4. FAC: 0-0. FLC: 0-0. Others: 0-0. Total: 12-4.

Bert came onto the scene when Rounce was injured and out of the side; scoring twice on his debut. It is not known what happened to him after 1930.
Debut: 15.12.1928 v. Coventry City (H).3-1. Div.3 (S).

ROGERS Donald E.

(O.L.) Wing 5' 10" 12st 10lbs
b. Paulton, Somerset 25.10.1945
Swindon Town Oct 1962
Crystal Palace (£150,000) Nov 1972
Q.P.R. (Exchange deal) Sep 1974
Football League: 18-5. FAC: 1-0. FLC: 0-0. Others: 0-0. Total: 19-5.
Swindon Town (Ex-deal + £33,000) Mar 1976

Honours: England youth caps. 2 U23 caps. Football League cap. FA Youth cup runners-up medal. 3rd Div. runners-up medal. League Cup winners medal. Anglo-Italian cup winners medal. Anglo-Italian Inter-League winners medal.

The spectators at Loftus Road were given the treat of watching one of the best wingers in the country at that time. Don combined an electrifying turn of speed with silky skills on the ball. An exchange for Ian Evans brought him to Shepherds Bush and an exchange again brought Peter Eastoe from Swindon Town. Don still lives in Swindon where he runs his own sports shop as he has for the last thirty-odd years.
Debut: 24. 9.1974 v. Everton (H). 2-2. Div.1.

ROGERS Martyn

(R.B.) Def 5' 9" 11st 4lbs
b. Nottingham 26. 1.1960
South Nottingham schools
Manchester United Jan 1977
Q.P.R. Jul 1979
Football League: 2-0. FAC: 0-0. FLC: 0-0. Others: 0-0. Total: 2-0.

Honours: 9 England schoolboy caps.

When Tommy Docherty became manager of Q.P.R. for the second time, he persuaded Martyn to join him. He played for the club twice before Terry Venables sacked him when he became manager in May 1981. Sadly Martyn's promise as a junior was never fulfilled, and h was to die tragically in a fume-filled hire car.
Debut: 26. 4.1980 v. Newcastle United (H).2-1. Div.2.

RONALDSON Duncan McKay

(C.F.) Striker 5' 8" 12st 3lbs
b. Glasgow 21. 4.1879d. Glasgow 20. 9.1947
Vale of Clyde
Rutherglen Glencairn
Q.P.R. Dec 1900
Southern League: 18-8. FAC: 0-0. FLC: 0-0. Others: 0-0. Total: 18-8.
Grimsby Town May 1901
Bury May 1903
Q.P.R. May 1904
Southern League: 21-6. FAC: 1-0. FLC: 0-0. Others: 0-0. Total: 22-6.
Norwich City May 1905
Brighton & Hove Albion May 1907
Southend United May 1908
Norwich City May 1909
Dunfermline Athletic 1911

Honours: Scottish Junior International.

Duncan was a 'have boots will travel', sort of player whose brainy manoeuvres on the pitch made him a wanted man throughout his career. Quick off the mark with an unselfish attitude, plus a sixth sense for openings in the opponents defence. It was said that he had a good deep singing voice. Duncan was a tinsmith by trade.
Debut: 1.12.1900 v. New Brompton (A).1-2.SLDiv. 1.

ROSE John

(R.B.) Def
b. Sheffield, Yorkshire 25.10.1921
Peterborough United
Q.P.R. Mar 1943
Football League: 17-0. FAC: 1-0. FLC: 0-0. Others: 0-0.
Total: 18-0.

Jack dominated the right back position during the latter part of the 1946/47 season. He then suffered three cartilage operations within a year, which proved too much for this likeable player, so he decided to quit the game in 1948.
Debut: 31. 8.1946 v. Watford (H). 2-1. Div. 3. (S).

ROSE Matthew David

CD 5' 11" 11st 1lb
b. Dartford, Kent 24. 9.1975

Arsenal		Jul 1994
Q.P.R.	(£500,000)	May 1997

Football League:169-6. FAC: 1-0. FLC: 7-0. Others: 2-0.
Total:179-6.

Honours: 2 England U21 caps. FA Youth cup winners medal.

Matt was the captain of Arsenal's Youth team when they won the 1994 FA Youth Cup, and three years later Q.P.R. paid a substantial fee for his signature. A relatively stylish and good tackler with passing skills, Matt began as a midfield player but moved to centre back or sweeper. He is an excellent defender but has often been hit by injuries, although he has gradually earned himself a more or less regular slot in the first team. By the end of the 2002/03 season he had been with the club for six years and made a very creditable 169 Football League appearances, and at this time he was the club's longest serving player.
Debut: 9. 8.1997 v. Ipswich Town (H).0-0. Div.1.

ROSENOIR Leroy

(C.F.) Striker 6' 1" 11st 10lbs
b. Balham, London 24. 8.1964

Fulham		Aug 1982
Q.P.R.	(£50,000)	Aug 1985

Football League: 38-8. FAC: 4-0. FLC: 5-2. Others: 0-0.
Total: 47-10.

Fulham		Jun 1987
West Ham United	(£275,000)	Mar 1988
Fulham	(Loan)	Sep 1990
West Ham United		Dec 1990
Charlton Athletic	(Loan)	Nov 1991
Bristol City		Mar 1992

Honours: England Schoolboy International.

A bustling type of player who sometimes seemed to lack a bit of refinement to his game. On other occasions Leroy could be very effective and was especially good in the air and quick on the ground. In 1994 he went to Fleet Town as coach and two years later moved on to Gloucester City as the player/ manager. Leroy is now currently the manager of Torquay United.
Debut: 3. 9.1985 v. Arsenal (H). 0-1. Div. 1.

ROUNCE George Alfred

(I.L.) Striker 5' 8" 10st 7lbs
b. Grays, Essex in 1905 d. London 2.10.1936
Tilbury
Uxbridge Town
Q.P.R. Jun 1928
Football League:171-58. FAC: 17-12. FLC: 0-0. Others: 0-0.
Total:188-70.

Fulham	(£450)	Mar 1933
Bristol Rovers	(£150)	Jun 1935

Honours: 2 appearances for the Middlesex Amateurs.

George was a direct player with a very hard shot who unfortunately was struck down with tuberculosis shortly before signing for Bristol Rovers. Aged just 31 he died in Victoria Park Hospital, Hackney.
Debut: 25. 2.1928 v. Merthyr Town (A). 4-0. Div.3 (S).

ROWE Alfred James

(O.L.) Wing 5' 8" 10st 7lbs
b. Poplar, London

Barking	
Plymouth Argyle	1921
Q.P.R.	1925

Football League: 4-1. FAC: 0-0. FLC: 0-0. Others: 0-0. Total: 4-1.

Bob Jack, the manager of Plymouth Argyle signed three players from Barking Town in 1921. Frank Richardson attained instant fame, Jack Leslie, after a slower start became an Argyle legend, but Alf Rowe spent four years at Home Park without becoming an automatic choice. At Q.P.R. Alf played on the wing instead of at half back and managed to score on his debut. However, within a year he was gone.
Debut: 5.4.1926 v.Bournemouth & B.A.(A).1-4. Div.3 (S)

ROWE Jonathan

(L.B.) Def 5' 8" 10st 10lbs
b. Packmoor, Manchester in 1907

Manchester Central	1929
Reading	1932
Q.P.R.	1935

Football League: 52-0. FAC: 4-0. FLC: 0-0. Others: 1-0. Total: 57-0.

Port Vale	1937

Jonty was a very experienced player who could fill either full back positions with ease. He retired during the ill-fated 1939/40 season when Port Vale's future went into abeyance because of the start of the War. Jonty appeared as a guest player for Crewe Alexandria once during the conflict.
Debut: 31. 8.1935 v. Millwall (H). 2-3.Div.3 (S).

ROWLAND Keith

Mid 5' 10" 10st 0lbs
b. Portadown, Northern Ireland 1. 9.1971

AFC Bournemouth		Oct 1989
Farnborough Town	(Loan)	Aug 1990
Coventry City	(Loan)	Jan 1993
West Ham United	(£110,000)	Aug 1993
Q.P.R.	(Part/Ex.deal)	Jan 1998

Football League: 56-3. FAC: 2-0. FLC: 2-0. Others: 0-0. Total: 60-3.

Luton Town	(Loan)	Jan 2001
Chesterfield		Aug 2001
Barnet		Mar 2003

Honours: 18 N.Ireland caps. 3 B caps. Youth caps.

A left-sided player who can who can operate either as a wing back or in a more traditional midfield role. Keith usually delivers one great cross during the course of the match. He came to Q.P.R. as part of the Trevor Sinclair deal with West Ham United. He stayed at Loftus Road for three years, during which time he made 60 senior appearances. He then moved on to Barnet (Transferred to Hornchurch July 2003)
Debut: 31. 1.1998 v. Stockport County (A).0-2. Div.1.

ROYCE Simon Ernest

(G.) 6' 2" 13st. 2lbs.
b. Newham, Northumberland 9. 9.1971

Heybridge Swifts		
Southend United	£35,000)	1991
Charlton Athletic		1998
Leicester City		2000
Brighton & Hove Albion	(loan)	2001
Manchester City	(Loan)	2002
Leicester City		2002
Q.P.R.	(loan)	Aug 2002
Charlton Athletic		June 2003

Football League: 16-0. FAC: 0-0. FLC: 0-0. Others: 0-0. Total: 16-0.

Loaned from Leicester City while Colkin and Day were injured, Simon was the third choice goalkeeper behind Flowers and Walker. Q.P.R. were so impressed with him when they played against him at Brighton & Hove on Boxing Day 2001, that this led to the loan deal. He stayed for much of the 2002/03 season, before eventually moving on the Charlton.
Debut: 24. 8.2002 v. Peterborough Utd.(H).2-0. Div. 2.

RUDDOCK Neil

CD 6' 2" 12st 2lbs
b. Wandsworth, London 9. 5.1968

Millwall		Mar 1986
Tottenham Hotspur	(£50,000)	Apl 1986
Millwall	(£300,000)	Jun 1988
Southampton	(£250,000)	Feb 1989
Tottenham Hotspur	(£750,000)	Jul 1992
Liverpool	(£2,500,000)	Jul 1993
Q.P.R.	(Loan)	Mar 1998

Football League: 7-0. FAC: 0-0. FLC: 0-0. Others: 0-0. Total: 7-0.

West Ham United	(£100,000)	Jul 1998
Crystal Palace		Jul 2000
Swindon Town		Aug 2001

Honours: 1 England cap. 1 B cap. 4 U21 caps. Youth caps. League Cup winners medal.

Neil is a very effective defender, his seven match loan spell from Liverpool saving Q.P.R. from relegation in 1998. His imposing physical presence is supported by powerful tackling, strength in the air, and a great left foot.
Debut: 28. 3.1998 v. Huddersfield Town (A).1-1. Div.1.

RUSSELL Sydney E. J.

(L.B.) Def 6' 0" 12st 7lbs
b. Feltham, Middlesex 1.10.1911

Tunbridge Wells	1931
Q.P.R.	1933

Football League: 42-0. FAC: 1-0. FLC: 0-0. Others: 2-0. Total: 45-0.

Northampton Town	1936

After three years Sid only made 45 first team appearances for the Rangers, and he moved on to Northampton Town. Tragically for Sid, he broke a leg at the end of the 1938/39 season while he was playing for the Cobblers at Southend on Easter Saturday. He was stretchered off and at Southend Infirmary he had to have the leg amputated after complications had set in. The brotherhood that exists in football showed itself with manager David Jack telling Northampton that he would let Southend help in any way possible, and Everton agreeing to play a charity match.
Debut: 4. 2.1933 v. Watford (A).2-2. Div. 3 (S).

RUTHERFORD Michael A.

Mid 5' 9" 11st 10lbs
b. Sidcup, Kent 6. 6.1972

Q.P.R.	1989

Football League: 2-0. FAC: 0-0. FLC: 1-0. Others: 0-0. Total: 3-0.

Welling United	1993

A Q.P.R. trainee who was released at the end of the 1993/94 season. Mike became a valued member of the Welling United club that were at that time in the Vauxhall Conference.
Debut: 21.10.1989 v. Charlton Athletic (H).0-1. Div.1.

RUTTER Keith G.

(C.H.) CD 6' 0" 11st 7lbs
b. Leeds, Yorkshire 10. 9.1934

Methley United	
Q.P.R.	Jul 1954

Football League:339-1. FAC: 18-0. FLC: 5-0. Others: 7-0. Total:369-1.

Colchester United	Feb 1963
Romford	1964

Consistent, reliable and unflappable were the words used about this outstanding defender. Keith was arguably the best centre half of the 3rd Division in the early sixties, missing just seven matches in six seasons, which included three occasions when he was an ever-present. He ousted Taylor from the centre half position to proved himself in that position. His stay at Loftus Road lasted nearly nine years, when he made an impressive 369 first team appearances in total, a very high average of around 40 per season. Yet he only ever scored one League goal, in his first season at Loftus Road. He moved to Colchester in 1963, and during the 1963/64 season scored another goal - this time for the opposition (an own goal versus Reading)! Even at age 40, he was able to sign for another club, Romford of the Southern League, after 20 years as a full time professional. 1964/65 was the last for Keith as a player.
Debut: 24. 8.1954 v. Southend United (A).2-2. Div.3 (S).

S

RYDER George S. D.

(I.L.) Mid 5' 8" 11st 10lbs
b.
Q.P.R. 1904
Southern League: 69-20. FAC: 4-1. FLC: 0-0. Others: 0-0. Total: 73-21.
Bolton Wanderers 1907
Leyton 1909
Croydon Common 1914

Honours: Toured South Africa with the Corinthians.

George had the reputation of being a fast and tricky player at Oxford University where he was studying law. At Q.P.R. he ended the 1905/06 season as the top goalscorer.
Debut: 1.10.1904 v. Northampton T. (H).0-1. SLDiv.1.

SALES Arthur Alfred

(R.H.) Mid
b. Lewes, Sussex 14. 3.1900d. Lewes, Sussex 5. 5.1977
Redhill
Chelsea Sep 1924
Q.P.R. 1930
Football League: 35-0. FAC: 0-0. FLC: 0-0. Others: 0-0. Total: 35-0.
Bournemouth & Boscombe Athletic 1933

Arthur established a huge reputation for himself in the amateur football world, however, at Chelsea he was limited to just seven first team matches in five years. Upon leaving Stamford Bridge in May 1928 he played for several amateur clubs before joining Q.P.R. Arthur was a fine athlete and once ran the hundred yards in ten and a half seconds.
Debut: 11.10.1930 v. Swindon Town (A).1-4. Div.3 (S).

SALT Harold

(R.H.) Mid 5' 9" 11st 7lbs
b. Sheffield, Yorkshire
Sheffield Wednesday 1917
Ecclesfield United
Brighton & Hove Albion Mar 1921
Mexborough town May 1922
Peterborough & Fletton 1922
Ravensdale
Port Vale Dec 1925
Q.P.R. May 1926
Football League: 5-0. FAC: 0-0. FLC: 0-0. Others: 0-0. Total: 5-0.
Grays Thurrock United 1927
Crystal Palace Jan 1928
Brentford May 1929
Walsall May 1932
Yeovil & Petters United 1933

This fair haired Yorkshireman was a centre half as well as an inside forward for Brighton & Hove, a left winger for Port Vale and a wing half at Q.P.R. Bob Hewison was trying to build a side that wouldn't have to apply for re-election again, but Salt didn't fit the bill.
Debut: 2.10.1926 v. Bournemouth. (A).2-6.Div. 3 (S).

SALVAGE Barry J.

Mid 5' 11" 11st 10lbs
b. Bristol 21.12.1947 d. Eastbourne in 1986
Eastbourne United
Fulham Sep 1967
Millwall Mar 1969
Q.P.R. (£9,000) Mar 1971
Football League: 21-1. FAC: 1-0. FLC: 1-0. Others: 0-0. Total: 23-1.
Brentford Feb 1973
Millwall Aug 1975
St. Louis Stars, USA 1977
Hastings United

Barry was a tall orthodox left footed player who was most successful at Brentford and Millwall. At these clubs he found regular senior squad football. Tragically he died of a heart attack while he was on a charity run in Eastbourne, and still in his thirties.
Debut: 21. 8.1971 v. Middlesbrough (A).2-3. Div. 2.

SAMUEL Daniel John

(I.L.) Mid 5' 7" 10st 7lbs
b. Swansea, Wales in 1911
Llanelly
Southend United Aug 1932
Reading May 1933
Q.P.R. 1935
Football League: 9-3. FAC: 0-0. FLC: 0-0. Others: 0-0. Total: 9-3.
Tunbridge Wells 1936
Barrow 1937

Dan was just one of five players to be tried in this position during the season. But he quickly faded from the Football League, and it became evident that he was better suited playing the summer game of cricket.
Debut: 31. 8.1935 v. Millwall (H). 2-3. Div. 3. (S).

SANDERSON Keith

Mid 5' 10" 11st 8lbs
b. Hull, Humberside 9.10.1940

Bath City		
Plymouth Argyle		Aug 1964
Q.P.R.	(£5,000)	Jun 1965

Football League: 104-10. FAC: 9-2. FLC: 11-0. Others: 0-0. Total: 124-12.
Goole Town

Honours: League Cup winners medal. 3rd Div. championship medal. 2nd Div. runners-up medal.

Malcolm Allison recruited Keith, a former Cambridge football blue, as soon as he became manager of Bath City, and when he became the manager of Plymouth Argyle, the player followed him there, where he became a part-time pro. Keith had his critics at Plymouth, those arguing that as a part-timer he ought not to receive full wages, but he was championed by manager Malcolm Allison who maintained that the player's value to the side was not appreciated from the terraces. Alec Stock stepped in to buy Sanderson as soon as Allison left Plymouth, and he became an integral part of the Q.P.R. side and also the captain. Keith had a tireless attitude to the game and was a huge favourite with the spectators at Loftus Road. His time at Loftus Road lasted four seasons, whereupon he moved down into non-League football.
Debut: 21. 8.1965 v. Brentford (A). 1-6. Div. 3.

SANGSTER J.

(O.R.) Wing
b.
Southall

Q.P.R.	1912

Southern League: 4-0. FAC: 0-0. FLC: 0-0. Others: 0-0. Total: 4-0.

A reserve player who stood in for Bill Thompson on four occasions during the season and never once appeared on the losing side.
Debut: 21. 9.1912 v. Northampton T. (H). 3-2. SLDiv. 1.

SANSOM Kenneth Graham

(L.B.) Def 5' 6" 11st 8lbs
b. Camberwell, London 26. 9.1958

Crystal Palace		Dec 1975
Arsenal	(£1,250,000)	Aug 1980
Newcastle United	(£300,000)	Dec 1988
Q.P.R.	(£300,000)	Jun 1989

Football League: 64-0. FAC: 10-2. FLC: 7-0. Others: 1-0. Total: 82-2.

Coventry City	Mar 1991
Everton	Feb 1993
Brentford	Mar 1993
Petersfield Town	Aug 1993
Wycombe Wanderers	Sep 1993
Luton Town	Oct 1993
Bromley	Nov 1993
Chertsey Town	Dec 1993
Watford	Aug 1994
Sydenham Sports	Oct 1995
Slough Town	Mar 1996

Honours: South London, Surrey and England schoolboys. 5 Youth caps. 8 U21 caps. 3 B level. 86 full England caps. FA youth cup medal. 2nd Div. championship medal. League Cup winners medal. League Cup runners-up medal.

Kenny was regarded as the best left back in the country at the time Arsenal paid a world record fee to secure his transfer. What made him a great player was his remarkable consistency, being very fast over short distances and the accuracy of his distribution of the ball. Spectators all agreed that his touchline sorties were a picture to behold. At 31 years old he still cost Q.P.R. a large transfer fee, and over 80 games and two years later he once again moved on. A succession of clubs still saw home playing in non-League football at 41.
Debut: 19. 8.1989 v. Crystal Palace (H). 2-0. Div. 1.

SAPHIN Reginald Francis Edward

G
b. Kilburn, London 8. 8.1916
Hayes

Walthamstow Avenue
Ipswich Town 1945
Q.P.R. May 1946
Football League: 30-0. FAC: 2-0. FLC: 0-0. Others: 0-0. Total: 32-0.
Watford Jul 1951
Hayes

While serving in the Navy during World War Two, Reg played for Ipswich Town as an amateur. On being signed by Q.P.R. he turned professional and became the understudy to Reg Allen, until he left for Manchester United. With the arrival of Harry Brown, Reg moved to Watford to join ex-patriot Dave Underwood and stayed until 1954. He then became assistant trainer of Watford until March 1957. He was later the youth team manager from 1960 until 1963.
Debut: 4.12.1946 v. Poole Town(A).6-0.1st Rd Rep.

SAUL Frank Lander

(C.F.) Striker 5' 10" 11st 12lbs
b. Canvey Island, London 23. 8.1943
Tottenham Hotspur Aug 1960
Southampton(£125,000 + Chivers) Jan 1968
Q.P.R. May 1970
Football League: 43-4. FAC: 3-0. FLC: 6-2. Others: 0-0. Total: 52-6.
Millwall Mar 1972
Dagenham Mar 1976

Honours: 7 England youth caps. Young England cap. FA Cup winners medal.

Something of a 'Boy Wonder', playing for the Spurs reserves when only fifteen years of age and then making his League debut at just seventeen. He was the stand-in for Bobby Smith, notching three goals in six matches in the famous Spurs double season. Frank was strong and eager and not lacking in skill, a fair haired youngster that always grafted hard, giving everything. After two years at Southampton he spent the next two or so at Loftus Road, when he notched up over 50 first team appearances. After his retirement from football he ran a building and decorating concern in Billericay in Essex and later a small fashion and knitwear business in London's East-End during the 1990s.
Debut: 15. 8.1970 v. Birmingham City (A).1-2. Div.2.

SCULLY Anthony Derek Thomas

(O.L.) Wing 5' 7" 11st 12lbs
b. Dublin, Eire 12. 6.1976
Crystal Palace Dec 1993
AFC Bournemouth (Loan) Oct 1994
Cardiff City (Loan) Jan 1996
Manchester City (£80,000) Aug 1997
Stoke City (Loan) Jan 1998
Q.P.R. (£155,000) Mar 1998
Football League: 40-2. FAC: 1-0. FLC: 5-0. Others: 0-0. Total: 46-2.
Walsall (Loan) Mar 2000
Cambridge United Jul 2001
Southend United (Loan) Nov 2002
Peterborough United (Loan) Mar 2003

Honours: Rep.of.Ire school & youth caps.10 U21 caps. 1 B cap.

Although he was a skilful ball player, Tony was unable to command a regular first team place. He was loaned to Walsall but did not appear in any of the Saddlers line-ups.
Debut: 21. 9.1998 v. Stoke City (A). 1-2. Div. 1.

SEALY Anthony John

(C.F.) Striker 5' 8" 11st 10lbs
b. Hackney, London 7. 5.1959
Wallsend schools
Wallesend boy club
Southampton May 1977
Crystal Palace (£50,000) Mar 1979
Port Vale (Loan) Feb 1980
Q.P.R. (£75,000) Mar 1981
Football League: 63-18. FAC: 1-0. FLC: 4-0. Others: 0-0. Total: 68-18.
Port Vale (Loan) Feb 1982
Fulham (Loan) Dec 1983
Fulham (Loan) Aug 1984
Fulham (£80,000) Jan 1985
Leicester City (£60,000) Sep 1985
AFC Bournemouth (Loan) Mar 1987
Sporting Braga, Portugal May 1987
Brentford Mar 1989
Bristol Rovers Sep 1989
Finland May 1991
Brentford Oct 1991

Honours: League Cup runners-up medal. 2nd Div. championship medal. 3 3rd Div. championship medals.

A hero straight out of the "Boys Wonder Comic" , he scored no less than 224 goals in schools and boys club football during the 1974/75 season. Tony signed for Southampton and made his reserve team debut at the age of sixteen years. Sealy was a strong bustling player who was the leading scorer for Q.P.R. in their championship season of 1983. An astonishing record held by Tony is that of four Championship medals, won by him with four different clubs in the space of ten years.

As he played out the twilight years of his career in Hong Kong, he also trained as a physio. However, Tony is now employed by the Hong Kong FC as the Sporting manager.
Debut: 21. 3.1981 v. Derby County (H). 3-1. Div. 2.

SEAMAN David Andrew

G 6' 2" 14st 10lbs
b. Rotherham, Yorkshire 19. 9.1963

Leeds United		Sep 1981
Peterborough United	(£4,000)	Aug 1982
Birmingham City	(£100,000)	Oct 1984
Q.P.R.	(£225,000)	Aug 1986

Football League:141-0. FAC: 17-0. FLC: 13-0. Others: 4-0. Total: 175-0.

Arsenal	(£1,300,000)	May 1990

Honours: 73 England caps. 10 U21 caps. 6 B caps. 1ST Division championship winners medal. 2 Premiership championship winners medals. 3 FACup winners medals. League Cup winners medals. European Cup winners medal. Charity Shield winners medal.

Relaxed and composed both on and off the pitch, he was still the number one choice for England until 2002, despite his age. David is a strong, brave goalkeeper who is fast off his line, has a safe pair of hands and a strong kick. Seaman's distribution is excellent, varying between long and short to the wing backs or long kicks to the strikers. Many attacking moves originate from his foresight and he is a great shot-stopper being exceptionally agile for a big man. In four seasons at Loftus Road, David was a first team fixture in the side and in 1989 he won the first of his 73 England caps when appearing against Scotland. It cost Peterborough United a modest fee to buy him from Leeds United.

But a more realistic idea of his value was required for his signature at Birmingham City. George Graham, then manager of Arsenal, paid out a British record fee (£1.3m.) for a goalkeeper - and nearly six times what he had cost Q.P.R. from Birmingham City - when he obtained Seaman's signature.
Debut: 23. 8.1986 v. Southampton (A). 1-5. Div.1.

SEARY Raymond M.

(L.B.) Def 5' 9" 10st 7lbs
b. Wallingford, Buckinghamshire 18. 9.1952

Q.P.R.		Sep 1970

Football League: 1-0. FAC: 0-0. FLC: 0-0. Others: 0-0. Total: 1-0.

Cambridge United	(£3,000)	Mar 1973

Ray's only appearances for the club was as a substitute in September 1971. His contract was not renewed at Cambridge United in 1976, so he ended his days in non-League football.
Debut: 4. 9.1971 v. Swindon Town (A). 0-0. Div. 2.

SEELEY George Alfred

Wing 5' 6" 11st 7lbs
b. Ventnor, I.O.W. in July 1877 d. Ventnor 15.10.1921

Gordon Avenue	
Southampton St. Marys	1896
Bristol St. Georges	
Eastville Rovers	
Southampton	1898
New Brompton	Jul 1899
Q.P.R.	1901

Southern League: 19-2. FAC: 3-0. FLC: 0-0. Others: 0-0. Total: 22-2.

Southampton Wanderers	1902
Clapton Orient	1903
Leyton	1905

A speedy, versatile and very tricky player who could centre the ball with remarkable precision. George was known as 'the Lion Tamer', due to his once having entered a lions cage in a circus in Southampton. Although he was marked down as a right winger, he could also play on the left.
Debut: 7. 9.1901 v. Watford (H). 0-1. SLDiv. 1.

SHANKS Donald

(R.B.) Def 5' 11" 10st 8lbs
b. Hammersmith, London 2.10.1952

Fulham		
Luton Town		Jul 1970
Q.P.R.	(£35,000)	Nov 1974

Football League:180-10. FAC: 11-1. FLC: 14-0. Others: 1-0. Total: 206-11.

Brighton & Hove Albion	Aug 1981
Eastern club, Hong Kong	1983
Wimbledon	1983
U.S.A.	
Zurrieq, Malta	

Honours: 7 England youth caps

Don was a regular defender who missed very few matches through injury. Arriving at Loftus Road in late 1974, it was three seasons or so before he established a regular place in the Q.P.R. line-up. Eventually, after seven seasons, he made over 200 appearances, and helped Q.P.R. to the runners-up spot, behind Liverpool, in 1976. Following his time at Loftus Road, he first stopped off at Brighton for two years, before moving around the world, playing in the Far East, America and Malta, before returning to England. But he is also remembered for his reputation as a playboy on the London gambling scene and had a former Miss World, Mary Stavin, as his girlfriend. Don now works for a well known horse-racing family

Debut: 7.12.1974 v. Burnley (A). 0-3. Div. 1.

SHAW Charles

G 5' 6" 12st 0lbs

b. Twechar, Scotland 21.9.1885

d. New York, USA 27.3.1938

Bailleston Thistle		
Kirkintilloch Harp		
Port Glasgow Athletic		Apl 1906
Q.P.R.		May 1907

Southern League:232-0. FAC: 16-0. FLC: 0-0. Others: 3-0. Total: 251-0.

Celtic		May 1914
Clyde	(Loan)	Feb 1925
New Bedford, U.S.A.		Jun 1925

Honours: Represented the Football League v. Irish & Scottish Leagues. Scottish X1 v. English X1. Scottish League v. Football League. 2 caps for the Southern League v. Football League. 2 Southern League championship medals. 5 Scottish League championship medals. 2 Scottish Cup winners medals.

Charlie was on a par with the rest of the goalkeeping greats that Q.P.R. have had in the history of the club. He was only 5' 6" tall with a small build but despite this he had a solid frame which kept him from being charged into the net, as was the norm in those far off days. A 'wondrous little goalkeeper', was the cry from Q.P.R. & Celtic fans alike. After seven years with Rangers, he moved north to Scotland. At Celtic he was idolised and made a club total of 436 appearances and kept 240 clean sheets. He took over as skipper in Sept. 1916 and *"His voice could be heard shouting advice all over the pitch."* Charlie died in New York, USA of pneumonia at the age of 52 years.

Debut: 2. 9.1907 v. Tottenham H. (H). 3-3. SLDiv.1.

SHEPHERD Ernest

(O.L.) Wing 5' 7" 11st 8lbs

b. Wombwell, Yorkshire 14. 8.1919

Dearne Valley schools		
Bradford Rovers		
Fulham		Apl 1938
W.B.A.		Dec 1948
Hull City	(£4,200)	Mar 1949
Q.P.R.		Aug 1950

Football League:219-51. FAC: 12-2. FLC: 0-0. Others: 1-0. Total: 232-53.

Hastings United

An old fashioned attacking winger, who was very fast and could beat the full back with deft ball control and tricky play. There was certainly no doubting his speed off the mark for it had served him well during sporting events while in the RAF and it had also won him money in invitation races. The crowd at Loftus Road enjoyed his antics and he became their firm favourite. When Ernie retired from playing he became the Bradford Park Avenue trainer in 1957, the same at Southend United in, 1959, then the assistant/manager in 1969, before becoming the physio/coach at Orient in 1973. Shepherd retired at the age of 61 years in 1979 after coaching for 2 years in the United Arab Emirates.
Debut: 13. 8.1950 v. Chesterfield (H). 1-1. Div. 2.

SHEPPARD William

(I.L.) Mid 5' 11" 11st 4lbs
b. Ferryhill, Durham in 1906 d.Hem.Hempstead 27.12.1950

Ferryhill		
Chilton Colliery		
Crook Town		
Liverpool		Dec 1925
Watford		Jul 1927
Q.P.R.		Jun 1930

Football League: 13-4. FAC: 0-0. FLC: 0-0. Others: 0-0. Total: 13-4.

Coventry City		Jul 1931
Walsall		Dec 1932
Chester	(Loan)	1935
Walsall		
Tunbridge Wells Rangers		
Odhams		1937

Bill scored some sixty goals in two years at Ferryhill Athletic and did the same at Chilton Colliery as well as Crook Town. He was never in the Liverpool line-up but Sheppard scored 25 goals for Watford in his first season and 14 in the next, after that he seemed to fade out of the picture, except when scoring that famous penalty against Arsenal in 1933. Bill died of a heart attack on a Christmas visit to his local "King Henry Eighth" in Hemel Hempstead aged 46 years.
Debut: 25.10.1930 v. Northampton T. (H). 0-2.Div. 3. (S)

SHERON Michael Nigel

Striker 5' 10" 11st 13lbs
b. Liverpool 11. 1.1972

Manchester City		Jul 1990
Bury	(Loan)	Mar 1991
Norwich City	(£1,000,000)	Aug 1994
Stoke City	(£450,000)	Nov 1995
Q.P.R.	(£2,750,000)	Jul 1997

Football League: 63-19. FAC: 2-0. FLC: 4-1. Others: 0-0. Total: 69-20.

Barnsley	(£1,000,000)	Jan 1999

Honours: 16 England U21 caps.

A player with vision and skill to go with his sharpness around the box. A very skilful player linking up well with his colleagues and with the ability to beat opponents with ease. Mike Sheron was a £2.75 million move to Q.P.R. (a record for both Stoke Q.P.R.), but he suffered a recurrence of a back injury and, after only 18 months, in January 1999, he moved to Barnsley.
Debut: 2. 9.1997 v. Reading (A). 2-1. Div. 1.

SHITTU Daniel Olusola

CD 6' 3" 13st 0lbs
b. Lagos, Nigeria 2. 9.1980

Carshalton Athletic		
Charlton Athletic		Sep 1999
Blackpool	(Loan)	Feb 2001
Q.P.R.	(£250,000)	Oct 2001

Football League: 94-9. FAC: 1-0. FLC: 1-0. Others: 0-0. Total: 96-9.

Honours: 1 cap for Nigeria.

Signed by Q.P.R. after two fans funded his quarter of a million pound deal. Danny is a big solid central defender who won his first cap v. Paraguay, whilst at Loftus Road, and had a memorable debut for Q.P.R., being sent off. He soon became a popular player at Loftus Road. And was a near ever-present in the first team during the 2002/03 season.
Debut: 23.10.2001 v. Peterborough Utd. (A).1-4. Div.2.

SHUFFLEBOTTOM Thomas

(L.H.) Mid
b. in 1881

Stoke	Jun 1901
Brentford	Jun 1902
Chesterfield Town	Jun 1903
Q.P.R.	May 1904

Southern League: 1-0. FAC: 0-0. FLC: 0-0. Others: 0-0. Total: 1-0.

Rotherham Town	Dec 1906
Workington	Jun 1907
Oldham Athletic	Oct 1907
Lincoln City	Nov 1907
Nuneaton Town	Jul 1908
Ilkeston United	Nov 1908

A young and enthusiastic player who was a reserve at most of his clubs. Tom travelled to Swindon along with John Bowman and played alongside him in his only match for the club.
Debut: 18. 3. 1905 v. Swindon Town (A).0-0. SLDiv.1.

SIBLEY Frank Phillip

(L.H.) Mid 5' 10" 12st 4lbs
b. Uxbridge, Middlesex 4.12.1947

Q.P.R.	1965

Football League:143-3. FAC:10-1. FLC: 15-1. Others: 0-0. Total: 168-5.

Honours: 4 England youth caps. Captain of the U18 squad. 3 U23 caps. 3rd Div. championship winners medal. League cup winners medal.

It was highly unfortunate that Frank received a severe knee injury which forced him to retire early in his career in 1974. He was immediately given the job of club coach and in 1977 followed on with the manager's job after Dave Sexton had left. When Steve Burtenshaw came onto the scene in 1978, Frank reverted to club coach again but then took the manager's job at Walsall, but only for a short time. He became the coach at Hounslow Town and in 1984 reverted to the job of caretaker/manager at Q.P.R. once again after Alan Mullery left the club. Jim Smith arrived in 1985 and Frank resumed the job as coach to the club becoming assistant/manager to Trevor Francis in 1988. In the 1990s he became the assistant/manager of Millwall. However, yet again he then returned to the job of coach at Q.P.R.
Debut: 4. 9.1963 v. Aldershot (A).1-3. FLCup 1st Rd.

SILKMAN Barry

Mid 5' 8" 10st 13lbs
b. Stepney, London 29. 7.1952

Fulham		
Wimbledon		
Barnet		
Hereford United		Aug 1974
Crystal Palace		Aug 1976
Plymouth Argyle	(£53,000)	Oct 1978
Luton Town	(Loan)	Feb 1979
Manchester City	(£60,000)	Mar 1979
Brentford	(£50,000)	Aug 1980
Maccabi, Tel Aviv		
Q.P.R.	(£5,000)	Oct 1980

Football League: 23-2. FAC: 2-0. FLC: 0-0. Others: 0-0. Total: 25-2.

Orient	(£15,000)	Sep 1981
Southend United		Jul 1985
Crewe Alexandria		Sep 1986
Staines Town		
Wingate & Finchley		
Harrow Borough		2000

Honours: 3rd Div. championship medal winner.

Barry was a flamboyant character who on his day was unstoppable. In November 2000, Silkman received plenty of plaudits after his 75th minute appearance for Harrow Borough (versus Wycombe Wanderers) made him the oldest player at 48 years, to play in the FACup since Sir Stanley Matthews turned out for Stoke City in the 1960s. He later became a football agent and also greyhound trainer in Kent.
Debut: 1.11.1980 v. Grimsby Town (A). 0-0. Div. 2.

SILVER Alan

G
b.

Q.P.R.	1954

Football League: 0-0. FAC: 1-0. FLC: 0-0. Others: 0-0. Total: 1-0.

Tunbridge Wells	1955

Just two days before the second replay of a 1st round FACup match, Harry Brown the goalkeeper was injured in a League match at Bristol City. Silver was the only goalkeeper available to fill the gap. With a goalless first half on a mud churned pitch, all seemed well at the start of the second. Yet by 73 minutes Q.P.R. were down 0-4. Alan never played for the club again, in fact Brian Nicholas, the regular right half was in goal for the next League match!
Debut: 29.11.1954 v. Walthamstowe A.(A).0-4. FACup.

SIMONS Henry Thomas

(I.R.) Mid 5' 8" 11st 4lbs
b. Hackney, London in October 1887 d. in 1956

Peel Institute	
Clapton Orient	
Leyton	Mar 1906
Tufnell Park	
Doncaster Rovers	
Sheffield United	Jul 1907
Halifax Town	
Merthyr Tydfil	Aug 1912
Brentford	Aug 1913
Fulham	Apl 1914
Q.P.R.	Aug 1914

Southern League: 19-7. FAC: 3-1. FLC: 0-0. Others: 0-0. Total: 22-8.

Tottenham Hotspur	Nov 1918
Norwich City	Sep 1920
Margate	

Honours: Southern Counties Amateur championship medal.

Simons was very much respected in London amateur circles, showing uncanny anticipation in matches, often mastering the opposing defender. Tommy was one of several brothers who were prominent among amateur clubs around this time and was the son of a one-time groundsman at Clapton Orient.
Debut: 14.11.1914 v. Exeter City (H).0-2. SLDiv. 1.

SINCLAIR Trevor Lloyd

Mid 5' 10" 11st 2lbs
b. Dulwich, London 2. 3.1973

Blackpool		Aug 1990
Q.P.R.	(£750,000)	Aug 1993

Premier/Football League:167-16. FAC: 10-2. FLC: 13-3. Others: 0-0. Total: 190-21.

West Ham United	(£2,300,000)	Jan 1998

Honours: England youth caps. 1 B cap. 14 U21 caps. 9 full caps.

Trevor's appetite for running at defenders is backed-up by an indefatigable work rate which marks him out as a modern rarity. He is very much a skilful player who is difficult to dispossess when he is in full flight. Despite being a Londoner by birth, he was brought up in Manchester (where he became a City fan), and started in the Football League at Blackpool. After three seasons he became a big money Q.P.R. signing. After a further five years, and nearly 200 appearances, his value had trebled with his move across London. One of his best performances was for West Ham United against Derby County on Boxing Day 2002 when he scored with a spectacular 12 yard volley. By the end of the 2002/03 season, he had also played around 200 matches for the Hammers.
Debut: 18. 3.1993 v. Liverpool (H). 1-3. PL.

SINGLETON Harold Bertram

(O.L.) Wing 5' 9" 12st 3lbs
b. Prescot, Lancashire in 1877d. Macclesfield 5. 7.1948

Stockport County	1900
Bury	1901
Everton	1901
Grimsby Town	1902
New Brompton	May 1903
Q.P.R.	1904

Southern League: 19-0. FAC: 0-0. FLC: 0-0. Others: 0-0. Total: 19-0.

Leeds City	Jun 1905

The left wing spot was filled by Harry with capability during his time with the club, although he normally shared it with John Stewart.
Debut: 3. 9.1904 v. Plymouth Argyle (H).2-1. SLDiv. 1.

SINTON Andrew

Mid 5' 7" 10st 7lbs
b. Newcastle 19. 3.1966

Cambridge United		Apl 1983
Brentford	(£25,000)	Dec1985
Q.P.R.	(£350,000)	Mar 1989

Premier/Football League:160-22. FAC: 13-2. FLC: 14-0. Others: 3-1. Total: 190-25.

Sheffield Wednesday (£2,750,000)	Aug 1993
Tottenham Hotspur (£1,500,000)	Jan 1996
Wolverhampton Wanderers	Jul 1999

Honours: School caps. 3 B caps. 12 England caps. League Cup winners medal.

A left sided midfield player who added width to the attack and made things happen. Andy was an early ball specialist who could place an accurate cross into the heart of the penalty area. A bargain buy from Cambridge United, still aged under 18, he quickly became a great favourite at Griffin Park, and the fans were very disappointed when he moved the few miles to Loftus Road. Over four years, and 160 appearances later he moved north to Sheffield, then south again to Spurs. A radio reporter once boldly stated that, *"It could be bad news for Andy Sinton - his knee is locked-up in the dressing room."*! Another player who tried to show off his silky skills at Cambridge United, at the same time as Sinton didn't meet with quite the same success. He kept falling over on an icy pitch and was promptly rejected. His name was Peter Beardsley!
Debut: 25. 3.1989 v. Sheffield Wednesday (A).2-0. Div.1.

SKILTON Percy G.

(C.F.) Striker 5' 10" 12st 2lbs
b. Harrow, Middlesex
Harrow
Q.P.R. 1903
Southern League: 62-22. FAC: 0-0. FLC: 0-0. Others: 2-0. Total: 64-22.

Honours: Southern League championship medal.

A first class amateur, who played for the club over a number of years. Percy gave many fine performances but perhaps his best was in the 5-1 defeat of Swindon Town at Park Royal in 1909 in which he scored a hat trick.
Debut: 30. 4.1904 v. Millwall (H). 2-1. SLDiv.1.

SKINNER Henry

(L.H.) Mid 5' 9" 12st 0lbs
b. Middlesex in 1875
Windsor F.C.
Uxbridge Town 1897
Q.P.R. 1899
Southern League: 40-1. FAC: 6-0. FLC: 0-0. Others: 0-0. Total: 46-1.
Grimsby Town May 1901

Q.P.R.
Honours: F.A. Amateur Cup winners medal.

According to contemporary writers, Henry, was a man with a pleasant disposition who could cope with the swiftest opponents. Quick on his feet he could hold his own with the fastest of wingers.
Debut: 16. 9.1899 v. New Brompton (H).2-0. SLDiv.1.

SLACK Rodney Geoffrey

G
b. Farcett, Cambridgeshire 11. 4.1940
Fletton youth club
Leicester City Sep 1958
Q.P.R. Mar 1961
Football League: 1-0. FAC:0-0. FLC:0-0. Others: 0-0. Total: 1-0.
Cambridge United 1962

Honours: Southern League runners-up medal. Southern league Championship winners medal. Southern League Cup winners medal.

Rodney was the understudy to Gordon Banks at Leicester City but he only made a single appearance for Q.P.R. At Cambridge United, Rodney, made over 350 League & Cup appearances, and won the 'Player of the year award' on three separate occasions - 1963, 1965 and 1966.
Debut: 3. 5.1962 v. Halifax Town (A).1-1. Div. 3.

SLADE Steven Anthony

Striker 6' 0" 11st 2lbs
b. Hackney, London 6.10.1975
Tottenham Hotspur Jul 1994
Q.P.R. (£350,000) Jul 1996
Football League: 68-6. FAC: 3-0. FLC: 7-1. Others: 0-0. Total: 78-7.

Brentford	(Loan)	Feb 1997
Cambridge United		Aug 2000
Luton Town		Apr 2001
Hayes		Aug 2001

Honours: 4 England U21 caps.

A right sided attacker who also plays as a central striker. Steve is a hard runner who looks to create opportunities for others. Released in the summer of 2000 he joined Cambridge United on a weekly contract but was released in November 2000. Steve subsequently re-emerged at Luton Town in April 2001 where he had a trial with their reserves.
Debut: 28. 8.1996 v. Wolverhampton W.(A).1-1. Div.1.

SMITH Albert W.

(L.H.) Mid
b. Stoke-on-Trent, Staffs. 27. 8.1918 d. 9. 6.1992
Shirley Juniors
Birmingham City
Q.P.R. May 1939
Football League: 62-2. FAC: 7-0. FLC: 0-0. Others: 0-0. Total: 69-2.
Ashford
Dover
Sittingbourne

Honours: 3rd Div. (South) championship winners medal.

A tough, uncompromising and aggressive player who challenged hard for the ball. During the war he was awarded the B.E.M. at Dunkirk for bravery. Later in the war he served in the Middle East and then in Germany where he played for an army team, the winners of two cups. Unfortunately a broken leg ended his career after a tackle by Fulham's Pat Beasley at Craven Cottage in October 1948. Later, Bert qualified as an F.A. coach and for forty years was emplotyed in that role at Harrow Borough F.C. Later on he set up a fish and chip shop near Loftus Road with ex-team mate Arthur Jefferson.
Debut: 7. 9.1946 v. Walsall (A). 2-0. Div.3. (S).

SMITH Arthur R.

(O.R.) Wing
b. Stourbridge, Nr. Birmingham in 1887
Brierley Hill Aliance
Q.P.R. 1911
Southern League: 35-8. FAC: 1-0. FLC: 0-0. Others: 1-0. Total: 37-8.
Birmingham Jun 1912
Brierley Hill Alliance

Honours: Southern League championship winners medal.

A small and very fast winger who was a master of the early cross. Arthur was an amateur who was training at a London College to become a schoolteacher. Later he tutored at St. Peters college, in Saltley, Birmingham. He became a very efficient and respected administrator in non-League football as secretary of Brierley Hill Alliance, before retiring in 1934.
Debut: 2. 9.1911 v. Plymouth Argyle (A).1-0. SLDiv.1.

SMITH Edward William Alfred

(I.L.) Mid 5' 9" 12st 2lbs
b. Marylebone, London 23. 3.1929
d. London in April 1993

Chelsea	Aug 1946
Wealdstone	
Chelsea	May 1950
Bournemouth & Boscombe Athletic	Aug 1952
Watford	Jul 1953
Northampton Town	Jan 1955
Colchester United	Jun 1956
Q.P.R.	Jul 1957

Football League: 17-1. FAC: 1-1. FLC: 0-0. Others: 2-0. Total: 20-2.
Chelmsford City May 1958

Eddie was an aggressive player who was only a part-time professional, as he owned a chain of newsagents shops in London, which kept him out of full time football.
Debut: 24. 8.1957 v. Brentford (H). 1-0. Div.3. (S).

SMITH Frank A.

G
b. Colchester, Essex 30. 4.1936
Colchester Casuals
Tottenham Hotspur Feb 1954
Q.P.R. May 1962
Football League: 66-0. FAC: 3-0. FLC: 2-0. Others: 0-0. Total: 71-0.
Wimbledon (£1,500) 1965

Manager Alec Stock, considered Peter Springett was too young to play regularly for the senior squad, so he signed Smith, the Spurs reserve goalkeeper to share the position with him. Hence over his three years at Loftus Road he played 66 League games, almost exactly half the total number of matches possible.
Debut: 24. 9.1962 v. P.N.E. (H). 1-2. FLCup. Rd.1.

SMITH George Casper

(C.H.) CD 6' 1" 12st 2lbs
b. Bromley-by-Bow, London 23. 4.1915
d. Bodmin in Oct 1983

Hackney schools	
Army Football	
Bexleyheath & Welling	1937
Charlton Athletic	Aug 1938
Brentford	Nov 1945
Q.P.R.	Jun 1947

Football League: 75-1. FAC: 8-0. FLC: 0-0. Others: 0-0. Total: 83-1.

Ipswich Town	Sep 1949

Honours: 3rd Div. (South) championship medal.

George made his Football League debut in the final match before World War Two for Charlton Athletic. Much of his playing career, he was aged 25, and his chance of honours were negated by the conflict. He did win an England cap and a Cup winners medal during this period, but these are not generally acknowledged, and in addition he appeared in many representative matches. George was a tall, unflappable centre half who captained Q.P.R. to the championship in 1948. A year later he became the assistant/manager of Ipswich Town but resigned within three months. In 1950 Smith became the Chelmsford City manager, then the Redhill manager, and the boss of Eastbourne United followed. He then became the FA youth manager, the Sheffield United coach, then the Sutton United manager in 1957. In 1958 he became the manager of Crystal Palace and in 1960 the Sheffield United coach again. Finally he became the Portsmouth manager in 1960 culminating in the general manager's job at Portsmouth in 1970.
Debut: 23. 8.1947 v. Norwich City (H). 3-1. Div.3 (S).

SMITH John William

(C.F.) Striker 5' 8" 11st 0lbs
b. Derby in 1890

Burton United		
Manchester City		Nov 1909
Chesterfield Town		May 1912
Third Lanark		May 1913
Q.P.R.		Apl 1919

Southern/Football League:117-43. FAC: 5-2. FLC: 0-0. Others: 0-0. Total: 122-45.

Swansea Town	(£250)	Jun 1922
Brighton & Hove Albion	(£150)	Aug 1924

Honours: 3rd Div. (South) championship medal.

Jack played for the club during the latter part of the war under the 'guest' player system and signed for Q.P.R. directly peace had resumed . Neat and quick in all his actions he was a firm favourite of the crowd. An ever-present in their last season in the Southern League, Jack was in the side for the entire first season of the Football League. Dogged by injuries at his final club, Brighton & Hove Albion, he was released in May 1925 and left the first class game.
Debut: 30. 8.1919 v. Bristol Rovers (A). 2-0. SLDiv. 1.

SMITH Norman

(R.B.) Def 5' 8" 11st 1lb
b. Durham 20. 9.1897 d. Newcastle 18. 5.1978

Usworth Colliery		
Tottenham Hotspur		
Wedworth Colliery		
Charlton Athletic	(£250)	May 1922
Q.P.R.		May 1937

Football League: 68-2. FAC: 3-0. FLC: 0-0. Others: 0-0. Total: 71-2.

Honours: 2 3rd Div. (South) championship winners medal.

Norman was a solid old fashioned full back, who was made captain upon his arrival at the club. In July 1939 he became the Chelsea assistant/trainer and in May 1946 he was then made the head trainer for around seven years. After his retirement from football, Norman bought a newsagents in the Tottenham area of London.
Debut: 28. 8.1937 v. Brighton & H.A.(H). 2-1. Div.3 (S).

SMITH Norman

(L.H.) Mid 5' 8" 10st 9lbs
b. Newburn Newcastle-on-Tyne 15.12.1897
d. Newcastle-on-Tyne 5.1978

Mickley F.C.	
Ryton United	
Huddersfield Town	May 1923
Sheffield Wednesday	Dec 1927

Q.P.R. Aug 1930
Football League: 26-0. FAC: 1-0. FLC: 0-0. Others: 0-0. Total: 27-0.

Norman was made team captain as soon as he arrived at Loftus Road. When he left the club he took up coaching, and in 1933 joined the Swiss club Kreuzlingen. After two years he took a job at St. Gallen, Switzerland until 1938 when he joined Newcasle United as trainer; he also trained England and the English representative sides. After the war, Norman was a vital part of the Newcastle United set-up which clinched promotion and won three FACup finals. In 1961 at the age of 64 he became manager, until he stepped down in 1962.
Debut: 30. 8.1930 v. Thames Ass. (H).3-0. Div. 3 (S).

SMITH Stephen Charles

(O.L.) Wing
b. Hednesford, Staffordshire 27. 3.1896
d. Chichester in 1980

Portsmouth	1915
West Ham United	1919
Charlton Athletic	1922
Southend United	May 1925
Clapton Orient	May 1927
Q.P.R.	May 1928

Football League: 24-1. FAC: 1-0. FLC: 0-0. Others: 0-0. Total: 25-1.

Mansfield Town	Jun 1929

The son of an English international of the same name, who played for Aston Villa in the late 19th Century. Like his father, Steve was an outside left who was a good passer of the ball and accurate with his crosses.
Debut: 6. 9.1928 v. Newport County (A). 0-0. Div.3 (S).

SMITH Stephen R.

G
b.
Guildford United
Q.P.R. 1925
Football League: 2-0. FAC: 0-0. FLC: 0-0. Others: 0-0. Total: 2-0.
Guildford United
Mansfield Town

An amateur goalkeeper who was on trial with the club and played in the last two matches of the 1925/26 season - the second re-election campaign for the club.
Debut: 24. 4.1926 v. Aberdare Ath. (A). 0-1.Div. 3 (S).

SMITH Thomas S.

(O.R.) Wing 5' 9" 11st 6lbs
b. Ashton-in-Makerfield, Lancashire in 1877

Ashton Athletic	1893
Ashton Town	1895
P.N.E.	1897
Southampton	1898
Q.P.R.	1899

Southern League: 13-1. FAC: 8-3. FLC: 0-0. Others: 0-0. Total: 21-4.

P.N.E.	1900

Tom arrived at Southampton from Preston North End, his new club thinking they had signed a star player. It was discovered that there were two Tom Smiths at the Lancashire club and that Spurs had signed the true star. Nevertheless Q.P.R. were only too happy to sign him for their initial season in the Southern League.
Debut: 9. 9.1899 v.Tottenham H. (A). 0-1. SLDiv.1.

SMITH William Conway

(I.R.) Striker 5' 7" 10st 12lbs
b. Huddersfield, Yorkshire 13. 7.1926

Huddersfield Town	May 1945
Q.P.R.	Mar 1951

Football League:174-81. FAC: 6-3. FLC: 0-0. Others: 1-0. Total: 181-84.

Halifax Town	Jun 1956

Always known by his second given name, Conway, he was the son of W.H.Smith, the old England and Huddersfield Town player who formed a celebrated partnership with Clem Stephenson.

Conway was certainly a chip off the old block, although not reaching his father's standards, he nevertheless possessed a sizzling shot. Denied an earlier Football League playing career due to the war, he didn't make it at his home town team, and joined Rangers in 1951. He immediately became a near automatice first team choice, and in four out of the next six seasons that Smith was with Q.P.R. he topped the scoring list, and during this time made 181 appearances in total. In 1956, aged 30, he finished his League career with Halifax.
Debut: 17. 3.1951 v. Leeds United (A). 2-2. Div.2.

SNELGROVE George W.

(I.R.) Mid 5' 8" 11st 0lbs
b. in 1886
Chatham

New Brompton	1905
Sittingbourne	1906
Q.P.R.	1907

Southern League: 11-1. FAC: 0-0. FLC: 0-0. Others: 0-0. Total: 11-1.

George was a reserve who appeared on three occasions during the 1908 championship year, taking the place of Cannon. During the following season, he was given an extended stay in the first team but to no avail.
Debut: 18. 4.1908 v. Northampton T. (H). 2-3. SLDiv. 1.

SOMMER Juergen Peterson

G 6' 4" 15st 12lbs
b. Manhatton, New York, U.S.A. 27. 2.1969

Luton Town		Aug 1991
Dunstable	(Loan)	1991
Brighton & Hove Albion	(Loan)	Nov 1991
Torquay United	(Loan)	Oct 1992
Kettering Town	(Loan)	Feb 1993
Wycombe Wanderers	(Loan)	Mar 1993
Luton Town		1993
Q.P.R.	(£600,000)	Aug 1995

Premier/Football League: 66-0. FAC: 3-0. FLC: 2-0. Others: 0-0. Total: 71-0.

Columbus Crew, U.S.A.	(£175,000)	1998

Honours: 5 USA caps.

The son of a former SV Hamburg player who emigrated to America. Juergen showed signs of brilliance at Q.P.R. and he was virtually impregnable in the air. Although this huge goalkeeper was a good shot-stopper he came under some pressure when Q.P.R. were relegated, nonetheless holding on to his first team place, but - perhaps suprisingly - was passed over for the U.S. Olympic squad in 1996.
Debut: 16. 9.1995 v. Leeds United (A). 3-1. PL.

SPACKMAN Nigel James

Mid 6' 1" 12st 4lbs
b. Romsey, Hampshire 2.12.1960
Andover

AFC Bournemouth		May 1980
Chelsea	(£40,000)	Jun 1983
Liverpool	(£400,000)	Feb 1987
Q.P.R.	(£500,000)	Feb 1989

Football League: 29-1. FAC: 0-0. FLC: 2-1. Others: 2-0. Total: 33-2.

Glasgow Rangers	(£500,000)	Nov 1989
Chelsea	(£485,000)	Sep 1992
Sheffield United		Jul 1996

Honours: 2nd Div. championship winners medal. League Cup winners medal. 3 Scottish Premier League championship medals. Scottish League cup winners medal. Scottish Cup winners medal.

Nigel was a tall, hefty character with a tremendous shot. He had a good sense of humour which was loved by the fans and his colleagues alike. In 2001 he took over the manager's job at Barnsley but he was relieved of it shortly into the season.
Debut: 4. 2.1989 v. Millwall (H). 1-2. Div. 1.

SPENCE William Joseph

(C.H.) CD
b. Hartlepool 10. 1.1926

Portsmouth	Mar 1947
Q.P.R.	Dec 1951

Football League: 56-0. FAC: 4-0. FLC: 0-0. Others: 0-0. Total: 60-0.

Bill was made team captain on his arrival at Loftus Road and the spectators saw a classy performance, although they were shocked to see such a small central defender. However, his ball control was pure class. Injury was the cause of his early retirement in July 1955.
Debut: 22.12.1951 v. Coventry City (H).1-4. Div.2.

SPENCER John

Striker 5' 6" 11st 7lbs
b. Glasgow, Scotland 11. 9.1970

Glasgow Rangers		Sep 1986
Morton	(Loan)	Mar 1989
Chelsea	(£450,000)	Aug 1992

Q.P.R. (£2,500,000) Nov 1996
Football League: 48-22. FAC: 6-2. FLC: 2-0. Others: 0-0. Total: 56-24.
Everton (£1,500,000) Mar 1998
Motherwell 1998

Honours: School & youth caps. 3 U21 caps. 14 full Scottish caps.

John was confined for long spells to the Glasgow Rangers reserve side but managed to score 18 goals in 49 appearances, before his initial big money move which took him to Chelsea. He became Rangers' second highest purchase when he moved to Loftus Road in 1996. A small, lively, bustling striker with a good finish, who had strength and a shrewd footballing brain which served him well. John was skilful and quick thinking, who turned defenders to make space for shooting. He also had the ability to retain the ball in tight situations.
Debut: 23.11.1997 v. Reading (A). 1-2. Div. 1.

SPOTTISWOODE Joseph

(O.L.) Wing 5' 9" 12st 0lbs
b. Carlisle, Cumberland in 1894
Carlisle United
Manchester City
Bury
Chelsea 1919
Swansea Town (£500) Jan 1920
Q.P.R. Jun 1925
Football League: 22-2. FAC: 0-0. FLC: 0-0. Others: 0-0. Total: 22-2.

Honours: 3rd Div. (South) championship winners medal.

Joe was a winger of considerable ability but he had slowed down somewhat by the time he reached Q.P.R. He settled into the side which finished the season bottom of the table for the second time in three years.
Debut: 25. 8.1925 v. Gillingham (A). 0-3.Div. 3 (S).

SPRATLEY Alan S.

G 5' 9" 11st 0lbs
b. Maidenhead, Surrey 5. 6.1949
Q.P.R. May 1967
Football League: 29-0. FAC: 2-0. FLC: 1-0. Others: 0-0. Total: 32-0.
Swindon Town Jul 1973

The arrival of Phil Parks ended the period in which Alan was given to prove himself. Transferred to Swindon Town in 1973, his contract was terminated at the end of the following season, having played just seven matches for the Wiltshire club.
Debut: 4. 1.1969 v. Aston Villa (A).1-2.FAC.3rd Rnd.

SPRINGETT Peter J.

G 5' 10" 11st 6lbs
b. Fulham, London 8. 5.1946 d. Sheffield 28. 8.1997
Q.P.R. May 1963
Football League:137-0. FAC: 10-0. FLC: 13-0. Others: 0-0. Total: 160-0.
Sheffield Wednesday (£40,000) May 1967
Barnsley Jul 1975
Scarborough 1980

Honours: 6 England youth caps. 6 U23 caps. 3rd Div. championship winners medal. League Cup winners medal. 4th Div. promotion medal.

Peter arrived aged just seventeen, and the highlight of his career at Loftus Road was being in the Q.P.R. side that came from behind to beat Jimmy Hagan's West Bromwich Albion in Wembley's first ever League Cup Final. He went on to play 160 first team matches over four years. An exceptionally brilliant custodian who was quick to get down to a shot, confident in collecting the ball from a centre, and was never overshadowed by his brother's reputation. After retiring from the game he became a policeman, and died aged just 51 from a long term illness.
Debut: 18. 5.1963 v. Peterborough Utd. (H).0-0. Div. 3.

SPRINGETT Ronald Deryk G.

G 5' 10" 12st 6lbs
b. Fulham, London 22. 7.1935

Victoria United

Q.P.R.		Feb 1953

Football League: 88-0. FAC: 1-0. FLC: 3-0. Others: 3-0. Total: 97-0.

Sheffield Wednesday	(£9,000)	Mar 1958
Q.P.R.	(£16,000)	Jun 1967

Football League: 45-0. FAC: 1-0. FLC: 3-0. Others: 0-0. Total: 49-0.

Ashford Town

Honours: 33 England caps. 9 Football League caps. 4 caps v. Young England. 2nd Div. championship winners medal. 1st Div. runners-up medal. FACup runners-up medal. 2nd Div. runners-up medal.

Ron kept goal with a mixture of brilliance, dependability and cat-like agility and with phenomenal anticipation. His first term at Loftus Road lasted five years, when he moved, like his older brother later, to Sheffield Wednesday. Nine years on, a unique deal in 1967 took his brother, Peter, to Sheffield Wednesday and Ron back to Loftus Road for a fee of £16,000. Ron had the distinction of being Sheffield Wednesday's most capped England player, having gained 33 between 1959 and 1966. In 1970 Ron owned a sports shop in Shepherds Bush.

Debut: 5.11.1955 v. Norwich City (H). 2-3. Div.3 (S).

STAINROD Simon Allan

Striker 6' 1" 11st 11lbs

b. Sheffield, Yorkshire 1. 2.1959

Sheffield schools

Sheffield United		Jul 1976
Oldham Athletic	(£60,000)	Mar 1979
Q.P.R.	(£275,000)	Nov 1980

Football League: 145-48. FAC: 12-5. FLC: 17-5. Others: 3-3. Total: 177-61

Sheffield Wednesday	(£250,000)	Feb 1985
Aston Villa	(£250,000)	Sep 1985
Stoke City	(£90,000)	Dec 1987
Strasbourg, France	(Loan)	1989
Rouen, France	(£100,000)	1989
Falkirk		1990
Dundee		
Ayr United		

Honours: 3 England youth caps. 2nd Div. championship winners medal. FACup runners-up medal.

Simon was a popular character at Q.P.R. enriching the game with a touch of class that didn't show at any of his other clubs, having a subtle style of play and scoring many memorable goals, Simon's only negative attribute was a fiery temper. He fitted in well at Q.P.R., with his game developing under the coaching of Terry Venables. His stay at Loftus Road lasted just over five years during which time he made 145 Football League appearances, whereupon his career continued in England, France and Scotland. At Dundee he became the player/manager and then manager, in 1992, followed by the same at Ayr United, which lasted just two months before he was sacked. Later he bcame a partner in a football advertising at football grounds company.

Debut: 22.11.1980 v. P.N.E. (A). 2-3. Div. 2.

STANDLEY Thomas L.

(C.F.) Striker

b. Poplar, London 23.12.1932

Basildon

Q.P.R.	May 1957

Football League: 15-2. FAC: 0-0. FLC: 0-0. Others: 0-0. Total: 15-2.

Bournemouth & Boscombe Athletic	Nov 1958

Tom was the fifth of eight centre forwards to be tried during the 1957/58 season. At Bournemouth he was turned into a very reliable half back and stayed until he retired in 1965, notching up over 160 first team appearances.

Debut: 21.12.1957 v. Brentford (A).1-1.Div. 3 (S).

STEER William Henry Owen

(C.F.) Striker 5' 8" 11st 6lbs

b. Kingston-upon-Thames in 1888

Old Kingstonians

Kingston Town

Q.P.R.	1909

Southern League: 68-31. FAC: 8-6. FLC: 0-0. Others: 0-0. Total: 74-37.

Chelsea	1911

Newry County, Ireland

Honours: 6 Amateur caps for England. London League v. Birmingham League. 2 caps for Southern League v. Football League.

Bill was an amateur at Q.P.R. but turned professional at Chelsea. He played throughout the 1st World War and retired in 1918.

Debut: 1.10.1909 v. Watford (H).4-3. SLDiv. 1.

STEIN Mark Earl Sean

Striker 5' 6" 11st 10lbs

b. Cape Town, South Africa 29. 1.1966

Luton Town		Jan 1984
Aldershot	(Loan)	Jan 1986
Q.P.R.	(£300,000)	Aug 1988

Football League: 33-4. FAC: 3-1. FLC: 4-2. Others: 4-0. Total: 44-7.

Oxford United		Sep 1989
Stoke City	(£1,00,000)	Aug 1991
Chelsea	(£1,400,000)	Oct 1993
Stoke City	(Loan)	Nov 1996
Ipswich Town	(Loan)	Aug 1997
AFC Bournemouth		Mar 1998
Luton Town		Jul 2000
Dagenham & Redbridge		Aug 2001

Honours: England youth cap. League Cup winners medal. Full members cup runners-up medal. Auto Trophy winners medal. 2nd Div. championship winners medal.

One of three footballing brothers, he is a nimble opportunist and quick off the mark. Mark made several big transfer moves, and at 37 years of age is still playing in senior non-League football.
Debut: 27. 8.1988 v. Manchester United (A).0-0. Div.1.

STEINER Robert Herman

Striker 6' 2" 13st 5lbs
b. Finsprong, Sweden 20. 6.1973
Norrkoping, Sweden

Bradford City	(Loan)	Oct 1996
Bradford City	(£500,000)	Jul 1997
Q.P.R.	(Loan)	Nov 1998

Football League: 8-1. FAC: 0-0. FLC: 0-0. Others: 0-0. Total: 8-1.

Q.P.R.	(Loan)	Mar 1999

Football League: 4-2. FAC: 0-0. FLC: 0-0. Others: 0-0. Total: 4-2.

Walsall	(Loan)	Mar 1999
Q.P.R.	(£215,000)	Jul 1999

Football League: 24-6. FAC: 2-0. FLC: 1-0. Others: 0-0. Total: 27-6.

Honours: 4 Swedish International caps.

Steiner was at Q.P.R. on three separate occasions, twice as a loan player from Bradford City, and the last time a permanent £215,000 deal from the same club. But injuries blighted his career, and whilst with Q.P.R. Rob suffered a serious back injury which required surgery. Unfortunately he was unable to recover from it and had to prematurely retire.
Debut: 7.11.1998 v. Bolton Wanderers (H).2-0. Div.1.

STEJSKAL Jan

G 6' 3" 12st 0lbs
b. Czechoslovakia 15. 1.1962
Sparta Prague

Q.P.R.	(£625,000)	Oct 1990

Premier/Football League:108-0. FAC: 3-0. FLC: 11-0. Others: 1-0. Total: 123-0.

Sparta Prague	1994

Honours: 4 Czech International caps. 1 U21 cap.

Jan was a very tall goalkeeper who was quickly confirmed as a favourite of the crowd at Loftus Road. Brought in to replace David Seaman, he generally shared the number one spot with Welsh International Tony Roberts, although Jan was a Czech International himself. During his four seasons at Loftus Road, he appeared in 108 League matches (missing only one in the 1991/92 season). In 1994 he returned to his former club, Sparta Prague, and later became the coach of rivals Slavia.
Debut: 20.10.1990 v. Leeds United (A). 3-2. Div.1.

STEPHENSON Herbert L.

(I.R.) Mid 5' 11" 11st 0lbs
b. London

Q.P.R.	1930

Football League: 2-0. FAC: 0-0. FLC: 0-0. Others: 0-0. Total: 2-0.

Both of the matches Herbert played in were against the same opposition, Southend United, and both matches ended in 2-0 defeats for the London club. Bert never turned out again for the Rangers, and detailed research has failed to reveal any further information.
Debut: 15.11.1930 v. Southend United (A).0-2. Div.3(S).

STEPHENSON James

(O.R.) Wing 5' 6" 11st 2lbs
b. New Delaval in Feb 1895
d. Newcastle-upon-Tyne Feb 1960
New Delaval Villa

Aston Villa	1914
Sunderland	1921
Watford	1922
Q.P.R.	1927

Football League: 18-0. FAC: 0-0. FLC: 0-0. Others: 0-0. Total: 18-0.

Norwich City	
Boston	1928
New Delaval Villa	1929
Ashington	1931
New Delaval Villa	

A class act on the right wing, Jimmy was one of a famous footballing family which included the great Clem, he was also the uncle of the cricketer/ footballer, Bob Stephenson. Jimmy, who was the licencee of a public house in Watford had to be persuaded to sign for Q.P.R. at the time.
Debut: 27. 8.1927 v. Newport County (H).4-2. Div.3(S).

STEVENS Ronald Frederick

(O.L.) Wing
b. Luton, Bedfordshire 26.11.1914
Hitchen Town
Luton Town 1936
Q.P.R. 1938
Football League: 0-0. FAC: 0-0. FLC: 0-0. Others: 1-0.
Total: 1-0.

The only match that Ron played, in Q.P.R. colours, was a 3rd Division (South) Cup match which resulted in a draw. The replay was never played owing to the outbreak of War.
Debut: 4. 5.1939 v. Port Vale (H).0-0.Div.3 (S). Cup.

STEWART George

(I.R.) Mid
b. Chirnside, Durham 16.10.1920
Hamilton Academicals
Brentford Aug 1946
Q.P.R. Mar 1948
Football League: 38-5. FAC: 2-0. FLC: 0-0. Others: 0-0.
Total: 40-5.
Shrewsbury Town Jan 1953

A quality player who was quick witted and clever on the ball. George was a real asset to the team in their final run-in to the championship of 1948. He was often kept out of the side by the brilliance of Freddy Ramscar.
Debut: 13. 3.1948 v. Ipswich Town (H).2-0. Div.3 (S).

STEWART Ian Edwin

(O.L.) Wing 5' 6" 11st 9lbs
b. Belfast, N.Ireland 10. 9.1961
Q.P.R. May 1980
Football League: 67-2. FAC: 3-0. FLC: 14-2. Others: 3-0.
Total: 87-4.

Millwall	(Loan)	1983
Newcastle United	(£150,000)	Aug 1985
Portsmouth		Dec 1987
Brentford	(Loan)	1988
Leicester City	(Trial)	Dec 1988
Aldershot		Jan 1989
Colchester United		1992
Harrow Borough		Nov 1992

Honours: N.Ireland schools & youth caps. 31 full caps for N.Ireland. 2nd Div. championship winners medal.

Early impressions at Loftus Road of Ian's talent were most favourable. He had a clever but direct style of play with complete control of the ball. However, he was labelled with the inconsistent tag, which stayed with him throughout his career.
Debut: 12.12.1981 v. Barnsley (H). 1-0. Div.2.

STEWART John

(O.L.) Wing
b.
Hibernian
Q.P.R. 1901
Southern League: 23-3. FAC: 3-1. FLC: 0-0. Others: 0-0.
Total: 26-4.
Hibernian 1902
Q.P.R. 1904
Southern League: 13-2. FAC: 0-0. FLC: 0-0. Others: 0-0.
Total: 13-2.

Scoring on his debut for the club, this fast and tricky winger, was the most popular of the players. John could play on either wing but he had to return home to Scotland for domestic reasons. After 1905 all trace of him disappears.
Debut: 5.10.1901 v. Swindon Town (H).4-0.SLDiv. 1.

STOCK Alexander William

(C.F.) Striker 5' 9" 10st 10lbs
b. Peasedown, Somerset 30. 3.1917 d. 2001
Redhill
Tottenham Hotspur
Charlton Athletic 1936
Q.P.R. 1938
Football League: 16-3. FAC: 0-0. FLC: 0-0. Others: 1-2.
Total: 17-5.
Yeovil Town

As happened to so many players the war disrupted his career. Alec was drafted into the army in 1939 and became a Major in the Royal Armoured Corps and saw plenty of action, but played no serious football until 1947. On demobilisation he became the player/manager of Yeovil Town and masterminded that famous defeat of 1st Division Sunderland in the FACup of 1949. This catapulted him into the limelight and in August that year, Alec was appointed manager of Leyton Orient and he led them to the championship of the 3rd Division (South) in 1956. Stock turned down an offer from Middlesbrough and joined Arsenal, staying there for just 53 days before returning to Orient. In August 1957 Roma of Italy offered him a job, and he returned to England in 1958. A year later he moved to Q.P.R. and so began one of the most exciting periods in the club's history. Alec later managed Luton Town, Fulham, became a Q.P.R. director, and then the caretaker/manager for a spell in 1978. He finally managed AFC Bournemouth in 1979 before becoming a director from 1981 to 1986.
Debut: 26. 2.1938 v. Reading (H).3-0. Div. 3 (S).

STRUGNELL H. H.

(I.F.) Mid
b.
Aston Villa

Q.P.R.	1913

Southern League: 11-0. FAC: 0-0. FLC: 0-0. Others: 0-0. Total: 11-0.

Hartlepool United	1914

Nothing is known about Strugnell except that he was a reserve inside forward who stood in for relevant players when they were injured.
Debut: 1. 9.1913 v. Swindon Town (A). 0-3. SLDiv.1

SUGDEN Sidney H.

(I.R.) Mid 5' 9" 10st 2lbs
b. Battersea, London in 1880

Ilford	1898
West Ham United	1902
Nottingham Forest	1903
Q.P.R.	Jan 1905

Southern League: 65-23. FAC: 2-0. FLC: 0-0. Others: 0-0. Total: 67-23.

Brentford	1908
Southend United	1909

'*A wonderfully dashing player with a splendid turn of speed and a deadly shot. However, he is not a good team man*'; Sidney Sugden was so described by a contemporary reporter. Sid played just nine League matches during the first championship season of 1908 which was also his last.
Debut: 2. 9.1905 v. New Brompton (H).4-0. SLDiv.1.

SUTCH W. H.

(I.L.) Mid
b.

Q.P.R.	1919

Southern League: 1-2. FAC: 0-0. FLC: 0-0. Others: 0-0. Total: 1-2.

A reserve who came into the side in place of the injured John Gregory, the captain, and scored two goals in a 7-1 victory against Bristol Rovers.
Debut: 3. 1.1920 v. Bristol Rovers (H).7-1.SLDiv.1.

SWAN John (formerly Swann)

(I.L.) Mid 5' 10" 11st 7lbs
b. Easington, Durham 19. 7.1892 d. Hendon in Jan. 1990
Seaham Harbour

Huddersfield Town		May 1919
Leeds United		Nov 1921
Watford	(£1,000)	Sep 1925
Q.P.R.	(£300)	Feb 1927

Football League: 28-5. FAC: 0-0. FLC: 0-0. Others: 0-0. Total: 28-5.

Thames Athletic	Jul 1928
Lovalls Athletic	Oct 1929

Honours: FACup runners-up medal. 2nd Div. championship medal.

John possessed a very hard left footed shot and boasted that his right foot was just to stand on, his heading was not so bad either. However, there is a downturn to the story. Suspended by Leeds United for going absent without leave, John was transferred to Watford and was again suspended, this time *sine die*, along with another player, who was dismissed at the same time. Nothing was ever revealed as to the nature of his misdeed but in those days most indiscretions were alcohol related. In 1986 John was living in Hendon and it was believed at the time that there was no one still alive that had played in an earlier FACup Final.
Debut: 12. 2.1927 v. Bristol City (A). 0-1.Div. 3 (S).

SWANN Herbert A.

(I.R.) Mid 5' 7" 11st 8lbs
b. Lytham, Lancashire 28. 3.1882

Lytham Institute	1898
Bury	1903
Plymouth Argyle	1906
Crystal Palace	1907
Q.P.R.	1909

Southern League: 4-1. FAC: 0-0. FLC: 0-0. Others: 0-0. Total: 4-1.

Not much is known about this player, except that he once scored all five goals for Plymouth Argyle in a match v. Millwall, in the Western League in 1906.
Debut: 9.10.1909 v. Millwall (H). 1-2. SLDiv. 1.

SWEETMAN Sidney C.
(R.B.) Def 6' 0" 12st 12lbs
b. London
Hampstead Town
Q.P.R. 1925
Football League:100-0. FAC: 2-0. FLC: 0-0. Others: 0-0.
Total: 102-0.
Millwall 1929

Honours: Willesden schools representative.

A Q.P.R. discovery who turned professional in 1925. Sid was a stylish full back who could play on either flank, he was powerfully built and attracted much attention among the big clubs. Eventually Sid was transferred to Millwall and stayed there until the mid-thirties. He was also an expert billiards and table-tennis player.
Debut: 7. 2.1925 v. Merthyr Town (A).3-2.Div. 3 (S).

SWINFEN Reginald
(R.B.) Def
b. Battersea, London 4. 5.1915 d. October 1996
Civil Service 1935
Q.P.R. 1936
Football League: 26-5. FAC: 3-0. FLC: 0-0. Others: 4-0.
Total: 33-5.
Yeovil Town 1947
Tonbridge
Crawley Town

A stocky, bustling player, who never really found his true position. Reg, unfortunately owing to the 2nd World War, had his most promising career interrupted.
Debut: 19. 9.1936 v. Clapton Orient (H).2-1. Div. 3 (S).

SYMES Ernest Herbert Charles
(L.B.) Def 5' 9" 11st 10lbs
b. Acton, London 22. 8.1892 d. 1977
Fulham Mar 1917
Aberdare Athletic May 1923
Q.P.R. 1924
Football League: 26-0. FAC: 4-0. FLC: 0-0. Others: 0-0.
Total: 30-0.

Ernie was one of the players dismissed after the club's second re-election year in three seasons.
Debut: 8.11.1924 v. Gillingham (H).1-1. Div. 3 (S).

TAGG Anthony
CD 6'1" 11st 0lbs
b. Epsom, Surrey 10. 4.1957
Q.P.R. Mar 1975
Football League: 4-0. FAC: 0-0. FLC: 0-0. Others: 0-0.
Total: 4-0.
Millwall Jul 1977
Wimbledon Jul 1982

Honours: 4th Div. championship medal winner.

Tony Tagg played in the, arguably, best Q.P.R. side ever when they were beaten into second place on the last day of the season, by Liverpool, in the 1975/76 season. His debut match was the 5-1 defeat of Derby County at the Baseball Ground. Tony went on to play over a hundred matches for Millwall.
Debut: 23. 8.1975 v. Derby County (A). 5-1. Div. 1.

TAYLOR
(H.B.) Mid
b.
Q.P.R. 1905
Southern League: 2-0. FAC: 0-0. FLC: 0-0. Others: 0-0.
Total: 2-0.

Lost in the mists of time is any record of this man. He played right half in place of Yenson when Millwall defeated Q.P.R 7-0. He then played centre half, in place of McLean in the 2-0 defeat by Spurs.
Debut: 26. 1.1907 v. Millwall (A). 0-7. SLDiv. 1.

TAYLOR Brian
(F.B.) Def
b. Hammersmith, London 2. 7.1944
Q.P.R. 1962
Football League: 50-0. FAC: 0-0. FLC. 2-0. Others: 0-0.
Total: 52-0.
Romford 1965

Brian stepped into Roy Bentley's position once the latter had retired. He was a very good defender who stood in for all the first class players such as Keen, Angell and the Brady brothers. Even so he managed to accrue 50 League matches at Q.P.R., before dropping down to the non-League scene, after three years.
Debut: 23. 3.1963 v. Watford (A). 5-2. Div. 3.

TAYLOR Gareth Keith

Striker 6' 2" 13st 8lbs
b. Weston Super Mare, Somerset 25. 2.1973
Broadoak school
Milton Nomads
Avon schools
Stoke City

Southampton		1988
Weston Super Mare		1990
Bristol Rovers		Jul 1991
Gloucester City	(Loan)	1992
Weymouth	(Loan)	1992
Crystal Palace	(£750,000)	Sep 1995
Sheffield United		Mar 1996
Manchester City	(£400.000)	Nov 1998
Port Vale	(Loan)	Jan 2000
Q.P.R.	(Loan)	Mar 2000

Football League: 6-1. FAC: 0-0. FLC: 0-0. Others: 0-0. Total: 6-1.

Burnley	Feb 2001

Honours: 9 Welsh caps. 7 U21 caps.

His style is limited but usually effective and he gets his fair share of yellow cards. Gareth is very much in the mould of the old fashioned centre forward, his goals coming mainly from his head.
Debut: 18. 3.2000 v. Walsall (A). 3-2. Div. 1.

TAYLOR Geoffrey Arthur

(O.L.) Wing 5' 8" 10st 0lbs
b. Henstead, Suffolk 22. 1.1923
City of Norwich school
Bungay Grammar school
CNSOBU
R.A.F.

Norwich City	Aug 1946
Reading	Mar 1947
Lincoln City	Aug 1947
Brighton & Hove Albion	Aug 1948
Stade Rennais, France	Dec 1949
Bristol Rovers	Sep 1951
S.C.Bruhl, Switzerland	May 1952
Q.P.R.	Nov 1953

Football League: 2-0. FAC: 0-0. FLC: 0-0. Others: 0-0. Total: 2-0.

VFR 07 Kirn, Germany	1955
F.C.Soberheim, Germany	1958

In an astonishing career, Geoff appeared for six different Football League clubs, in a 11 year period, but made a total of only ten outings, which must be a record of sorts. He spoke both fluent French and German and also carved out a career in both countries, first as a player/coach, then as a coach with German clubs F.C.Idar Oberstein (from 1964), VFL Weierback (1967), VSV Schwarzerden (1975) and SV Bundenbach (1984).
Geoff finally retired at the age of 61 years.
Debut: 25.12.1953 v. Colchester Utd. (A). 0-5. Div.3 (S).

TAYLOR James Guy

(C.H.) CD
b. Cowley, Middlesex 5.11.1917
Hillingdon

Fulham	Mar 1938
Q.P.R.	Apl 1953

Football League: 41-0. FAC: 3-0. FLC: 0-0. Others: 0-0. Total: 44-0.

Tunbridge Wells Rangers	1954

Honours: 2nd Div. championship winners medal. Football League cap. 2 England caps. (At the age of 34).

Jim originally signed for Fulham as an inside forward just before the 2nd World War, in which he served in the Navy, and this delayed his introduction to the first class game. He was 28 years old when he made his debut in August 1946, as a wing half. Eventually he replaced the regular centre half and became one of the best defenders in the country. Jim was well liked at Loftus Road and was made captain as soon as he arrived at the club. He was likened to Neil Franklin by reason of his strong, quick tackles and his good use of the ball, although he was regarded as rather weak in the air. Jim later became manager of Yiewsley, in 1958 and then the same at Uxbridge, in 1959.
Debut: 19. 8.1953 v. Brighton & H.A. (H).1-2. Div.3 (S).

TEAL Richard G.

G 6' 1" 13st 7lbs
b. Millam, Sussex 27. 2.1952
Walton & Hersham
Slough Town

Q.P.R.	Jul 1973

Football League: 1-0. FAC: 0-0. FLC: 1-0. Others: 0-0. Total: 2-0.

Fulham	Aug 1976
Wimbledon	Aug 1977

Slough Town
Staines Town
Carshalton Athletic
Walton & Hersham

Honours: Amateur Cup final winners medal.

Dick was a consistent and a commanding goalkeeper who covered for Phil Parkes. He came to the notice of Q.P.R. in the Amateur Cup final of 1973. Now he runs a building firm and plays veteran football, although outfield rather than in goal.
Debut: 7. 9.1974 v. Birmingham City (H).0-1. Div.1.

TEMBY William
(I.R.) Mid
b. Dover, Kent 16. 9.1934
Rhyl
Q.P.R. Feb 1955
Football League: 7-3. FAC: 0-0. FLC: 0-0. Others: 0-0.
Total: 7-3.
Dover

Bill's first two matches for the club were played at right half. However, the following season he played at inside right and scored three goals in his last three matches. He was then enticed into Kent League Football.
Debut: 5.11.1955 v. Norwich City (H).2-3. Div.3 (S)

TENNANT William
(C.H.) CD 5' 10" 12st 7lbs
b. Coatbridge, Scotland in 1874
Caledonian F.C.
Athurelie
Q.P.R. 1899
Southern League: 12-5. FAC: 3-0. FLC: 0-0. Others: 0-0.
Total: 15-5.
Third Lanark 1900

Honours: A Scottish junior cap.

Bill was a clever player who came to the club with a great reputation. Although his position was centre half he played at centre forward on four occasions and scored five goals.
Debut: 9. 9.1899 v. Tottenham H. (A). 0-1.SLDiv. 1.

THOMAS David
(O.R.) Wing 5' 8" 10st 10lbs
b. Kirkby-in-Ashfield, Nottinghamshire 5.10.1950
Burnley Oct 1967
Q.P.R. (£165,000) Oct 1972
Football League:182-28. FAC: 14-2. FLC: 17-3. Others: 7-1.
Total: 220-34.
Everton (£200,000) Aug 1977
Wolverhampton Wanderers Oct 1979
Vancouver Whitecaps, Canada 1981
Middlesbrough Mar 1982
Portsmouth Jul 1982

Honours: Schoolboy International. 5 England youth caps. 11 U23 caps. 8 full caps. 2nd Div. runners-up medal. 1st Div. runner-up medal.

The capture of David Thomas was probably Gordon Jago's best signing for Q.P.R. He was part of the team that ended the season as runners-up in the First Division.

Dave was a two-footed winger who could centre the ball with immaculate precision from any angle. Fast and direct he could destroy his opponent with a sleight of foot or a swerve of his body. He left Q.P.R. in 1977, and played for several clubs during the ensuing five years. On retiring as a player, he took up coaching, first at Bognor Regis Town then at Brentford, and later became a landscape gardener, living in Prinsted, Sussex.
Debut: 21.10.1972 v. Sunderland (H). 3-2. Div. 2.

THOMAS Jerome William
W 5' 10" 11st. 10lbs.
b. Wembley 23. 3.1983
Arsenal Jul 2001
Q.P.R. (loan) Mar 2002
Football League: 4-1: FAC: 0-0. FLC: 0-0. Others: 0-0.
Arsenal 2002
Q.P.R. (loan) Aug 2002
Football League: 6-2. FAC: 0-0. FLC: 0-0. Others: 0-0.
Arsenal 2003

Despite twice coming on loan to Q.P.R., Jerome only played a handful of games on each occasion, although he was recognised as an exciting prospect.
Debut: 30.3.2002 v. Tranmere Rovers (A) 3-2 Div.2

THOMPSON A.
(O.R.) Wing
b.
Q.P.R. 1905
Southern League: 23-7. FAC: 1-0. FLC: 0-0. Others: 0-0.
Total: 24-7.

Thompson was a reserve who scored a hat-trick when he replaced Neil Murphy. But when Pentland moved to Q.P.R. Thompson was released.
Debut: 28.10.1905 v. Plymouth Argyle (H).2-0. SLDiv.1.

THOMPSON Charles

(R.B.) Def
b. Bighton Banks, Hampshire

Birtley	
Newcastle United	1920
Q.P.R.	1921

Football League: 1-0. FAC: 0-0. FLC: 0-0. Others: 0-0. Total: 1-0.

Charlie made his one and only appearance for Q.P.R. in a match v. Brentford, replacing Ben Marsden in defence.
Debut: 29.10.1921 v. Brentford (H).1-1. Div. 3. (S).

THOMPSON Garry Linsey

Striker 6' 2" 13st 3lbs
b. Birmingham 7.10.1959

Coventry City		Jun 1977
W.B.A.	(£225,000)	Feb 1983
Sheffield Wednesday	(£450,000)	Aug 1985
Aston Villa	(£450,000)	June 1986
Watford	(£325,000)	Dec 1988
Crystal Palace	(£200,000)	Mar 1990
Q.P.R.	(£125,000)	Aug 1991

Premier/Football League: 19-1. FAC: 0-0. FLC: 5-3. Others: 1-0. Total: 25-4.

Cardiff City	Aug 1993
Northampton Town	Feb 1995

Honours: 6 England caps at U21 level. League Cup runners-up medal.

Garry was a tall, well built target man who was extremely strong in the air. He was released from Northampton Town in the summer of 1998.
Debut: 21. 8.1991 v. Norwich City (H).0-2. Div.1.

THOMPSON J.

(R.H.) Mid
b. Willesden

Bristol City	1920
Yeovil & Petters	1922
Q.P.R.	1924

Football League: 22-0. FAC: 4-0. FLC: 0-0. Others: 0-0. Total: 26-0.

An ex-right winger and now a right half and called upon to play in many positions, including centre half and inside right.

This was the second time in three years that the club had finished bottom of the table, and Thompson was released at the end of the season.
Debut: 27.12.1924 v. Newport County (H).4-3. Div.3 (S).

THOMPSON Oliver

(L.H.) Mid 5' 8" 11st 2lbs
b. Gateshead 11. 5.1900 d.Chesterfield 24. 7.1975

Spen Black & White	
Merthyr Town	Mar 1922
Spennymore United	
Chesterfield	May 1922
Q.P.R.	May 1928

Football League: 18-0. FAC: 0-0. FLC: 0-0. Others: 0-0. Total: 18-0.

York City	Jun 1929
Halifax Town	Jun 1932
Chesterfield	1933

Oliver was a constructive member of the team whose expertise at the time was invaluable. At Chesterfield, along with Shirley Abbott, he became the mainstay of the club. He coached the team and during the war took over as the first team trainer. He held the post until 1966 whereupon he took a slightly less active role as the club's masseur.
Debut: 1. 9.1928 v. Gillingham (H).1-0. Div.3 (S).

THOMPSON William T.

(O.R.) Wing 5' 7" 11st 0lbs
b. Morpeth in Aug. 1886 d. Byker 28.12.1933

Morpeth & Ashington schools	
Byker boys	
Grangetown	
Middlesbrough	1905
Morpeth Harriers	1906
W.B.A.	Mar 1908
Sunderland	May 1911
Plymouth Argyle	1912
Q.P.R.	1912

Southern League:119-6. FAC: 11-0. FLC: 0-0. Others: 0-0. Total: 130-6.

Carlisle United	
Newport County	1920
Hartlepool United	1921
Jarrow	1922

Honours: Southern League v. Football League.

Billy was known as 'Rubber' because of his elastic-type stature and spring-heeled displays down the right wing. He was brilliant at times but he could be very frustrating and temperamental too by all accounts. A very speedy and clever winger.
Debut: 5. 9.1912 v. Plymouth Argyle (H).2-1 .SLDiv.1

THOMSON Andrew

Striker 5' 10" 10st 13lbs
b. Motherwell, Scotland 1. 4.1971
Jerviston boys club

Queen of the South		Jul 1989
Southend United	(£250,000)	Jul 1994
Oxford United		Jul 1998
Gillingham	(£25,000)	Aug 1999
Q.P.R.		Mar 2001

Football League: 90-29. FAC: 4-2. FLC: 2-2. Others: 1-0.
Total: 97-33.

Andy became the top goalscorer in the 2001/02 season although it was clear that he suffered from a back injury and was not fully fit when playing. He played in around half the matches in the 2002/03 season but lost his goalscoring form, netting just two in League matches, and he was not retained. (Signed for Partick Thistle July 2003)
Debut: 24. 3.1991 v. Burnley (A). 1-2. Div.1.

THORNTON H. V.

(I.L.) Mid
b.
Q.P.R. 1911
Southern League: 35-10. FAC: 1-0. FLC: 0-0. Others: 1-0.
Total: 37-10.

Honours. Southern League championship winner medal.

Thornton joined the 'Footballers Battalion' and became one of the casualties of the First World War, being killed in France.
Debut: 9.10.1911 v. Reading (H). 3-0. SLDiv.1.

TILLSON Andrew

CD 6' 2" 12st 10lbs
b. Huntingdon, Cambridgeshire 30. 6.1966
Peterborough United
Kettering Town

Grimsby Town		Jul 1998
Q.P.R.	(£400,000)	Dec 1990

Football League: 29-2. FAC: 0-0. FLC: 2-0. Others: 1-0.
Total: 32-2.

Grimsby Town	(Loan)	Sep 1992
Bristol Rovers	(£370,000)	Nov 1992
Walsall	(£10,000)	Aug 2000
Rushden & Diamonds		Feb 2002

A good, dependable central defender whose heading and passing abilities from defence contributed enormously to a sound back four. A big money signing, he was only at Rangers for less than two years, but remained at his next club for nearly eight.
Debut: 23.12.1990 v. Derby County (A). 1-1. Div.1.

TOMKYS Michael G.

(O.R.) Wing 5' 8" 11st 6lbs
b. Kensington, London 14.12.1932
Fulham
Q.P.R. Nov 1951
Football League: 91-19. FAC: 8-2. FLC: 0-0. Others: 2-0.
Total: 101-21
Yeiwsley 1959

Honours: English Youth International.

Mike was a genuine player who would give his all during a match, sometimes interchanging with the other winger or centre forward. He made his debut at the age of nineteen and was last heard of as the manager of Harrow Borough in 1978.
Debut: 17.11.1951 v. Cardiff City (A).1-3. Div. 2.

TOSSWILL John Speare

(I.R.) Mid 5' 11" 12st 0lbs
b. Eastbourne in 1890 d. Brighton 28. 9.1915
Eastbourne
Hastings & St. Leonards
Aberdare
Tunbridge Wells Rangers
Maidstone United
Q.P.R. May 1911
Southern League: 3-1. FAC: 0-0. FLC: 0-0. Others: 0-0.
Total: 3-1.

Liverpool	Jun 1912
Southend United	May 1913
Coventry City	Nov 1913

John joined the Royal Engineers at the outbreak of the 1st World War and was serving as a dispatch rider on the Western Front when he was wounded. He was brought home to Brighton but tragically died on the operating table.
Debut: 5.4.1912 v. Southampton (H). 1-1. SLDiv.1.

TOWERS Edwin James

(C.F.) Striker 5' 10" 12st 2lbs
b. Shepherds Bush, London 5. 4.1933

Brentford		May 1951
Q.P.R.	(Francis & Towers £8,000)	May 1961

Football League: 28-15. FAC: 3-0. FLC: 2-1. Others: 0-0.
Total: 33-16.

Millwall	(£5,000)	Aug 1962
Gillingham	(£4,000)	Jan 1963
Aldershot		Jul 1963
Romford		

Jim was a powerfully built, direct hustler for goals, who spelt danger to all opposing defenders. He was the other half of the duo that was known as the 'Terrible Twins', the other half being George Francis. The 'Terrible Twins' were the leading goalscorers for Brentford for seven seasons between 1955 and 1962. It is the only partnership traced in League Football to have scored twenty goals each in three consecutive seasons.
Debut: 19. 8.1961 v. Brentford (H). 3-0. Div. 3.

TRAVERS James Edward

(C.F.) Striker 5' 8" 11st 6lbs.
b. Birmingham 4.11.1888 d. Birmingham 31. 8.1946
Birchfield Road school

Bilston United	1904
Rowley United	1905
Wolverhampton Wanderers	1906
Birmingham	Aug 1907
Aston Villa	May 1908
Q.P.R.	May 1909

Southern League: 34-7. FAC: 7-1. FLC: 0-0. Others: 0-0. Total: 41-8.

Leicester Fosse	Aug 1910
Barnsley	Jan 1911
Manchester United	Feb 1914
Swindon Town	1919
Millwall Athletic	Jun 1920
Norwich City	Oct 1920
Gillingham	Jun 1921
Nuneaton Town	Sep 1921
Cradley Heath	Nov 1922
Bilston United	1929

Honours: FACup winners medal.

George, as he preferred to be called, was the son of Hyram Travers, the old-time music hall comedian known as the 'Pearly King'. His birth is still shrouded in mystery as a couple of other club histories have him born in different places, indeed the Athletic News states that he was born in Bow, London. It is known that he enlisted in the army in 1915 and it is said that he caught malaria while serving in the Far East, while others say he served in Salonika where he played for the British Army. He made six appearances for Spurs in wartime matches and retired from playing in 1931 aged 42.
Debut: 1. 9.1909 v. Watford (H). 4-3. SLDiv.1.

TRODD William H.

(R.H.) Mid
b.
Leyton

Q.P.R.	1934

Football League: 6-0. FAC: 0-0. FLC: 0-0. Others: 1-0. Total: 7-0.

Trodd took over from Dickie March when he was injured. This was at the time when one manager left the club and another arrived, and this proved to be his first and last season.
Debut: 13. 4.1935 v. Exeter City (H). 1-1. Div. 3. (S).

TURNBULL Peter

(I.L.) Mid 5' 7" 11st 5lbs
b. Lanquhar, Scotland in 1875
Glasgow Thistle

Burnley		Mar 1893
Bolton Wanderers	(Loan)	Mar 1895
Blackburn Rovers		Apl 1895
Glasgow Rangers		May 1896
Blackburn Rovers	(Loan)	Apl 1898
Millwall Athletic		May 1898
Q.P.R.		Aug 1899

Southern League: 19-6. FAC: 6-7. FLC: 0-0. Others: 0-0. Total: 25-13.

Brentford	Nov 1900
Barrow	1901

Blessed with natural athleticism, Peter knew how to control the ball at speed, a hard man to dispossess, yet he had to be in the mood, for not only did he show his brilliance at times but his inconsistency in other games. At Brentford he finished the season as top goalscorer in the Southern League with fifteen goals.
Debut: 9. 9.1899 v. Tottenham H. (A). 0-1. SLDiv.1.

TURNER William

(L.H.) Mid 5' 10" 12st 0lbs
b.Southmoor, Nr. Durham 22.12.1894 d. 1970

Dipton United		1913
Scotswood		
Leadgate Park		
Southampton	(£200)	Sep 1919
Bury		Apl 1924
Q.P.R.		Jul 1927

Football League: 38-0. FAC: 1-0. FLC: 0-0. Others: 0-0. Total: 39-0.

Honours: 3rd Div.(S) championship winners medal. F.A.X1 v. The Army.

Bill was a full back who was quickly turned into a half back at Southampton after an injury crisis. His last season as a professional was spent at Loftus Road. He was said to have been a very reliable player.
Debut: 27. 8.1927 v. Newport County (H). 4-2. Div.3 (S)

TURPIE Robert P.
Mid 5' 7" 10st 8lbs
b. Hampstead, London 13.11.1949
Q.P.R. Nov 1967
Football League: 2-0. FAC: 0-0. FLC: 0-0. Others: 0-0. Total: 2-0.
Peterborough United Jul 1970

Bob was the substitute for Watson, who played at full back for the club, and never really had a chance in a midfield position.
Debut: 13. 9.1969 v. Portsmouth (A). 3-1. Div. 2.

TUTT Walter R.
(O.L.) Wing
b.
Canterbury Waverley
Q.P.R. 1930
Football League: 7-3. FAC: 0-0. FLC: 0-0. Others: 0-0. Total: 7-3.

Walter was one of the many left wingers tried during this period. Eventually he became the substitute for Cribb.
Debut: 14. 1.1931 v. Bristol Rovers (A).0-3. Div.3 (S).

UNDERWOOD Edmund David
G 6' 1" 13st 5lbs
b. St. Pancras, London 15. 3.1928 d. South Africa in 1989
Kingsbury Town 1948
Q.P.R. Dec 1949
Football League: 2-0. FAC: 0-0. FLC: 0-0. Others: 0-0. Total: 2-0.

Watford		Feb 1952
Liverpool	(£7,000)	Dec 1953
Watford	(£1,250)	Jul 1956
Dartford		Aug 1957
Watford		Apl 1960
Fulham		Jul 1963
Dunstable Town		Jul 1965
Hastings United		Jun 1966

Dave was a genial and bubbly character who was the third choice goalkeeper at Loftus Road, after Harry Brown and Stan Gullen. He was given a free transfer to Watford, but within eighteen months, Liverpool bought him to replace their regular keeper, Sidlow. However, when they dropped into the 2nd Division in 1954, Dave returned to Watford. He retired at the age of 37 and became the player/manager of Hastings United, followed by Barnet in 1968, then the same at Wealdstone. In 1977 Dave became the Barnet chairman, while carrying on his work as a haulage contractor. He later emigrated to South Africa where he died at the age of 60.
Debut: 19. 1.1952 v. Luton Town (H). 1-0. Div. 2.

VAFIADIS Odysseus
Wing
b. London 8. 9.1945
Chelsea
Q.P.R. Nov 1962
Football League: 15-4. FAC: 0-0. FLC: 0-0. Others: 0-0. Total: 15-4.
Millwall Sep 1964
Hillingdon Borough 1965

After two years at Loftus Road, Odysseus first moved to Millwall before joining Jim Langley at Hillingdon Borough in 1965. He was with them when they sensationally beat Luton Town in the FACup in 1969.
Debut: 28. 9.1963 v. Millwall (H). 2-0. Div. 3.

VALLANCE Hugh Baird
(C.F.) Striker 5' 11" 11st 12lbs
b. Wolverhampton 14. 6.1905 d. Birmingham in 1973
Aston Villa Jan 1928
Q.P.R. May 1928
Football League: 1-0. FAC: 0-0. FLC: 0-0. Others: 0-0. Total: 1-0.

Brighton & Hove Albion	May 1929
Worcester City	Oct 1930
Evesham Town	Feb 1931
Tunbridge Wells Rangers	Jun 1931
Gillingham	Dec 1931
Kidderminster Harriers	May 1932
Nimes, France	Sep 1932
Basle, Switzerland	1933
Gillingham	1934

Hugh was a master at positioning himself, he also had a deceptive body swerve, but could not get into the side at Q.P.R. because of the form of record breaking George Goddard. So during the close season he was transferred to Brighton & Hove Albion, where he turned into a goalscoring phenomenon. He created a new club record, netting 30 in the League during the 1929/30 season. But his career took a rapid turn for the worse when he was dismissed following a very serious misdemeanour, the details of which were never revealed, but drink related problems during this period were common. Hugh joined the RAF in the middle 1930s and served throughout the war.
Debut: 16. 2.1929 v. Watford (A). 1-4. Div. 3. (S).

VANGO Alfred James
(C.H.) CD 5' 9" 11st 10lbs
b. Bethnal Green, London 23.12.1900d. Erith 24.11.1977

Walthamstow Avenue
Leyton
Gnome Athletic
Gillingham 1924
Walthamstow Avenue 1925
Barking Town 1926
Q.P.R. 1930
Football League: 12-0. FAC: 0-0. FLC: 0-0. Others: 0-0. Total: 12-0.
Walthamstow Avenue 1932
Clapton Orient 1932
London Paper Mills

Honours: F.A.Amateur cup runners-up medal.

Alf was an amateur who was a very clever attacking centre half but turned out for the club mostly at wing half. He was a motor mechanic by trade.
Debut: 13. 1.1931 v. Bristol Rovers (A). 0-3. Div.3 (S).

VARCO Percy Seymour

(C.F.) Striker 5' 9" 13st 0lbs
b. Fowey, Cornwall 17. 4.1904d. Fowey 29. 1.1982
Fowey school
Torquay United Aug 1923
Aston Villa (£200) Dec 1923
Q.P.R. Jun 1926
Football League: 16-4. FAC: 0-0. FLC: 0-0. Others: 0-0. Total: 16-4.
Norwich City Jul 1929
Exeter City Feb 1930
Brighton & Hove Albion Jun 1932
St. Austell 1933
St. Blazey 1935

Percy was a powerfully built player who was speedy and very hard to knock off the ball. Unfortunately at Q.P.R. he was out of the side for a long period owing to a fractured patella (knee-cap). When he recovered he was given a free transfer to Norwich City where he became very popular. On retirement from first class football he became a very successful fish merchant and later the Mayor of Fowey twice. He also became the official A.F.A coach in Cornwall in 1938.
Debut: 28. 8.1926 v. Crystal Palace (A).1-2. Div.3 (S).

VENABLES Terence Frederick

(R.H.) Mid 5' 8" 11st 8lbs
b. Dagenham, Essex 6. 1.1943
Dagenham schools
Essex schools
London schools
Chelsea Aug 1960
Tottenham Hotspur (£80,000) May 1966
Q.P.R. (£70,000) Jun 1969
Football League:177-19. FAC: 14-1. FLC: 15-2. Others: 0-0. Total: 206-22.
Crystal Palace Sep 1974
St. Patricks Athletic, Dublin

Honours: England school caps. 1 amateur cap. 7 youth caps. Football League v. Irish League. Young England v. England 4 caps at U23 level. 2 full England caps. F.A.Youth Cup winners medals. 2nd Div. runners-up medal. League Cup winners medal.

Terry was the first player to be capped by his country at all levels. On the field he was an accurate long range passer of the ball who had great vision for the game. Much of his career was spent at Chelsea and Spurs and at Loftus Road, but for only a little over five years, where he managed more than 200 first team appearances, an average of 40 per season. After retiring from playing, Terry became the Crystal Palace manager in 1976, the same at Q.P.R. in 1980, and then Barcelona in 1984. The Spurs managership followed in 1988, the same for England in 1992, Australia in 1995, and Portsmouth in 1997, after which he became a T.V. football pundit. In 2002 he was appointed the manager of Leeds United, but was dismissed during the season.
Debut: 9. 8.1969 v. Hull City (H). 3-0. Div.2.

VIGRASS John

(C.H.) CD
B. Leek, Derbyshire
Leek Alexandria
Q.P.R. 1921
Football League: 66-1. FAC: 5-0. FLC: 0-0. Others: 0-0. Total: 71-1.

Macclesfield Town:

John was a wing half who was converted into a centre half but when the club ended the season bottom of the 3rd Division (South) in 1924, he, along with many others was sacked.
Debut: 22. 4.1922 v. Merthyr Town (H).0-0. Div.3 (S).

VINCENT Ernest

(R.H.) Mid 5' 9" 11st 9lbs
b. Washington, Durham 28.10.1907
d. Doncaster 2. 6.1978

Dawdon Colliery		1923
Ryhope Colliery		1925
Seaham Harbour		1926
Washington Colliery		1929
Southport		Jul 1930
Manchester United	(£1,000)	Feb 1932
Q.P.R.		Jun 1935

Football League: 28-0. FAC: 2-0. FLC: 0-0. Others: 1-0. Total: 31-0.

Doncaster Rovers		May 1937
Stamford		1940

Honours: Durham County schoolboy caps. Rest of the League v. Wearside champions.

Ernie proved to be a strong and vigorous tackler who could play as a central defender in an emergency. He suffered a fractured ankle at Manchester United and on his recovery moved to Q.P.R. where he made 28 League appearances in two seasons. After his career in football Ernie worked at Haworth Colliery and later became the security officer there, retiring in 1972. He died six years later of cancer of the stomach. Ernie's brother played in the Football League for Durham City.
Debut: 31. 8.1935 v. Millwall (H). 2-3. Div. 3 (S).

WADDOCK Gary Patrick

Mid 5' 10" 11st 12lbs
b. Kingsbury, Nr. London 17. 3.1962

Kingsbury		
Q.P.R.		Jul 1979

Football League:203-8. FAC: 14-0. FLC: 22-2. Others: 1-0. Total: 240-10.

Royal Charleroi, Belgium		Dec 1987
Millwall	(£130,000)	Aug 1989
Q.P.R.		Dec 1991

Football League: 0-0. FAC: 0-0. FLC: 0-0. Others: 0-0. Total: 0-0.

Swindon Town	(Loan)	Mar 1992
Bristol Rovers	(£100,000)	Nov 1992
Luton Town		Sep 1994

Honours: Eire youth caps. 2 caps at B level. 1 cap at U21 level. 1 cap at U23 level. 21 full caps. 2nd Div. Championship medal. FACup runners-up medal.

Gary was very much a defensive type of midfield player with a ferocious tackle, distributing the ball very quickly and accurately. He became one of the most popular Q.P.R. players at the time, qualifying to play for the Rep. of Ireland through parentage, his father having been born in County Wexford. Locally born Gary's first club was Q.P.R., where he stayed for over eight years, before he moved to Belgium. Very occasionally a professional footballer returns from a serious injury after a long period out of the game and is able to make a complete recovery. At one time it was widely believed that Gary's career was over after such an injury, yet his recovery was so complete that he won his nineteenth cap for Eire in 1990. Gary was released from Luton Town in 1998.
Debut: 15. 9.1979 v. Swansea City (A). 2-1. Div. 2.

WAKE William

(L.H.) Mid 5' 9" 12st 0lbs
b. Bamburgh, Nr. Newcastle in 1887

Bamburgh Castle	
North Sunderland	
Morpeth Harriers	
Newcastle United	1905
Plymouth Argyle	1907
Exeter City	1908
Q.P.R.	1909

Southern League:175-1. FAC: 16-0. FLC: 0-0. Others: 1-0. Total: 192-1.

Honours: 2 caps for London League v. Birmingham League. Southern League v. Scottish League. Southern League championship winners medal.

Bill played for Q.P.R. for ten years in total, turning-out for them throughout the First World War, until retiring from the game in 1919. Hence four crucial years in his career were curtailed by the hostilities. By the end of the conflict he was aged around 32 and so just missed out (by a year or so) on appearaning for the Rangers in their early Football League days.
Debut: 1. 9.1909 v. Watford (H). 4-3. SLDiv.1.

WALKER Arthur

(C.F.) Striker 5' 9" 11st 0lbs
b. Ripley, Derbyshire in August 1888
Ripley Athletic
Nottingham Forest
Q.P.R. 1907
Southern League: 28-15. FAC: 2-1. FLC: 0-0. Others: 0-0. Total: 30-16.
Notts County 1908

Honours: Southern League championship medal.

Arthur was one of the top strikers of his day playing outside the Football League. He became the club's second top goalscorer in the 1907/08championship season having been transferred from Nottingham Forest. He left for Notts County the following season but he was not as successful at his new club.
Debut: 14. 9.1907 v. Tottenham H. (A). 2-3.SLDiv. 1.

WALKER Clive

(O.L.) Wing 5' 8" 11st 4lbs
b. Oxford 26. 5.1957
Chelsea Apl 1975
Fort Lauderdale, USA 1979
Sunderland (£75,000) Jul 1984
Q.P.R. Dec 1985
Football League: 20-1. FAC: 4-0. FLC: 3-1. Others: 0-0. Total: 27-2.
Fulham Oct 1987
Brighton & Hove Albion (£20,000) Aug 1990
Woking Aug 1994
Brentford Aug 1997
Cheltenham Town Nov 1997

Honours: Oxford and England representative. 3 FA Trophy medals. Conference player of the year 1995. FA Representative X1 v. Isthmian League.

Clive was quick and had an unpredictable flair for scoring spectacular goals. In just under two years he made only 27 appearnces for Rangers before moving on. Released by Brighton in May 1993, he had trials with Swansea City and Slough Town before joining Woking. For a short period Clive was the full-time player/assistant manager to Eddie May at Brentford in the 1997/98 season. He remained active in the GM Vauxhall Conference, not retiring from playing until May 1999, just a few days short of his 42nd Birthday.
Debut: 17.12.1985 v. Aston Villa (H). 0-1. Div.1.

WALLACE Barry D.

Def 5' 9" 11st 4lbs
b. Plaistow, Essex 17. 4.1959
Q.P.R. Aug 1976
Football League: 25-0. FAC: 2-0. FLC: 1-0. Others: 0-0. Total. 28-0.
Tulsa Roughnecks, USA 1980
Minnesota Strikers, USA 1987

After an unremarkable 25 League appearances in four years at Loftus Road, Barry visited, and then stayed on in the USA as a player during the 1980s.
Debut: 26.10.1977 v. Aston Villa (A). 0-1. FLCup.Rd.1.

WALLER William

(I.L.) Mid
b. Bolton, Lancashire
Nelson 1921
Burnley 1922
Scunthorpe United 1923
Chorley 1923
Q.P.R. Feb 1924
Football League: 2-0. FAC: 0-0. FLC: 0-0. Others: 0-0. Total: 2-0.

No fewer than six different players filled the position of inside left in this re-election season, and Billy was sacked at the end of it.
Debut: 1.3.1924 v.Bournemouth & BA.(H).0-1. Div.3 (S)

WALSH Michael A.

Striker 5' 9" 11st 5lbs
b. Chorley, Lancashire 13. 8.1954

Blackpool		Nov 1971
Everton	(£325,000)	Aug 1978
Q.P.R.	(Exchange P.Eastoe)	Mar 1979

Football League: 18-3. FAC: 1-0. FLC: 1-0. Others: 0-0. Total: 20-3.

Porto, Portugal	(£175,000)	Sep 1980
Sal Gueiros, Portugal		1985
Espinho, Portugal		1986
Rio Avenue, Portugal		1987

Honours: 21 caps for the Republic of Ireland.

At his best Micky was brave, quick and could control the ball at speed. However, he failed to show the fans at Loftus Road the sort of talent that they knew he had. On his return to England in 1989 he joined the backroom staff at non-League Slough Town where he remained until 1991. In February 1995 he was appointed joint manager of Chertsey Town. Micky was the proud father of quads in 1985.
Debut: 31. 3.1979 v. Derby County (H).2-2. Div.1.

WALSH Paul Anthony

Striker 5' 7" 10st 8lbs
b. Plumstead, London 1.10.1962
Blackheath schools
South London schools
London schools

Charlton Athletic		Oct 1979
Luton Town	(£250,000 + player)	Jul 1982
Liverpool	(£700,000)	May 1984
Tottenham Hotspur	(£550,000)	Feb 1988
Q.P.R.	(Loan)	Sep 1991

Football League: 2-0. FAC: 0-0. FLC: 0-0. Others: 0-0. Total: 2-0.

Portsmouth	(£400,000)	Jun 1992
Manchester City	(£750.000)	Mar 1994
Portsmouth	(Ex. player)	Sep 1995

Honours: 5 England caps. 9 youth caps. 4 at U21 level. London FA X1 v. England. European runners-up medal. Championship winners medal. Football League Cup runners-up medal. FACup winners medal.

Paul was loaned to Q.P.R. with a view to a permanent transfer. After an incident with Ray Clemence on the Spurs training ground, it did not materialise.

Voted young player of the year in 1984, he was tricky with the ball and was highly popular, with an excellent work rate and 100% committal throughout his career. Finally in December 1997 he had to give up playing after an injury he sustained in February 1996.
Debut: 17. 9.1991 v. Luton Town (A). 1-0. Div. 1.

WALSHE Benjamin Matthew

Wing 6' 1" 12st 12lbs
b. Hammersmith, London 24. 5.1983

Q.P.R.	Jul 2000

Football League: 2-0. FAC: 0-0. FLC: 0-0. Others: 0-0. Total: 2-0.

Ben made his League debut in the closing weeks of the 2000/01 season. He is a fast and direct winger who was a member of the U19 team that reached the final of the FA Premier Academy.
Debut: 28. 4.2001 v. Stockport County (H). 0-3. Div.1.

WARBURTON Arthur

(I.R.) Mid 5' 8" 10st 7lbs
b. Whitefield, Nr. Bury, Lancashire 30.10.1903
Sedgley Park

Manchester United	May 1929
Burnley	Dec 1933
Nelson	May 1934
Fulham	Oct 1934
Q.P.R.	Jun 1938

Football League: 17-0. FAC: 4-0. FLC: 0-0. Others: 0-0. Total: 21-0.

Southport	Oct 1945

Arthur was a hard working midfield player who showed boundless energy and put in some useful performances for the club in the last full season before the 2nd World War. He joined the RAF and became a PT instructor. As a guest during the hostilities he played for Rochdale, Bradford, Middlesbrough, Lincoln City and Bury.
Debut: 10. 9.1938 v. Brighton & HA.(A).1-3.Div. 3 (S).

WARD Darren Phillip

CD 6' 0" 12st 6lbs
b. Harrow, Middlesex 13. 9.1978

Watford		Feb 1997
Q.P.R.	(Loan)	Dec 1999

Football League: 14-0. FAC: 1-0. FLC: 0-0. Others: 0-0. Total: 15-0.

Millwall	(£500,000)	Oct 2001

Darren was loaned from Watford on a three months spell after an operation to remove a metal plate from his leg, and the move proved to be the making of him. Regaining his appetite for the game he soon became popular with the fans. But his loan period at an end, he returned to Watford in March 2000.
Debut: 18.12.1999 v. Charlton Athletic (H).0-0. Div.1.

WARDLE George

(O.R.) Wing 5' 8" 11st 7lbs
b. Kimbleworth, Durham 24.10.1919
Durham boys club

Middlesbrough		May 1937
Exeter City		Jun 1939
Cardiff City	(£30,000)	May 1947
Q.P.R.		Jan 1949

Football League: 53-4. FAC: 1-0. FLC: 0-0. Others: 0-0. Total: 54-4.

Darlington	Aug 1951
Crook Town	1953

George was a very skilful player whose career was marred by the 2nd World War. He probably reached his summit during the conflict as a guest player, turning out in two Wembley Cup Finals for Chelsea and in one scored a goal. Returning to Exeter City at the end of the war, George showed that he was in a class of his own. Often he would beat three or four players with the ball but his colleagues would not react quickly enough to take advantage. Accommodation was a problem in post-war Britain and unable to find a house in Exeter, he was transferred to Cardiff City. Two years later, aged nearly 30, he appeared for Q.P.R. for over two seasons during which time he appeared in over 50 matches.
Debut: 29. 1.1949 v. Southampton (H). 1-3. Div.2.

WARDLEY Stuart James

Mid 5' 11" 12st 7lbs
b. Cambridge 10. 9.1975
Saffron Waldon Town

Q.P.R.	(£15,000)	Jul 1999

Football League: 87-4. FAC: 5-3. FLC: 2-0. Others: 1-0. Total: 93-7.

Rushden & Diamonds	(Loan)	Jan 2002

Gerry Francis, who plucked Les Ferdinand and Andrew Impey from non-League football, appeared to have found another gem of a player, for Stuart was voted the "Player of the Year" for the 1999/2000 season. He is mainly a right-sided midfield player but is extremely versatile and even took over in goal for Q.P.R. when Chris Day was injured. But after less than three years at Loftus Road, and nearly100 apearances, he joined Rushden & Diamonds, after a loan period, in April 2002, and scored on his home debut.
Debut: 7. 8.1999 v. Huddersfield Town (H).3-1. Div.1.

WARREN Christer S.

Mid 5' 10" 11st 10lbs
b. Weymouth, Dorset 10.10.1974
Cheltenham Town

Southampton	(£40,000)	Mar 1995
Brighton & Hove Albion	(Loan)	Oct 1996
Fulham	(Loan)	Mar 1997
AFC Bournemouth	(£50,000)	Oct 1997
Q.P.R.		Jun 2000

Football League: 36-0. FAC: 1-0. FLC: 1-0. Others: 0-0. Total: 38-0.

Bristol Rovers	Sep 2002

Chris came into the side when Paul Bruce was injured, but was unable to hold on to his place. He was one of four players to be tried in the left-back position by Q.P.R. in 2001/02 but after only a handful of appearances, and just two as substitute early in 2002/03 season, he moved on to Bristol Rovers
Debut: 28. 8.2000 v. W.B.A. (A). 1-2. Div.1.

WASSELL Harold

(L.B.) Def
b. Stourbridge, Shropshire 21. 9.1879
Brierley Hill Alliance

Small Heath	1901
Bristol Rovers	1903
Q.P.R.	1905

Southern League: 3-0. FAC: 0-0. FLC: 0-0. Others: 0-0. Total: 3-0.

A reserve defender who was never on the losing (first team) side at Q.P.R. Harry was the cover for Newlands, and his final match was the 7-0 home defeat of Bristol Rovers.
Debut: 18.11.1905 v. Watford (A).4-3. SLDiv.1.

WATERALL Albert

(C.H.) CD 5' 7" 11st 11lbs
b. Nottingham 1. 3.1889 d. in 1963
Sneinton

Notts County	1910
Stockport County	Jun 1913
Q.P.R.	1926

Football League: 2-0. FAC: 0-0. FLC: 0-0. Others: 0-0. Total: 2-0.

Clapton Orient	1926

Honours: 3rd Div. (North) championship winners medal.

While Albert was clearly not lacking in skill, his greatest asset was his unquenchable thirst for the game. Following a disagreement with Notts County he went to Stockport County and developed into a versatile player who was equally adept as a wing half as well as a centre half. Both he and his football playing brother, Tommy, were called-up in February 1918, and Albert continued to play for Stockport until he was 37 years old. He made just two appearances for Rangers before his last move, to Clapton Orient. He retired in 1927 and returned to Nottingham where he became a pub landlord.
Debut: 18. 9.1926 v. Charlton Athletic (A).0-2. Div.3 (S).

WATSON Edward

(R.B.) Def
b. Shotton, Durham in 1899
Sunderland West End
Sunderland Jan 1920
Dundee Hibs May 1921
Q.P.R. May 1922
Football League: 8-0. FAC: 0-0. FLC: 0-0. Others: 0-0. Total: 8-0.
Rochdale 1923

A reserve defender who usually covered the right back position when injuries occurred.
Debut: 11. 9.1922 v. Brentford (A). 3-1. Div.3 (S).

WATSON George Edward

(O.L.) Wing 5' 7" 9st 2lbs
b. Shotton Colliery, Durham in 1914
Durham City
Q.P.R. 1934
Football League: 8-1. FAC: 0-0. FLC: 0-0. Others: 0-0. Total: 8-1.

George had won several medals and trophies at junior level for the winter game but his more renowned for his ability at cricket in the summer.
Debut: 15. 9.1934 v. Brighton & H.A.(H).2-1. Div.3 (S).

WATSON Ian L.

(R.B.) Def 5' 11" 11st 11lbs
b. Hammersmith, London 7. 1.1944
Chelsea Feb 1962
Q.P.R. (£10,000) Jul 1965
Football League:202-1. FAC: 16-0. FLC: 14-0. Others: 0-0. Total: 232-1.
Honours: 3rd Div. championship winners medal. 2 2nd Div. runners-up medals.

Ian signed professional forms for Chelsea after being at the club for two years. He never achieved a permanent place in the their senior squad and was snapped-up for a song by manager Alec Stock, when he was languishing in the Chelsea reserve team. Ian was a well built, burly defender, who gave great service to the club for nine years and played in the top three divisions of the Football League. However, he had a baptism of fire, being on the losing end of a 6-1 drubbing by local rivals Brentford. He was an ever-present in the First Division during the 1968/69 season, and missed just a few games on three other occasions. Just one solitary goal was scored, in the League, in 1969/70. Discounting his time at Chelsea, Ian was a true one club man, for he retired in 1974, aged 30.
Debut: 21. 8.1965 v. Brentford (A). 1-6. Div.3.

WATTS T. Frederick

(L.B.) Def
b. London
Q.P.R. 1919
Southern/Football League: 5-0. FAC: 0-0. FLC: 0-0. Others: 5-0.
Yeovil & Petters 1923

An amateur full back who occasionally turned out for the club when required to do so.
Debut: 3. 4.1920 v. Norwich City (H).1-0.

WAUGH Lyle Sidney

(C.H.) CD
b. Newcastle-on-Tyne in 1899
Bedlington Colliery
Q.P.R. 1923
Football League: 5-0. FAC: 0-0. FLC: 0-0. Others: 0-0. Total: 5-0.
West Cramlington Welfare

Lyle was an amateur reserve centre half, who was not retained at the end of the season. He was one of many that suffered in the clear-out at the club at that time.
Debut: 12. 9.1923 v. Newport County (H).0-3. Div.3(S).

WAUGH William L.

(O.R.) Wing
b. Edinburgh, Scotland 27.11.1921
Bathgate Thistle
Luton Town Sep 1944
Q.P.R. Jul 1950
Football League: 77-6. FAC: 2-0. FLC: 0-0. Others: 0-0. Total: 79-6.
Bournemouth & BA Jul 1953

Billy's early football career was disrupted by the start of the Second World War and his permanent introduction to English League football was not made until 1944, unusually during hostilities, at Luton Town. After six years he moved to Q.P.R. He was an extremely fast and tricky winger who drifted past the opposition with ease. But his time at Loftus Road was limited to just three seasons Billy retired from the game in May 1954.
Debut: 19. 8.1950 v. Chesterfield (H). 1-1. Div.2.

WEARE Ross Michael

Striker 6' 2" 13st 6lbs
b. Perivale, Middlesex 19. 3.1977
East Ham United
Q.P.R. (£10,000) Mar 1999
Football League: 4-0. FAC: 1-0. FLC: 0-0. Others: 0-0. Total: 5-0.
Bristol Rovers Jul 2001

Gerry Francis discovered Ross playing for East Ham United and promptly captured him for Q.P.R. Unfortunately he later sustained an injury which has since forced him to retire from the game.
Debut: 20.11.1999 v. Walsall (H). 2-1. Div.1.

WEBB David James

Def 5' 11" 12st 11lbs
b. Stratford, London 9. 4.1946
West Ham United
Leyton Orient May 1963
Southampton (£23,000) Mar 1966
Chelsea (£40,000 + player) Feb 1968
Q.P.R. (£100,000) Jul 1974
Football League:116-10. FAC: 8-0. FLC: 14-2. Others: 8-2. Total: 146-14.
Leicester City Sep 1977
Derby County Dec 1978
AFC Bournemouth Mat 1980

Honours: FACup winners medal. European Cup winners medal. League Cup runners-up medal. Charity Shield appearance.

A strong, robust and very versatile performer, who could play in almost any position on the field. Dave had a swashbuckling attitude to the game and was a favourite with players and spectators alike. When he joined Q.P.R. he partnered Frank McLintock at the back, as the club came within a whisker of clinching the championship of the old Division One. The pair were reunited at Leicester City as manager McLintock attempted to shore up a hard-pressed defence. Disappointment was part of David's lot at both Leicester City and Derby County, but he was back on the promotion trail at AFC Bournemouth during his first stint at management in 1980. David also managed Torquay United in 1984, Southend United in 1986 and 1988, Milford in 1988, Chelsea in 1993 and Brentford from 1993 to 1997.
Debut: 17. 8.1974 v. Sheffield United (A).1-1. Div.1.

WEBB Issac

G 6' 1" 12st 0lbs
b. Worcester 10.10.1874 d. Birmingham in March 1950
Worcester Park school
St. Clemants Rangers
Berwick Rangers (in the Worcester league)
Worcester Olympic
Evesham Town
Mansfield Town
Lincoln City
Mansfield Town
Wellington Town

Small Heath		1898
W.B.A.		May 1901
Sunderland	(£250)	Dec 1904
Q.P.R.		1907

Southern League: 10-0. FAC: 0-0. FLC: 0-0. Others: 0-0.
Total: 10-0.

W.B.A.	Aug 1908

Honours: 2nd Div. championship winners medal.

Issie was a thoroughly reliable custodian, who had quick reflexes and was spectacular and agile. His early career was with various home town clubs, before 1904 when Sunderland paid £250 to West Brom. for his services. Just 10 games for Rangers followed before a return to the Hawthorns. He retired in May 1910 to join the Army as a catering orderly. However, in August 1918, he made a comeback at the age of 43, when he turned out for West Brom.
Debut: 11. 3.1907 v. Brentford (H). 1-1. SLDiv. 1.

WEBLIN F. T.

(R.B.) Def
b.
West Norwood

Q.P.R.	1912

Southern League: 11-0. FAC: 0-0. FLC: 0-0. Others: 0-0.
Total: 11-0.

Weblin stood in for McDonald when he was injured.
Debut: 14.12.1912 v. Merthyr Town (A). 0-0.SLDiv.1.

WEGERLE Roy Connon

Striker 5' 8" 10st 2lbs
b. Johannesburg, South Africa 19. 3.1964

Tampa Bay Rowdies		1981
Chelsea	(£100,000)	Jul 1986
Swindon Town	(Loan)	Mar 1988
Luton Town	(£75,000)	Jul 1988
Q.P.R.	(£1,000,000)	Dec 1989

Football League: 75-29. FAC: 11-1. FLC: 5-1. Others: 1-0.
Total: 92-31.

Blackburn Rovers	(£1,200,000)	Mar 1992
Coventry City	(£1,000,000)	Mar 1993

Honours: 2 full caps for USA plus U21 caps. League cup runners-up medal.

On his day a very exciting player who could be relied upon to pull something out of a dull match to brighten up the proceedings. Roy learnt his trade under the guidance of Rodney Marsh at Tampa Bay Rowdies. A wonderfully talented striker whose brilliant individualism was later sought after by a number of clubs in the nineties. Roy was discovered in South Africa by the former Ipswich Town goalkeeper, Roy Bailey. He began to show his true potential while at Luton Town, which was sufficient to persuade Q.P.R. to pay a million pounds for him. It was here that he began to live up to his fee. His ability to twist and turn defenders inside out and score the most spectacular goals made him a great favourite with the crowd. His stay at Loftus Road lasted just over two years before he moved on for an even bigger transfer fee.
Debut: 16.12.1989 v. Sheffield Wed. (A). 0-2. Div. 1.

WELTON Patrick Roy

G 6' 0"
b. Eltham, Kent 3. 5.1928
Chislehurst

Leyton Orient	May 1949
Q.P.R.	Mar 1958

Football League: 3-0. FAC: 0-0. FLC: 0-0. Others: 0-0.
Total: 3-0.

Honours: 3rd Div.(South) championship medal.

30 years old Pat was transferred to Q.P.R. after turning out for Orient on nearly 300 occasions. He later went on to manage St. Albans City and then Walthamstow Avenue before becoming the England youth team coach, and in 1969 Pat took the same role at Spurs, until 1976. He coached abroad for a time before becoming a P.E. Teacher at a public school.
Debut: 31. 1.1959 v Norwich City (A). 1-5. Div. 3.

WENTWORTH F.

(R.H.) Mid
b.

Q.P.R.	1909

Southern League: 7-0. FAC: 0-0. FLC: 0-0. Others: 0-0.
Total: 7-0.

A young solid player who only played for Q.P.R. during a single season. Wentworth was Archie Mitchell's stand-in.
Debut: 11. 9.1909 v. Clapton Orient (H).2-1. SLDiv.1.

WESTWOOD Daniel R.

Striker 5' 10" 11st 5lbs
b. Dagenham, Essex 25. 7.1953
Billericay

Q.P.R.		Jul 1974

Football League: 1-1. FAC: 0-0. FLC: 0-0. Others: 0-0.
Total: 1-1.

Gillingham	(£17,000)	Nov 1975
Barnet		1982

Danny came on as a substitute in the Boxing day match v. Leicester City and scored in the 4-2 victory, in his only appearance for the club.
Debut: 26.12.1974 v. Leicester City (H). 4-2. Div.1.

WHATMORE Ernest L.

(L.H.) Mid 5' 9" 11st 6lbs
b. Kidderminster 25. 4.1900 d. Kidderminster 30. 7.1991

Stourbridge	1921
Wolverhampton Wanderers (Trial)	1922
Shrewbury Town	Feb 1923
Bristol Rovers	Jul 1923
Q.P.R.	Jun 1928

Football League: 78-3. FAC: 4-0. FLC: 0-0. Others: 0-0.
Total: 82-3.

Shepherds Bush	Feb 1933
Stourbridge	1933

Honours: Shropshire senior cup winners medal. Birmingham & District league winners medal.

His style of play led him to take more knocks during the course of a match than one can expect all season. Ernie was distinctive on the field of play with his bald head and there was no more an honest player on the pitch than this man. Ernie died a fortnight afer breaking his hip in a fall at a Kidderminster nursing home.
Debut: 25. 8.1925 v. Torquay United (A).4-3. Div.3 (S).

WHELDON George Frederick

(I.L.) Mid 5' 8" 11st 5lbs
b. Langley Green 1.11.1869 d. Worcester 14. 1.1924
Langley St. Michael's school
Road End White Star
Langley Green, Victoria

W.B.A.	(Trial)	1888
Small Heath		Feb 1890
Aston Villa	(£100 + £250 from match)	Jun 1896
W.B.A.	(£100)	Aug 1900
Q.P.R.		Dec 1901

Southern League: 14-6. FAC: 0-0. FLC: 0-0. Others: 0-0.
Total: 14-6.

Honours: 2nd Div championship winners medal. 3 League Championship winners medal. FACup winners medal.(The famous double) 4 English caps. 4+ Football League caps.

Freddie was the youngest in a family of ten and was a brilliant footballer, with an exceptional talent, and a great goalscorer, who simply loved the game. His intricate footwork often bemused the best defenders in the country. Fred also developed the art of the daisy-cutter shot; on bumpy pitches at this time, such a shot was a goalkeeper's nightmare and a high proportion of his goals were scored in this way! Fred was also a fine cricketer and played for Worcestershire from 1899 until 1906, and Carmarthenshire in 1910. In later life he became the landlord of the Farriers Arms in Worcester for a number of years. His brother, Sam, played for W.B.A.
Debut: 16.11.1901 v. Reading (A). 1-7. SLDiv.1.

WHITAKER Colin

(O.L.) Wing 5' 10" 11st 6lbs
b. Leeds, Yorkshire 14. 6.1932

Sheffield Wednesday		Nov 1951
Bradford Park Avenue		Jun 1953
Shrewsbury Town		Jul 1956
Q.P.R.		Feb 1961

Football League: 8-0. FAC: 0-0. FLC: 0-0. Others: 0-0.
Total: 8-0.

Rochdale		May 1961
Oldham Athletic	(Player exchange)	Oct 1962
Barrow		Aug 1964
Ashton United		Nov 1964
Buxton		1965
Heanor Town		Aug 1966

Honours: League Cup runners-up medal.

A speedy, skilful and confident winger who achieved some outstanding scoring feats. Colin recorded a century of goals from the wing in his League career, including eight hat-tricks, although ironically none for Q.P.R. in his brief career with the club. He was an all-round sportsman playing minor counties cricket for Shropshire and a single handicap golfer. He purchased a 46 acre farm and transformed it into a golf course. An RAF posting in Germany meant that he missed an England U23 cap while he was on Bradford Park Avenue's books. Colin is now retired and lives part of the year in Spain.
Debut: 18. 2.1961 v. Hull City (H). 2-1. Div.3.

WHITE Devon Winston

Striker 6' 3" 14st 0lbs
b. Nottingham 2. 3.1964

Radford Olympic		
Arnold Town		
Lincoln City	(£2,000)	Dec 1984
Boston United	(Loan)	
Naxxar, Malta	(Loan)	
Boston United		Oct 1986
Shepshed Charterhouse		
Grantham		
Bristol Rovers		Aug 1987
Cambridge United	(£100,000)	Mar 1992
Q.P.R.	(£100,000)	Jan 1993

Premier League: 27-9. FAC: 0-0. FLC: 2-0. Others: 0-0. Total: 29-9.

Notts County	(£110,000)	Dec 1994
Watford	(£100,000)	Feb 1996
Notts County		Mar 1997
Shrewsbury Town	(£30,000)	Sep 1997

Honours: Anglo-Italian Cup winners medal. 3rd Div. championship winners medal.

Devon was a big, cumbersome, awkward to mark striker, who was twice taken out of non-League football to play in the professional ranks. After numerous transfers he was released in the summer of 1998 at the age of 34.
Debut: 27. 1.1993 v. Chelsea (H). 1-1. PL.

WHITE John W.

(R.B.) Def 5' 10" 12st 6lbs
b. Manchester in 1880

Ollenshaw United	
Grays Anchor	
Swanscombe	
Grays United	
Q.P.R.	May 1901

Southern League:133-1. FAC: 7-0. FLC: 0-0. Others: 0-0. Total: 140-1.

Leeds City	May 1908
Merthry Tydfil	1911

Honours: Southern League championship winners medal.

Although christened, Jabez, he always used the first name John. He was a ferocious tackler with a powerful kick. A football writer of the day wrote, *"He had a cool and resourceful temperament about him."* Brought out of non-League football, John spent seven years at Q.P.R. during which time he averaged exactly 20 first team matches per season.
Debut: 28. 1.1909 v. Portsmouth (A).0-1.SLDiv.1.

WHITE William

(I.F.) Mid 5' 9" 12st 7lbs
b. Scotland in 1877

Heart of Midlothian	
Woolwich Arsenal	May 1897
New Brompton	Mar 1899
Q.P.R.	1899

Southern League: 20-7. FAC: 5-1. FLC: 0-0. Others: 0-0. Total: 25-8.

Liverpool	1901
Middlesbrough	1902
Dundee	1903

Bill hailed from the Scottish club Hearts and was good enough to walk straight into the Arsenal side and score on the opening day of the 1897/98 season. On his debut for Liverpool, Bill did the same again, scoring in the 2nd minute of a Merseyside derby at Goodison Park.
Debut: 11.11.1899 v. Chatham (A). 3-5. SLDiv.1.

WHITEHEAD William Thomas

(C.F.) Striker
b. Saffron Waldon, Cambridgeshire 11. 9.1897

Swansea Town	1924
Q.P.R.	1926

Football League: 25-5. FAC: 4-0. FLC: 0-0. Others: 0-0. Total: 29-5.

Manchester City
Boston Town
Yeovil & Petters United

Bill was at Swansea Town when they won the 3rd Division (South) championship, but didn't play enough matches to qualify for a medal. Conversely at Q.P.R., Bill was part of Bob Hewison's squad that had to apply for re-election for the second time in two years.
Debut: 17.10.1925 v. Watford (H). 2-0. Div.3 (S).

WHITELAW George

(C.F.) Striker 6' 0" 12st 6lbs
b. Paisley, Nr. Glasgow 1. 1.1937

St.Johnston	
Sunderland	Feb 1958
Q.P.R.	Mar 1959

Football League: 26-10. FAC: 0-0. FLC: 0-0. Others: 1-0. Total: 27-10.

Halifax Town	Oct 1959
Carlisle United	Feb 1961
Stockport County	Jan 1962
Barrow	Aug 1963
St. Johnston	

Honours: Scottish Amateur International cap.

George was just one of six centre forwards to be tried this season. He did, however, score on his debut for the club.
Debut: 15. 3.1959 v. Bradford City (H). 3-0. Div.3.

WHITFIELD Kenneth

(I.F.) Mid 5' 10" 12st 0lbs
b. Durham City 24. 3.1930.

Shildon Colliery		
Wolverhampton Wanderers		Dec 1947
Manchester City	(£13,000)	Mar 1953
Brighton & Hove Albion	(£6,500)	Jul 1954
Q.P.R.		Jul 1959

Football League: 19-3. FAC: 4-0. FLC: 0-0. Others: 0-0. Total: 23-3.

Full of promise in his early football days, just after the war, Ken was in an exciting Q.P.R. side that ended the season in third place in Division 3. One year later, in 1961, he became the manager of Bideford Town for a time, then the coach of Luton Town and finally the assistant/manager of Cardiff City from 1974 until 1978.
Debut: 26. 9.1959 v. Tranmere Rovers (A).3-0. Div.3.

WHITTAKER Richard

(R.B.) Def 5' 9" 11st 0lbs
b. Dublin, Eire 10.10.1934

St. Marys boys club, Dublin	
Chelsea	May 1952
Peterborough United	Sep 1960
Q.P.R.	Jul 1963

Football League: 17-0. FAC: 0-0. FLC: 1-0. Others: 0-0. Total: 18-0

Stamford	1967

Honours: Irish schoolboy caps. 1 U23 cap. 1 full cap. 4th Div. championship winners medal.

This compact full back became player/coach under Alec Stock, filling the gap left by Roy Bentley. Finally, in 1967, Dick became player/coach at Stamford.
Debut: 24. 8.1963 v. Oldham Athletic (A). 1-2. Div.3.

WHYMAN Alfred

(I.L.) Mid 5' 10" 12st 0lbs
b. Edmonton, London 31.10.1884
d. South America in 1955

Edmonton Rovers	
Tottenham Hotspur	Apl 1905
New Brompton	1908
Q.P.R.	May 1909

Southern League:153-22. FAC: 15-2. FLC: 0-0. Others: 1-0. Total: 169-24.

Honours: Southern League championship medal.

Alf was a talented player who could fill any position except for goalkeeper. He gave Q.P.R. great service during the period leading up to the 1st World War. On retirement, Alf emigrated to South America in 1920.
Debut: 1. 9.1909 v. Watford (H). 4-3. SLDiv. 1.

WICKS James R.

G 5' 6" 11st 0lbs
b. Reading in 1899

Wycombe Wanderers	1920
Nottingham Forest	1921
Reading	Jun 1923
Q.P.R.	1924

Football League: 5-0. FAC: 0-0. FLC: 0-0. Others: 0-0. Total: 5-0.

Honours: Spartan League championship medal. Berks & Bucks senior cup winners medal.

When Jim was at Q.P.R., the club suffered a goalkeeper crisis and for a short period he was the only custodian available owing to injuries.
Debut: 8.11.1924 v. Gillingham (A). 1-1. Div.3 (S).

WICKS Steven John

(C.H.) CD 6' 2" 13st 2lbs
b. Reading, Berkshire 3.10.1956

Chelsea		Jun 1974
Derby County	(£275,000)	Jan 1979
Q.P.R.	(£300,000)	Sep 1979

Football League: 73-0. FAC: 3-0. FLC: 6-0. Others: 0-0. Total: 82-0.

Crystal Palace	(£250,000 + Clive Allen)	Jun 1981
Q.P.R.	(£250,000)	Mar 1982

Football League:116-6. FAC: 2-0. FLC: 17-0. Others: 4-0. Total: 139-6.

Chelsea	(£450,000)	Jul 1986
Wycombe Wanderers		Jul 1989

Honours: 7 England youth caps. 1 U23 cap. 2nd Div. championship winners medal. Football League Cup runners-up medal.

Steve graduated to the professional ranks from Chelsea juniors and was a first-team regular at the age of nineteen years old. A tall, solid and powerfully built player, who was dominant both in the air and on the ground. Steve was at the club twice for a total of six years. He eventually retired in 1988 after an injury which won him £262,000 in compensation, although a very brief comeback in non-League football was made the following year. Steve became the assistant manager at Portsmouth in 1989, the manager of Crawley Town in 1992, Scarborough in 1994, and had spells scouting for Lincoln City and Newcastle United. He finished his football career by coaching in the USA.
Debut: 25. 9.1979 v. Mansfield Town (A). 3-0. FLCup.

WILCOX Jonah Charles

(C.F.) Striker 5' 11" 12st 0lbs
b. Coleford, Somerset 19. 1.1894 d. Shipham, 5. 8.1956

Coleford Athletic	Sep 1912
Frome Town	Sep 1913
Welton Rovers	Nov 1913
Abertillery	1914
Bristol City	Aug 1919
Bradford Park Avenue	Sep 1922
New Brighton	Jun 1924
Bristol Rovers	May 1925
Q.P.R.	May 1926

Football League: 9-2. FAC: 0-0. FLC: 0-0. Others: 0-0. Total: 9-2.

Gillingham	Aug 1927
Kidderminster Harriers	Jul 1929

Jonah was a natural goalscorer, although he didn't turn it on at Loftus Road. Scoring on his debut for Coleford, he later totalled thirteen goals in eight matches for Bristol City during the 1st World War. At New Brighton he netted thirty five goals in forty two League matches, which set a new club scoring record. At Bristol Rovers, Jonah became the top marksman in the 1925/26 season and the same for Gillingham in 1927/28 with twenty five goals. In retirement he became the landlord of The Vine Hotel in Kidderminster until 1938, then the Golden Bowl in Bristol, followed by The New Inn at Blagdon for fourteen years until 1955.
Debut: 28. 8.1926 v. Crystal Palace (A).1-2.Div. 3 (S).

WILDE J.

(C.H.) CD
b.
Q.P.R. 1913
Southern League: 13-0. FAC: 0-0. FLC: 0-0. Others: 0-0. Total: 13-0.

The reserve centre half who turned out in place of Archie Mitchell before the 1st World War. It is known that during the hostilities, he joined the 'Footballers Battalion'.
Debut: 23. 4.1914 v. Reading (A). 1-0. SLDiv.1.

WILES George Harold

(F.B.) Def 5' 9" 11st 4lbs
b. East Ham, London in 1905
East Ham School
London Schools
Sittingbourne
Q.P.R. May 1929
Football League: 18-0. FAC: 0-0. FLC: 0-0. Others: 0-0. Total: 18-0.

Walsall	Mar 1933
Halesowen Town	1938

A splendid all-round footballer, who during his career hardly ever committed a bad foul. George joined Q.P.R. as an amateur and embraced professionalism in 1930. He was physically a strong man who could battle it out with the toughest of characters, and usually coming off best.
Debut: 5. 9.1929 v. Walsall (H). 2-2. Div. 3. (S).

WILES Henry S.

(C.F.) Striker 5' 8" 11st 0lbs
b. East Ham, London
R.A.F.
Sittingbourne
Q.P.R. 1929
Football League: 42-25. FAC: 1-0. FLC: 0-0. Others: 0-0. Total: 43-25.
Walsall 1932

Honours: Represented the United Services team in Egypt while in the R.A.F.

In the 1931/32 season at Loftus Road, Harry scored eleven goals in eleven matches. When he was transferred to Walsall the following campaign he notched sixty four goals playing in the Midland Midweek League, the Birmingham Combination and various minor cup competitions, plus in a handful of Third Division matches. He eventually left Fellows Park in 1935.
Debut: 31. 8.1929 v. Crystal Palace (A).1-1.Div. 3. (S).

WILKINS Dean Mark

Mid 5' 10" 12st 4lbs
b. Hillingdon, Middlesex 12. 7.1962

Q.P.R.	May 1980

Football League: 6-0. FAC: 0-0. FLC: 1-0. Others: 0-0. Total: 7-0.

Myllykosken Pallo, Finland	1982
Brighton & Hove Abion	Aug 1983
Leyton Orient	Mar 1984
PEC Zwolle, Holland	1985
Brighton & Hove Albion (£10,000)	Jul 1987
Worthing	1996
Crawley Town	1997
Bognor Regis Town	1998

Honours: Capped for Middlesex.

The younger brother of Ray. Dean was a stylish player who was dangerous at dead ball situations and was also an excellent passer of the ball. He retired in 1999 through injury.
Debut: 1.11.1980 v. Grimsby Town (A). 0-0. Div.2.

WILKINS Raymond Colin (M.B.E.)

Mid 5' 8" 11st 2lbs
b. Hillingdon, Middlesex 14. 9.1956

Chelsea		Oct 1973
Manchester United	(£875,000)	Aug 1979
AC Milan	(£1,500,000)	Jul 1984
Paris St. Germain	(£500,000)	1986
Glasgow Rangers	(£250,000)	Nov 1987
Q.P.R.		Nov 1989

Football/Premier League: 154-7. FAC: 13-2. FLC: 13-0. Others: 2-1. Total: 182-10.

Crystal Palace	May 1994
Q.P.R.	Nov 1994

Football/Premier League: 21-0. FAC: 1-0. FLC: 3-0. Others: 0-0. Total: 25-0.

Wycombe Wanderers	Sep 1996
Hibernian	Sep 1996
Millwall	Jan 1997
Leyton Orient	Feb 1997

Honours: England schoolboy caps. 6 Youth caps. 1 U21 cap. 2 U23 caps. 84 full caps. FACup winners medal. Scottish Premier Division winners medal.

Ray became Chelsea's youngest ever captain in April 1975 at the age of 18. Throughout his career he plied his services all around Europe. An elegant midfield general, he was at Q.P.R. twice, on the second occasion as the player/manager, during those last frantic seasons when he tried to keep the club in the Premier League. A regular in the England team, he made 84 appearances, and in total played in 200 matches for the Rangers. Ray resigned as Q.P.R. manager in 1996 and moved on to the same position at Fulham for a short time. From his TV appearances he was known for the overuse of the word 'super' which led to a nickname of 'Super Ray! He finally finished his football career as the Chelsea coach.
Debut: 16.12.1989 v. Sheffield Wed. (A). 0-2. Div.1.

WILKS Alan

Striker 5' 11" 11st 0lbs
b. Slough, Buckinghamshire 5.10.1946

Chelsea	Aug 1964
Q.P.R.	May 1965

Football League: 50-14. FAC: 1-0. FLC: 3-5. Others: 0-0. Total: 54-19.

Gillingham	(£5,000)	Jul 1971
Folkestone Town		Jan 1976
Canterbury City		1979
Chatham Town		Jul 1981

Honours: 3rd Div. championship winners medal. 2nd Div. runners-up medal. 4th Div. runners-up medal. England schoolboy caps.

A quiet and unassuming person off the pitch and on it he was cultured, gifted and sometimes a dazzling performer. Alan was a member of the squad that made the meteoric rise from the 3rd Division to the 1st in the late 1960s. In a League Cup match v. Oxford United in 1967 he scored all five goals.
Debut: 27.12.1966 v. Brighton & H.A. (A).2-2.Div. 3.

WILLIAMS Brian

(F.B.) Def 5' 8" 12st 12lbs
b. Salford, Lancashire 5.11.1955

Bury		Apl 1973
Q.P.R.	(£70,000)	Jul 1977

Football League: 19-0. FAC: 2-0. FLC: 2-0. Others: 0-0.
Total: 23-0.

Swindon Town	(£50,000)	Jun 1978
Bristol Rovers	(Player/Ex.)	Jul 1981
Bristol City		Jul 1985
Shrewsbury Town		Jul 1987
Alvechurch		1991

A very dependable full back but who was used mainly as a substitute at Loftus Road for just one season.
Debut: 20. 8.1977 v. Aston Villa (H). 1-2. Div. 1.

WILLIAMS Thomas Andrew.

Def. 6' 0" 11st. 8lbs.
b. Carshalton 8. 7.1980.
Walton & Hersham

West Ham United	(£60,000)	Aug 2000
Peterborough United	(Loan)	Mar 2001
Peterborough United		Mar 2001
Birmingham City	(£1,000,000)	Mar 2002
Q.P.R.	(Loan)	Aug 2002

Football League:29-1. FAC:2-0. FLC:1-0. Others:1-0.

Tommy quickly became a crowd pleaser at Q.P.R. during the 2002/03 season with his charges from full back and skilful play on the ball. He is a very confident player who always seems to have time to spare.
Debut: 10. 8.2002 v. Chesterfield (H). 3-1. Div. 2.

WILLIAMS William Thomas

CD 6' 1" 13st 0lbs
b. Esher, Surrey 23. 8.1942
Esher schools
Surrey County

Portsmouth		Jun 1960
Q.P.R.		Jun 1961

Football League: 45-0. FAC: 2-0. FLC: 1-0. Others: 0-0.
Total: 48-0.

W.B.A.	(£10,500)	Jun 1963
Mansfield Town	(£10,500)	Jan 1966
Gillingham	(£7,000)	Sep 1967
Maidstone United		Jul 1972
Durban Celtic, S. Africa	(Player/Manager)	Feb 1973

Honours: England schoolboy caps. 8 England youth caps.

Bill was a powerful central defender, who was always dangerous from corners and free kicks in the opponents penalty area. He was converted into a central defender at W.B.A. where he remained for three years.

A long career in football followed, playing with several clubs, and then as coach to Sacramento Gold (U.S.A.) in 1979 and Atlanta Chiefs (1980). In 1981 he became the manager of Maidstone United, then the same in Durban (South Africa) in 1984. He returned to manage Maidstone eighteen months later, followed by Gillingham and Dover Athletic. In May 2001 he became the director of football at Kingstonian.
Debut: 16. 9.1961 v. AFC Bournemouth (H).1-1. Div.3.

WILLOCK Calum Daniel.

Sriker 5' 11" 12st. 7lbs.
b. London 29.10.1981.
ADT College, Putney

Fulham		Jul 2000
Q.P.R.	(Loan)	Nov 2002

Football League:3-0. FAC:0-0. FLC:0-0. Others:0-0.

An excellent young striker who came on loan from Fulham. Calum prefers the ball played to his feet where his speed off the mark enables him to get behind the opposing defences.
Debut: 9.11.2002 v. Northampton Town (H). 0-1. Div.2.

WILSON Andrew Nesbit

(I.F.) Mid 5' 7" 12st 5lbs
b. Newmains, Scotland 14. 2.1896 d. October 1973

Cambuslang Rangers		1913
Middlesbrough		Feb 1914
Heart of Midlothian		1918
Dumfermline Athletic		1920
Middlesbrough		Aug 1921
Chelsea	(£6,500)	Nov 1923
Q.P.R.		Oct 1931

Football League: 20-3. FAC: 3-0. FLC: 0-0. Others: 0-0.
Total: 23-3

Nimes, France		May 1932

Honours: 12 Scottish full caps. 13 goals.

In 1915 Andy enlisted in the 6th Highland Light Infantry and was posted to France, losing his lance-corporal's stripes following a 'disagreement' with another soldier. In 1918 a shell fragment shattered his left hand. Whilst in Stobhill Hospital, he was allowed out with the rest of the walking wounded to watch the Victory International between Scotland and England. Two of the Scottish players were delayed owing to a train breakdown., McMullan arriving in time, but not McNair, and Andy was drafted into a hurriedly re-arranged team, at centre forward, and scored two goals!

He went on to make the position his own. He scored 23 of Scotland's 36 goals during the tour of Canada in 1922. Chelsea paid a record fee for him and he stayed for eight years. Andy later became manager of Clacton Town, then the Walsall manager until 1937 and finally the same at Gravesend & Northfleet. Still in London, he became a fine golfer, billiards player, and played bowls for England. He was a familiar figure at Stamford Bridge almost until he died.
Debut: 10.10.1931 v. Norwich City (A). 1-2. Div.3 (S).

WILSON Clive Euclid Aklana

(L.B.) Def 5' 7" 10st 0lbs
b. Manchester 13.11.1961
Moss side amateurs

Manchester City		Dec 1979
Chester City	(Loan)	Sept 1982
Chelsea	(£250,000)	May 1987
Q.P.R.	(£450,000)	Jul 1990

Premier/Football League:172-12. FAC: 8-1. FLC: 16-1. Others: 3-1. Total: 199-15.

Tottenham Hotspur	Jun 1995
Cambridge United	1999
Wingate & Finchley	2000

Honours: 2nd Div. championship winners medal.

This highly talented defender possessed both speed and excellent passing ability as well as good ball control, and he was extremely popular with the fans. Clive was just as capable in midfield and was widely thought of as the best uncapped defender in the country at the time. Yet, somehow his talents were never fully appreciated or put to the best use at Loftus Road, although for four of his five seasons he was a near ever-present in League matches. He made just one short of 200 first team appearances for Rangers, before moving on to Spurs for a four year spell.
Debut: 25. 8.1990 v. Notts. Forest (A). 1-1. Div.1.

WILSON Thomas

(I.F.) Mid. 5' 8" 11st 2lbs
b. London in December 1879 d. Circa 1935
Millwall

Aston Villa	1901
London Caledonians	1902
Old Fleet	1904
Q.P.R.	1909

Southern League: 6-1. FAC: 0-0. FLC: 0-0. Others: 0-0. Total: 6-1.

Little is known about this man, except that he was an amateur and he made his debut for the club on Christmas Day 1909, scoring the only goal of the match. His other five matches ended in draws.
Debut: 25.12.1909 v. Norwich City (H). 1-0. SLDiv.1.

WILSON Thomas Carter

(O.L.) Wing 5' 6" 11st 6lbs
b. Preston, Lancs 20.10.1877 d. Blackpool 30. 8.1940
Fishwick Ramblers, Preston
Ashton-in-Makerfield
West Manchester
Ashton Town
Ashton North End

Oldham County	1896
Swindon Town	May 1897
Blackburn Rovers	May 1898
Swindon Town	May 1899
Millwall Athletic	May 1900
Aston Villa	Apl 1901
London Caledonians	
Q.P.R.	1902

Southern League: 59-3. FAC: 3-0. FLC: 0-0. Others: 0-0. Total: 62-3.

Kensal Rise United	
Bolton Wanderers	May 1904
Leeds City	Dec 1906
Manchester United	Feb 1908

Honours: South v. North International trial match.

Although he was on the small side, Tommy was sturdily built and was strong in possession. His forte was an ability to cross accurately from the wing and he was made captain as soon as he arrived at the club. A very popular player, he was described by one London correspondent as *"One of the best outside lefts in the Southern League."* He married the daughter of an Oldham publican, and whilst with Bolton Wanderers was a publican himself. He became manager of Chorley of the Lancashire Combination in 1912 and finally was elected Chairman of the board of Directors at Rochdale in October 1919, running the club until 1923. Wilson also became proprietor of the Wellington Hotel in the town centre.
Debut: 3. 9.1902 v. Wellingborough T. (H).2-0.SLDiv.1

WINGROVE Joseph S.

(R.B.) Def
b. Southall, Middlesex
Uxbridge

Q.P.R.	1912

Southern League: 73-0. FAC: 3-0. FLC: 0-0. Others: 0-0. Total: 76-0.

Joseph survived the conflict of the 1st World War after serving in the 'Footballers Battalion' throughout, but retired in 1921.
Debut: 23. 4.1913 v. Plymouth Argyle (A). 0-2. SLDiv.1.

WITTER Anthony Junior

CD 6' 1" 13st 0lbs
b. London 12. 8.1965
Grays Athletic

Crystal Palace	(£10,000)	Oct 1990
Q.P.R.	(£125,000)	Aug 1991

Premier League: 1-0. FAC: 0-0. FLC: 0-0. Others: 0-0.
Total: 1-0.

Plymouth Argyle	(Loan)	Jan 1992
Reading	(Loan)	Feb 1994
Millwall	(£100,000)	Oct 1994
Northampton Town		Aug 1998
Torquay United		Nov 1998
Welling United		Dec 1998
Scunthorpe United		Feb 1999
Hayes		Jul 2000

A tall, fast and mobile central defender who could use both feet and had a very fast turn of speed, keeping cool and calm under pressure. Tony was an expensive buy, for he was earlier rejected as a youngster, then made only one appearance in the first team. Three years later most of the transfer fee was recouped when he moved to Millwall. Tony was released in the summer of 1998 and became a cover player on a semi-permanent basis, but a knee injury in 1999 saw him dropping down to semi-pro level.
Debut: 14. 8.1993 v. Aston Villa (A). 1-4. PL.

WOOD Arthur Basil

(I.F.) Mid 5' 10" 11st 1lb
b. Southampton, Hampshire 8. 5.1890
St. Marys Athletic
Eastleigh Athletic

Fulham	Apl 1911
Gillingham	1918
Hamilton Academicals	1922
Newport County	Nov 1922
Q.P.R.	1923

Football League: 20-0. FAC: 0-0. FLC: 0-0. Others: 0-0.
Total: 20-0.

A robust forward, who scored on his debut for Newport County against Q.P.R. which probably influenced the club to sign him the following season. However, Arthur had the misfortune to play for four seasons out of five for the club that came bottom of the League. Gillingham - Southern League and the 3rd Division (South) - Newport County and finally Q.P.R. Arthur finally retired from playing at the age of 37, due to a knee injury.
Debut: 15.12.1923 v. Merthyr Town (H).3-0. Div.3 (S).

WOODHOUSE George F.

(R.H.) Mid
b.

Q.P.R.	1920

Southern League: 1-0. FAC: 0-0. FLC: 0-0. Others: 0-0.
Total: 1-0.

George Woodhouse 'junior' played just one game for the club, his farther George 'senior', was an original member of the boys club, Christchurch Rangers, in 1882. Although moving to Berkshire, George senior, often journeyed to London to play, and was one of the pioneers responsible for the formation of Q.P.R. in 1886. Both father and son share what must be a unique distinction of having at various times been both player and director of the same club.
Debut: 3. 4.1920 v. Newport County (A). 0-3. SLDiv.1.

WOODS Christopher Charles Eric

G 6' 2" 13st 5lbs
b. Swineshead, Lincolnshire 14.11.1959
Swineshead
Priory Celtic

Nottingham Forest		Dec 1976
Q.P.R.	(£250,000)	Jul 1979

Football League: 63-0. FAC: 1-0. FLC: 8-0. Others: 0-0.
Total: 72-0.

Norwich City	(£250,000)	Mar 1981
Glasgow Rangers	(£600,000)	Jul 1986
Sheffield Wednesday	(£1,200,000)	Aug 1991
Reading	(Loan)	Oct 1995
Colorado Rapids, USA		May 1996
Southampton	(Loan)	Nov 1996
Sunderland	(Loan)	Mar 1997
Burnley		Jul 1997

Honours: 9 England youth caps. 6 U21 caps. 43 full caps. 2nd Div. championship winners medal. 2 Football League winners medals. 4 Scottish Premier Division championship winners medals. 3 Scottish League Cup winners medals.

Chris seemed an ideal replacement for Phil Parkes, possessing lightning reflexes and he could execute all the crafts of goalkeeping. Yet he lost his place to John Burridge. Chris later admitted that he lived too far from the Q.P.R. training ground, and after 18 months he was transferred to Norwich City.
Debut: 18. 8.1979 v. Bristol Rovers (H).2-0. Div. 2.

WOODS Patrick J.

(R.B.) Def 5' 7" 11st 6lbs
b. Islington, London 29. 4.1933

Q.P.R.	Jun 1950

Football League:304-15. FAC: 20-0. FLC: 2-0. Others: 7-1.
Total: 333-16.

Pat was described by many critics as a fearless tackler and was noted for his well-timed clearances. A fine full back and a cheerful character who left the club in 1961 to emigrate to Australia. During his 11 year long spell at Loftus Road, he made well over 300 appearances, and was an ever-present in the 1959/60 season Division Three side. In the three previous seasons he missed just five League matches. Pat returned to England some two years later to play for Colchester United for the 1963/64 season, where he appeared in most of the 'U's' Third Division matches, at both left and right back. But he was soon to return to Australia.
Debut: 12. 9.1953 v. Walsall (H). 2-0. DIV. 3. (S).

WOODWARD Horace John

(C.H.) CD 5' 10" 11st 11lbs
b. Islington, London 16. 1.1924

Tottenham Hotspur juniors		
Tottenham Hotspur		Mar 1939
Finchley		
Tottenham Hotspur		May 1946
Q.P.R.	(£10,500)	Jun 1949

Football League: 57-0. FAC: 1-0. FLC: 0-0. Others: 0-0.
Total: 58-0.

Tonbridge	
Snowdon Colliery	
Walsall	Jul 1953
Stourbridge	

After signing for Spurs straight from school, Horace was originally signed as a centre forward and played as such as a seventeen year old in the London War League. However, in 1942, he was sent to Finchley and turned out regularly for them.

While serving in the Navy he was converted into a centre half and made his debut in that position in September 1946. He was immediately made captain on his arrival at Q.P.R. in 1949 Leaving after two years, Horace finished his playing career at Stourbridge, then became the Kingsbury Town manager in 1966 until 1971. He later worked as a bus driver for the British Oxygen Company.
Debut: 20. 8.1949 v. Leeds United (A). 1-1. Div.2.

WOODWARD Joseph Henry

G 6' 1" 12st 0lbs
b. Catford in February 1904 d. Lewisham in 1974

Catford	
Watford	Aug 1926
Southend United	Aug 1927
Clapton Orient	Oct 1927
Q.P.R.	Feb 1928

Football League: 10-0. FAC: 1-0. FLC: 0-0. Others: 0-0.
Total: 11-0.

Merthyr Town	Jun 1929
Bexleyheath & Welling	Jan 1931
Canterbury Waverley	Aug 1932

Joe was signed as cover for Joel Cunningham and indeed was generally the reserve goalkeeper at his other League clubs.
Debut: 17.11.1928 v. Brighton & H.A.(H).3-2. Div.3(S).

WRIGHT Ernest

(I.L.) Mid 5' 9" 11st 7lbs
b. Middleton, Lancashire in 1912

Sedgley Park	
Q.P.R.	Oct 1934

Football League: 1-0. FAC:0-0. FLC: 0-0. Others: 0-0.
Total: 1-0.

Crewe Alexandria	Jun 1935
Chesterfield	May 1937
Oldham Athletic	Jun 1938

Ernie joined the club as an amateur but afetr two months he became a professional. He was a schemer who could draw an opponent to create an open space before giving an accurate pass. The 'Notts Post Football Annual' for 1937/38 described him as a *"dextrous dribbler and a splendid shot."*
Debut: 26. 1.1935 v. Brighton & H.A.(A). 1-5. Div.3(S).

WRIGHT Paul H.

Striker 5' 8" 10st 8lbs
b. East Kilbride, Scotland 17. 8.1967

Aberdeen		1983
Q.P.R.	(£275,000)	Jul 1989

Football League: 15-5. FAC: 2-0. FLC: 2-1. Others: 0-0. Total: 19-6.

Hibernian	(£300,000)	1990
St. Johnston		1991
Kilmarnock		1995

Honours: Scottish youth caps. 3 U21 caps.

Paul, a phenomenal Scottish striker and scorer of over one hundred goals in 350 Scottish matches, could not settle into the English game, so was soon transferred back to Scotland.
Debut: 19. 8.1999 v. Crystal Palace (H). 2-0. Div.1.

WYATT A. G.

(O.R.) Wing
b.

Q.P.R.	1909

Southern League: 10-0. FAC: 0-0. FLC: 0-0. Others: 0-0. Total: 10-0.

A reserve player who stepped into the side when McNaughton was injured, and only played in the latter part of the 1909/10 season.
Debut: 12. 3.1910 v. Exeter City (A). 0-0. Div. 3 (S).

WYPER Henry Thomas Harley

(O.R.) Wing 5' 7" 10st 3lbs
b. Calton, Glasgow 8. 10.1900 d. Coatbridge, Scotland.

Glengarnock Vale	
Army Football	
Southport	Feb 1921
Motherwell	Sep 1922
Southport	Nov 1922
Wallasey United	Sep 1923
Burscough Rangers	Jul 1924
Accrington Stanley	Aug 1925
Hull City	Feb 1927
Charlton Athletic	Sep 1928
Q.P.R.	Jun 1931

Football League: 11-0. FAC: 0-0. FLC: 0-0. Others: 0-0. Total: 11-0.

Chester	Feb 1932
Bristol Rovers	Jan 1933
Accrington Stanley	May 1933
Crewe Alexandria	May 1935
Rossendale United	Aug 1935

Honours: 3rd Div. (South) championship winners medal.

Harry was a lightweight winger with sleek black hair and twinkling feet, who played for ten clubs before Q.P.R. and moved on to five clubs after. On his retirement from the game, he took over the Peel Park Hotel (opposite the ground) in Accrington. He served in the RAF during the war, took over a guest house in Bournemouth, then emigrated to Australia in 1949.
Debut: 28. 8.1931 v. Brentford (A). 0-1. Div.3 (S).

YATES John

(L.H.) Mid
b. Manchester 27.11.1903

Manchester Central	
Boston Town	
Coventry City	1925
Chesterfield	1926
Aston Villa	1927
Q.P.R.	1929

Football League: 10-0. FAC: 0-0. FLC: 0-0. Others: 0-0. Total: 10-0.
Stourbridge

He was a player who bounded about the pitch like an *"india-rubber man."* John was a mobile left half who deputised for Andy Neil during the 1929/30 season.
Debut: 9. 9.1929 v. Walsall (A). 0-4. Div. 3 (S).

YATES Stephen

CD 5' 11" 11st 0lbs
b. Bristol 29. 1.1970

Brislington schools		
Bristol Rovers		Jul 1988
Q.P.R.	(£650,000)	Aug 1993

Premier/Football League:134-2. FAC: 7-0. FLC: 8-0. Others: 0-0. Total: 149-2.

Tranmere Rovers	Aug 1999
Sheffield United	Jul 2002

Honours: 3rd Div. championship winners medal.

Steve's career with Bristol Rovers was almost ended before it began. The club was in severe financial trouble in 1988 and without the generous offer of the supporters club, who agreed to pay his wages in the first year of his career, he would have been released. Calm and solid, Steve had a no nonsense approach to the game and showed good aerial skills. He was voted 'The Young Player of the Year' in 1989 at the age of 17. Steve was a big money buy by Rangers in 1993, and at Loftus Road he was noted as a fair opponent and a tough tackler.
Debut: 18. 8.1993 v. Liverpool (H). 1-3. PL.

YENSON William

(R.H.) Mid 5' 9" 12st 0lbs
b. Kingston Bagpuze, Oxfordshire in 1880

West Ham United	1901
Bolton Wanderers	1903
Q.P.R.	1905

Southern League: 90-4. FAC: 4-0. FLC: 0-0. Others: 0-0. Total: 94-4.

West Ham United	1908
Croydon Common	1909
Crystal Palace	
Brentford	

Honours: FACup runners-up medal. Southern League championship winners medal.

A tall, well built player who captained the side to the Championship of the Southern League. Bill could use his strength in the tackle and was fond of throwing his weight about.
Debut: 2. 9.1905 v. New Brompton (H). 4-0.SLDiv. 1.

YOUNG Herbert

(O.L.) Wing 5' 8" 11st 7lbs
b. Liverpool 4. 9.1899
Liverpool youth football

Everton	1921
Aberdare Athletic	1923
Brentford	1925
Bangor City	Jun 1926
Newport County	Jul 1927
Q.P.R.	Jul 1929

Football League: 14-1. FAC: 1-0. FLC: 0-0. Others: 0-0. Total: 15-1.

Bristol Rovers	Jul 1930
Swindon Town	1932

Bert was a fast and forceful winger, who was a consistent performer and a first team choice wherever he played. He shared the left wing spot with Howe at Q.P.R., who was inclined to score more goals than Young.
Debut: 31. 8.1929 v. Crystal Palace (A).1-1. Div.3 (S).

YOUNG John

(L.B.) Def 5' 10" 12st 8lbs
b. Whitburn, Tyne & Wear in 1895 d. in 1952
Whitburn Villa
South Shields

Southend United		1919
West Ham United	(£600)	Apl 1920
Q.P.R.		May 1926

Football League: 89-12. FAC: 2-0. FLC: 0-0. Others: 0-0. Total: 91-12.

Accrington Stanley	Aug 1929

Honours: FACup runners-up medal. 2nd Div. runners-up medal.

A left winger who was converted into a full back with considerable success. Upon his arrival at Q.P.R. he was given the captaincy and also became something of a penalty king. However, John was plagued by ill health and after a short spell with Accrington Stanley he decided to retire from the game which enabled him to take over a farm near Sunderland.
Debut: 28. 8.1926 v. Crystal Palace (A).1-2. Div.3 (S)

YOUNG William A.

(I.R.) Mid 5' 9" 11st 6lbs
b. Ferrybridge, Durham in 1898
Tyneside district football

Q.P.R.	1924

Football League: 8-2. FAC: 0-0. FLC: 0-0. Others: 0-0. Total: 8-2.

Kettering Town	1926
Jarrow	
Barnsley	1931
Gillingham	
Carlisle United	Sep 1932
Barnsley	May 1933
Jarrow	1933

Bill was an amateur who was released after the team ended the season bottom of the League for the second time in three years.
Debut: 21. 3.1925 v. Bournemouth .(H).0-2.Div.3 (S).

ZELIC Nedijeljko

Def 6' 2" 13st 8lbs
b. Sydney, Australia 4. 7.1971
Sydney Croatia

Borussia Dortmund, Germany		1992
Q.P.R.	(£1,250,000)	Aug 1995

Premier League: 4-0. FAC: 0-0. FLC: 0-0. Others: 0-0. Total: 4-0.

Eintracht Frankfurt, Germany(Loan)	
Eintracht Frankfurt, Germany(£1,000,000)	Dec 1996
Auxerre, France	1996
Munich 1860, Germany	1997

Honours: 33 Australian caps.

A big, strong midfield defender, who was captain of his country, and did an excellent job as a sweeper. Ned had to undergo an operation on his knee which was followed by a virus.
Debut: 23. 8.1995 v. Wimbledon (H).0-3. PL.

Nicknames:

Many players over the years are given nicknames, either in their normal domestic life or those devIsed by the fans. A good number of course are just common abbreviations or derivatives, those such as David - Dave, Charles - Charlie, William - Bill, etc. which have been ignored here. Below is a list of the popular and more memorable ones that have been applied to the Q.P.R. players over the years, but this should not be regarded as a full definitive list.

ALLEN...ANDREW...ARCHIBALD...BARRY...BRIAN....CHARLES...CHRISTOPHER...COLIN...DAVID DEAN...DENNIS... DONALD...ERIC...EDWARD...FRANK...FRED...GARETH...GEORGE...GRAHAM...HARRY...HENRY...HUBERT... IAN...JACK...JAMES...JOHN...KEITH...KENNETH...KARL...LAWRENCE...LUKE...MICHAEL...MORRIS...NICHOLAS...NORMAN...OLIVER... PAUL...PETER...RAYMOND...REGNALD...SAMUEL...SIMON...TIM....THOMAS...VERNON...VINCENT....WILLIAM...

Player		Nickname
Allen James	-	JAS
Allen John	-	IAN
Andrews Cecil	-	ARCHIE
Ardiles Osvaldo	-	OSSIE
Balogun Jesilmi	-	TESI
Bankole Ademola	-	ADE
Blackman John	-	JACK
Bradshaw John	-	JACK
Brazier Matthew	-	MATT
Clark Clive	-	CHIPPY
Clark William	-	WILLY
Crawford John	-	JACKIE
Dichio Daniele	-	DANNY
Francis Gerald	-	GERRY
Gardner William	-	WALLY
Gilmore Henry	-	PAT
Givens Daniel	-	DON
Gregory John	-	JACK
Hamilton William	-	WILLY
Hill Charlie	-	MIDGE
Holloway Ian	-	OLLY
Jobson John	-	JACK
Johnson Henry	-	HARRY
Jones Vincent	-	VINNIE
Leigh Thomas	-	GINGER
Lewis James	-	SENIOR
Maddix Daniel	-	DANNY
McLintock Francis	-	FRANK
Mikloska Ludek	-	LUDO
Milward George	-	PADDY
Newbiggin Alexander	-	SANDY
Parker Richard	-	DICK
Pearson Harold	-	TITCH
Pullen Henry	-	HARRY
Revill Edward	-	TEDDY
Ridley John	-	MICK
Rose John	-	JACK
Smith Athur	-	NIPPER
Smith Stephen C.	-	JUNIOR
Swan John	-	JACK
Travers James	-	GEORGE
Vafliadis Odysseus	-	TESSI
Varco Percy	-	SACCHO
Vincent Ernest	-	GINGER
Warren Christer	-	CHRIS
Webb Issac	-	ISSIE
Wheldon George	-	DIAMOND
White Devon	-	BRUNO
Wiles Henry	-	HARRY
Wilkins Raymond	-	BUTCH
Wyper Henry	-	HARRY
Woodhouse George	-	JUNIOR
Young John	-	JACK
Zelic Nedijeljko	-	NED

~ The Managers: 1907 - 2003 ~

COWEN James 1907-1913

b. Scotland 17.10.1868 d. Scotland 12.12.1918

Highest Achievement with Q.P.R.
Southern League championships: 1908 and 1912

After James had retired from playing in June 1902, he coached the youngsters at Aston Villa for a while before taking the decision to move to Q.P.R. in 1907. The club had just moved to a new ground at Park Royal and had appointed their first ever manager. Jimmy Cowen gathered together eight new men and fitted them into a team. They were transformed it into a title winning combination even drawing with Manchester United in the new F.A.Charity competition. Q.P.R. and Cowen repeated the feat four years later, and in the summer of 1912 the club undertook their first continental tour by visiting France and Germany, where all their matches were won. As the world was getting ready for hostilities, Jimmy offered his resignation on the grounds of ill health in 1913 to which the directors agreed. He went home to Scotland and died peacefully in his sleep at the age of 47 years.

HOWIE James 1913-1920

b. Aryshire, Scotland 19. 3.1878 d. London January 1963

Highest Achievement with Q.P.R.
6th in the Southern League 1920

After playing for Kimarnock, Kettering Town, Bristol Rovers, Newcastle United and Huddersfield Town, James was offered the job of manager at Q.P.R. in November 1913. Although the club was active throughout the 1st World War, the army commandeered the Park Royal ground in February 1915. So the club had to play out the rest of the war on their old Kensal Rise ground in Harvest Road. At the end of the war Rangers moved to the old Shepherds Bush ground at Ellerslie Road in 1919, now known as Loftus Road. It was there that they played their last season of Southern League football. Howie left Q.P.R. in the spring of 1920 to manage Middlesbrough. Later he returned to London, where he ran a tobacconist's business. Howie died in January 1963.

LIDDELL Ned 1920-1924

b. Whitburn, Nr. Sunderland in April 1877 d. 22.11.1968

Highest Achievement with Q.P.R.
3rd in Division 3 (South) 1921
Q.P.R. 2. Arsenal 0. F.A.Cup 1921

Ned was a centre half who stood over 6' 0" tall and played his football for Sunderland, Southampton, Gainsborough Trinity, Clapton Orient, Southend United and Arsenal. Having retired from playing at the end of the 1st World War, Ned became manager of Southend United in their last season in the Southern League. He then became manager of Q.P.R. and discovered the likes of O'Brien and Chandler. Liddell was sacked in the close season of 1924 after the club had to seek re-election. Subsequently he was employed by Fulham as a scout and later he became manager. Ned guided Luton Town to promotion in 1937 and he was still actively involved in the game at the time of his death.

HEWISON Robert 1925-1930

b. Newcastle-upon-Tyne 25. 3.1889 d. Bristol 1964

Highest Achievement with Q.P.R.
3rd in Division 3 (South) 1929-30

Before Bob Hewison took over the managerial seat at Q.P.R. the temporary manager, who was also acting as secretary, Will Wood, ran the club. Hewison had been a wing half in the Newcastle United team until after the 1st World War. In May 1920, Northampton Town paid £250 for Bob and made him their player/manager, he was there for five years. Q.P.R. secured him in 1925 and he managed the first side to play in the new blue and white hoops. Notably Hewison signed George Goddard, the club's all-time record goalscorer. Bob left Q.P.R. in the summer of 1931and in March 1932 joined Bristol City where he spent 18 years, although from October 1938 until May 1939, he was suspended after a joint F.A./League enquiry found several members of the club guilty of being involved in illegal payments. Hewison went on to manage Guildford City and Bath City.

Bob Hewison

MITCHELL Archie 1931-1933

b. Smethwick, Staffs 15.12.1885 d. in April 1949

Highest Achievement with Q.P.R.
13th in Division 3 (South) 1932

The original man to take over from Bob Hewison was John Bowman, an ex-player, ex-manager of Norwich City and Croydon Common and was at that time a Q.P.R. director. The club's move to the White City stadium was imminent and Bowmen was appointed manager in the summer of 1931. He was forced to stand down through illness before the new season had begun. However, the man who eventually took over from Bowman was Archie Mitchell, the ex-captain of Q.P.R., who had managed Brentford from 1921 to 1925, then coached abroad and finally managed non-League Dartford before joining Q.P.R. again to coach the reserve team. The move up Wood Lane to the White City Stadium proved disastrous and although the new manager brought new blood into the side, attendances dropped dramatically and the club was forced to move back to Loftus Road. Within 18 months of taking over the managership of the club, Mitchell had gone, never to manage in the League again.

O'BRIEN Michael 1933-1935

b. Kilcock, Ireland 10. 8.1893 d. Uxbridge October 1940

Highest Achievement with Q.P.R.
4th in Division 3 (South) 1934

Upon retiring from playing, O'Brien was immediately given the job of managing Q.P.R. in May 1933. He cleared out half the team and brought in six new players, but after the team ended the season in fourth position it suddenly collapsed to thirteenth in the following year of 1935. O'Brien left the club in April, and later worked as the assistant/manager at Brentford, before taking up the job as manager of Ipswich Town, who were at that time in the Southern League and brought them into the Football League.

BIRRELL William 1935-1939

b. Cellardyke, Fife, Scotland 13. 3.1897 d. November 1968

Highest Achievement with Q.P.R.
3rd in Division 3 (South) 1937-38.

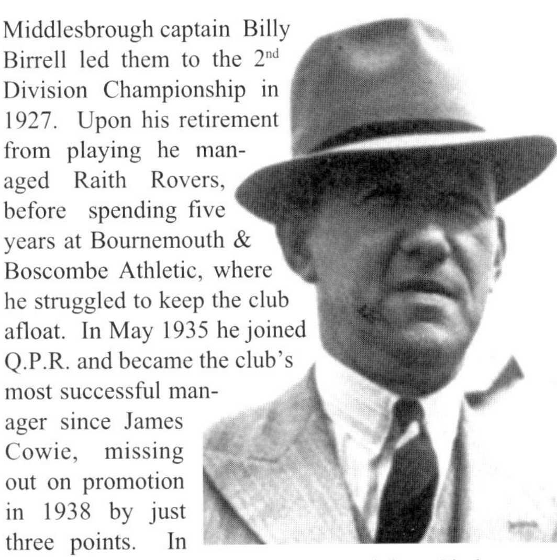

Middlesbrough captain Billy Birrell led them to the 2nd Division Championship in 1927. Upon his retirement from playing he managed Raith Rovers, before spending five years at Bournemouth & Boscombe Athletic, where he struggled to keep the club afloat. In May 1935 he joined Q.P.R. and became the club's most successful manager since James Cowie, missing out on promotion in 1938 by just three points. In May 1939 he took on the manager's job at Chelsea and steered the club to two wartime cup finals plus two FA Cup semi-finals, before retiring in May 1952.

VIZARD Edward 1939-1944

b. Cogan, Wales 7. 6.1889 d. Wolverhampton 25.12.1973

Highest Aceivement with Q.P.R.
Won wartime ' B ' South League in 1940

As a youth, Ted played football for Cogan Old Boys and rugby for Penarth, before joining Bolton Wanderers where he enjoyed a meteoric rise to fame. He soon made his debut for the senior squad and won his first international cap. Ted became the mainstay of the international side and was the caretaker/manager of Bolton Wanderers for a spell in 1919. In the first Wembley final, he won an F.A.Cup medal in 1923 and another three years later. He played his last match in March 1931at the age of 41 years. In 1933 he became the first full time manager of Swindon Town, before, in the summer of 1939, taking over at Q.P.R.; but, alas, he only had wartime football to compete in. Nevertheless, the club was relatively successful throughout the war, and in April 1944 he was offered the manager's job at Wolves, for which over 100 applicants had applied. He was sacked in 1948 and finally took the job as manager of Cradley Heath in 1949.

MANGNALL David **1944-1952**
b. Wigan, Lancs. 21. 9.1905 d. Penzance, 10. 4.1962

Highest Achievement with Q.P.R.
Champions Division 3 (South) 1948
13th in Division 2 1949

In his playing days, Dave was a bustling centre forward who had a deceptive body swerve and was a prolific scorer. He once scored ten goals in a reserve match for Leeds United but could not find a regular first team place, but was more successful after his move to Moving to Huddersfield Town. Dave Mangnall joined Q.P.R. in May 1939 and played for the club throughout the 2nd World War scoring many goals. He was reluctant to take the job of manager towards the end of the war, but in the end he accepted the offer and went on to build a fine side. The gradual break-up of the team, including Allen to Manchester United and Powell to Aston Villa, saw Mangnall leave the club after their relegation.

Alec Stock

TAYLOR Jack **1952-1959**
b. Barnsley 15. d. Barnsley 22. 2.1978

Highest Achievement with Q.P.R.
10th in Division 3 (South) 1957 & 1958

As a player Jack joined Wolves in 1931 staying with the club until 1938 when he joined Norwich City. After the war he played for Hull City and became the Weymouth player/manager in 1950 before becoming the Q.P.R. manager in 1952. At Loftus Road he was a solid if unspectatacular manager who often picked up useful players from around the Leeds area. Taylor left Q.P.R. in May 1959 to take over the managership at Leeds United, who were relegated in 1960, but he resigned in March 1961, never to manage again.

STOCK Alec **1959-1968**
b. Somerset 30. 3.1917 d. Somerset 16. 4.2001

Highest Achievement with Q.P.R.
League Cup winners 1967
Division 3 Champions 1967
2nd in Division 2 (promoted to Division 1) 1968

Alec, a miner's son, signed for Charlton Athletic, then joined Q.P.R. on loan in 1938, before signing permanently a year later. During the war he became a Captain, and later Major (after being wounded in the 1944 D Day landings). In the summer of 1946, Alec became the player/manager of Yeovil Town, and led them on their famous F.A.Cup run of 1949. That same year he joined Leyton Orient, won them the championship of the 3rd Division (South) in 1956, and had Short spells at Arsenal and A S Roma. The managership of Q.P.R. followed, in August 1959, and one of the most exciting periods in the club's history unfolded during the next few years. By finishing eighth in the old 3rd South, he secured a place in the new Third Division in 1960, with a third final placing a year later. Four moderate seasons followed, before another third place in 1966, and at last the Championship a year later plus the capture of the League Cup. Amazingly Alec immediately secured the runners-up place in the Second Division the following season, just one point behind Champions Ipswich Town, and so up to the First Division for the first time in the club's history. But after this nine year stint in charge, and before even selecting a First Division team, Stock resigned, and second in command, Bill Dodgin Jnr., took over as caretaker/ manager. Stock later became the manager at Luton own and Fulham, and a Q.P.R. director in 1977.

DODGIN William Jnr. **June 1968 - Nov. 1968**
b. Wardley, Durham 4.11.1931

Highest Achievement with Q.P.R.
(No complete season)

Coach Jimmy Andrews took over the managership for a very short period, before former Arsenal and Fulham player Bill Dodgin Jnr. became caretaker/ manager until the arrival of Tommy Docherty in December 1968. Bill went on to manage Fulham, Northampton Town in 1973 (and again in 1980), Brentford in 1976, and Woking.

DOCHERTY Thomas Nov. 1968 and 1979-80
b. Glasgow, Scotland 24. 8.1928

Highest Achievement with Q.P.R .
5th in Division 2 1979-80.

In November 1968, Scot and former Preston and Arsenal player Tommy Docherty was lured to Loftus Road. he wanted a move back to London and wished for 1st Division football again. But he soon realised he had made a mistake and sensationally quit the club after 28 days. Tommy had resented the influence of chairman Jim Gregory who had wanted control over the signing of players and Docherty was refused permission to sign Brian Tiler from his former club Rotherham United. The ex-Chelsea manager was not out of work long for he was snapped up by Aston Villa the following month. On his appointment as manager for the second time, in 1979, the much travelled and by now controversial Docherty stayed longer and the club ended the season fifth in the 2nd Division. However, by November of the following season and with the club in the relegation zone Tommy was sacked.

ALLEN Leslie 1968-1971
b. Dagenham, Essex 4. 9.1937

Highest Achievement with Q.P.R.
9th in Division 2 in 1970.

Les was one of the legendry Spurs players of the early 1960s who was part of the famous ‘double team’. He was transferred to Q.P.R. in a £21,000 deal from the north London club. Allen was made player/manager after the tempestuous 28 day reign of Tommy Docherty. He sold Roger Morgan to Spurs for £110,000 and then bought Terry Venables for £50,000, both transfer fees breaking Q.P.R. records. Les remained at Q.P.R. until January 1971 after suffering immediate relegation back to the Second Division and two moderate seasons at that level.

Dave Sexton

JAGO Gordon 1971-1974
b. Poplar, London 22.10.1932

Highest Avievement with Q.P.R.
Runners-up in Division 3 1973
8th in Division 1 1974

Former Charlton player Gordon Jago was Les Allen’s assistant and it was natrual that he took over the hot seat. He sold Rodney Marsh to Manchester City for £90,000, and took Q.P.R. into the 1st Division in 1973 followed by a very creditable 8th in the table a year later. In October 1974 Jago took over the managership of the Millwall club until 1978 when he emigrated to the USA. and became a successful soccer coach there.

Gordon Jago

SEXTON David 1974-1977
b. Islington, London 6. 4.1930

Highest Achievement with Q.P.R.
Runners-up to the League Champions 1976

Former West Ham, Leyton Orient and Brighton player of the 1950s Dave Sexton became the manager of Q.P.R. thirteen days after being sacked from Chelsea. In 1976 the club had its best ever season when they came second to Liverpool with only one point separating them. The club entered Europe and reached the quarter-finals of the UEFA Cup in 1977. The League Cup semi-finals were reached in the same year, but come the summer and Dave was tempted away, with a lucrative offer, to Manchester United.

SIBLEY Frank **1977-1978 and 1984-1985**
b. London 4.12.1947

Highest Achievement with Q.P.R.
19th in the 1st Division

Former Q.P.R.player Frank Sibley, who had to retire prematurely due to injury, was promoted from head coach to manager after the departure of Sexton to Manchester United. Following the most successful period in the history of Q.P.R., a season of woe was about to unfold. The club were lucky to cling on to their 1st Division status, but Sibley was at least responsible for the signing of Leighton James and Dave Needham. In July 1978 Sibley resigned and was replaced initially by Alec Stock, who was by then a director of the club, and eventually by Steve Burtenshaw. Frank, who on and off has spent a lifetime at Q.P.R., made a brief return to the hot seat for a few months in 1985.

BURTENSHAW Steve **1978-1979**
b. Portslade, Brighton, Sussex 23.11.1935

Highest Achievement with Q.P.R.
20th in Division 1 in 1978-79

The former Brighton and Arsenal player Steve Burtenshaw was the next in line. Steve's only season in charge at Loftus Road ended in disaster with Q.P.R. being relegated. Chairman Jim Gregory sacked him after only ten months of his three year contract. Burtenshaw had been in charge at Hillsborough when they suffered the same fate. At Everton he lasted just a month as caretaker/manager in 1977.

Jim Smith

VENABLES Terry **1980-1984**
b. Bethnal Green, London 6. 1.1943

Highest Achievement with Q.P.R.
F.A.Cup final runners-up in 1982, after a replay
Championship of Division 2 in 1983
5th in Division 1 in 1984

After the second departure of Tommy Docherty, came the arrival of Terry Venables. The story of his career is well documented among the players. He is well known for his abilities as a coach and for man management. The championship of the 2nd Division was won in 1983 with ten points to spare over their nearest rivals. A huge offer to manage Barcelona was received from Spain and so Venables left the club with his assistant Allan Harris.

MULLERY Alan M.B.E. **1984**
b. Notting Hill, London 23.11.1941

Highest Achievement with Q.P.R.
(No complete season)

Chairman Jim Gregory wished Terry Venables the best of luck and promptly appointed Alan Mullery in his place in June 1984. Alan had managed Brighton & H.A., Charlton Athletic, Crystal Palace and now Q.P.R. Jago stood-in for a short while but Mullery was sacked by Gregory in December 1984. Sibley once again took over for the rest of the season.

SMITH James **1985-1988**
b. Sheffield 17.10.1940

Highest Achievement with Q.P.R.
League Cup runners up 1986
5th in the 1st Division 1988

Within a year Smith had taken Q.P.R. to the League Cup final at Wembley. He brought many fine players to Loftus Road including David Seaman, Paul Parker and Dean Coney. The other teams to be managed by Jim Smith had been Boston United, Colchester United, Blackburn Rovers, Birmingham City and Oxford United and after leaving Q.P.R. he went on to manage Newcastle United, Portsmouth and Derby County.

FRANCIS Trevor 1988-1989

b. Plymouth, Devon 19. 4.1954

Highest Achievement with Q.P.R.
9th in the 1st Division 1989

A schoolboy wonder, he was the first sixteen year old to score four goals in a League match. Later he became the first English player to be transferred for £1,000,000. Francis had an unhappy spell as a player/manager and the club struggled in the 1st Division during his spell in charge. Trevor tried to be a disciplinarian which really didn't suit his temperament and the players did not respond. There was also some adverse publicity after the firing of a player who had decided to attend the birth of his first born rather than appear in the first team squad. It was an error of judgment on Trevor's part and he was sacked shortly afterwards.

HOWE Donald 1989-1991

b. Wolverhampton, Staffs. 12.10.1935

Highest Achievement with Q.P.R.
11th in the 1st Division 1990

At the time of his appointment Don was the coach at Q.P.R.. As well as a former player, he had been the manager of Arsenal as well as the England assistant/ manager. Don had worked in Turkey and in Saudi Arabia and despite his qualifications and respect in the game, and a reasonable record at Loftus Road, he did not enjoy the job, and after only 18 months, he left and moved across London to Wimbledon.

FRANCIS Gerald 1991-1994 and 1998-2001

b. Chiswick, Mddx. 6.12.1951

Highest Achievement with Q.P.R.
5th in the Premier League 1993

Gerry Francis (who hardly needs an introduction) was appointed, and under him Q.P.R. ended their first season in the Premier League in 5th position, becoming the top London club in 1992/93. But his future at Loftus Road was in some doubt after talk of the possibility of selling his stars, Les Ferdinand and Andy Sinton to balance the books. Francis was reluctant to sell despite pressure from the boardroom. He was also in charge in 2001 when they dropped into Division 2 and went into administration.

WILKINS Raymond 1994-1996

b. Hillingdon, Mddx 14. 9.1956

Highest Achievement with Q.P.R.
8th in the Premier League 1995

Much travelled and then current player (since 1989), former England captain Ray Wilkins took over the combined player/manager job when Gerry Francis left for Spurs in 1994. At the end of his first season he lifted the team from near bottom to a very respectable 8th. But relegation genuinely hit him hard, and it became too much for this elegant midfield general and so he left the club.

HOUSTON Stewart 1996-1997

b. Dunoon, Scotland 20. 8.1949

Highest Achievement with Q.P.R.
8th in the 1st Division 1997

Ex-Manchester United defender Stewart Houston sat in the managerial seat at Q.P.R. during this period when caretaker boss Frank Sibley moved aside in September 1996. His one complete season was moderately successful, but in December 1997 he stepped down to make way for Ray Harford.

Gerry Francis

HARFORD Raymond **1997-1998**
b. Halifax, Yorkshire 1. 6.1945

Highest Achievement with Q.P.R.
21st in the 1st Division 1998

Ray was the most successful manager ever to lead Luton Town, yet he still ended up getting the sack, with the chairman stating that he didn't smile enough. Retiring as a player in 1976, he became the youth team coach at Fulham and eventually became their manager. He managed Wimbledon and also he was part of the Blackburn Rovers set up when they won the Premiership. His time as manager at Q.P.R. was both limited and disastrous despite his high pedigree elsewhere. (Ray died on the 9th August 2003)

HOLLOWAY Ian **2001 To Date**
b. Kingswood 12. 3.1963

Highest Achievement with Q.P.R.
4th in the 2nd Division 2003

When the club went into administration in 2001, Gerry Francis was sacked from the manager's job and Ian Holloway was brought in. Once a player with Q.P.R., he had played alongside a number of former Bristol Rovers team-mates, Dennis Bailey, Gary Penrice, Devon White and Steve Yates. He is the son of the well-respected local amateur, Bill Holloway. Ian is a great credit to his profession on and off the field and remains so at Q.P.R. as one of the club's most popular of characters, and there can be no finer example for any young footballer to emulate. Ian exceeded all expectations, and performed marvels at the club when he guided the club to the divisional play-off final at Cardiff in 2003.

Ray Harford

Ian Holloway

The Complete Role Call: 1907 - 2003

Manager	Years	Manager	Years
COWEN James -	1907-1913	SIBLEY Frank -	1977-1978
HOWIE James -	1913-1920	BURTENSHAW Steve -	1978-1979
LIDDELL Ned -	1920-1924	DOCHERTY Thomas -	1979-80
HEWISON Robert -	1925-1930	VENABLES Terry -	1980-1984
MITCHELL Archie -	1931-1933	MULLERY Alan M.B.E. -	1984
O'BRIEN Michael -	1933-1935	SIBLEY Frank -	1984-1985
BIRRELL William -	1935-1939	SMITH James -	1985-1988
VIZARD Edward -	1939-1944	FRANCIS Trevor -	1988-1989
MANGNALL David -	1944-1952	HOWE Donald -	1989-1991
TAYLOR Jack -	1952-1959	FRANCIS Gerald -	1991-1994
STOCK Alec -	1959-1968	WILKINS Raymond -	1994-1996
DODGIN William Jnr. -	June-Nov 1968	HOUSTON Stewart -	1996-1997
DOCHERTY Thomas -	Nov. 1968	HARFORD Raymond -	1997-1998
ALLEN Leslie -	1968-1971	FRANCIS Gerald -	1998-2001
JAGO Gordon -	1971-1974	HOLLOWAY Ian -	2001 To Date
SEXTON David -	1974-1977		

QUEENS PARK RANGERS F.C.
1882
LOFTUS ROAD

We specialise in football books (only), normally with an historic theme.

Especially: Comprehensive **Football League club histories**, over 30 to date, including: Reading, Bolton Wanderers, Partick Thistle, Rochdale, Torquay United, Scarborough, etc.

Also players **'Who's Who' books**, recent clubs include:
Oldham Athletic, Portsmouth, Hull City, Chesterfield, etc.

Other titles of a more unusual nature include:
'The Ultimate Directory of English and Scottish Football League Grounds" (an impressive encyclopaedia detailing every ground on which a League match has been played)

'Through The Turnstiles Again' (A history of football related to attendances)

'Rejected F.C.' (A series of books providing the histories of former Football League clubs.

Plus non-League - The **'Gone But Not Forgotten'** series
(histories of defunct non-League clubs and former grounds)

Free newsletters (for details of these and many other titles) are issued biannually,
for your first copy please send a s.a.e. to:
Yore Publications, 12 The Furrows, Harefield, Middx. UB9 6AT
(website: www.yore.demon.co.uk)